Teaching Children with Dyslexia

Teaching Children with Dyslexia is essential reading for any teacher, parent, Special Educational Needs Co-ordinator, teaching assistant or student who needs an incisive, up-to-the-minute account of the best ways to successfully tackle dyslexia and dyspraxia – at home and in the classroom.

This book is packed with photocopiable checklists, activities, recommendations for resources and tests, advice and suggestions for strategies and techniques that are instantly transferable to teaching environments. Written by one of the most well-regarded and experienced practitioners in the field, the author's 'hands-on' experience makes this an indispensable teaching companion. It includes chapters on:

- dispelling the myths about the existence of dyslexia and dyspraxia with help for early recognition
- creating dyslexia-friendly environments
- suggestions for establishing good home–school partnerships
- when, why and how to teach synthetic and analytic phonics
- essential principles and processes for teaching reading
- a rationale for the most effective use of the different spelling methods
- guidelines for developing confidence and overcoming difficulties for reluctant writers.

Philomena Ott has a well-deserved reputation for cutting through the jargon, explaining complex scientific theories and research findings in a palatable and accessible way. She provides a succinct overview of the most recent research about the characteristics of dyslexia, as well as ways of dealing with it by using well-established methods. Written specifically to bolster experienced teachers' confidence and to empower Newly Qualified Teachers (NQTs) with the key to unlocking literacy problems in challenging pupils, this resource book should be on the shelf of every staff room.

Philomena Ott is an internationally recognised expert on teaching pupils with specific learning difficulties. She is currently an independent educational consultant, trainer and speaker on dyslexia, and has conducted seminars and given lectures worldwide.

Related titles from Routledge:

How to Manage Spelling Successfully
Philomena Ott

Activities for Successful Spelling
Philomena Ott

Day-to-Day Dyslexia in the Classroom (2nd edition)
Joy Pollock, Rody Politt and Elisabeth Waller

Helping Children with Reading and Spelling: A Special Needs Manual
Rene Boote and Rea Reason

Teaching Children with Dyslexia

A practical guide

Philomena Ott

Routledge
Taylor & Francis Group

LONDON AND NEW YORK

First published 2007 by Routledge
2 Park Square, Milton Park, Abingdon, Oxon OX14 4RN

Simultaneously published in the USA and Canada
by Routledge
270 Madison Ave, New York, NY 10016

Routledge is an imprint of the Taylor & Francis Group, an informa business

Typeset in Goudy by Keystroke, 28 High Street, Tettenhall, Wolverhampton
Printed and bound in Great Britain by The Cromwell Press, Trowbridge, Wiltshire

British Library Cataloguing in Publication Data
A catalogue record for this book is available from the British Library

Library of Congress Cataloging in Publication Data
Ott, Philomena.
   Teaching children with dyslexia : a practical guide / Philomena Ott.
      p. cm.
   Includes bibliographical references and index.
   ISBN 0–415–32454–8 (pbk. : alk. paper) 1. Dyslexic children–Education.
   2. Dyslexic children–Ability testing. I. Title.
   LC4708.O88 2006
   371.91′44–dc22   2005035758

ISBN10: 0–415–32454–8 (pbk)
ISBN13: 978–0–415–32454–0 (pbk)

ISBN10: 0–203–35696–9 (ebk)
ISBN13: 978–0–203–35696–8 (ebk)

To my husband Michael for his love, encouragement and support, without which this would not have been written.

Contents

Foreword by Sir Richard Branson

Dyslexia is an issue frequently in the media spotlight. It arouses passionate debate including diverse opinions about the condition and its characteristics. Sceptics dismiss it as a mythological condition found among the well-heeled classes. Academics removed from the day-to-day realities argue about definitions. The reality is that many individuals are haunted by a lifelong incapacity with certain aspects of language which does not diminish with age or experience. Evidence is reported globally and in multi-lingual settings from those with a specific pattern of difficulties.

Scientists using MRI scans show individual differences in brain architecture and function when different tasks are undertaken. Studies show that some dyslexic people activate their right brain more frequently which explains why they have artistic, creative and spatial abilities, whereas they often struggle with language activities which are associated with left brain activities.

Talents and creativity are sometimes unrecognised, undervalued or stifled during school days in environments where literacy and numeracy are prized and prowess in these constantly assessed. Those who struggle to jump through the academic measurement hoops often fall behind, feel inferior and worthless because they cannot pass routine tests and frequent examinations. Confidence is eroded and self-belief ebbs because of constant exposure to repeated failure with tasks that the majority take in their stride.

I was one of these. My school days were a struggle. I never forgot the day when I was taking an IQ test and just looked at the sheet of paper for one hour without being able to answer anything. My mother refused to accept that I was just careless and lazy and encouraged me in all kinds of out of school activities, and fortunately I ended up being top in sports. At my senior school I opted out of the challenge of writing essays. In those days computers were not readily available for word processing and spellchecking. And the problems didn't end when I started Virgin! Amusingly it wasn't until my 50th birthday that I could finally tell the difference between 'net' and 'gross'. You can imagine. The Virgin Group board meetings. Results £10 billion gross, 'no Richard that's NOT profit, you can't spend it. It's turnover!' A friend sat me down and said 'Think of a fishing net in the ocean. The fish you have in your net is what you've earned not your profit'.

Hey presto, I had it!

Technology, when used appropriately, has revolutionised the lives of those who struggle to spell. The Internet has made the contents of library shelves accessible at the touch of a button. Multimedia resources enable text to be read and speech recognition technology transfers words to the page. Computers enable people now to train for careers and allow them to do jobs that at one time would have been unthinkable because of handwritten requirements.

The challenge for parents and teachers is to identify the signs of dyslexia before it blights confidence. This book offers practical advice about what readers need to know, and when they dip into it, it provides sensible answers. It is derived from real-life experience and based on up-to-date international research. The key facts are accessible and easily located for the general reader. Early recognition of dyslexia and dyspraxia empowers parents and teachers who want to support and encourage the ten per cent of children who learn differently and it will help to prevent a further increase in the 16 million adults in the workforce with low literacy levels. Understanding specific needs and providing support has shown that prevention of problems results in many talented and successful dyslexic people reaching stellar goals in many walks of life.

Richard Branson

London, July 2006

Preface

Like millions of viewers round the world while watching the marriage of the Prince of Wales to Lady Diana Spencer in July 1981 my telephone rang, just as the Archbishop of Canterbury solemnised the union. The caller was a primary school teacher who was 'worried about her dyslexic son's lack of progress at school'. Her call and concerns were not unique as shown later by an e-mail I received from a parent in Buenos Aires who too was worried because 'his teachers do not know how to help him because of his dyslexic difficulties'. This resulted in an invitation to Argentina where the seminars I conducted became the nucleus of a book. I was prompted to expand on the contents because of continuing concerns about how to teach those who fail to learn to read and write.

The House of Commons Education and Skills Committee ordered an inquiry in 2005 because of the 'unacceptably high numbers entering secondary school with poor levels of literacy. Former Ofsted director Jim Rose consulted practitioners, visited schools and considered scientific research findings. These included the Universities of York and Sheffield's review of the research which acknowledged the importance of the United States National Reading Panel's Reports that 'based on the scientific evidence, the essential components of any reading programme must include systematic and direct instruction in phonemic awareness, phonics, reading fluency, vocabulary development and comprehension strategies'. The Rose Review recommended in 2006 that 'systematic phonic work should start by the age of five'. This book argues for the inclusion of these teaching principles.

Meanwhile, a dedicated group of teachers who have had specific training in Orton-Gillingham methods had been using programmes which have had systematic, synthetic phonics as a core element to teach dyslexic children, for over forty years in the USA and UK. Their contribution was largely ignored and dismissed by many mainstream educationalists in the 1980s. The wheel has turned a full circle because the teaching principles and methods used for teaching children with dyslexia have been established as effective. The Government has announced that special needs co-ordinators (SENCOs) will have to complete a nationally accredited qualification to provide the right expertise in the classroom and it is to establish a dyslexia trust to provide specialist support in all schools which will include many of the recommendations discussed later. This is something that the various dyslexia organisations have campaigned for, for three decades.

Acknowledgements

My thanks to colleagues who have answered queries, shared their knowledge and experience and commented on chapters in the manuscript, including Professor Greg Brooks, Ann Cooke, Dr Nata Goulandris, Jean Hutchins, Ian Litterick, Bernadette McLean, Elaine Miles, Penny Rose, Professor Maggie Snowling and Dr Benita Thomson. I am indebted to Steve Cuthbert, Peter Dale, Alison Foyle, David Jefferson and Lesley Munroe for their advice and support. Thanks are due to the pupils I have taught, from whom I have learned so much, and especially to their parents for their faith and fortitude for following many of the recommendations and suggestions given here. A special thank you to Cecilia Malbran and her son Jose for making it possible for me to lecture in Argentina. Much of the content was prepared for this occasion.

Note

For convenience, the learner is 'he' and the teacher is 'she' throughout the book, but 'she' and 'he' could be substituted in every case.

Abbreviations

ACID	Arithmetic, Coding Information and Digit Span
ADD	Attention Deficit Disorder
ADHD	Attention Deficit Hyperactivity Disorder
AMBDA	Associate Member of the British Dyslexia Association
ASN	additional support needs
BAS	British Ability Scales
BDA	British Dyslexia Association
BPS	British Psychological Society
BSA	British Skills Agency
COP	Code of Practice
COPP16	Code of Practice for Providers of Post-16 Education and Related Services
COPS	Cognitive Profiling System
COPSH	Code of Practice for Schools
CSP	co-ordination support plans
c-v-c	consonant-vowel-consonant
DCD	Developmental Co-ordination Disorder
DDA	Disability Discrimination Act 1995
DDAT	Dyslexia, Dyspraxia and Attention Deficit Disorder
DECP	Division of Educational and Child Psychology
DfES	Department for Education and Skills
EAL	English as an additional language
EP	educational psychologist
GCA	general conceptual ability
IALS	International Adult Literacy Survey
ICT	information and communication technology
IDEA	Individuals with Disabilities Education Act
IEP	individual education plan
INSET	In-Service Education and Training
IPS	Independent Parental Support
IPSEA	Independent Panel for Special Education Advice
IQ	Intelligence Quotient
ITA	Initial Teaching Alphabet
JCQ	Joint Council for Qualifications
LEA	local education authority
LSA	learning support assistant

NAA	National Assessment Agency
NAEP	National Assessment of Educational Progress
NARA	Neale Analysis of Reading
NLS	National Literacy Strategy
NPPN	National Parent Partnership Network
NRP	National Reading Panel
OECD	Organisation for Economic Co-operation and Development
Ofsted	Office for Standards in Education
OCR	Oxford, Cambridge and RSA Examinations
Patoss	Professional Association of Teachers of Students with Specific Learning Difficulties
PDA	personal digital assistant
PGCE	Post-Graduate Certificate in Education
PIRLS	Progress in International Reading Literacy Study
PRD	*Preventing Reading Difficulties in Young Children*
PTA	parent–teacher association
QCA	Qualifications and Curriculum Authority
RAN	Rapid Automatised Naming
REA	Reading Excellence Act
SATs	Standard Achievement Tasks
SCAD	symbol search, coding, arithmetic and digit span
SEN	special educational needs
SENCO	special educational needs co-ordinator
SENDA	Special Educational Needs and Disability Act 2001
SENDIST	Special Educational Needs and Disability Tribunal
SLI	specific language impairment
SMS	short messaging service
SpLD	specific learning difficulty
SPS	School Psychological Service
STEPS	Spelling Test to Evaluate Phonic Skills
WISC	Wechsler Intelligence Scale for Children
WORD	Wechsler Objective Reading Dimensions
wpm	words per minute
WRAT	Wide Range Achievement Test

Chapter 1

The really useful guide for parents, carers, teachers and professionals dealing with dyslexia and dyspraxia at home and in pre-school settings

---

Outline

- What is dyslexia?
- What are the early warning signs of SEN? Guidelines for concerned parents and carers
- Who's who of educational and healthcare professionals
- What is the significance of early intervention for those with SpLD?
- Extrinsic factors that may affect language acquisition
- Checklist to help identify children at risk of dyslexia/dyspraxia
- What speaking and listening skills do children need to function effectively?
- Speech and language disorders indicative of SEN with suggestions to help compensate and overcome them.
- Activities to help with sequencing and with fine and gross motor difficulties
- What is dyspraxia (DCD)?
- Indications of dyspraxia with suggestions to help
- Difficulties associated with laterality, directionality and time; suggestions to help compensate and overcome them
- Terms and conditions to include in a happy family's 'homework treaty'
- Websites for pre-school activities, homework and revision
- Checklist for resources and a shopping list for dyslexic and dyspraxic pupils
- Hints on why and how to use ICT resources
- Summary and conclusions

The word 'dyslexia' has entered into mainstream conversation and is commonly used, but it still generates controversy. A crossword puzzle in *The Times* gave the letters 'dy', 'x' and 'a' as a clue for 'dyslexia' and the answer was 'a reading disorder'. This pinpoints the inaccuracies, misinformation and folklore that still surround a condition that:

> implies vastly more than a delay in learning to read, which is but the tip of the iceberg. [It also should be applied to] the use of words, how they are identified, what

they signify, how they are handled in combination, how they are pronounced and how they are spelt.

(Critchley, 1981)

Years after this was written, a Working Party of the Division of Educational and Child Psychology (DECP, 1999) of the British Psychological Society (BPS) concluded that 'dyslexia is evident when accurate and fluent reading and/or spelling develops very incompletely or with great difficulty. This focuses on literacy learning at the "word level" and implies that the problem is severe and persistent despite appropriate learning opportunities.' This definition forms the basis for LEAs' policies. Its narrowness and superficiality dismayed practitioners (Johnson et al., 2001), resulting in strong criticism from fellow psychologists. Pumfrey (2002) conceded that 'even at the level of single word decoding it is unlikely that all workers would agree that this represents a comprehensive analysis of the situation'. Fawcett (2003) pointed out that it 'overlooks research findings'. Thomson (2003) broadened the argument, saying: 'it is my view that children are being misidentified and barred from receiving appropriate help due to misconceptions arising from the BPS Working Party Report.' He quoted evidence from an LEA psychologist's report which argued that a child was not dyslexic according to the BPS definition because it was not necessary to have 'a significant discrepancy between cognitive ability and attainments scores' and 'a particular pattern of cognitive scores'. Educational policies are based on definitions, and assessment and provision depend on interpretation. McGuinness (1998) admonished readers to 'clear your minds of notions like "dyslexia" and "learning difficulties"' and claimed that 'there is no validity to the diagnosis of dyslexia'. Elliott's (2005) claim, in an interview for the Channel 4 documentary Dispatches: The Dyslexia Myth, that 'dyslexia is no more than a snobbish label and a myth which hides the scale and scandal of the reading disability' caused world-wide reaction including rage among academics and insult among sufferers.

This shows that the condition is still shrouded in misunderstanding and polarised opinions about causation, the nature of the condition, and the extent of the problem; there is no universally accepted definition. Some would argue that different definitions serve different purposes including identification, assessment, research and legal issues.

What is dyslexia?

The word dyslexia is derived from dys, which is a Greek prefix meaning 'poor' or 'inadequate', and lexis which is Greek for 'words' or 'language', and so means literally a 'trouble with words' (Cox, 1985).

The International Dyslexia Association (1998) expanded this, saying:

Dyslexia is a learning disability characterised by problems in expressive or receptive, oral or written language. Problems may emerge in reading, spelling, writing, speaking or listening. Dyslexia is not a disease, it has no cure. Dyslexia describes a different kind of mind, often gifted and productive, that learns differently. Dyslexia is not the result of low intelligence. Intelligence is not the problem. An unexpected gap exists between learning aptitude and achievement in school. The problem is not behavioural, psychological, motivational or social. It is not a problem of vision; people with dyslexia do not 'see backwards'. Dyslexia results from differences in the structure and function of the brain. People with dyslexia are unique, each having individual strengths and weaknesses. Many dyslexics are creative and have unusual talents in areas such as art, athletics, architecture, graphics, electronics, mechanics, drama, music or engineering. Dyslexics often show special talent in areas that require visual, spatial, and motor integration. Their problems in language processing distinguish them as a group. This means that the dyslexic has problems translating languages into thought (as in listening or reading) or thought into language (as in writing or speaking).

The British Dyslexia Association (BDA) says:

> Dyslexia is best described as a combination of abilities and difficulties which affect the learning process in one or more of reading, spelling and writing. Accompanying weaknesses may be identified in areas of speed of processing, short-term memory, sequencing, auditory and /or visual perception, spoken language and motor skills. It is particularly related to mastering and using written language, which may include alphabetic, numeric and musical notation. Some children have outstanding creative skills, others have strong oral skills. Dyslexia occurs despite normal teaching, and is independent of socio-economic background or intelligence. It is, however, more easily detected in those with average or above average intelligence.
>
> (Peer, 1999)

What are the early warning signs of SEN? Guidelines for concerned parents and carers

The Education Act 1996 defines a child as having a learning difficulty if 'he has a significantly greater difficulty in learning than the majority of children of his age' and if he 'has a disability that either prevents or hinders him from making use of educational facilities of a kind generally provided for children of his age in schools within the area'. In the USA the term 'learning disability' is used to describe a wide range of disorders in listening, speaking, reading, writing and mathematics. The terms 'specific learning difficulty' and 'specific learning disability' are interchangeable and both apply to individuals with dyslexia and dyspraxia.

Parents are usually the first to notice that a child has unexpected difficulties in acquiring specific skills. Parents have rights and needs when dealing with children with special educational needs, including knowing what help is available, and how and where this help can be obtained. Parents also have responsibilities according to the Children's Act 1989, including a 'collection of duties, rights and authority'.

The Code of Practice (COP) (DfEE, 1994) highlighted the importance of partnership between professionals and parents. The revised COP (DfES, 2001a), stated that

> all parents of children with special educational needs should be treated as partners and should:

- Play an active role in their children's education.
- Be informed of their children's entitlement within the SEN framework.
- Make their views known about their children's education.

- Have access to advice and support during assessment and education decision making for their children.

This resulted in the setting up of a parent partnership scheme which offers support, advice and information to parents including access to an independent parental supporter who is often a voluntary worker or an LEA Parent Partnership Officer. The SEN Disability Discrimination Act (2002) gives parents the right to appeal to the SEN Tribunal in cases of unlawful discrimination against those with SEN.

What should parents do when they are concerned about their child's progress and when should they do it?

- Parents are best placed to recognise their child's strengths and weaknesses. For example, a child may be verbally bright but have inexplicable expressive and receptive language difficulties such as saying familiar words, naming everyday objects or remembering simple instructions.
- Comparisons between difficulties with academic, social and emotional skills are unexpected and not consistent. For example, 8-year-old Charlie could not write his address or a birthday card to his granny but won a gold medal for poetry recitation at a local arts festival and subsequently was asked to audition for a part in *Oliver*, a West End production.
- Parents need to be aware of the characteristics of dyslexia, including difficulties with literacy, sequencing, organisation, information processing, short-term and working memory and the automisation of skills.
- Parents can find information about assessment and intervention by contacting voluntary organisations such as the BDA's helpline (0118 966 2677) and website (http://www.bdadyslexia.org.uk). Publications include *How to Detect and Manage Dyslexia* (Ott, 1997) and *Dyslexia: a Complete Guide for Parents* (Reid, 2005).
- Initially they should discuss their concerns and their own observations with the child's class teacher. The Code of Practice (COP, 2001) states that 'parents hold key information and have a critical role to play in their children's education' and 'positive attitudes to parents, user-friendly information and procedures and awareness of support needs are important'.

  The Code promotes a new, enlightened approach which augurs well for meeting the needs of children who somehow do not fit the norm because something is 'not quite right' about their performance and/or behaviour. It should become ever less likely that parents are dismissed as 'being over anxious', 'pushy', 'thinking that all their geese are swans' or having 'unrealistic expectations for their not very bright child' who may be 'thick, clumsy and bone idle'.
- It may be possible to arrange a meeting with the school's SEN co-ordinator (SENCO). All maintained schools are legally bound to produce a special educational needs policy document which should point the way forward for parents with concerns about their child's progress or lack of progress.
- Other physical factors such as hearing, speech, eyesight and the development of gross and fine motor skills should be considered and checked.

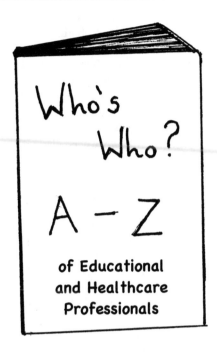

Figure 1

Who's who of educational and healthcare professionals

Educational psychologists (EPs) are involved in the study of mental, emotional, physical and social behaviour in children and adults. They usually have a degree in psychology, a Post-Graduate Certificate in Education (PGCE) teaching qualification followed by two years' teaching experience culminating in a master's degree in educational psychology. They are then able to carry out assessments. To practise they have to be registered by the British Psychological Society as chartered psychologists (www.psych-ed.org).

The LEAs employ about 2,000 EPs but there is a shortage, with a number of advertised posts not being filled. Turner (1997a) pointed out that there are 'perhaps 300 teachers for every educational psychologist'. Referral to the School Psychological Service (SPS) for psychological assessment may be made by:

- *the head teacher* often on the recommendation of the school's SENCO
- *community paediatricians*
- *parents,* who may ask the school to make the necessary arrangements or write directly to the LEA to request an appointment.

There is often a long waiting list and it can take up to twelve months to be given an appointment. However, if the school in consultation with the parents decides that a statutory assessment needs to be made 'the LEA normally have six weeks to decide whether to do so' and the timetable for the assessment should 'not normally exceed 26 weeks'.

Some parents seek help from an independent educational psychologist. The Psychological Society (www.bps.org.uk) has a list with details of chartered psychologists who can be contacted in the appropriate geographical location.

Dyslexia Action (DA) formerly the Dyslexia Institute (www.dyslexiaaction.org.uk) arranges for assessments to be carried out by independent consultant psychologists. It has over seventy-five who work at all the main DA centres throughout the UK.

The BDA local dyslexia associations have helplines which can offer information about centres and individuals such as specialist teachers, healthcare professionals and psychologists who carry out assessments (http://www.bdadyslexia.org.uk; e-mail: info@ dyslexiahelp.org.UK).

Education welfare officers are employed by the LEA and are education social workers who provide support and counselling for parents and children, including those with SEN, regarding school attendance.

General practitioners (GPs) are often the first contact for parents of children with special educational needs. They can make referrals to the Clinical Medical Health Officer at a clinic or Child Development Centre which can involve other healthcare professionals.

Health visitors usually see children in their own homes and can arrange for a child to be seen by other healthcare professionals such as the Special Needs Health Visitor.

Learning support assistants (LSAs) work with an individual child or a small SEN group who are usually withdrawn from the classroom. Critics say that this makes children feel 'different' and can affect self-esteem. Ofsted (1997) reported on the effectiveness of in-class support, especially for secondary pupils.

Optometrists diagnose and treat children with eye disease and vision abnormalities such as:

- myopia (short-sightedness)
- hyper-myopia (long-sightedness)
- astigmatism, which causes blurred vision
- strabismus (lazy eye), when the eyes are misaligned
- binocular instability, when eye movement is irregular which can cause letters to jump about on the page (treated with eye exercises)
- lack of a fixed reference eye can cause problems when reading (treated by patching the unstable reference eye)
- Meares-Irlen Syndrome (MIS) – sensitivity to glare and colour (treated with coloured glasses or coloured overlays). The Assessment with the Intuitive Overlays Test (Wilkins, 2001) and Wilkins Rate of Reading Test (MRC, 1996) use coloured overlays for people with reading difficulties and visual discomfort. There are less expensive and more widely available than the Wilkins Intuitive Colorimeter which is an instrument to test for preferred hue, saturation and brightness of a large range of colours to alleviate some of the symptoms of MIS.

Paediatric occupational therapists see children at Child Development Centres or hospitals. Referrals are usually made by a medical officer. They assess, plan and deliver programmes for children with everyday problems, for example with dressing, feeding, playing and walking. They also assess underlying skills such as fine motor and gross motor as well as movement difficulties often associated with developmental co-ordination disorders including dyspraxia. They use a combination of activities to strengthen muscles, co-ordination and balance.

Parent partnership officers are appointed by the LEA as part of the Parent Partnership Scheme to provide 'a menu of flexible services for parents whose children have SEN in order to empower them to play an active and informed role in their child's education' (DfES, 2001a). LEAs must give information about the parent partnership service when they decide whether or not to make a statutory assessment. Some parents may prefer an Independent Parental Support (IPS). The National Parent Partnership Network (NPPN) has a database of information (www.parent.partnership@hertscc.gov.uk).

Physiotherapists see children in Child Development Centres, hospitals or privately. Referrals are usually made by a medical officer. They treat children with physical conditions such as cerebral palsy and orthopaedic problems arising from accidents or injuries, using methods including exercises, manipulation, massage and heat treatments.

Special needs advisory teachers are employed by LEAs and advise schools on early identification and provision for SEN children. They co-ordinate the support given to parents by the health authority and other agencies such as the social services.

Special educational needs co-ordinators (SENCOs) are responsible for the day-to-day implementation and management of the school's SEN policy. They liaise with parents, co-ordinate staff involvement, and manage learning support assistants and external agencies such as the LEA and educational psychology services. They are also responsible for in-service training of staff to increase awareness and effectiveness in dealing with pupils with SEN according to the Code of Practice (COP, 2001). Some SENCOs also provide learning support to pupils and give advice to parents and teachers about SEN resources. They must keep records and monitor, identify and assess progress including children's individual education plans (IEPs).

Specialist teachers have undertaken a recognised training course such as a BDA-accredited course to qualify for associate membership of the BDA (AMBDA) or approved teacher status (ATS) (http://www.bdadyslexia.org.uk), Dyslexia Action's postgraduate diploma (http://dyslexia_inst.org.uk) or the Oxford, Cambridge and RSA (OCR) examinations diploma or certificate (www.patoss-dyslexia.org). They teach and some assess children with SpLD including dyslexia and dyspraxia.

Speech and language therapists identify and assess children's receptive (listening) and expressive (spoken) language skills and developmental communication disorders. They devise and implement programmes to help children communicate and develop sub-skills necessary for literacy including understanding rhyme, alliteration and categorisation of sounds.

Teaching assistants work either with individual children such as those with a statement or with a small group of children, giving in-class support as well as helping when the curriculum has been modified or differentiated. Some work with pupils who are withdrawn for additional support and help with the planning and implementation of IEPs.

What is the significance of early intervention for those with SpLD?

- It can prevent lack of self-confidence, low self-esteem or secondary emotional and behavioural problems from developing as a result of repeated failure and frustration.
- Basic skills can be taught including language, motor, auditory, visual and literacy skills which may lessen or prevent a loss of motivation.
- Research studies from the US government's programme Project Head Start showed

that early intervention is effective. A fifteen-year longitudinal study showed the long-term effects of early intervention. Children did not have to repeat a grade, did not have to be placed in special education classes, scored higher on IQ tests and were more likely to finish high school at 18 (Lazar and Darlington, 1982).

- Lyon (1998) pointed out that if reading difficulties are identified early and appropriate help is given, 90–95 per cent of pupils catch up, but only 75 per cent catch up if problems are not identified until they are 9 years old.
- The gap between attainment and underachievement is often smaller initially. It gradually widens with age. Usually the greater the gap the more difficult it is to catch up.
- Early intervention is more cost effective for schools and society.
- Early intervention can ultimately reduce the numbers of students who drop out of college because of low literacy skills.
- Early identification and appropriate intervention can lessen the chance of unemployment and delinquency in adolescence and adulthood.

However, intervention is often delayed because legislators in the UK have based their criteria for support for an individual with a 'learning disability' on 'a severe discrepancy between the student's apparent potential for learning and his low level of achievement'. This has resulted in what is known as the discrepancy formula, in other words a 'wait and fail' policy. In practice this means that children have to be given the opportunity to learn to read and write before they can be formally assessed as having difficulties, requiring a document called a 'statement of special education needs'.

Extrinsic factors that may affect language acquisition

Language is an innate skill in humans but develops through practice and experience. The child needs plenty of exposure to language to lay solid foundations for future growth. The following factors may inhibit language acquisition:

- a lack of parental interaction and communication such as talking during family meals or chatting about school and friends
- poor-quality child minding or day nurseries where physical needs are taken care of but little time is spent on language development through either play or social interaction
- carers such as nursery assistants, child minders, au pairs or nannies who do not speak the child's mother tongue and consequently may be poor role models for language, even if they are good carers in the physical sense
- excessive use of slang and 'short hand' rather than 'proper' conversation, perhaps impairing language development
- watching television or videos or playing computer games to the exclusion of social interaction and conversation. The National Literacy Trust (Close, 2004) reported that too many 'inappropriate TV programmes' inhibit language development in 3–5-year-olds. But viewing shared with an adult improves vocabulary as does the repetition element in video and children's television programmes.

Medical problems

Medical problems such as hearing loss due to otitis media (glue ear) should be eliminated as underlying causes of difficulties. This inflammation of the middle ear causes a build-up of fluid in the ear and a discharge due to infections or inflamed tonsils and adenoids. It may also be caused by swimming and diving and is sometimes linked to allergies. Grommets are sometimes inserted to help ventilate the eardrum and to improve hearing loss. However, after the grommets are removed some children have bouts of intermittent hearing loss even from a common cold. A history of hearing loss due to middle ear infections and fluctuations in hearing can exacerbate the difficulties of dyslexic children. Intermittent hearing loss can interfere with language and learning even though it is not the primary cause of difficulties. Up to 25 per cent of 5-year-olds entering school will have suffered from glue ear at some time (Macpherson, 1995) affecting their understanding of speech and language and use of language. They may be unable to remember instructions, follow a story, or join in playground games/conversations often resulting in behavioural problems. The child who consistently turns the volume up very high on the television set and frequently says 'What did you say?' may need to have his hearing tested.

Checklist to help identify children at risk of dyslexia/dyspraxia

Name:

Date of birth:

School:

Class teacher:

Is consent given for this information to be used by other professionals? □

- Was the pregnancy normal? □
- Did you have any illness requiring medication? □
- Was he a full-term, late or premature baby? □
- Was the delivery normal, forceps or by Caesarean section? □
- Was oxygen required? □
- What weight was the child at birth? □

Family history □

- Did either parent have difficulties with reading, spelling or writing? □
- Did maternal/paternal grandparents have similar difficulties? □
- Do any other siblings or relatives have similar difficulties? If so, enumerate. □

Speech and language development

- How old was he when he said his first words? □
- How old was he when he spoke properly? □
- Did he frequently mispronounce words? □
- Did he reverse words or put words in the wrong order in sentences? □
- Did he find it hard to remember the names of familiar objects or people when he wanted to explain or describe something? □
- Did he tend to give one-word answers? □
- Did you teach him to say nursery rhymes? □
- Was he able to say nursery rhymes? □

Developmental milestones

Gross motor skills

- Did he crawl? □
- How old was he when he learned to walk? □

- Did he have difficulties climbing down stairs? □
- Did he frequently fall over or bump into objects? □
- Did he find it hard to learn to ride a bicycle? □
- Did he find it difficult to turn door handles? □
- Did he find it difficult to walk in a straight line? □
- Was he able to join in and play childhood games such as musical chairs or Simon says? □
- Was he able to skip, hop and jump in time to musical games? □

Fine motor skills

- How old was he when he used the same hand consistently? □
- Did he tend to spill his food and knock over drinks? □
- Did he continue to feed himself with his fingers or a spoon long after his peers were using a knife and fork? □
- Did he find it difficult to feed himself? □
- Did he find it hard to cut up the food on his plate with a knife? □
- Did he find it hard to sit still? □
- How old was he when he was able to write his own name? □
- At what age was he able to colour in pictures and do dot-to-dot activities? □
- Was he constantly falling off his chair? □
- Did he find it difficult to dress himself? □
- Did he find it difficult to learn to tie shoelaces? □
- Did he sometimes put his clothes on back to front? □
- Did he find it hard to button and unbutton his clothes? □
- Did he find it difficult to cut with scissors? □

Auditory memory

- Did he sometimes confuse similar-sounding words? □
- Did he forget to do what he was asked to do? □
- Was he able to remember and follow simple instructions? □
- Was he able to remember and say the names of close family members? □
- Was he able to remember the words of simple songs or ditties? □
- Was he able to fetch an item when asked to when shopping in a supermarket? □
- Was he taught to say the alphabet and can he remember it? □

Visual memory

- How old was he when he recognised his own name? ☐
- Could he play simple board games involving matching pairs of pictures? ☐
- Was he able to do jigsaw puzzles? ☐
- Was he able to sort objects according to shapes and sizes? ☐
- Was he able to thread beads? ☐
- Was he able to remember where he left an object such as a favourite toy? ☐

Temperament

- Was he good at occupying himself? ☐
- Did he remain on task? ☐
- Did he get on well with siblings and other children? ☐
- Was he able to sit and listen to a story being read to him? ☐
- Was he able to remember and follow a story when it was read to him? ☐
- Was he able to sit with an adult and watch children's television? ☐
- Was he able to interact with the characters in the story? ☐

Please list the activities he enjoys doing:

Please list activities he is good at:

Include any further relevant information or comments including details of illnesses requiring hospitalisation or serious accidents.

Do these results warrant further investigation and an assessment? ☐

What speaking and listening skills do children need to function effectively?

- They need vocabulary to make sense of what they see and hear, including specific vocabulary for names of people, toys, household objects, food, pets.
- They need to know and understand the differences between fact, fantasy and reality in stories.
- They need to be able to give, process and understand information.
- They need to be able to use questioning for understanding and clarification with words such as: *how, what, when, where, why*.
- They need to be able to find out about why and how things happen.
- They need to be able to express emotions and feelings with words such as: *like, love, happy, hate, horrid, nasty*.
- Skills to tell and listen to stories and give a recount or a report with words such as: *before, after, later, this morning, last night, yesterday, tomorrow*.
- An ability to communicate with family and friends as well as being able to listen to a conversation. The responses may indicate that a diagnostic assessment is required.

Speech and language disorders indicative of SEN with suggestions to help compensate and overcome them

- Some children have a language delay and their speech is indistinct or unintelligible until they are about 2.06 years. This may warrant a referral to a speech therapist. A normal 3-year-old child has a vocabulary of about 1,000 words and a 5-year-old can use 3,000 words. Children can learn vocabulary by looking at picture books with a parent modelling the words which the child repeats. Stories can be read to them.
- He may have constantly mispronounced words and said things like 'I've lost my teddy dare' when his teddy bear went missing or when asked what his barrister father's job was he replied 'My dad's a banister'.
- He may have had hesitant or laboured speech and a tendency to use circumlocution because he cannot find the word he wants to use. He said 'Give me the thingamy for cutting paper' when he wanted to say the word 'scissors'. Or perhaps he had a word retrieval problem: for example, when his mother pointed to her watchstrap and asked 7-year-old Brian, 'What's this?' he replied 'Oh! it's a belt mum.' There is a large body of scientific research which has found evidence of difficulties with word naming at speed (Wolf *et al.*, 1986). Denckla and Rudel's (1974) Rapid Automatised Naming (RAN) theory showed that some children have difficulty with word naming. Help the child by showing him a collection of objects on a tray. Then ask him to name as many as he can in one minute. Have a game to see how many he remembers on successive occasions. Use a variety of objects such as food, toys, clothes. Commercial resources are available from www.nesarnold.co.uk.

  Some children switch off when asked what they got for Christmas or their birthday. They may say 'I don't know' because they cannot find the words they want to use. These are the children who give one-word answers to questions. They put up their hand in class and then forget the answer. Others give muddled or indistinct answers, for example when asked to describe what they have just watched on *The Simpsons* or *Blue Peter*.

- Their use of grammar may be poor even when surrounded by a language-rich environment. They say things like 'Do you remember the time at we went to the shop and I boughted ours Lego?'
- Many of these children are literal thinkers and find sentences such as 'My dad has a pair of crocodile shoes' perplexing. Idioms like 'pull your socks up' are similarly mystifying, and proverbs such as the 'early bird catches the worm' can be very confusing for them. They need explicit teaching of the meanings.
- Some children are described as having a 'semantic-pragmatic disorder', meaning they have difficulties with the meaning of words (semantics) and with using language socially (pragmatics). Others fail to understand the subtle nuances of language when censured or reprimanded. They may smile when they should appear contrite. Others totally ignore a reprimand and carry on doing what they have just been told not to do.
- Others confuse words with similar sounds, like 8-year-old Thomas who said, 'I had a great time at Auntie Sue's wedding, when I was a page and I had to wear a quilt.' He was in fact wearing a kilt.
- Remembering a series of instructions can be problematic because of short-term and working memory problems. When asked to get his shoes, his football kit and his coat from his bedroom, a boy went to the top of the stairs and said, 'What did you say?' Just ask him to do a maximum of two things at a time. Encourage oral repetition and keep in eye contact with him to monitor his reactions. Use role-play for this. He can pretend to be a robot. Then he can, for example, tell the robot how to change the baby's nappy. He can play a matching pairs game. The object is to find and say the missing words such as: 'He put salt and . . . on the table' (pepper).
- Bradley and Bryant's (1983) work showed that some children find it difficult to say nursery rhymes and play games involving rhythm or rounds such as 'Old Macdonald had a farm' or 'Ten green bottles standing on the wall'. Teach them these as they help with sequence and phonological awareness (awareness of the sounds in words). Teach them to identify sounds by recording, for example, a dripping tap, a kettle boiling, a fire engine. Clapping out sound patterns, bouncing a ball, playing a drum all develop awareness of rhythm.
- Songs such as 'The twelve days of Christmas' help improve sequencing and numeracy skills.
- The researchers tell us that children should learn 'chants, action, verses, poetry and stories'. Children's radio and television programmes such as the American series *Sesame Street* and the BBC's CBeebies have many ideas for teaching language through play.
- Practise these communication skills. Ask your child to tell his little brother about Tom's party. He can pretend he is a news reporter on TV when he tells Dad about the football match he played in at school that afternoon.

- Try to avoid the situation where the non-dyslexic brother or sister does all the talking and interrupting and is always answering the question.
- Repeat instructions if necessary and give the child time to process the information – speak slowly. There is research evidence which shows that he processes language slowly (Tallal *et al.* 1997).
- Do not put him on the spot by asking him a question if you know he has not been listening or if it is something you cannot help him answer.

Delamain and Spring's *Speaking, Listening and Understanding: Games for Young Children* (2003) includes many useful activities (www.speechmark.net).

Tests

Hatcher, P. (1994) *Sound Linkage* (Whurr Publishers; www.whurr.co.uk) is suitable for 7+ years.

Wagner, R., Torgesen, J. and Rashotte, C. (1999) *Comprehensive Test of Phonological Processing* (*CTOPP*) (www.harcourt-uk.com) is suitable for 5–24 years.

Activities to help with sequencing and with fine and gross motor difficulties

The muscles that perform motor skills are controlled by the brain. Problems may occur with some or all of the following:

- gross motor skills involving the arms, large muscles of the legs, neck and body, such as are used when kicking or throwing a ball
- fine motor skills involving the small muscles in the tongue, toes or fingers, such as are used when repeating a nursery rhyme, names, cutting with scissors, colouring in or tracing over lines
- graphomotor function involving the hands and fingers, used when tracing, drawing and doing handwriting or keyboarding
- oromotor function involving the music motor memory such as is used when remembering a tune or slogan or saying a poem.

Some find doing jigsaw puzzles very difficult. These children have difficulties with visual perception such as seeing the difference between the size and form of objects and shapes. It is helpful to start with puzzles with large wooden pieces. Those with a knob on the individual pieces are initially useful. It is important to be aware of a wide discrepancy between dyslexic children's skills and weaknesses. Some are excellent with Lego and Meccano and construction toys; others find these difficult or have no interest in them. The mother of a very bright 9-year-old said that when she had new brake shoes fitted in her car her son was watching. The mechanic was having difficulty fitting them. Her son suggested pushing the spring rather than pulling it. To their surprise Austin's suggestion was right and it worked.

Others find games with pegboards or matching geometric shapes difficult. They find it hard to pick up small objects or sort beads by either shape or size because they have low muscle tone or may not have the manual dexterity to do this. Others lack spatial awareness of figures and shapes as well as visual perception which later may affect their ability to recognise letters and words when learning to read. The golden rule is always to begin with large shapes, then gradually move on to smaller ones. Dancing and walking around plastic hoops or different-shaped objects helps to establish the concept of a circle, rectangle or square.

When putting the shopping away after a visit to the supermarket talk about the different shapes while touching and looking at the packaging to develop language and visual skills. Use concrete objects to teach the names and shapes of, for example, the square box of tissues or the round tub of cottage cheese. Count the eggs in the carton as they are put in the fridge. Commenting on the litre of milk or Dad's pint of Guinness helps to develop recall of names and the ability match them to objects. Games involving classification are useful for this. Denckla and Rudel (1974, 1976) showed that naming colours, letters and digits is a core difficulty for some children. Resources include: Place a Shape and Geometrix (www.nesarnold.co.uk).

Some children are slow at dressing, especially at doing up shoelaces or buttons. Nicolson and Fawcett's study (1994) of 126 dyslexic children and a control group aged 8–16 showed that some dyslexic and dyspraxic children have problems with motor skills including balance. They found evidence of a lack of automaticity in motor skills in the dyslexic subjects which they ascribed to a cerebellar deficit. Help to develop manual dexterity by activities like threading a string through a cardboard butterfly. Logic string beads are available from www.nesarnold.co.uk. Buy football boots which use Velcro rather than the 'dreaded' football laces which dyslexic children struggle to tie. Often they are 8–9 years old before they master this skill. Try sew-over cards, such as those available from Early Learning Centres. Use Velcro and zips on clothing whenever possible.

Some find it hard to learn to ride a bicycle because of a poor sense of balance. Parents of 7-year-old Oliver reported that he was very upset because his 4-year old brother learned to ride a bike at almost the same time as he did. Having found it difficult to learn to ride a bicycle, when they do learn, they are often accident-prone. For example, 14-year-old Adam arrived at school one day with a black eye and a severely grazed cheek. His teacher asked him how it had happened. He said that when he was on his mountain bike he had gone round a corner and a 'tree hit me'.

Unlike most children who open doors automatically and remember how to without having to think about it, your child may find it difficult to turn door handles. It helps to put a sticker with a red arrow on to remind him of the way he should turn the handle – then he won't get locked in the loo. Later such children may find memorising the layout of a keyboard or learning to drive a car challenging. They struggle when they have to 'think' about the QWERTY sequence of letters when touch-typing or about what to do when changing gear.

He is untidy and slow at packing, unpacking and tidying up his toys or belongings. The buzzword applied to this is that he lacks 'organisational skills' both in planning and implementation. Show him how to do these things for himself and develop a routine such as always putting the scissors in the kitchen drawer by the cooker after use. Do not do it for him.

Fine and gross motor skills such as those involved in using scissors or drinking through a straw are usually instinctive and reflexive responses. Most children develop these skills easily. However, some children are 9–10 years old before the motor skills become internalised and used spontaneously. Losse *et al.* (1991) conducted a longitudinal study of children with difficulties with co-ordination and concluded that they did not grow out of them. Fawcett and Nicolson (1995) found evidence of difficulties with motor skills in 17-year-olds and Wolff *et al.* (1990) found evidence in adults.

What is dyspraxia (DCD)?

Dyspraxia is the term most commonly used in the UK, Ireland and New Zealand whereas Developmental Co-ordination Disorder (DCD) is the preferred term in the USA and elsewhere to describe those with gross and fine motor difficulties.

The American Psychiatric Association (1994) defined it as:

> performance in daily activities that require motor co-ordination substantially below that expected given the person's chronological age and measured intelligence. This may be manifested by marked delays in achieving motor milestones (e.g. walking, crawling, sitting), dropping things, 'clumsiness', poor performance in sports and hand-writing.

Difficulties are associated with balance, movement and co-ordination involving two simultaneous activities. Speech may also be affected. These difficulties are unexpected for the individual's age and development.

The word comes from the Greek *dys* which means 'difficulty' or 'malfunction' and *praxis* which means 'doing', 'acting' or 'practising'. Some children have an impairment of gross or fine motor skills.

Kaplan *et al.* (2001) showed that there was a 50 per cent chance of co-occurrence in children with specific learning difficulties of two of seven disorders such as Attention Deficit Disorder (ADD), Asperger's Syndrome or Specific Language Impairment (which included dyslexia) and dyspraxia. In a study conducted by Kaplan *et al.* (1998), 63 per cent of dyslexic children were reported to be dyspraxic. Portwood (1999) and Kirby (1999) showed co-existence of dyslexia and dyspraxia in 50 per cent of cases. Estimates of dyspraxia are that it affects up to 6 per cent of the population. The Dyspraxia Foundation (www.dyspraxiafoundation.org.uk) is the national organisation which provides information and support.

Indications of dyspraxia with suggestions to help

- A child may have problems using a spoon and use his fingers instead. Later, long after his peers, he finds using a knife and fork challenging. He may find it difficult to cut up food and may often knock over drinks. He is often a messy eater. It is possible to tell what he had for lunch at school by looking at what he has spilled down the front of his shirt. Role-play with tea sets and make-believe cooking help. Using playdough and plasticine helps to develop tactile and manual dexterity. Hand and finger exercises and play can help to develop muscle tone.

- Some children find it difficult to walk in a straight line. They can practise this by walking along the car park spaces outside the supermarket or when walking on the pavement on the way to school. Games can include walking on stepping stones, using place mats which are laid on the floor. A musical element can be incorporated: the child walks around the mats, and when the music stops he has to stand with both feet together inside one of them. As skill develops he could be asked to stand on one leg, then on the other leg. A chalked straight line 12 feet long and 1 inch wide can be marked on the floor or outdoor hard surface, then a zigzag. The child can practise walking heel-to-toe along this with his arms by his side.
- Some children are frightened to get on and off an escalator.
- Encourage the use of different writing implements long before the child can write. Scribbling with crayons, felt tips, pencils or roller-ball pens all develop pre-writing skills, as does using paints. Ask the child to place his arms on either side of a double-sided easel blackboard. Then give him two pieces of chalk and let him scribble using both hands simultaneously to develop arm and shoulder muscles.
- Some find skipping and hopping involving balance, rhythm and motor co-ordination difficult. Let them practise by jumping on a trampoline or an old mattress. Later on, using roller skates may also be difficult.
- Childhood games such as hopscotch, marching to music and songs such 'One, two, three, four, five, Once I caught a fish alive' help develop number recognition, rhyme and rhythm.
- Playing musical instruments such as a drum, percussion instrument or castanets is beneficial. Using a metronome develops awareness of rhythm.
- Throwing and catching a ball may be problematic – practise this using a beach ball first, then gradually reduce the size to a tennis ball. Practise throwing balls into a bucket – this helps to develop visuo-motor skills. Begin by standing at close range, gradually increasing the distance from the object.
- Using a 'fishing rod' with a magnet placed at the end of a bit of string to fish metal objects from a bucket helps develop eye–hand co-ordination.
- Using finger puppets and catching and throwing beanbags helps to develop manual dexterity.
- If the child constantly bumps into other people or objects, playing musical chairs is a useful activity.
- If stairs have to be negotiated in a nursery use big arrows to show which side to use. Children going up the stairs keep to the left and follow the arrow pointing upwards. The words 'left' and 'right' may lead to confusion. When 10-year-old George was having his eyes tested the optician said 'Look left' and George said, 'I can't remember which way left is to look at it'. Concrete objects such a large sign with an arrow are better than abstract language which may be confusing to those with directionality difficulties. Asked if he found telling left and right difficult, 12-year-Mohammed said, 'No, I don't because I

always stick up my finger and thumb and make an "L", then I know this is the left side.'

- Some when using playground equipment such as a climbing frame are unable to co-ordinate their arms and legs. They fall and hurt themselves because they are unable to calculate the distance between the top of the equipment and the ground. Others find crawling through a tunnel difficult, like 10-year-old Jane. She was unable to make her way out of her sleeping bag which she had slid down in her sleep on a school camping trip and woke the whole group up with her screams.
- Make different shapes and later objects to develop finger and thumb control and develop finger muscles using sand, clay, paints, plasticine, pastry or playdough. Turning a skipping rope helps develop the wrist muscles and helps arm and shoulder movements. Use a cardboard weaving loom to make a pattern or design by weaving through holes with a cord or a shoelace. Commercial lacing cards of animals, bugs and seashore shapes with extra long plastic tip laces are available from www.LDAlearning.com.
- Visual-perceptual skills can be practised through games and activities such as those supplied by Ann Arbor Publishing (www.annarbor.co.uk) and the Happy Puzzle Company (www.happypuzzle.co.uk).
- Letter shape recognition and writing can be introduced using finger paints and different surfaces such as carpet tiles or sandpaper. This is a good multi-sensory activity. It is fun to begin with the first letter of the child's own name. A piece of cardboard 30 by 20 cm can be used. Put the correct letter on the card. The child then says A for Amy/Aaron and traces over the letter. Then he can trace over the shape with a glue stick and decorate this by applying stardust or sand.
- Practise pincer movement between finger and thumb first using clothes pegs or bulldog clips to hang doll's clothes on a washing line. It is fun to make designs by putting pegs around the polystyrene base on pizza packaging. Teach children to use scissors and to cut and paste. Use left-handed scissors for left-handed children (available from www.taskmasteronline.co.uk). There are a variety of non-conventional scissors on the market such as 'easy-grip' and 'self-opening' scissors which makes use easier (www.LDAlearning.com).

Handy hints for using scissors and teaching cutting skills:

- Choose the most appropriate pair depending on individual needs and teach the child how to hold them.
- Practise cutting out pictures of favourite animals, pets and footballers. Put these on a poster and make them into a collage. The *Developing Scissor Skills Book* includes photocopiable activities (www.taskmasteronline.co.uk).
- When learning to swim the synchronised movements involving arms, legs and breathing are difficult. Tell the swimming instructor about the child's difficulties with co-ordination and following instructions.

Tests

Portwood, M. (1996) *Motor Skills Screening (7 Years–Adult) in Developmental Dyspraxia* (David Fulton Publishers; www.fultonpublishers.co.uk).

Beery, K.E, Buktenica, N.A. and Beery, N.A. (2004) *Beery Buktenica Visual Motor Integration Test* (Ann Arbor Publishers; www.annarbor.co.uk) is suitable for ages 2–18.

Difficulties associated with laterality, directionality and time; suggestions to help compensate and overcome them

Laterality refers to the side of the body used for a set task or function and applies to the eyes, ears, hands and feet.

- A 39-year-old adult dyslexic parent said, 'When I'm laying the table I always have to stand by the place I'm setting to get the cutlery right'. Many playground games depend on language involving directionality and listening skills. Help by playing games such as Simon says, or the hokey cokey (in which you say 'Put your right leg in, your right leg out, in, out, in, out, and shake it all about'). Younger children can play 'Heads, shoulders, knees and toes' which they touch in sequence. The words 'right' and 'left can be problematic. Some children are unable to remember which hand or foot is the right and which the left. Hannah was preparing for a ballet examination and became very upset when she was told to take 'five steps to the right', then 'five steps to the left'. Her mother observed the dilemma and noticed that the 'bar' was on the right and the piano was on the left. Hannah could remember that the bar side was right and the piano side was left. This mnemonic solved the problem.
- People with these problems have difficulty with the prepositions and adverbs involving sequencing and direction such as 'up' and 'down', 'before' and 'after', 'backwards' and 'forwards'. Games, numeracy and science often involve the use and understanding of these words.

The significance of handedness and brain lateralisation have long been considered as a cause or a correlate of developmental disorders in speech and language including dyslexia and auto-immune disorders (Geschwind and Behan, 1982). Orton (1937) argued that mixed handedness indicates that the brain is not strongly lateralised and this accounts for reading and spelling difficulties. He did not regard left-handedness as having any adverse effect and said that 'there is no real reason to consider the straight left-handed individual in any way inferior to the right-handed except by reason of those inconveniences which are forced upon them by the custom and usage of the right-handed majority'. It was the lack of fixed dominance manifested in ambidexterity that was significant. Zangwill (1960) subscribed to the theory that left-handedness indicates that there is imperfect brain lateralisation and this makes the individual vulnerable to language and reading disorders.

Tests of laterality involving the hand, eye, ear and foot were included in assessments and for SpLD test batteries such as the Aston Index (Thomson and Newton, 1979). Bishop (1990) examined sixteen studies for links between crossed eye–hand dominance and reading problems and established that cross-lateralisation is just as high in normal readers.

Bishop (1990) reviewed the literature because of 'stagnation of research in this area' and the 'controversy and confusion' surrounding this 'controversial topic' (Satz, 1990). She reported that:

- Most people are right-handed.
- There are slightly more male than female left-handers.
- There is some evidence that handedness is inherited. A family study of dyslexia showed that there was not an association between dyslexia and left handedness in relatives of dyslexic subjects (Pennington et al., 1987).
- Babies are normally bilateral until they are about 7 months old. Gradually a consistent preference is established. By the age of 3 years handedness in right-handers is stabilised (Hildreth, 1949). Handedness preference stabilises with age but there is disagreement about when this occurs.

An informal test for preferred handedness includes establishing the hand used to:

- bounce a ball
- catch a bean-bag
- throw a bean-bag
- draw a picture.

Should unfamiliar or infrequent activities be included in the assessment of handedness? Should handedness be measured by the use of the writing hand as well as the use of the preferred writing hand? Miles et al. (1996) used five categories of handedness including consistent right and consistent left, inconsistent right and inconsistent left and ambidexterity. They studied 981 10-year-olds, of whom 235 were dyslexic. Of the dyslexics 74.9 per cent were consistently right-handed and 5.5 per cent consistently left-handed; 7.7 per cent inconsistently right-handed and 5.5 per cent inconsistently left-handed and 5.5 per cent were ambidextrous. They concluded that 'routine reporting of the handedness of dyslexic children appears to have little to commend it' but 'we do not claim that the issue of handedness in relation to dyslexia is dead'.

Bishop (1990) reviewed over twenty studies of handedness in dyslexics and found that 11.2 per cent of the dyslexics and 5.8 per cent of the controls were left-handed. She hypothesised that as a result 'we should expect to find poorer motor performance overall in dyslexics compared to controls'.

Evidence to support this hypothesis was found by Nicolson and Fawcett (1994) in the cerebellum. Brain imaging technology such as functional magnetic resonance imaging (fMRI), magnetoencephalography (MEG), both of which are non-invasive measures, and Positron Emission Tomography (PET) scans can be used to measure activity in the brain while a certain function is being carried out; this is then converted into three-dimensional pictures. These images show the differences between brain architecture and regional functional organisation in dyslexics and controls. Stein (2004) when studying genetics using brain imaging techniques reported that 'hand motor skill is significantly inherited' in 41 per cent of dyslexic subjects.

Lack of dominant handedness may yet turn out to be another useful early indicator of SpLD. The existence of mixed laterality is as yet only a small piece of the big puzzle dyslexia and dyspraxia present when causes, theory, identification and intervention are being considered.

Some dyslexics have a poor sense of time as well as poor language associated with time. Words such as 'today', 'tomorrow', 'yesterday' and 'next week' are challenging and cause confusion. On a Wednesday, 12-year-old Sholto said to his piano teacher, 'I am going to see you yesterday next week.' In fact he wanted to say, 'I'm going to see you on Tuesday, next week.'

When a 16-year-old pupil wanted some help with revision for a re-sit of his English GCSE examination he was asked when he had to submit the coursework by. He said that it had to be in 'by the *last* Monday in November'. Subsequently his father made a frantic phone call to the teacher, saying that Steven had got the dates wrong. The coursework should have been handed in by the *first* Monday in November. This scuppered his chances of an autumn re-sit. He had to wait until June to retake his exams.

Reading a clock and telling the time can be problematic for some. Often they are 9–10 years old before they can do this. They are confused because twenty to eleven and ten forty are the same time. Use an old-fashioned analogue clock rather than a digital one. Use a watch and clock with Arabic rather than Roman numerals on the face. The language associated with time can be confusing. Children can master five o'clock or half past five but recognising ten to five and twenty past five may cause a problem. They may also have difficulties with calculating or estimating how long it will take to do something. 'You have ten minutes left before you go to school' may not mean anything. If the child who uses English as his first language has problems with learning about time he will have even greater difficulties when he is learning about it in French or in mathematics. The Teaching Clock and Digital Teaching Clock (www.taskmasteronline.co.uk) help deal with 'to' and 'past' and 'digital' and 'analogue' confusions. Problems associated with time do not disappear when telling the time has been mastered. Residual difficulties persist even for adults including:

- calculating how long it will take to complete a task such as an essay or how long a routine car journey will take, resulting in constantly missed deadlines or appointments
- time management, including prioritising tasks – for example, spending too long on research on the Internet and on making notes, then not having enough time to write up the assignment
- losing track of time, including the major markers in the day – breaktime, lunchtime and hometime – consequently being totally disorientated and never being in the right place at the right time

- reluctance to use a diary and a failure to check deadlines, resulting in homework not being handed in on time.

Terms and conditions to include in a happy family's 'homework treaty'

Check with the school and obtain a copy of its 'home learning policy' document, if available. This should be a blueprint for enforcement and help when questions or disputes arise concerning homework assignments. A 'homework treaty' can then be drawn up.

- It should specify times when work is to be done, probably between 6.30 and 7.30 on Monday to Friday evenings and between 9.30 and 11.00 on Saturday mornings. It should state when holiday homework is to be done, such as in the first week of the holidays, not the night before the first day of term.
- Keep a record on a kitchen bulletin board of the days on which homework is set, for example maths and history on Monday, English and science on Tuesday. Both parties should check on Friday what the weekend assignments are rather than leaving it until eight o'clock on Sunday evening.
- Include the school guidelines and the recommended times for each subject However, be realistic because dyslexic pupils often take three times as long as their peers to complete written work.
- The place where the work is to be done should be agreed, whether the kitchen table or a desk in the child's bedroom.
- Display copies of the homework treaty prominently for easy reference for both parties.
- Highlight special events or recurring 'bones of contention', such as the day of the weekly spelling test.
- No discussion or changes are permissible for six weeks.
- Fresh talks and renegotiation of the terms are then permissible, if necessary.
- Both parties should sign and date the written copy of the treaty and shake hands on it.
- A homework diary for the younger child is essential. If they can programme it themselves, older pupils could use a personal digital assistant (PDA) such as the Palm Zire 21. It is suitable for 11 years–adult. Others prefer small micro cassette recorders such as a Sony M-670V which is suitable for 7 years–adult.

Figure 2

- Maria's mother said that a very simple but very effective form of support for her 13-year-old daughter was given when she had to report to her form teacher each morning before class. The teacher quickly checked when homework had to be handed in, for example maths on Friday morning. She then directed Maria to the subject teacher's classroom, thus ensuring that the work was put in the correct place.

- Try to make an arrangement with the teacher whereby she or the teaching assistant checks that all-important messages are copied down correctly. The adult should check that the spellings for the weekly spelling test have been copied correctly. James was given a detention because he did not copy out the spellings for the weekly test. Many parents are dyslexic themselves and may be unaware of spelling errors. A dyslexia-friendly option is to give the child a computer print-out of the list of spellings to be leaned. This can be done easily by users of an interactive whiteboard. Messages or instructions written down incorrectly can be a source of irritation or confusion. Hannah had to do two lots of homework because she wrote page 18 instead of page 81 in her maths book. Her teacher made her do the second lot next evening because she said, 'You were careless and it will teach you a lesson.' A tape recorder prevented further misunderstanding.

- Keep a list of telephone numbers and e-mail addresses of parents of children in your child's class on the pin-board to use when details of homework are lost or forgotten. Dyslexia-friendly schools now put homework on-line via the school network. They are also useful to check the time he needs to be ready for the school trip to the Science Museum.

- Schools should have a whole-school homework policy document including recommendations for time spent, particularly for children at senior level so that they are not overloaded by individual subject teachers or expected to do four subjects on one night.

- It is also important that children know and understand the homework that has been set. It can be useful to buy copies of set textbooks to help with further explanation or parts missing from notes taken during the lesson. Teachers in dyslexia-friendly schools give print-outs of key vocabulary so that the science experiment can then be written up at home. Christopher sobbed his heart out when trying to do his history homework, writing a report about a video he had watched in the morning at school about the Nile in ancient Egypt. He could not remember the names of the gods, cities, rulers.

- Provision should be made to differentiate between children of different ability. A teacher can come to an agreement with parents whereby they sign the homework book when half an hour has been spent on a subject even if it is not completed. This should ensure that the child is not kept in at breaktime or given a detention next day. Pupils with SpLD should be provided with modified assignments which make allowances for their particular learning difficulties. For instance, the dyspraxic child might be allowed to give one-word answers rather than complete sentences when doing a history questionnaire or the dyslexic child could be asked to learn ten of the twenty spellings. Spelling tests cause dyslexic children more stress and grief than almost any other activity they have to do. Tackle the list of words a few at a time each day rather than in one marathon session the night before the test.

- Parents and teachers should agree at the beginning of the academic year about the type and quantity of help to give. The SENCO could convene a meeting of parents and teachers and run a homework 'surgery'. George's mother finished copying geography notes for her son because it had taken him half an hour to do one-third of the work set. The teacher objected to seeing the adult's work in his book. His mother argued that finishing the copying meant he would be able to revise for exams.

The compromise was that in future a word-processed version could be made and stuck in the exercise book. Dictionary work often takes a dyslexic pupil ages to do because he gets lost when saying the alphabet. A dyslexia-friendly option is to allow the use of an electronic dictionary such as the Franklin Literacy Word Bank which is linked to the requirements of the National Curriculum. It has a very well-laid-out keyboard (www.dyslexic.com/franklin). Coursework and project work provide a significant proportion of marks in many subjects in, for example, GCSE. Teachers and examining boards have to establish what is legitimate help and what is cheating. 'It is acceptable for parents and others to act as primary sources or to give guidance on sources. But they must not be involved in the execution of the work, whether in written form or artefact' (TES, 2004b). This directive is open to abuse and it is difficult to draw up the parameters for policing it. What about the parent who 'tells' a pupil the correct spelling and helps with punctuation and syntax when he is editing a first draft? Teachers are forbidden by the examining boards to 'improve' children's work except by drawing attention to 'general defects' and are required to sign a validation declaration stating that the work to the best of their knowledge has been carried out by the pupil without outside help. This is becoming ever more difficult with Internet sites which include model examination answers and essays for students.

- Have a colour-coded copy of your child's school timetable printed as large as possible on a pin-board in the kitchen and in his bedroom. Keep another in his homework diary and another in his locker. Include details of extracurricular clubs or activities, giving times, venues, equipment needed and the organiser's telephone number. Joanna was very upset when she had forgotten to bring her swimming things to school and then wasn't able to go swimming. Check the timetable every evening before bedtime. Highlight days when your child has to take specialist equipment to school. Colour coding helps: for example, use a green pen to remind him that he has to take his PE equipment on Tuesdays and Fridays. Use a red pen to help him remember to take the overalls he needs for science lessons on Mondays and Wednesdays. Use blue for Cub or Scout uniform on Mondays. Buy five different-coloured plastic stacking boxes and place one on top of the other. Label the front and the lid of each box with the days of the week. Itemise the contents to be included in each box by checking on the timetable. Colour code where appropriate. Write on the label what is needed for each day so that it is clearly visible. Pin a colour-coded master timetable with a picture of a wizard on the wall above the stacked boxes. Each evening when the pupil gets back from school he must empty the contents of the school bag into the correct box before dashing to watch television or disappearing to ride his bicycle. This could be included in the homework treaty. Colour-coded files, exercise books and textbooks with removable sticky labels are useful. Geography books could be green. This helps to make them immediately recognisable and is another reminder to put them in Tuesday's box which also has a green sticky label.
- The school bag and games kit should be packed from the 'Boxing Wizard's Boxes' (Figure 3) the night before and put by the front door so that they are not forgotten in the morning rush. Post-it notes can be put on the inside of the front door with reminders such as 'Don't forget the lunch box in the fridge'.

- Before going upstairs to bed your child can use the following checklist instead of the 'Boxing Wizard's Boxes' system to ensure that the following have been packed:

  - completed homework
  - homework diary, checked and signed by a parent/carer
  - textbooks
  - exercise books or files for next day's lessons
  - pencil case and calculator, laptop if used.

- Keep a copy of the school calendar on the pin-board.
- Mark the dates of tests, examinations and deadlines for coursework. School trips can be denoted with a highlighter pen including requirements, for example a packed lunch. Dyslexic children need longer to revise and need adequate notice of tests and exams.
- Have a routine clear-out of your child's school bag. Decide whether the contents are 'trash or treasure'. Keep an eye out for undelivered notes or letters or homework that has not been handed in to be marked.
- Designate a day and a time for a weekly spring clean which will include separating worksheets, handouts and work into individual files.
- Put coursework on CD-Roms as back-up in case the computer crashes. Label and date these clearly. Keep them in a designated box on a shelf where they are clearly visible. Keep hard copies of work in individual files. Date and number the pages of each piece of work.
- Some schools are now using e-mail to correspond with parents. A very simple, cheap and effective method used by one school is to have a Jiffy bag which is used for the whole term for all correspondence between home and school. Both home and school check the contents regularly and initial it when an item has been received. If not using this brown envelope system, put a sticker on your child's pencil case or a red cross on his hand to help him to remember to deliver the letters from home. Another useful suggestion is to encourage him to put notes or 'tear-off' slips in his lunch box. These will be found when the lunch box is being washed even not until the next morning. It's better late than never.

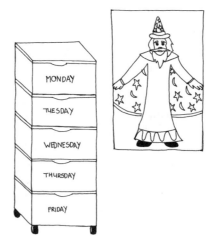

Figure 3 Boxing Wizard's Boxes.

- It is better to email or send photocopies of notes and circulars. Verbal messages are a recipe for disaster for dyslexics because they have problems with short-term memory. The pupil will often not be able to follow a series of instructions because the teacher gave too much information or spoke too quickly. Research evidence shows that dyslexics process language more slowly (Tallal *et al.* 1997). Older pupils can use a handheld tape recorder to record messages including details about homework. MiniDisc recorders are easier to use but are more expensive. iANSYST is a useful source for information and sales (www.dyslexic.com).
- Make a train or bus timetable and stick this inside the front cover of your child's homework notebook. Put times FROM in red so that he does not confuse them with times TO, if he has to phone to say he is coming home on a later train or bus or that he is playing in an 'away' match. Enlarge it on a photocopier and laminate it to ensure that the print is large enough to be seen clearly. Older pupils who have PDAs can set the alarm and include these details.
- Give the child a phone card when he is old enough to use it. At the beginning of the year help him practise using a public phone so that he is able to do this in emergencies. If he has a mobile phone, pre-programme key numbers so that he can use them quickly and easily. Stick his own mobile number on the back of the phone in case he needs to tell someone what it is.
- Name all equipment and clothing as boldly as possible and on the surface or outside of garments. Commercial nametapes can have lettering as big as 2 cm. These make it difficult for someone else to 'borrow' clothing or equipment. They are great for socks, sweaters and shirts and they also make it easier for your child to find his clothes in the scrum in the cloakroom after a PE lesson or games. Or else mark everything with indelible pens. It helps a child who cannot read or does not know his left from his right if right-footed shoes are marked with a red pen and left with a green pen.
- Check that you know the school rules about uniform before buying expensive trainers and then discovering that these cannot be worn except perhaps for games.
- Schools usually provide a list of uniform clothing, equipment and books needed. Keep a copy of this to hand for reference throughout the year.
- Parents should hand in payment for school trips to the school secretary themselves to avoid tears.
- If the pupil has a lesson with a specialist teacher or a music lesson, put it in his homework diary. Also put a sticker on his hand and perhaps write the time and the venue such as the room number on his wrist to help him to remember. Older pupils can set the alarm on their PDAs providing they do not disturb other pupils.
- Try to establish a routine time for doing homework, for example after watching *Neighbours*, if your child has not already signed a 'homework treaty'. Allow him time to relax after school. He should work with the television off. Some pupils can concentrate better if they can simultaneously listen to background music. The music should be soft and not have a strong rhythm. Preference will depend on individual learning styles. Children should work early in the evening rather than late when they are too tired.
- Do supervise and help and check the homework, particularly the instructions. Don't just send your child up to his bedroom to 'get on with it'. He often won't get started or will get distracted and waste time. Remember that many dyslexics have a poor sense of time and lack organisational skills. Some will spend thirty-five minutes colouring in a picture for geography and then run out of time to do the written response. It is helpful

to use a timer. This helps to develop time management and is a transferable skill, useful, for example, in examinations.

- Read the text and instructions for those with poor reading skills. Poor readers are often poor comprehenders because of working memory difficulties. They will often forget the contents of what they read because of the mental effort they require to decode the words. Help them by encouraging them to highlight keywords. It helps to do a summary to learn and later revise the contents for a test or examination. ICT can be used such as the Reading Pen (www.scanningpens.co.uk) which scans a single word or full line of text on a page which it displays and reads aloud. It can also spell a word aloud and give the *Concise Oxford English Dictionary* definition. It stores the last eighty words which can be used to revise and review word recognition and spelling skills. It is battery operated and suitable for age range 11–adult. It requires good fine motor skills to operate. It can also be used for translation into over twenty languages.

  Tell your child a spelling when he needs it. Discuss with his teacher at an open evening if she would be prepared not to deduct marks for spelling errors, particularly in writing tasks. An inability to spell inhibits creativity and interferes with the thought process. Ignoring spelling errors when marking writing assignments will do wonders for a child's self-esteem and vocabulary.

- Encourage him to use a ruler to help him keep his place on the line when he is copying from a textbook. Tinted reading rulers help those children who suffer from visual stress resulting in distortions and a sensitivity to white paper (www.crossboweducation.com).

Websites for pre-school activities, homework and revision

Websites for pre-school activities include:

www.club-web.com/kids/storytime/nurse-rhymes
www.ash.udel.edu/ash
www.randomhouse.com/seussville
www.bbc.co.uk/schools/preschool
www.bbc.co.uk/schools/laac
www.bbc.co.uk/cbeebies (this includes activities and games based on CBeebies characters such as the Teletubbies, Fimbles, Tweenies and Bob the Builder and is suitable for children up to 6 years).

Websites for homework include:

www.homeworkhigh.co.uk
www.learn.co.uk
www.nc.uk.net
www.topmarks.co.uk
www.bbc.co.uk/education/revision (this breaks subjects into the bare essentials, includes graphics and examples of examination questions)
www.bbc.co.uk/schools (information)
www.bbcschoolshop.com (publishing)
www.dfes.gov.uk

Checklist for resources and a shopping list for dyslexic and dyspraxic pupils

- Duplicate pens and extra cartridges if ink pens are used; pencils, rubbers and sharpeners, compass, protractor, a selection of different-coloured 'jel' pens and different-coloured highlighters including fine and broad line pens. It is worth the expense of having a second pencil case at home with all the necessaries. Keep these all together in a box or drawer which is out of bounds for other family members. See-through pencil cases are time savers because the pencil sharpener is immediately visible when needed

- file paper, dividers, plastic A4 wallets

- supply of A4 ring binder files of different colours and stick-on labels for the front cover and spine

- card index box with alphabetic cards and cards; these are useful for definitions and revision notes. Glue stick, post-it notes, large paper clips, scissors, ink eradicator, non-opaque rulers, 15 and 30 cm. The smaller ruler can also be used to help track words and when following lines of text

- large format calculator and a scientific calculator for older pupils

- spellchecker with a speech option and thesaurus

- laptop computer, disks, storage system for disks

- tape recorder and blank tapes

- good-quality headphones to use with PC

- subject dictionaries

- revision guides

- washable ink, which should always be used; it can be rubbed out with a rubber eraser and does not stain clothes or belongings

- a list of the 100 words most often misspelt (Ott, 1997: 403) and the NLS (1998) high frequency lists. Put this on the inside of your child's school desk for easy reference. Highlight his particular *bêtes noires*

- Digital watches can also be useful if the alarm can be set and if they do not disrupt the rest of the class. Set the alarm before school

Books

Dyslexic children generally read less than their peers because they find it difficult and may read very slowly. Children need literature which they can read with ease and fluency if they are to enjoy and benefit from it. Sources for audio books include:

- commercial outlets
- local lending libraries
- listening books: the National Listening Library (www.listening-books.org.uk) is a postal audio library service for anyone who has an illness or disability. Individual membership is currently £70 a year and £150 for organisations such as schools which are entitled to borrow up to four titles at any one time. The fee includes book lists and the loan of up to two audio tapes. Postage is free to and from the recipient. It has an extensive range of titles.

Hints on why and how to use ICT resources

- Watching a video of a Shakespeare play before reading it helps children to understand the plot and memorise the characters' names which can otherwise be problematic. Watching a first-class production with Oscar-winning actors in the leading roles often brings a play alive for those who struggle to follow the plot when pupils take it in turns to read the text in the class room.
- Read the textbook to your child to help his comprehension of history homework. Recap the main points – he will then be able to find the answers more quickly. Ask the teacher to allow him to dictate his answers on tape. She may also allow the pupil to dictate his answers if he has weak writing skills.
- Encourage him to learn and use a variety of planning strategies such as a storyboard plan or a mindmap. The computer is a great ally for the poor planner who struggles to organise and sequence his ideas. A computer package such as Kidspiration will produce a variety of plans in a variety of layouts.
- Ensure that he has a handheld spellchecker which is appropriate for his age. Encourage him to use it and to add to it the words he frequently misspells.
- Encourage him to proofread all written work by using the mnemonic C-O-P-S to check for Capital letters, Omissions, Punctuation and Spelling (Ott, 2007b). Remind him to check for spellings of words he always gets wrong such as 'they' or 'said'. You could keep a list of these on a pin-board or at the back of his homework diary. Highlight the problematic letters.
- Encourage your child to use information and communication technology (ICT) whenever possible.
- Playing on the computer develops skills. Games can be educational as well as entertaining.
- Those who use a computer at home are more confident or efficient when using it at school.
- ICT enables pupils to work at their own pace and public exposure of failure is minimised.

- It builds confidence when packages give feedback and encouragement and are appropriate to pupils' interest level and skills. Self-esteem is established when pupils produce a final copy that is error free.
- ICT develops language skills, enabling pupils to use the vocabulary they want but do not dare to use because they are unable to spell the words.
- Writing skills develop and are enhanced by the ability to edit, revise and cut and paste work.
- The use of multimedia improves learning and matches individual learning styles.
- It allows those with poor motor skills such as dyspraxia to produce legible work which can be marked for knowledge, ideas and understanding.
- Speech recognition technology is a godsend for those with poor motor skills. It allows pupils to keep pace with their peers by making it possible for them to finish their work on time. It levels the playing field because the word processor deals with the secretarial skills, thus freeing the learner's mental space to concentrate on the cognitive aspects of writing. Dragon Naturally Speaking is the market leader and supersedes Dragon Dictate as the best speech recognition package.
- The spellchecker, dictionary, thesaurus and CD-ROMs are often the key to a rich treasure trove of knowledge and experience.
- Use a tape recorder to listen to a set text or play, particularly if your child cannot read easily or reads very slowly. Buy a cassette recorder such as the Sony TCM which has a speech control facility for those with poor short-term and working memory. It has a voice-operated recording (VOR) facility as well as a tape counter which is helpful when doing revision. Suitable for age range 11 years–adult, it has a 'slow' button as an option to help the child assimilate or repeat information or learn, for example, French or English vocabulary. Parents could record their child's science work, for example, so that he can then play it back and listen to it when he revises for exams.

  Read & Write 8 GOLD (www.texthelp.com) is an expensive top-of-the-range computer package. It claims to be the 'one-stop solution' for literacy, language and learning. It has been developed to help SEN and dyslexic individuals. It can read back text as it is typed or later. It scans and reads text on screen. It keeps a log of spelling errors which is useful for review. It has a word prediction feature and a speaking spellchecker (age range 7 years–adult).
- Many books are now available on CD-ROM so these can be read on the built-in screen reader, as can information from the Internet. There is a zoom facility on Microsoft Word which will magnify text for those with poor visual perception. The background and the colour of the screen can be changed, so too can the font style and size. Word also has a highlighter facility.
- Taped stories – audio books – are stimulating (www.audiobookcollection.com). Often they can spark a child's interest in reading. The most effective way to use audio books is for the parent and child to follow the text while simultaneously listening to the story.

- Buy audio tapes or CD-Roms of set books for examination candidates. There are now software packages of talking books available for the computer such as the following: Start-to-Finish Books (www.donjohnston.co.uk) and Clicker Books (www.cricksoft.com).
- Spellcheckers have revolutionised the lives of many dyslexic people and come to the rescue of beleaguered editors. Some snags still arise, as when homophones are used incorrectly. The speech option spellchecker can overcome these difficulties by giving definitions and using them in sentences for clarification and meaning. Some find it helpful if the spellchecker is turned off when they are doing their first draft of a piece of writing, otherwise the frequent interruptions (because of their many spelling errors) interfere with their train of thought.
- If your child can use the computer and word processor encourage him to do so, especially for coursework. Essays can be drafted, revised and edited and the spellchecker and grammar checker used. Co-writer 4000 is a talking word processor package which, when the first letter of a word is pressed, will predict and write the rest. This is useful for those with poor word retrieval, poor word naming skills and poor spelling. It can also read the words so that the pupil can simultaneously hear and see what he writes. It is for age range 5–adult. There is also a foreign language version (www.donjohnston.co.uk).

One of the best investments in time is to learn to touch-type. It is a lifelong skill that helps learners. It should be compulsory for SEN pupils to be given a short course in touch-typing. However it is important to consider the following issues:

- Some dyslexic/dyspraxic pupils quickly learn the keyboard and quickly build up speed. Jayme aged 12 years had ten one-hour lessons once a week and practised for ten minutes five days a week. At the end of the short course he was able to type 42 words per minute (wpm). James, 13 years old, worked for five terms one hour a week and followed this up with daily practice at home. He was pleased to be able to type 19 wpm at the end of the course.
- Some dyslexic pupils have enormous difficulties memorising the QWERTY keyboard because of their sequencing difficulties and may end up needing to look at the keyboard.
- Touch-typing should become an automatic skill like changing the gears on a car.

There are a number of commercial packages to teach touch-typing such as:

- Mavis Beacon Teaches Typing
- Typing Instructor Deluxe, which uses colour, music and animation and gives immediate feedback during the lessons, games and tests (age range 7 years–adult) award winner
- Type to Learn V3, which uses real words and incorporates teaching phonics and grammar skills (www.dyslexic.com).

With good keyboarding skills a child can handle the secretarial aspects of projects and coursework efficiently. In practice this will often make the work easier for him to do. It will be legible, neater and often of a higher standard. Being able to choose a larger font and different font styles also helps. A font no smaller than 12 point should be used. Litterick (2005) recommends 'Trebuchet and Verdana which are both standard Microsoft fonts (which they went to a lot of trouble to develop) to ensure they are legible on screen at different sizes'. Some individuals prefer Arial and younger users like Comic Sans because it looks more like cursive writing. 'There have been some fonts designed for users with dyslexia but no serious research has been done to test their validity'. A survey conducted on line (Smythe, 2005) reported that of 6,500 voters 28 per cent prefer white, 22 per cent blue and 19 per cent prefer cream backgrounds and 50 per cent preferred Arial font. When the physical slog of writing by hand is removed and the confidence and comfort of the spellchecker provided, often reluctant and restricted writers blossom and their ideas and opinions then flow onto the page.

When buying a word processor package try to choose one that has a speech option. Nelson and Parker (2004) replicated a study carried out by O'Hare and McTear (1997) on a sample of eleven pupils of a chronological age of 12–14 years and a reading age of 9–10 years. They carried out the following tasks on the same piece of text:

- handwritten dictation
- typed dictation
- voice recognition.

The results showed that 'voice input was on average, up to eight times faster than typing, and five times faster than handwriting'. The pupils' output was: fifteen wpm for handwriting; nine wpm for typing; seventy-nine wpm when using voice recognition. However, a survey of 220 dyslexic users found that 62 per cent of those who had used voice recognition software found it difficult or unhelpful. This could be due to inadequate training and/or poor expressive language skills.

The speech option is a useful multi-sensory device because the text can be seen and heard by the user.

The Internet is proving to be a great boon for research for projects and coursework because it is more accessible than a thick encyclopaedia.

Summary and conclusions

- Parents and children who are faced with the realities of dyslexia in their daily lives know that it is much more than a reading disorder.
- Dyslexia and dyspraxia are part of a continuum of 'specific learning difficulties' which are defined as:

  - impaired ability to develop a skill (or set of skills) to an age-apppropriate level or to a level consistent with other abilities

-   difficulties which interfere significantly with academic achievement and in daily life
-   not caused by a medical condition.

Adequate opportunities to develop the skills have been made available (American Psychiatric Association, 1994).

•   Disagreement still exists in the international scientific community and in the education world about definitions. Some existing working definitions may need updating due to evolving evidence about the characteristics of the condition.

•   The earlier the identification of specific learning difficulties the better the prognosis (Foorman *et al.*, 1998).

•   Parents' opinions, observations and concerns are now encouraged and accepted as being an integral part of early intervention and identification. Research by Sylva and Evangelou (2003) showed clear evidence that pre-school 3–5-year-olds benefit when parents are involved in their education. Advantages include better vocabulary and understanding of language and of books and print.

•   Education and healthcare professionals play distinct but frequently overlapping roles in the diagnosis of learning difficulties.

•   The role of language is central to child development. Oral language skills are the bedrock of future literacy. There is increasing evidence for the importance of interaction and stimulation between the child and adult carers.

•   Children need to learn and develop skills through the medium of play and games.

•   Evidence about the impact of dyspraxia on the short-term and long-term development of fine and gross motor skills is more readily available.

•   Parents and children need to arrive at a consensus about doing homework. Ground rules are essential for family harmony. Ideally schools and parents should be mutually supportive about homework arrangements.

•   Modern technology is making dramatic changes to all our lives as well as empowering those who learn differently and enhancing their prospects.

•   Help with organisation and practical support is part and parcel of good parenting for all children but is crucial for a successful outcome to dyslexia. The best investment is time rather than money.

•   ICT support has had a major impact on the lives of those who embrace what is on offer. Speech recognition software is the most empowering tool of communication yet to be developed for dyslexic and dyspraxic individuals. Training and support are necessary to maximise the benefits and potential of technology.

Chapter 2

Why good home–school partnerships promote better relationships and further understanding of special educational needs

Outline

- Practical implications of SEN legislation for parents, teachers and professionals
- Provision in Scotland
- Provision in Northern Ireland
- Provision in the Republic of Ireland
- Provision in the United States of America
- Provision in England and Wales
- The implications of the Disability Discrimination Act (DDA) 1995 for those with SEN
- The duties and responsibilities of maintained and independent schools arising from SENDA 2001
- The SENDIST guidelines for making a claim
- What are special educational needs?
- A SEN parents' charter of needs
- The Parent Partnership Service
- Guidelines for the content of IEPs
- What do parents find useful to know about the school's provision for SEN pupils?
- What is a statement of special educational needs and what provision should it include?
- The implications of the Children Act 2004
- Summary and conclusions

Practical implications of SEN legislation for parents, teachers and professionals

Children have rights and parents have duties and responsibilities towards them, including care and protection. These principles are enshrined in legislation.

The Warnock Report, *Special Educational Needs: Report of the Committee of Inquiry into the Education of Handicapped Children and Young People* (DES, 1978), was the catalyst for change in policy and provision for children and young people with 'special educational needs' and changed much of the terminology and the exclusion policies used previously. Many of the recommendations of the report were included in the Education Act 1981. It stated that 'the successful education of children with special educational needs is dependent on the full involvement of their parents; indeed unless the parents are seen as equal partners in the education process, the purpose of our report will be frustrated'. The Education Act 1986 stipulated that schools should have parent representatives on the governing body. The Education Act 1988 required schools to send parents an annual progress report about their child.

The United Nations (UN) Convention on the Rights of the Child 1989 had a significant impact on educational policy. It set standards which sovereign states were obliged to meet and influenced the formulation of legislation. The UK government ratified this UN policy and human rights became increasingly important. It resulted in legislation including the Disability Discrimination Act (DDA) 1995. The Education Act 1992 set out proposals for establishing the Office for Standards in Education (Ofsted).

In 1994 a World Conference on Special Needs Education was held in Salamanca at which ninety-two governments and twenty-five international organisations were represented. Its main findings included parental involvement and it prescribed inclusion. These were enshrined in the *Salamanca Declaration and Framework for Action* (UNESCO, 1994). It endorsed a move towards 'educating all children including those who have serious disadvantages and disabilities' in mainstream schools because 'regular schools with this inclusive orientation are the most effective means of combating discriminatory attitudes . . . and it assumes human differences are normal and that learning must be adapted to the needs of the child, rather than the child fitted into the process'. It stated that 'schools have to find ways of successfully educating all children', including those with 'serious disadvantages and disabilities'. It recommended that governments should promote the view that the education of children with special educational needs should be a shared task between parents and professionals.

Provision in Scotland (www.dyslexiascotland.com)

A Parent's Guide to Special Educational Needs (SOEID, 1996) involved parents and parent organisations such as Dyslexia Scotland in discussion with education authorities. Scotland did not have a National Curriculum and as a result schools had greater autonomy in provision and allocation of resources for SEN. The Education (Additional Support for Learning) (Scotland) Bill 2005 highlighted partnership and collaboration including co-ordination support plans (CSP) which replaced Record of Needs (RON) which was a document setting out an individual's special educational needs. Children were only given a Record of Needs if their learning needs could not be met by the school's resources. The CSPs set out the provision to be made for pupils with 'additional support needs' (ASN). However, some parent groups were concerned that only children with co-ordination support plans could have recourse to the Additional Support Needs Tribunals when disputes arose.

Provision in Northern Ireland (www.nida.org.uk)

The Code of Practice for Identification and Assessment Needs (DENI, 1998) had different time limits to those in England for assessing pupils who might require a statement. In 2002 the Department of Education Northern Ireland set up a task group to look at provision for dyslexia. The Minister for Education, Martin McGuinness, pointed out that its conclusions:

> highlight[s] very real concerns and challenges for all of us in education, particularly the need for training for classroom teachers in recognising where children have or may have dyslexia and in putting in place the means to address their difficulties and, most importantly, to ensure that the obstacle which their difficulties present in accessing the rest of the curriculum is minimised. Equally, there are challenges for further and higher education, for employers and for society, because dyslexia is not a condition that disappears with maturity.

Parents were to be sent a 'good practice guide'.

Provision in the Republic of Ireland (www.dyslexia.ie)

The Education Act 1998 states that every person in the state, including a person with a disability or other special educational needs, is legally entitled to an 'education . . . which is appropriate to their abilities and needs in line with their human rights entitlement'. The Government of Ireland (2000) produced *Learning-Support Guidelines*. Its keynote was 'supplementary teaching' which 'denotes teaching provided by a learning-support teacher, that is additional to a pupil's regular classroom programme'.

It also guaranteed learning support especially to 'those pupils who are performing at or below the 10th percentile on nationally standardised tests of English reading and/or mathematics'.

> Other pupils whose persistent learning difficulties may be associated with a general or specific learning disability, will normally be referred for psychological assessment, in consultation with parents, and may then be supported by a resource teacher or by some other form of special educational provision. Pending such provision, these pupils should receive support from the learning support teacher.

A Task Force on Dyslexia (2001) was appointed by the Minister of Education. It received written submissions from 399 individuals (the vast majority were parents of dyslexic children), organisations and 896 oral submissions. Its summary of recommendations included:

- Pre-service and in-career development training should be provided to meet the needs of those with learning difficulties.
- The number of places for training educational psychologists should be increased and funding should be provided for assessment by educational psychologists.
- Grants should be given to parents to purchase assistive technology.
- Advice and information on dyslexia should be made available to schools on the identification of dyslexia.

- Parents and guardians should be involved in assessments.
- 'Reasonable accommodations' should be made in state examinations.
- Primary and post-primary schools should incorporate a policy in their School Plan to address the needs of those with specific learning difficulties.
- An exemption from the study of Irish (Gaelige) should be granted when parents submit an educational psychologist's report showing that the student is at or below the tenth percentile on a standardised norm referenced test of reading and spelling.

An on-line programme has been set up to train teachers to work with dyslexic pupils.

Provision in the United States of America (www.interdys.org/DA)

The term 'learning disability' is used to describe those who have special educational needs. The key legislation includes the following:

- Education for All Handicapped Children Act 1975
- Individuals with Disabilities Education Act (IDEA) 1990
- Individuals with Disabilities Education Act (IDEA) 1997

The term 'handicapped' is no longer used as it is considered pejorative. The legislation draws attention to the civil rights of children and inclusion in mainstream classrooms. IDEA (Public Law 105–17) tabulates parents' rights as follows:

- education for their child
- to request an evaluation (assessment) of their child
- to give consent to a school's request to evaluate their child and to teaching provision
- the child to be tested in his mother tongue
- to have access to school records
- to be informed of parents' rights
- to be involved in IEPs
- to be informed of progress and to request a reassessment.

In response to the federal government's continuing concerns about low literacy levels, the National Institute of Child Health and Human Development (2000) reported on the skills critical for reading proficiency and sought to establish scientifically how those skills are most effectively taught (Lyon *et al.*, 2004)

The findings were incorporated in the No Child Left Behind Act 2001 which includes recommendations for: (1) parental involvement; (2) recourse to research to show which teaching programmes are effective; (3) accountability for results, including publishing report cards for pupils; (4) greater local control and flexibility in the use of federal funding to improve schools.

Provision in England and Wales (www.bdadyslexia.org.uk)

The following is an overview of key legislation for SEN.

- Education Act 1981
- Education Act 1993 including the Code of Practice (COP) (1994)
- Disability Discrimination Act 1995
- Education Act 1996
- Special Educational Needs and Disability Act 2001 (SENDA)
- Special Educational Needs Code of Practice (2001)
- Code of Practice for Schools. Disability Discrimination Act (COPSH)
- Code of Practice for Providers of Post-16 Education and Related Services (COPP16).

The implications of the Disability Discrimination Act (DDA) 1995 for those with SEN

The Disability Rights Commission (helpline: 08457 622 633; www.drc-gb.org) provides information and advice for the 8.5 million disabled people in Britain. It highlights and increases awareness for disabled people about their rights. It informs employers and service providers about their obligations. It has produced Codes of Practice for schools and for providers of post-16 education.

Special educational needs, disability discrimination and human rights including inclusion have become burning issues in education. A culture of greater openness and accountability in education has developed.

The DDA 1995 defined disability as 'a physical or mental impairment which has a substantial and long-term adverse effect on [a person's] ability to carry out normal day-to-day activities'. 'Substantial' is taken to mean significant and 'long-term' as lasting for at least twelve months. The impairment must be 'physical or mental' and could be sensory such as blindness; hidden such as diabetes; 'clinically well-recognised' such as manic depression. It could have an effect on one or more of the following:

- mobility
- manual dexterity
- physical co-ordination
- continence
- ability to lift, carry or otherwise move everyday objects
- speech, hearing, eyesight
- memory or ability to concentrate, learn or understand
- perception of the risk of physical danger.

Some of these impairments apply to dyslexic people. To be protected against discrimination under the Act disabled persons must declare that they have a disability. This can be problematic, particularly for employers and employees. It raises issues about assessment, cost and availability of expertise as well as about employment including promotion prospects.

The DDA was amended and extended as the Special Educational Needs and Disability Act 2001 (SENDA). This made it unlawful to discriminate against a disabled pupil in education, training and any services provided wholly or mainly for students by:

- treating him 'less favourably'
- failing to make 'reasonable adjustments'
- failing 'to take steps to prevent disadvantage occurring'.

The duties and responsibilities of maintained and independent schools arising from SENDA 2001

All schools have duties and responsibilities arising from the legislation and the Code of Practice for Schools (COPSH, 2002). The ultimate responsibility for the action of its employees is the governing body, LEA or proprietor. The legislation applies to:

- maintained schools
- maintained nurseries
- pupil referral units
- independent schools
- special schools, both independent and maintained
- further education colleges
- higher education colleges and universities attended by full- or part-time students.

It applies to all areas of school life including extracurricular social, cultural and recreational activities and facilities for physical education and training designed to promote personal or educational development provided by a voluntary organisation (for example, a local branch of the Scouts or Guides).

The DDA 1995, Pt 4, Code of Practice for Schools (2002) draws attention to an example of 'less favourable treatment and discrimination' as follows.

Example 5.23B

A 12-year-old pupil sits and passes the entrance test for an independent school. He is subsequently refused a place when the school finds out that 'he has learning and behavioural difficulties'. Because his behavioural and learning difficulties were related to his disability, the school's course of action is not justified and would be considered to be in breach of the SENDA 2001.

The Code of Practice on School Admissions 1999 permits the following.

- Grammar schools are 'permitted [a] form of selection such as a selection test'.
- Specialist schools 'may give priority in their admissions criteria to a proportion of pupils who show a particular aptitude for the subject in which the school specialises'.
- Independent schools may select by means of ability or aptitude. The DDA 1995 Part 4 Code of Practice for Schools (2002) gives some examples and clarification.

What constitutes discrimination or less favourable treatment?

- Failure to modify examination papers such as enlarging font for a partially sighted pupil or a pupil with low literacy levels may be unlawful.
- Failure to give pupils who have been assessed and granted the additional time allowance of 15 minutes per hour in tests and examinations. Despite the extra cost

involved 'when a dyslexic student requests additional time for a class exam [if] the lecturer says this is not available' this is an unlawful act (COPP16, 2002).

- Failure to provide a reader or a scribe for those entitled to this.
- Failure to provide or permit the use in the examination room of assistive technology such as a computer or laptop for those who use these as their 'normal means of communication'.
- Failure by the school's Head of Centre or Director of Examinations to apply within the deadlines to the appropriate examination board for special arrangements to be made for candidates who are entitled to these because they have a statement or have been formally assessed as needing these. A claim of discrimination cannot be made against an individual working at the school. Claims are to be made against the governing body, LEA, school proprietor or management group.
- Failure to ensure that the technology such as the printer is working in the examination room. Candidates must be present when their work is printed out.
- Teachers who refuse dyslexic pupils permission to tape their lectures may well be acting unlawfully.
- Failure to accept work done on a computer and an insistence that a dyspraxic candidate has to write essays or notes by hand could well be seen as discriminatory.
- Pupils with physical disabilities as well as those with ADD/ADHD may well be discriminated against when they are not allowed 'rest breaks'. 'The reason why he has performed badly in his examination is related to his disability and so he has been treated less favourably'. The college acted unlawfully because it did not allow short rest breaks (COPP16, 2002).
- Failure by head teachers, school matrons or SENCOs to pass relevant information to other members of staff about the special needs of individual pupils may constitute unlawful discrimination.

COPSH (2002) gives an example of a pupil who told the school secretary about her diabetes. She explained that she needed to have a biscuit to hand in case her blood sugar level drops. Later her teacher refused to allow her to bring food into the classroom. The girl had a hypoglycaemic attack. COPSH (2002) argues that the school could not plead ignorance of her condition. It concludes that a lack of knowledge could not be claimed in defence.

Schools that will not allow candidates to choose certain courses or sit examinations in certain subjects because they do not want to jeopardise their place in, for example, the league tables may be guilty of unlawful discrimination. Similarly a student may only be allowed to enter for a lower level examination, for example in mathematics or science.

COPP16 (2002) gave an example of a student with inadequate literacy levels who wanted to do a course in journalism. The college acted lawfully in rejecting her because she did not meet the required academic standards to complete the course. However, it would probably be unlawful for it to introduce a policy rejecting all dyslexic students who want to study journalism. This is because such a policy does not consider 'different levels of dyslexia' or the 'ability of individual applicants'.

Pupils who are allowed additional time or who are permitted to use a word processor may need to be in a separate room to prevent them from being disturbed or distracted by other candidates.

There are a number of issues connected to the curriculum that will need addressing. For example, should a severely dyslexic pupil be exempt from studying a modern language if he cannot remember vocabulary or spell well enough for his work to be comprehensible?

There are many issues surrounding the marking and correcting of spelling that have not been resolved. 'My history teacher is horrible. I got spellings wrong and I now have to write them out ten times, 200 words – and I am dyslexic! I spoke to Mrs [SENCO] and she is trying to sort it out' (Audit Commission, 2002). Some individuals report that they were scarred for life by the humiliation of hearing their spelling test results read out publicly.

Institutions are deemed responsible and their arrangements should be 'anticipatory'. There are a number of unresolved issues and ambiguities concerning the fine details of 'education and associated services'. COPP 16 (2002) acknowledges that their list of criteria when determining what is reasonable is not 'exhaustive'. For example, some universities require dyslexic students to attach a form to an essay or a script which alerts the examiner to their condition. Some students object to this on the grounds of confidentiality, but others regard it as an insurance that their work will be marked for content and understanding.

This is an example about homework included in COPSH (2002):

> *At the end of each lesson, homework is written on the board. A pupil with dyslexia is unable to copy it down in the time. He is given a detention for not doing his homework. The reason he did not do his homework was because of his inability to write it down in the time available, which is part of his disability. More time could have been provided.*
>
> *The detention is likely to amount to unlawful discrimination.*

The Code also includes information about the following:

- preparation for entry to school
- the curriculum
- teaching and learning
- classroom organisation
- timetabling
- grouping of pupils
- homework
- access to school facilities
- activities to supplement the curriculum (for example, a drama group visiting the school)
- school reports
- school policies
- breaks and lunchtime
- serving of school meals
- interaction with peers
- assessment and exam arrangements
- school discipline and sanctions
- exclusion procedures
- school clubs and activities
- school trips
- the school's arrangements for working with other agencies
- preparation of pupils for the next phase of education.

The list is long and inclusive but falls short of fine detail which undoubtedly will be tested over time in the courts of law.

Initially some regulatory and examination bodies considered themselves exempt from DDA regulations. The DDA Amendment Regulations 2003 clarified the situation and a new bill has been proposed. Complaints can be made to the Disability Rights Commission which will provide advice and information. It has a conciliation service. If agreement cannot be reached the complainant has a right to instigate a civil action in a county court. 'Court action must be brought within six months of the alleged discrimination', according to the Special Educational Needs and Disability Tribunal (SENDIST) booklet.

The SENDIST guidelines for making a claim

Disability Discrimination in Schools: How to Make a Claim (DfES, 2002a) states that the claimant has to show the following:

- that your child is disabled
- that the alleged discrimination was connected with your child's disability
- that the alleged discrimination was unjustified
- ideally how best we can put things right.

(Discrimination helpline: 020 7925 5750; www.sendist.gov.uk.)

Special Educational Needs Code of Practice (DfES, 2001)

The revised Code of Practice was issued after lengthy consultation with various organisations involved in special educational needs practice, policy and provision. It takes account of the Education Act 1996 and the SENDA 2001. The key issues were the implementation of equal opportunities for all children and for meeting the needs of those with special educational needs, including a focus on preventive work to ensure that children's special educational needs are identified as quickly as possible and that early action is taken to meet these needs.

What are special educational needs?

'Children have special educational needs if they have a learning difficulty which calls for special educational provision to be made for them' (COP, 2001).

Definition of a learning difficulty (COP, 2001)

Children have a learning difficulty if they:

a) have a significantly greater difficulty in learning than the majority of children of the same age
b) have a disability which prevents or hinders them from making use of educational facilities of a kind generally provided for children of the same age in schools within the area of the local authority.

What does special education provision mean?

a) for children of two or over, educational provision which is additional to, or otherwise different from, the education provision made generally for children of their age in schools maintained by the LEA, other than special schools in the area

b) for children under two, educational provision of any kind.

The fundamental principles include the following:

- A child with special educational needs should have their needs met.
- The special educational needs of children will normally be met in mainstream schools or settings.
- The views of the child should be sought and taken into account.
- Parents have a vital role to play in supporting their child's education.
- Children with special educational needs should be offered full access to a broad, balanced and relevant education, including an appropriate curriculum for the foundation stage and the National Curriculum.

Since the publication of the Warnock Report (1978) and the legislation that it generated, the issuing of a statement of special educational needs was perceived by many as an assurance of additional help. Some parents regarded it as an insurance policy and a warranty for gaining access to a school of their choice or of resources such as ICT equipment as well as for obtaining the help and funds to meet the educational provision 'additional to, or otherwise different from' general provision.

Furthermore, having their child's needs documented and the provision to which they had a statutory right written down was seen as a copper-bottomed guarantee of delivery of the service which was included in the guidelines about the ways and means the child's special needs were to be met. There was an ever-increasing demand by parents for statements. The Education Act 1996 enshrined a right to appeal to the SEN Tribunal about issues involved in LEA assessments.

Those who were dissatisfied with the provision they were offered took the dispute to the SENDIST. The special needs budget rocketed, costs were spiralling and often the most needy children were not receiving help. According to Simmons (1997) a disproportionate number of parents who used the SENDIST were articulate and educated; relatively few were from poor backgrounds or ethnic minorities. The report of the House of Commons Select Committee (1996) highlighted the discrepancies in provision nationally measured by LEAs' appearances before the Tribunal, numbers of which ranged from no appearance from Middlesbrough LEA to eighty-nine by Kent's LEA.

In 1995, the House of Lords gave a judgement on three test cases about negligent failure to provide appropriate education by an LEA for pupils with SEN. Negligence was not proven in E v. Dorset County Council and Others but the case established the principle that educational psychologists, teachers and other similar staff may be held liable for negligence to the children for whom they are responsible. In the 1997 cause célèbre of Phelps v. London Borough of Hillingdon, Pamela Phelps won substantial damages because the High Court found that the LEA's educational psychologist had breached a 'duty of care' and, as a result, failed to 'provide a standard of education' appropriate for her in the light of her dyslexia difficulties which were not diagnosed. In 1998, the Court of Appeal reversed the decision and found that an individual EP does not owe a duty of care because he is part of a multidisciplinary team. In 2000 the House of Lords overturned the Court of Appeal's decision and found in favour of Phelps, making LEAs and schools vicariously liable for negligence by their staff including EPs, teachers and education officers (www.ipsea.org.uk/phelps.htm).

A revised Code of Practice was drafted and the government sought to diffuse the tension between parents and educational professionals. It consulted various organisations about the content. The government was mindful of the electorate, including the many parents who wanted the 'best' available provision for their children who had special educational needs. Their pleas for action became louder. Voluntary organisations and parent bodies were concerned about certain sections of the draft. The Independent Panel for Special Education Advice (IPSEA) took legal advice about the wording and the provision to be made. They succeeded in changing the content to: 'a statement should specify clearly the provision necessary to meet the needs of the child. It should detail appropriate provision to meet each identified need. Provision should normally be quantified (e.g. in terms of hours of provision, staffing arrangements). . . .'

A SEN parents' charter of needs

Russell (1997) encapsulated the parents' case by addressing their concerns. This was because many parents still felt unable to access what they considered to be the learning support and provision their children needed. He articulated the emotional responses felt by many parents by his pleas:

- Please accept and value our children (and ourselves as families) as we are.
- Please celebrate difference.
- Please try and accept children as children first. Don't attach labels to them unless you mean to *do* something.
- Please recognise your power over our lives. We live with the consequences of your opinions and decisions.
- Please understand the stress many families are under. The cancelled appointment, the waiting list no one gets to the top of, all the discussions about resources – it's *our* lives you're talking about.
- Don't put fashionable fads and treatments on to us unless you are going to be around to see them through. And don't forget families have many members, many responsibilities. Sometimes we can't please everyone.
- Do recognise that sometimes we are right! Please believe us and listen to what we know we and our children need.
- Sometimes we are sad, tired and depressed. Please value us as caring and committed families and try to go on working with us.

The revised COP (2001) has clearly been influenced by parents' needs as well as issues related to disability discrimination and human rights.

Schools and LEAs should 'ensure that parents have access to information, advice and guidance in relation to the special educational needs of their children so they can make appropriate informed decisions' (COP, 2001). This could include information about suitable literature such as:

- *Special Educational Needs Code of Practice* (COP, 2001) (210 pages)
- *Special Educational Needs (SEN): A Guide for Parents and Carers* (DfES, 2001a) (fifty-four pages of straightforward readable account, available in ten different languages including Bengali, Gujerati, Urdu)
- *SEN Toolkit* (DfES, 2001b) (a box with a collection of a dozen booklets on different aspects of managing SEN, available free from DfES Publications Centre, Nottingham, e-mail: dfes@prolog.uk.com).

The Parent Partnership Service

'The service should provide advice to the parents of all children with special educational needs, not only those with statements'. This could include information about other agencies such as health services, social services and voluntary organisations such as the British Dyslexia Association which trains independent volunteer parental supports (called befrienders at one time) who support and advise parents about SEN issues (www.bdadyslexia. org.uk), Advisory Centre for Education (www.ace-ed.org.uk), Dyspraxia Foundation (www. dyspraxiafoundation.org.uk) and Independent Panel for Special Education Advice (www. ipsea.org.uk).

'The prime role of the Parent Partnership Service is to help parents whose children have been identified as having special educational needs'. This includes contact with the Parent Partnership Service which LEAs have a statutory obligation to set up. The revised COP (2001) points out that the Parent Partnership Service should 'provide accurate and neutral information on the full range of options available to parents'. They should:

- provide information about other agencies
- seek out the views and wishes of the child
- publicise the services available; this could include holding public meetings or addressing parent–teacher association (PTA) meetings or the membership of a BDA local association
- provide information about SEN legislation and procedures such as the SEN Tribunal's appeal procedure. This is often included in a school's SEN policy document which all maintained schools must publish in a parent-friendly format
- provide information about the interpretation of documents published by the school. This could include help with understanding an educational psychologist's report for a statemented pupil or an explanation of the contents of an IEP.

Guidelines for the content of IEPs

An IEP is a planning, teaching and review resource. As a rule of thumb it should include information about:

- who will carry it out
- what help is to be given and what resources and strategies will be used
- when and how often the help will be given
- who the members of staff are who will implement and deliver the help

- how this will be done
- review dates and details.

The following factors should also be taken into consideration (adapted from DfES, 2001a, 2001b).

- Short-term targets should be specific and succinctly written such as 'memorising 20 words on the NLS high frequency list'. The revised COP recommends 3–5 targets at most with the priority written in bold font.
- Details should be given of the teaching strategies to be used, such as using the look-say-cover-write-check routine to practise spellings.
- Targets should be 'manageable and achievable' for both teacher and pupil. For example it could be unrealistic to set a target of finishing a set text or a class reader for a dyslexic pupil with very low reading skills. It would be preferable to suggest that he listens to an audio recording of the book. Unrealistic expectations such as writing legibly and on the line may be beyond the physical skills of the dyspraxic pupil. It would be preferable to suggest that he word-process his work. IEPs 'should usually be implemented, at least in part, in the normal classroom setting'.
- Provision should be put in place for help from a teaching assistant, for example. Parents should be told about help they can give, such as with brainstorming vocabulary when preparing a story.
- A date for when the plan is to be reviewed should be given and the views of the child should be heard. Parents as well as other parties involved such as the class teacher, learning support assistant, SENCO and subject teachers should meet to discuss progress.
- Success/progress such as the results of a standardised spelling or reading test should be recorded.

The COP reminds providers that 'it should only record that which is *additional to* or *different from* the differentiated curriculum provision, which is in place as part of provision for all pupils'.

What do parents find useful to know about the school's provision for SEN pupils?

- The name, contact telephone number and e-mail address of the SENCO so that they can seek information and advice such as clarification about access arrangements in examinations
- the content and aims of the school's SEN policy document
- how the school deals with complaints about special needs provision. Under the Education (Special Educational Needs) (Information) (England) Regulations 1999 all maintained schools are requested to 'publish information about any arrangements

made by the governing body relating to the treatment of complaints from parents of pupils with special educational needs'

- what the school does about passing on information when the child moves on to another school
- information about specialist teachers in the school such as a mathematics specialist who helps dyscalculic pupils
- the teachers who have undertaken additional training about SEN issues
- the name of the school governor responsible for special needs policy and its implementation.

The annual school report must include information about SEN policy and provision such as assessment, monitoring progress and how resources have been allocated to SEN children's needs.

What is a statement of special educational needs and what provision should it include? (adapted from DfES, 2001b)

This statement is a document laid out in six parts which describes the child's special educational needs. It includes information about how these needs are to be provided for.

Part 1 includes personal details and gives a list of contributory advice sent to the LEA.

Part 2 includes a clear and thorough description of the child's learning difficulties as established by the statutory assessment, including the views of an educational psychologist who 'must be employed or engaged for the purpose by the LEA'. The LEA's educational psychologist 'must consult and record any advice received from any other psychologist whom it is believed has relevant knowledge of, or information about the child'. It should also set out the implications these will have on performance in the classroom.

Part 3 includes the long-term objectives of the provision as well as specifying the appropriate provision to meet these needs. This should include details of the equipment needed, such as a laptop. It should state the amount of specialist teaching time or learning support assistance required, who this is to be delivered by and whether it is to be delivered one-to-one or in a small group. 'LEAs are required to be specific about provision' and this should normally be quantified, for example in terms of hours and frequency of support.

> Pupils with severe specific learning difficulties may have variations in performance in different curriculum areas and significant difficulties in literacy that impede access to the curriculum and so may need targets 1:1 support. If they are in a mainstream school it is likely that LSA time will be devoted to specific multi-sensory reading and spelling programmes, possibly based in National Literacy Strategy time, plus some support to access other curriculum areas requiring literacy.

Arrangements for monitoring progress on a regular basis need to be put in place.

Part 4 includes the type and name of school where provision is appropriate and is to be provided. 'Parents MUST be invited to consider their preference for any maintained school which can meet the needs.' Parents may choose to send their child to an independent school or to educate the child at home. The LEA is 'under no obligation to contribute towards the cost of educating' a child in an independent school but still has 'a duty to maintain the child's statement and to review it annually'.

Part 5 should include details about non-educational needs such as specialist medical intervention like occupational therapy or speech and language therapy.

Part 6 should include details about the non-educational provision.

Parents must be sent a draft copy of the statement and are allowed fifteen days to comment on arrangements and/or to meet the LEA to discuss the provision. If parents disagree with the contents of the statement they can meet with the LEA's Named Officer. Parents can be supported throughout the period of the statementing process by a Parent Partnership officer appointed by the LEA or by an Independent Parental Supporter who can give advice and support. They can also help if parents use the SEN Disagreement Resolution Process to resolve issues through an independent facilitator.

The Minimum Standards for Independent Facilitators in the Disagreement Resolution Process include the following guidelines. They should:

- be unbiased and always act in good faith
- have no vested interest in the outcome
- keep all the parties involved informed of progress
- have no personal involvement with any of the parties
- maintain confidentiality
- outline the procedures
- ensure all parties understand the outcomes
- not gain personally or accept gifts or hospitality in an attempt to influence outcomes
- have the necessary skills, expertise and knowledge to fulfil their role effectively.

The Special Educational and Disability Needs Tribunal

Parents who are still not happy with the statement have a legal right under the Special Educational Needs and Disability Act 2002 to use the disagreement resolution process and appeal to the Tribunal. This must be done 'no later than two months after the LEA makes its decision known to you'. The following are the grounds for an appeal if parents are dissatisfied with:

- the description of the child's SEN
- the help to be given
- the type and name of the school recommended.

The Tribunal is an independent body based at Procession House, 55 Ludgate Hill, London EC4M 7SW. It consists of a chairperson who is a lawyer and two other persons with experience of SEN issues. It will look at the evidence provided and parents are allowed up to two representatives to speak on their behalf. The Tribunal will write and say whether they can deal with the appeal. They will confirm the place, date and time of the hearing. They will send a written decision usually within ten working days of the hearing.

Special Educational Needs and Disability Tribunal: Special Educational Needs: How to Appeal (DfES, 2002b) states that the claimant can appeal if the LEA:

- refuses to carry out an assessment
- refuses to issue a statement of your child's special educational needs
- refuses to change the school named in the statement

- refuses to reassess your child
- decides to cancel your child's statement.
- decides not to amend the statement after reassessing your child.

The SEN helpline is 0870 241 2555 (www.sendist.gov.uk).

The SENDIST leaflet *Guidance for Coming to the Tribunal* (2003a) explains the following:

- who can come to the Tribunal as representative and witnesses
- the way the chairperson will conduct the hearing
- the presentation of both sides of the relevant facts
- the conclusion
- the decision about what should be done in the interests of the child.

The decision of the appeal will be sent by post within two weeks.

SENDIST (2003b) stated that:

- Of all claims, 98 per cent related to special educational needs and only 2 per cent to disability discrimination.
- Of all appeals, 75 per cent related to boys and 25 per cent to girls.
- Of all appeals, 40.4 per cent were about a refusal to do a statutory assessment with the next highest number, 21.9 per cent, about the contents of statements.
- SpLD (literacy) (dyslexia) was the type of disability (26.9 per cent) most frequently represented.
- Of appeals against LEA's refusal to assess the child, 54 per cent were upheld.
- Parents legally represented amounted to 30 per cent.

The Audit Commission is an independent watchdog which ensures that spending on public services is good value for money. Its report *Special Educational Needs: A Mainstream Issue* (2002) raises many important issues, as does its website (www.audit-commission. gov.uk). Its author, Anne Pinney, gives a clear overview and recommendations about issues needing to be resolved about SEN provision as well as reviewing current provision. It includes the following information:

- There are 1.9 million children with SEN who need some form of help in class: 22 per cent of pupils in England, 21 per cent in Wales.
- There are 275,000 children – 3 per cent of children – who have a statement because they 'need more support than their school can provide'.
- England and Wales spent £3.6 billion on SEN provision in 2001/2 which is 15 per cent of spending in schools. Of this 69 per cent was spent on the 'small minority [of] children with statements'.
- Because there is no 'common language' and no agreement among different professionals about different definitions of certain disabilities and learning difficulties, records of the individual type of needs of statemented children were not available for England. Data from the Scottish Executive and the Welsh Assembly show that specific learning difficulties accounted for 16 per cent – the second highest group of children with statements.

- Certain ethnic groups were under-represented often because English was not the parents' first language.
- Four-fifths of LEAs have initiatives to promote early identification but research shows that 'early intervention has yet to become the norm in terms of age or level of need'.
- Speech and language therapy, occupational therapy and child and adolescent mental health services were 'commonly unavailable or not available at all despite being specified in a statement' due to shortfalls in National Health and social services.
- SENCOs should be given more 'non-contact time' for managing and planning and greater access to information about school budgets.
- School governors should request regular updates on the work and progress of children with SEN.

The BDA (www.bda-dyslexia.org.uk/main/research) sought funding from the Frank Buttle Trust to establish what problems parents encountered when they sought help to address the needs of dyslexic children in school. The researchers (Griffiths *et al.*, 2005) sought to find models of 'best practice' in the five LEAs included in the study. They found that 'considerable variation exists with regard to such policies and provision between LEAs within a relatively compact geographic area'. They made sixteen main conclusions and recommendations including 'evidence of professionals not practising effective communication' and 'tension between parent partnership and [the] statement system'. 'A diagnosis of dyslexia by an LEA or independent expert does not necessarily mean that appropriate action will be taken by the child's current or future school.'

The implications of the Children Act 2004

The Act resulted in the government publication, *Every Child Matters*. It imposed new guidelines for collaboration between schools, health and social services, the police and voluntary services so that children are able to:

- be healthy
- stay safe
- enjoy and achieve
- make a positive contribution
- achieve economic well-being.

Summary and conclusions

- As a result of the Salamanca Statement made by UNESCO more pupils with special educational needs are being educated in mainstream schools. According to statistics published by the Organisation for Economic Co-operation and Development (OECD, 2004) the UK has 18.17 per cent of pupils with SEN in compulsory education, a higher proportion than almost any other member country.
- Recognition and provision including legislation for children with SEN varies in different countries.
- Disability legislation including SENDA is not statutory but schools are expected 'to take steps to prevent disadvantage occurring' and to help reduce discrimination in schools, colleges and educational services.

- The onus is on schools to ensure that adequate arrangements and provision are made for those with different kinds of special educational needs including cognitive behavioural/emotional communication difficulties and sensory/physical needs and disabilities including specific learning difficulties.
- The special educational needs of children must be met by schools working in partnership with parents who must be consulted and informed about provision for individual children as well as about the school's policy for SEN.
- The statementing process is well documented and a statement issued by the LEA in consultation with parents/carers is legally binding. The amount of support and provision indicated must be implemented in the way specified.
- Statutory assessment does not always result in a statement being issued. Disputes may arise about the provision, content and school placement. Parents have the right to appeal to the SENDIST when disputes arise with the LEA's SEN provision. The BDA found evidence that good practice and dyslexic-friendly schools depend on 'fostering positive parent–teacher relationships'.
- The Children Act 2004 includes legislation about the rights of children and it formalises collaboration between agencies involved in the provision for vulnerable children and young people.

Chapter 3

Dealing with dyslexia and dyspraxia at home and in dyslexia-friendly schools and classrooms

Outline

- The implications of gross and fine motor difficulties
- General principles and guidelines for teaching motor skills
- Practical suggestions for developing and improving motor skills using a multi-sensory approach
- Why children need explicit teaching of handwriting skills and how to teach them
- Guidelines for a 'whole-school' handwriting policy document
- Practical suggestions for classroom teachers and teaching assistants to support dyslexic and dyspraxic pupils
- Guidelines for assessment and the implementation of access arrangements in National Curriculum tests
- Guidelines for handwriting speed tests
- The issues and implications of writing speed for individuals
- Key findings from a DfES-funded project which established pupils' responses and needs in 'dyslexia-friendly' classrooms
- Summary and conclusions

The implications of gross and fine motor difficulties

Children who have problems with motor skills are frequently regarded as clumsy or awkward at home. They are poorly co-ordinated when doing PE and playing games and when writing, drawing and using a keyboard. Motor skills develop over time and usually progressively. Initially the child learns through play. Kephart (1963) identified children who had difficulties with space, time, directionality and orientation and developed motor training exercise programmes to help them. Occupational therapists in the USA such as Ayres (1972) and Fisher *et al.* (1991) devised physical activities and exercises to implement their sensory integration theories which claimed that physical exercises can modify brain function. In the UK Portwood (1996) and Kirby (1999) developed checklists for the detection of difficulties as well as developmental activities for what is known as dyspraxia in the UK. Internationally it is usually known as developmental co-ordination disorder (DCD). According to the American Psychiatric Association (1994) definition, dyspraxia includes:

- delays in the development of motor co-ordination and unexpected on-going poor motor skills in relation to chronological age and cognitive ability
- impaired performance in life skills such as when eating and dressing, in academic skills such as handwriting and computing, and in physical activities, to a significant degree
- a lack of co-ordination not due to an identifiable medical condition arising from brain injury or congenital conditions
- difficulties not due to a primary learning disability resulting in mental retardation.

Fawcett (2002) responded to a request from the DfES to review alternative therapies for children with SEN. She evaluated a number of therapies, including the Dyslexia, Dyspraxia and Attention Deficit Disorder (DDAT) centres whose work has frequently grabbed media headlines as a result of claims made by their providers and 'based on flawed research' (*Sunday Times*, 2003; Snowling and Hulme, 2003). They offer exercise-based programmes to retrain cerebellar skills, as originally described by Ayres (1972). Few of their claims have been scientifically evaluated by double-blind placebo-controlled studies. Fawcett concedes that 'it is clear that the usefulness of Occupational Therapists' intervention has been recognised. . . . In summary, a combination of traditional teaching and complementary therapy seems the most likely to be effective, producing truly multi-sensory teaching for children with difficulties'.

General principles and guidelines for teaching motor skills

- Try to make the activities enjoyable and fun. Treat the activities as games.
- Be aware that skills develop at a different rate for individual learners just as babies learn to walk at different ages and golfers have different levels of skills denoted by a handicapping system.
- Ensure that the chosen activity is within the child's current ability level. Begin with the easiest task. Success is paramount. Avoid failure.
- Activities should be short and successful. Five minutes is long enough for many activities.
- Muscle skill and muscle memory improve with use which is why the concert pianist continues to practise the scales and tennis champions continue to have coaching lessons.
- Daily practice is the ideal. A little and often is better than a weekly marathon session. Motor skills develop with maturation, practice and experience.
- Gradually, as strength develops, introduce a timed element to the activities with realistic targets based on individual skills.
- Choosing the 'right moment' is important. Interrupting a favourite television programme or a game with a favourite toy is not ideal. Tiredness is a factor that must be considered: the child who comes home from school exhausted first needs to relax and recuperate and have a snack to boost his energy levels.

- Pre-plan the activities for the session. Mix the activities to sustain interest and pleasure.

Practical suggestions for developing and improving motor skills using a multi-sensory approach

Child and adult stand side by side. The child looks at the adult who gives and repeats the verbal instructions while simultaneously demonstrating or modelling the action. Portwood (1996) recommended that the child should be given 'the easy part of the task first' so that he has 'success while trying to acquire the new skill', otherwise he can become frustrated by further failure.

The following exercises can be practised at home, in the nursery, playgroup or primary schools with the help of parents, teaching assistants or teachers. The bullet points give the instructions spoken by the adult.

Activities to develop shoulder muscles and strengthen upper arms and wrists (Adult instructions to the child are given in the bullet points.)

Activity 1

- Lie on the floor face downwards with your arms by your sides.
- Lift your hands above your head, keeping the palms of your outstretched hands facing downwards.
- Press down on your hands.
- Raise yourself up from the floor pressing down on your hands. (Repeat five times.)

Activity 2

The adult provides a skipping rope and ties the end to the handle of a closed door.

- Turn the rope ten times with your right hand.
- Then turn the rope ten times with your left hand.

Activity 3

The adult provides a yo-yo.

- Flick the yo-yo up and down ten times.
- Swing the yo-yo backwards and forwards.
- Put your arms by your side. Flick the yo-yo with your right hand then repeat with your left hand ten times.
- Swing the yo-yo over your head first with your right hand, then repeat with your left hand, five times.

Activity 4

The adult finds a yellow duster and a glass surface such as a coffee table or the lower window panes in a French door. She sprays it with a mild glass cleaner.

- Rub off the polish using the hand you write with.

Younger children can 'help' by dusting their toys, mirroring what parents or carers are doing when cleaning. There are a number of toys on the market to use for this.

Activity 5

The adult and child do a wheelbarrow race.

- Lie on the floor with the palms of your hands flat.
- With the adult holding your legs, take your weight on your hands and straighten your arms.
- Walk around the room on your hands while the adult counts how long you can do it for.

Activity 6

The adult takes a wind tunnel from the garden.

- Crawl through the tunnel on all fours.

Activity 7

The adult constructs an obstacle course. This could be indoors or outdoors, and could include objects such as inverted chairs and different surfaces such as a duvet, sheet of polystyrene or rubber rings. It could be done to taped music and as a variation of musical chairs.

- Crawl over and under these objects.

Activity 8

The adult provides wallpaper, a large soft paintbrush and washable emulsion paints (Cheap rolls of seconds or discontinued lines are often on sale for pence rather than pounds.) She cuts a piece of paper about 1.5 metres long, pins it horizontally to a wall with the pattern inwards, and covers the floor with plastic sheeting or an old dustsheet.

- Paint your room.

This is enormous fun and there are many variations on this type of activity, using different colours.

Activities to develop and strengthen wrists and hands

Activity 1

The adult provides a bean bag.

- throw it to another person.
- throw it in the air and catch it.
- catch it when it is thrown to you.
- throw it at a target such as a wastepaper bin. (This helps to develop eye–hand co-ordination skills.)

Activity 2

As above, the child throws, catches, retrieves and aims a ball at an object, initially using a large ball which is not very heavy such as a Spordas Bean Bag Ball (available from www.nesarnold.co.uk). He should use two hands at first, then throw with the dominant hand.

Activity 3

Two people each hold one handle of a skipping rope while the child skips. Then the child practises solo skipping, holding the rope with both handles. Some children take longer to learn this because the arms and the feet have to be synchronised.

Activity 4

A number of inexpensive games are available in supermarket chains and Early Learning Centres (www.nesarnold.co.uk) for practising skills, including: soft tennis sets; sticky bat and ball sets: one side of the bat has a Velcro-type surface for catching the ball and the other side can be used to bat; wizzle ball, a soft rocket-shaped object that whistles as it is thrown with a softball shaped end to make catching it easier.

Activity 5

Play 'Be the conductor'. A video clip of the Last Night of the Proms or of supporters singing before a World Cup rugby match could be shown. Ask the child to beat time with his hand. He should use the dominant hand first, then use both hands simultaneously. A variation is to use a baton such as a long-handled wooden spoon or drumstick.

Activity 6

Using a bat to bounce a rubber ball attached to its handle with a long piece of elastic is fun.

Activity 7

Use an aerosol with shaving foam in the bath. The child directs the foam on to the side of the bath or the tiled surround and makes different patterns.

Activity 8

The soap bubble factory game is fun. Take a large mixing bowl. Add some strong washing up liquid and a little water, then whisk to a foam. The child uses a wire hoop (made from a wire coat hanger) on a handle to blow big bubbles.

Activity 9

Play the clapometer game which is a group activity. Video *Top of the Pops* or *Pop Idol*. Play one song. Then ask the children to give their response by clapping and record this. Play and record the children's responses to two more songs. Play back and time the clapping. The song with the most claps is the winner.

Activity 10

Playing handball against a wall develops muscles and directionality skills.

Activity 11

Set up a skittle alley in the playground, gym or garden patio (if it has a smooth surface), or on a tiled floor indoors. The child uses a hard ball such as a cricket ball initially. Use different-sized bottles, starting with large ones such as empty squash bottles filled with sand. Gradually reduce the size of the bottles down to a plastic ketchup bottle half filled with sand.

Activity 12

To practise hand–eye co-ordination play hoop-la with a foam ring toss (available from www.nesarnold.co.uk). Five soft drinks cans are placed on a table. The player stands back and throws a hoop over a can. Gradually as the skill improves increase the distance between the player and the cans.

Activity 13

Junior ten pin bowling sets are available commercially in toyshops and retail outlets.

Activities to develop and strengthen fingers and hands as a precursor to handwriting and keyboarding skills

As previously, the adult's instructions to the child are given in the bullet points.

1 Objective: to practise exercising the wrists, first individually then in co-ordination

- Put your arms straight down by your sides.
- Raise your right hand.
- Stretch out your hand in front of you, palm facing downwards.
- Flick your hand up and down five times.

- Then repeat, using your left hand five times (repeat verbal instructions).
- Repeat, using both hands simultaneously.

2 Objective: to practise making a fist, stretching and squeezing the fingers in one hand, then the other, and finally in co-ordination

- Put your arms by your sides.
- Raise your right hand.
- Stretch out your hand in front of you with the palm facing downwards.
- Squeeze your fingers into a fist.
- Release them. Repeat five times.
- Then repeat, using your left hand (repeat verbal instructions) five times.
- Then repeat, using both hands simultaneously five times.

3 Objective: to exercise fingers individually, then in co-ordination

- Put your arms by your sides.
- Raise your right hand.
- Make it into a fist.
- Release your thumb and flick it five times.
- Release your index finger and flick it five times.
- Release your middle finger and flick it five times.
- Release your ring finger and flick it five times.
- Release your little finger and flick it five times.
- Raise your left hand and repeat the process for each finger (repeat verbal instructions).
- Raise both hands and repeat the process for both hands simultaneously (use the same verbal instructions).

4 Objective: to practise touching the individual fingers with the thumb

- Put your arms by your sides.
- Raise your right hand.
- Stretch out your hand in front of you with the palm facing downwards.
- With the thumb, touch the pad of each finger in turn. Repeat five times.
- Raise the left hand, repeat the process for each finger (repeat verbal instructions).
- Raise both hands and repeat the process for the fingers of both hands (use the same verbal instructions).

5 Objective: to raise one finger at a time, with the palm of hand prone on a flat surface

- Stand in front of a table, with your arms by your sides.
- Raise your right hand.
- Place it flat on the table with the palm facing downwards.
- Raise the thumb from the table and flick it about.
- Then raise each finger individually and flick it about while keeping the other fingers in contact with the table. Repeat five times.

- Then raise your left hand and repeat the process for each finger (use the same verbal instructions).
- Raise both hands and repeat the process for each finger (use the same verbal instructions).

6 Objective: to practise using a piano or keyboard

- Place the thumb of the right hand on the first note.
- Then play the next notes with the remaining fingers.
- Then play them in the reverse order.
- Repeat the sequence with the left hand forward and in reverse.
- Then use both hands to play the notes simultaneously.
- Do each exercise five times.

7 Objective: to practise scrunching material

- Pick up a piece of tissue paper.
- Scrunch into a ball using the right hand.
- Repeat using the left hand.
- Do the same things with newspaper.
- Do the same thing with bubble wrap.

8 Objective: play nurses and doctors using bandages (strips of an old sheet can be used but a bandage is best)

This can be done with another child/adult or doll. Use a crepe bandage initially because it is easier to manipulate.

- Wrap the bandage round the other person's wrist, hand, ankle and foot.
- Then unwind it.
- Then rewind the bandage.

9 Objective: to sew with a needle and thread

Use a large needle with a big eye such as those used for sewing leather and knitting wool or fine string.

- Do a running stitch on a line which has been traced on the fabric being sewn.
- Use an empty cotton spool, the largest size available.

10 Objective: to make patterns and shapes with playdough, plasticine, modelling clay, pastry

- Practise kneading the chosen substance.
- Roll it out into a continuous length.
- Cut or break off a suitable length.
- Make a basket shape using the fingers.

- Press down with the dominant thumb to make a hole in the centre.
- Then make half a dozen small round balls and place these 'egg' shapes in the basket (there is a wide variation of objects that can be made like this).

Use commercially available plastic or metal pastry cutters to make a variety of objects and shapes (www.nesarnold.co.uk).

Why children need explicit teaching of handwriting skills and how to teach them

Despite the advent of the National Curriculum which emphasises teaching a 'legible style' and 'joined-up' writing, heated debate still surrounds how, when and what handwriting style to teach. The NC (1999) stated that pupils should be taught:

- to start and finish letters correctly
- how to form lower- and upper-case letters
- how to join letters.

It stopped short of prescribing a national handwriting style and did not give precise instruction on how these targets should be achieved. The outstanding issues include whether all children should be taught a print script first or whether they should be taught the letters with entry and exit strokes, as this should make joining up writing easier at a later stage. The NLS (1998) advocated that children in Year 1 (5–6 years) should be taught 'to form lower-case letters correctly in a script that will be easy to join later'. It did not give a model or guidance for how this should be done. Another issue is whether children, especially those with SEN, should have to learn two different forms of writing such as printing and cursive styles. Addy (2004) argues that 'children should be taught joined up writing from day one'.

What basic skills are necessary for handwriting?

- There must be recognition of individual letter shapes. This includes an ability to discriminate between upper-case and lower-case letters as well as between cursive and printed forms.
- Gross motor skills need to have been developed so that the shoulder, arm, hand and fingers are co-ordinated.
- Fine motor skills, including the development of the tripod grip (made by flexing the thumb, forefinger and middle finger), need to be developed so that the pencil can be held correctly and moved smoothly across the page. The hand and eye need to be co-ordinated.
- Kinaesthetic motor memory needs to be trained to use individual letters shapes to a level of automaticity. Spatial awareness needs to be developed for space to be left between the words.
- Master teachers of dyslexic children such as Gillingham and Stillman (1956) and Cox (1980) argued that a fully cursive style is the most appropriate for dyslexic pupils. It leads to greater speed and fluency. Furthermore it is a crucial element in many multi-sensory teaching programmes because motor memory and spatial awareness are important kinaesthetic elements of the training.

The following arguments are deployed to explain why cursive writing is more appropriate than printing.

- Sheffield (1996) pointed out that 'the printed form of "l" starts at the top of the line, "i" starts in the middle of the line and "n" and "h" start in different places and are visually distinguished only by a short length of line'. She concluded that 'this delicatessen of motor forms may make a later switch into cursive overwhelming'. Consistency helps to establish and reinforce directionality skills. Therefore if all the lower-case letters begin on the line, these sources of confusion are eliminated.
- Being prompted to put the pencil on the line often acts as a trigger, reminding the child to join up the letters.
- It trains kinaesthetic memory. According to Zaporozhets and Elkon (1971), this is the strongest memory which is why motor skills such as swimming, riding a bicycle or touch-typing become automatic.
- It eventually leads to greater speed and fluency as the pen moves freely across the page rather than having to be lifted for each individual letter.
- It helps to reinforce the left-to-right orientation of the letters and to differentiate between the directionality of letters such as 'b' and 'd', 'p' and 'q'. It may also help to prevent a tendency to reverse these letters when writing them.
- A child who is taught to use an approach and exit stroke from the outset will not have to learn a different style later.

The NLS (1998) suggested that children in Year 2 (6–7 years) should practise what it calls 'four basic handwriting joins'. However, some children, especially children with dyspraxia, are not ready for joining up writing as early as this. Barnett and Henderson (2004) estimated that 10–15 per cent of the population has handwriting problems associated with dyspraxia. Lerner (2000) pointed out that in the USA the transfer to cursive writing is typically made somewhere in the third grade (8 years). Children with dyspraxia struggle to leave adequate space between letters and words. Others find it difficult to write on the line. Some find it difficult to visually distinguish between letters that have ascender strokes 'i'/'l'/'n'/'h'. Others have difficulties making different letter shapes.

Guidelines for a 'whole-school' handwriting policy document

- A 'whole-school' handwriting policy helps to ensure that in each year group individual teachers are using and encouraging pupils to use the same style as far as possible.
- It helps if there is a named member of staff who is the handwriting co-ordinator. She can arrange for model worksheets to be provided for new pupils and new members of staff.
- She can also arrange staff training or a workshop if necessary.
- The ideal is for 'feeder schools' to come to some consensus and for primary and secondary schools to adopt the same policy.

Handwriting is assessed as part of the National Curriculum tests in English. Marks are awarded for handwriting as part of the longer writing test.

The handwriting policy document should specify agreed shapes for upper- and lower-case letters. For example, should pupils write:

p p g f ?

Letters should be taught in groups according to their shapes and formation. It is important to remember that unless a looped descender is used writing cannot be fully cursive. The *Shorter Oxford English Dictionary* (1933) defines cursive script as 'written with a running hand so that the characters are rapidly formed without raising the pen'. Chambers (2000) describes it as 'flowing; having letters which are joined up rather than printed separately'. There has to be agreement on where the letters should begin, such as on the line with an entry stroke, and where they should end, such as with an exit stroke. Is the writing style fully cursive or semi-cursive? Do letters with a descender stroke such as 'g', 'j' and 'f' have a loop?

egg / egg ; jig / jig ; off / off

The NLS (1998) is curiously silent about letters with descenders. This is a core issue in the debate. Some teachers use a descender with a loop, others dislike loops. But unless the letter with a descender has a loop, the letters cannot be joined up. Loops are not necessary for letters with ascenders. Letters such as 'v' and 'w' should have ovoid shapes, so the hand can move cursively.

Leave alphabet wall charts displayed in classrooms until Year 4. They should give upper-case and lower-case cursive and printed forms side by side. Laminate copies of the alphabet and stick them on pupils' desks. These are also available from commercial sources. The *Handwriting File* (Balcombe, 1998) is photocopiable and also has a CD-ROM to teach cursive writing (www.kber.co.uk).

The following strokes need to be taught:

- the swing up stroke:

  i   n   u   *i n u*

- the swing straight up to the top of the line stroke:

  l   h   k   *l h k*

- swing up and over stroke:

  a   c   d   *a c d*

- the dip stroke:

  o   b   v   *o b w*

- the swing over and pull straight down to the bottom of the line stroke:

  g   j   y   *g j y*

Illustrations of the pencil hold for right- and left-handed pupils are helpful (Ott, 1997). Always use lined paper. Stop-Go Right-Line Paper uses colour to allow the pupil to see the lines and raised paper to feel the bottom line and top line (www.taskmasteronline.co.uk). Model the paper position. It should be tilted to the left at an angle of 20–35 degrees for a right-hander and slightly more to the right for a left-hander. Teach the child to anchor the paper with his non-writing hand. Guide-Write Raised Line Paper allows the user to feel the pencil touch the boundary of the lines or the outline of shapes when tracing and copying (www.taskmasteronline.co.uk).

Pencil control can be established and practised by using laminated cards and a felt pen (www.synergy-group.co.uk). Suggestions should be made for the writing tool. HB pencils should be used for all practice. H is too hard and does not move sufficiently freely across the page. B pencils help legibility for those who do not press firmly enough on the paper or for those who press too hard and dig into the paper. Ensure that each child has his own pencil sharpener and encourage the pupils to check that the pencil is sharp enough before writing commences. Do not allow pupils to use short, stubby pencils. The pencil should be long enough to rest in the space at the base of the thumb and between the thumb and forefinger. Those who do not put enough pressure on the pencil to make their writing legible can be helped by placing a sheet of carbon paper under the page and practising with this to help develop an awareness of legibility.

Encourage the correct pencil hold. Model the appropriate position for right- and left-handers. Try to encourage the child to hold the pencil below the line. Discourage the use of the 'hook' position because it puts additional strain on the wrist. It sometimes results in blotting the words. Furthermore it occludes letters, especially when copying text. The HandiWriter is an attachment fitted to the wrist and the pencil which helps the writer retain a correct hold (www.taskmasteronline.co.uk). Children who hold their pencils incorrectly sometimes complain that their fingers ache because of the pressure they use when writing. They can he helped by being asked to write their name. As they do so the teacher can attempt to remove the child's pencil from between his fingers. If the grip is too tight, pressure will have to be used to remove the pencil. If the correct pressure is being used the teacher can remove the pencil easily. This demonstration helps with awareness. Those who find it difficult to hold the pencil correctly, for example holding the pencil too close to the lead, can be helped with the use of a pencil grip fitted to the pencil. Ensure that it fits tightly so the pupil does not hold the pencil below the grip and it does not move about when in use. Finger grips that are moulded to the fingers such as the Stubbi Grip (www.taskmasteronline.co.uk) or Grippies (www.LDAlearning.com) which is moulded to keep the fingers in the correct tripod position all the time help to establish a comfortable and secure grip for right- and left-handers. Some children may need to continue to work in pencil long after their peers have moved on to using ink pens. Using a pencil develops confidence and kinaesthetic skills not least because work can easily be erased.

Agreement needs to be established about the size of the letters. Writing is usually a progressive skill. Initially children can use paper which has three lines. The top and bottom lines indicate where letters with ascenders and descenders should stop (www. taskmasteronline. co.uk). The middle line can be highlighted to develop even-sized letters.

Do not ask the dyslexic or dyspraxic child to use cursive writing until he has been taught and can use the individual lower-case letters. Some children's motor skills develop later and with greater difficulty. Some schools have a policy whereby all children have to do 'joined up' writing in Year 2 (6–7 year-olds). Some dyslexic and dyspraxic children are

8–9 years old before they have the underlying fine motor skills to begin to learn and use cursive handwriting. Earlier they do not have the necessary physical co-ordination skills. Differentiation and understanding of needs is the way forward. Some severely dyspraxic children do better when learning joined-up writing is postponed until they are 8 plus.

Cursive writing needs to be taught and practised as a discrete skill through methods including tracing and copying activities. Given time and practice, the majority of children will be able to use cursive writing for all their handwriting. Some writers struggle to write neatly and legibly when they have to simultaneously gather ideas, generate vocabulary, punctuate and think about syntax. Beringer (2004) points out that 'handwriting is not a pure motor skill – it is also language by hand. Representing the orthographic letter form precisely in memory and retrieving letter forms automatically and efficiently from memory are critical processes in learning to write'. This helps to explain why some children's writing becomes very messy and untidy when they write stories. These are the individuals for whom word-processing may be the answer. However, it is important to remember that these same individuals may encounter difficulties memorising the keyboard because of their poor fine motor skills. Learning to touch-type is the ideal but some individuals find it challenging because of additional poor visual memory and sequencing difficulties. Some dyspraxic pupils may have to be allowed to use speech recognition software to communicate. MacArthur and Graham (1987) conducted a study which examined the results when 10–12 year-old 'learning-disabled students' wrote a story by handwriting, by dictation and by using a computer. The results 'compared the quantity and quality of expressive writing under [the] three conditions. The average rate of production when dictating was nine times better than handwriting, but twenty times better than word-processing'. This also draws attention to the importance of teaching pupils to touch-type. Writing speed is another issue which needs consideration and should be measured. The number of words a child writes or copies per minute should be taken into account when setting homework and in tests and examinations.

Dyslexic and dyspraxic pupils may also need to be taught specific skills such as how to use a rubber and underline a word and to begin a sentence by the margin. Agreement on size, spacing and margins is essential. Rulers with a handle (which are used by architects and draughtsmen) make underlining easier. Those who find it difficult to begin a line next to the margin can be helped if a dot or an arrow is inserted on the line as a reminder. Children who have a tendency not to leave adequate space between words can be trained to place the index finger of the non-writing hand under the line, between the words. At the initial stages when handwriting is being taught it helps if the adult whispers 'Space'. This multi-sensory input is effective. Those who 'forget' to 'join up' their writing may be helped if they are given the prompt 'Pencil on the line' to trigger awareness of the approach stroke. It is also a reminder that all the lower-case letters begin on the line.

Some dyspraxic/dyslexic children may need to continue handwriting practice throughout primary school to retain the skills they have learned. The principle 'use it or lose it' applies. Teachers and parents are sometimes perplexed and dismayed by the pupil who can write neatly when he copies from the board and is reminded 'to write neatly', but who makes a complete mess when writing a story. This is often because multi-tasking is very difficult.

Those who have poor visual and spatial awareness and eye–hand co-ordination difficulties should be encouraged to continue to double space all their writing long after the majority of their peers no longer do.

Many schools follow a policy whereby all children in Year 3 have to use an ink pen for writing. Differentiate between individuals according to need and make reasonable adjustments. Do not insist that all children use an ink pen. Pilot Hi-Tecpoint V7 Fine works well and moves smoothly across the page. The tip of the pen seems to be almost indestructible even by children who use a lot of pressure when writing.

Ensure that the table and chair are at an appropriate height so that feet can be placed firmly on the ground. A sloped writing surface such as Writestart Desktop (www.LDA learning.com) may be helpful. A left-handed pupil should not be seated to the right of a right-handed pupil when desks are side by side.

Marking policy should allow for personal variations. Legibility must be the prime concern. Handwriting can be inordinately difficult for some pupils. Some children may continue to use printed writing because joining up their writing is too challenging. Others write relatively neatly when they have to copy. When other tasks such as composition are involved their handwriting deteriorates. They do not internalise the skill and it breaks down under pressure or because of failure to establish automaticity. Some children 'lose' a skill that they may appear to have acquired earlier. This may happen after lengthy breaks or holidays or when handwriting lessons no longer form part of the curriculum. Flexibility is the way forward in dyslexia-friendly classrooms. Each dyslexic child is an individual and has unique skills and weaknesses. The constellation of weaknesses that characterise the syndrome contains many variations. If a dyslexic or dyspraxic pupil of 8–9 years plus has a writing style which is legible or has already been taught a specific style such as Marion Richardson, it is unwise to attempt to change it.

Legibility is the prime consideration, particularly for older pupils. Realistic targets need to be set such as focusing on two or three letters for improvement to help with 'readability' such as closing the top of a lower-case 'a' so that it cannot be confused with a 'u' or putting a loop in the middle of a lower-case 'e' so that it cannot be confused with 'I' or using an ascender on 'h' and 'l' to avoid confusion with 'n' and 'i'. These targets could be included in a child's IEP.

Dyslexia-friendly classrooms differentiate and have a flexible approach to presentation skills in the light of individual SEN. Teachers should accept work which is handwritten or word-processed. Presentation in bullet points rather than in sentences could be acceptable in reports about a school trip, and mindmaps or flowcharts are acceptable when writing up a science experiment.

SEN is a whole-school issue and has to be included in policy, planning and provision. The governing body and head teacher are responsible for policy which the head teacher manages. Teachers are responsible for pupils with SEN in their class. The SENCO is responsible for the day-to-day operation and co-ordination of policy and provision. All in all SEN involves teaching and non-teaching staff. The Special Educational Needs Code of Practice (2001: 15) sets out a table of roles and responsibilities. All maintained schools must publish their SEN policy. It should include information about identification, assessment, monitoring and review procedures, which must have regard to the Code of Practice.

The Disability Rights Commission Code of Practice for Schools (2002), arising from the Disability Discrimination Act 1995, explains how discrimination against a disabled child can occur. Discrimination is 'failing to take reasonable steps to ensure that disabled pupils are not placed at a substantial disadvantage in comparison with non-disabled peers' and a 'failure to make reasonable adjustments to education and associated services' including 'the curriculum, classroom organisation, assessment and exam arrangements'. The legislation applies to maintained and independent schools.

The report *What are the Special Needs?* (DfES, 2004a) demonstrated that SEN is widespread with schools having 83,400 pupils with specific learning difficulties, 171,800 pupils with moderate learning difficulties and 31,900 pupils with severe learning difficulties.

Practical suggestions for classroom teachers and teaching assistants to support dyslexic and dyspraxic pupils

- Allow the dyslexic pupils to sit as close to the teacher's desk as possible so as to enable eye contact. The teacher can monitor the pupil's response and will be able to see when he has not followed an instruction or when he has lost the plot. The pupil can be reassured by a smile or a nod or a shake of the head when needed. The teacher can tell him a spelling straight away which may then help him to stay on task and remain focused. This is especially important for those those with poor working memory and sequencing difficulties. Dyslexic pupils should sit straight in front of the board, never at an angle – they often find copying accurately difficult because of poor visual sequential memory and/or poor eye–hand coordination.

- Do sit the dyslexic pupil next to a pupil who can tell him a word or give him a spelling when he gets stuck. Or else the teaching assistant can write this on a whiteboard for him. For many dyslexic pupils, using a dictionary may take a long time because some have inordinate difficulty saying the alphabet owing to sequencing difficulties. Let him use a handheld spellchecker or word bank or his own alphabetised spelling log. An address book with the letter clearly visible at the side makes for easier access. When using mnemonics to teach spelling include the 'cue' sentence on the page – for example 'the hen eats yoghurt' for the word 'they' – and an illustration. The illustration could be downloaded from the Internet (www.microsoft.com) and look for Clipart. These images can be stuck in and help strong visualisers. Some class teachers put lists of the high frequency words on posters on the wall. Others use a laminated mat with the high frequency words which is kept permanently on the pupil's desk for reference. Teach the regular sound/symbol words first. Irregular spellings are hard to remember, particularly for dyslexic pupils who have poor visual memory. It is important to be aware that thinking about correct spelling, particularly the irregular 'odd-bod' spellings, is very challenging for dyslexic writers and can affect the content and output of their written work. QCA (2005) has given a ruling on the use of spellcheckers in tests. This will presumably become 'normal practice' in future in classrooms. 'Spellcheckers are allowed in English (except in the spelling test), maths and science for pupils:

  - learning English as an additional language
  - with special educational needs
  - who use them as part of normal part of classroom practice.'

- Oral tests such as mental arithmetic are difficult for some dyslexic children who may struggle both to grasp the wording in the question because of short-term memory difficulties and to remember the content because of working memory difficulties while at the same time they have to search for the words to give the answer. It is important to allow them longer to process the information and to find the answer. Do not ask them to read aloud in class unless they volunteer to do so.

- Ensure that all writing is clear and legible on the board, in handouts and in activity worksheets. Some find it difficult to read cursive writing. The size of font is very important: 12–14 is recommended. Worksheets and handouts should have a clear layout and should be enlarged if necessary. Use two fonts at most. Double space or use 1.5 spacing. Use Arial or Comic Sans fonts. Use a left-aligned format. Keep illustrations clear and the page as uncluttered as possible.

- Give page or paragraph numbers when pupils have to check for information. Using a dictionary, reference book and reading for information on the Internet may be very slow. Use speech recognition technology such as Read and Write 7.1 Gold (www.texthelp.com) to read text for those with poor decoding skills.

- Speak clearly and distinctly. Be prepared to repeat or rephrase instructions or information for those who cannot keep up when listening because of poor working memory skills.

- Use consistent language, phrases and gestures. This is particularly important in subjects such as mathematics, modern foreign languages and science where vocabulary plays a pivotal role in meaning and understanding.

- Audio books level the playing field and give access to texts for poor readers. In the UK the National Listening Library has a wonderful collection of audio books (www.listening-books.org.uk). Talking books allow the user to look at the text on screen and to listen to the story simultaneously. They include Don Johnston's Start to Finish (www.donjohnston.co.uk), Crick's 'Clicker Find Out and Write About' (www.cricksoft.com), Sherston's 'Not So Naughty Stories' (http://www2.sherston.com) and Broderbund Living Books 'Just Grandma and Me' (http://www.taglearning.com). Many books are now available on CD-ROMs such as Don Johnston's 'Start to Finish'. Kurzweil 3000 (www.sightand sound.co.uk) software has a package which will read web pages. It has a facility to scan pages of text which will then be read back aloud. This supports the reading demands of poor readers and allows them to access the curriculum.

- Taking notes from dictation is difficult. Their handwriting may be illegible and slow, the contents inaccurate. Often history and science lessons involve writing notes and then writing a report or an explanation of an experiment. This can be a disaster for those with poor working memory and word naming difficulties, not to mention the difficulties for those with poor secretarial skills. A computer print-out may be the answer for the very poor or slow writer. Interactive white-boards have had a significant impact on learning for all pupils, but especially those with SpLD. Multimedia presentations appeal to different learning styles of individuals.

- Give photocopies of the teachers' notes. Handouts with overviews and summaries are helpful. *Grammar for Writing* (QCA, 1998) has highlighted the importance of using models and scaffolding including writing frames to support writing fiction and non-fiction.
- Do not expect mastery. Pupils will have good days and bad days when the skills they appeared to have mastered yesterday such as dictionary skills or handwriting or mathematical procedures or definitions and vocabulary will have disappeared. This is due to lack of automaticity of skills. Some children need longer and more frequent exposure when learning skills than the majority of their peers. The more complex the task the longer it may take individuals with dyslexia to perform it. They process information more slowly. This is not due to lack of effort or concentration. Skills break down when these pupils are under pressure, as when doing exams. This is why coursework and modular exams have proved helpful to them.
- Give print-outs of specialist subject vocabulary which can be laminated and stuck in at the front of files and stuck on to the inside cover of his desk. Important definitions and formulas can be stuck at the front of his file. They will also help to cut down on his spelling errors when he is doing written assignments. Give poor readers a computer print-out of keywords and specialist vocabulary when they have to write a report on a science experiment for homework.

   Many of these pupils have word retrieval problems so they find remembering definitions such as of the parts of speech very difficult. This is why Big Books have become such a useful teaching resource. Use multi-sensory aids such as posters. Pictorial Charts Education Trust do some colourful and exciting ones including for example *Top Dog's Plural Enforcers* (Ott, 2000) which includes visual images and reminders of the ten rules for plurals. Put the poster on the classroom wall and use photocopies of the rule from the teaching notes as a crib sheet. Stick these on the inside cover of exercise books and encourage pupils to look at these for reference when they want to spell.
- Allow extra time to copy from the board or from a textbook. Use good line spacing and colour whenever possible. Some teachers use different coloured board markers when writing on the board, for example green for headings, red for dates, blue for text. Do not rub work off the board too quickly.
- Another useful tip to help children who lose their place when copying is to number each line of a long passage.
- Number the lines on the text when possible. It saves having to re-read a whole paragraph to find a keyword for someone who does not scan quickly. It also helps those who find it difficult to retain the keyword in short-term memory while searching for information.
- Write clearly and use large writing rather than cramped, closely spaced work. Check that all the children can read joined-up writing. Do not underestimate the importance of size, clarity and colour.
- When important notices or spelling lists have to be copied down in the homework notebook do check that it has been done correctly. Teaching assistants can help with this. Give photocopies or print-outs whenever possible.

- Encourage double spacing for as long as possible. Some teachers complain when requests are made to continue double spacing or working in pencil or not using joined-up writing 'because he needed to try to keep up with the other children' or 'he must not be shown to be different'. These children are different and do have special educational needs. The Disability Discrimination Act 1995 makes it unlawful to fail to 'take reasonable steps' or make 'reasonable adjustments' related to the child's disability.
- Children who are allowed to use a word processor because of their SEN should be allowed to use it for 'normal classroom practice' and in internal and external tests. The laptop should not be regarded as giving an 'unfair advantage' any more than a hearing aid for a deaf pupil. It also makes proofreading and editing easier.

Provision for additional time

Arrangements for children with special educational needs became an issue when National Curriculum Key Stage tests were introduced. Initially there was little provision but it was gradually realised that special arrangements and special considerations needed to be made at this level, like those the JCQ made for GCE and GCSE examination candidates. The experience gained during the previous fifteen years at the senior level influenced provision at primary level and at Key Stage 3. The Professional Association of Teachers of Students with Specific Learning Difficulties (Patoss) has been at the forefront of the campaign to train teachers to carry out assessments for candidates who should be entitled to special arrangements because of their SEN.

A milestone was reached in 1998 when specialist teachers with appropriate qualifications were allowed to provide reports for candidates with SEN (Backhouse, 2000). Until then the examination awarding bodies required a recent report from an educational psychologist. This forward thinking move has had a significant impact nationally in view of the shortage of educational psychologists.

Guidelines for assessment and the implementation of access arrangements in National Curriculum tests

The DDA 1995 as amended by the SENDA 2001 Special Educational Needs Code of Practice for Schools came into effect in September 2002. It imposed a statutory duty on schools not to put pupils with special educational needs at a disadvantage. This resulted in the publication of statutory information and guidance for assessment and reporting arrangements in National Curriculum tests.

The QCA (2003a) booklet *Assessment and Reporting Arrangements. Key Stage 1, 2, 3* provided guidance and the answers to the following questions. The term 'access arrangements' replaced the term 'special arrangements' (QCA, 2004), as a result of a change in disability legislation. Access arrangements are based on a 'history of need' and should reflect 'normal classroom practice'. They should be the same in internal and external tests so that candidates can demonstrate what they know and understand as well as providing evidence of specific skills. They are regarded not as a concession but as an entitlement in an era when SEN have to be considered and accommodations made for disabilities.

Who is entitled to access arrangements?

- Children with statements of SEN and those who are currently undergoing statutory assessment.
- Children whose learning difficulty or disability significantly affects the speed of their reading or writing. This includes children whose needs are being addressed by the School Action or School Action Plus of the SEN Code of Practice 2002.

How are access arrangements requested? This depends on the circumstances of individual pupils.

- For maintained schools some permissions have to be obtained from the LEA.
- For independent schools some permissions have to be obtained from the NAA.

The deadline for applications for access arrangements was for example 5 p.m. on 1 March 2006. It is essential that the school checks the date for submission of requests which may change annually.

What provision is there for pupils who need help with reading the papers? Schools can make the following arrangements without permission if this is normal classroom practice and they can provide evidence of this.

- A reader can be provided 'where there is a significant disparity between the child's reading age and chronological age (a general guide is a reading age of 9 or below'.
- Generally readers should only help when requested by the pupil to read the occasional word or sentence. Occasionally some pupils will need to have the whole of the paper read to them.

Children allowed a reader need to practise with the reader. The reader also needs to be aware that her reading speed must be slow enough for the individual child to process the information. It helps if the paper is tackled in sections. For example, read Section A, then answer the questions on that section. Then proceed to read Section B and answer the questions on that. Many dyslexic pupils find the recommended fifteen minutes for reading the paper daunting, some because they read very slowly, others because they struggle to remember the content on account of working memory difficulties. These difficulties are compounded when they have to re-read the text then find the information to answer the questions.

Children who require the whole test paper read to them should be tested in a separate room.

Are there any access arrangements for specific needs?

- Taped versions can be made of mathematics and science papers.
- Papers can be photocopied on to coloured paper.

- Rest breaks or 'stopping the clock' are allowed for candidates who have attention problems (no permission is required for these arrangements).

What provisions are there for pupils who have writing difficulties and need an amanuensis?

- This is provided for children who write very slowly or for those with severe handwriting difficulties, including dyspraxia.
- The scribe must 'ensure that all the language, punctuation and phrasing are the child's own'.
- Evidence will be needed to show that this is a regular part of the child's normal classroom practice.

What provisions are there for children who word-process their work?

- They need to show that this is normal classroom practice for pupils with SEN. At Key Stage 3 they may be using a laptop.
- Pupils must have 'considerable writing difficulties' which means that they write very slowly and/or with physical discomfort.

On what grounds can requests be made for a child to be granted the additional time allowance?

- Children with a statement of SEN are allowed up to 25 per cent additional time without requesting it from the LEA. Maintained schools had to request permission for additional time from their LEA by 5 p.m. on 1 March in 2006. Independent schools had to apply by the same date to the NAA (www.naa.org.uk/test).
- To meet the criteria for 25 per cent additional time the pupil must meet three of the criteria in Section A or one of the criteria in Section B.
- Evidence must be provided using standardised test results. Results must have been obtained 'no earlier than the start of the previous school year'.
- The child must speak English as an additional language.
- The child must have a physical or motor disability or a named medical condition for which there is a recommendation from an appropriate professional such as an educational psychologist, physiotherapist or occupational therapist for additional time, which must have been obtained 'no earlier than the start of the previous school year'.
- 'Other exceptional circumstances', with detailed evidence of this.

Children need to rehearse how to use the time effectively by doing past papers and mock examinations. Many dyslexic/dyspraxic pupils have major problems with organisation and time management because of their constitutional difficulties. Critics such as Elkin argued in *How the Exam Rules Are Bent* (2001) that the additional time allowance confers unfair advantages on candidates who receive it.

In fact they need the extra time because they process language more slowly and their reading speeds are slower, impairing comprehension. Their writing speeds are often less than those of their peers because of poor fine motor skills as well as difficulties in processing information and sequencing their ideas and often because of their secretarial difficulties.

These will all require quantitative data as measured on standardised tests. Schools must keep the documentation to support the child's eligibility for arrangements on file for inspection if required.

Who can carry out these tests?

- 'All maintained schools have a statutory responsibility for administering the tests and teacher assessments.'
- Educational psychologists will have been involved in the formal assessment of children with statements.
- SENCOs will have assessed the needs of children at School Action or School Action Plus of the SEN Code of Practice.

Applications for additional time in Key Stage 2 tests for individual pupils have to be made on the Individual Pupil Request Form.
Pupils must meet at least three of the following criteria to be eligible:

1 Their reading comprehension age, single word reading age or accuracy with speed must be below a standardised score of 85. This is usually a reading age of below 9 years.
2 If their reading comprehension scores are increased by nine months or more when given the 25 per cent additional time in a timed reading test or if there is evidence of slow reading speed.
3 Their free writing speed must be ten words or less per minute in a ten-minute writing test.
4 They must have a processing speed of below a standardised score of 90.
5 They must have a difference of 20 points between verbal and performance scores on tests of cognitive ability, for example on an IQ test.
6 They must have average verbal reasoning and non-verbal reasoning with a standardised score of 90 or above with a below average standardised score of 85 in literacy tests.

Those who have specific learning difficulties may be granted additional time providing relevant information is provided about their condition.

Guidelines for handwriting speed tests

12–16-year-olds (adapted from Allcock 1999b)

- Choose a topic that is related to their interests and is age appropriate for candidates who are reluctant writers or who have word retrieval or word naming difficulties and/or spelling difficulties. Suggestions for suitable topics are: 'How I would spend the cash if I won the Lottery'; 'My summer holiday'; 'If I had three wishes'; 'My favourite sports personality'.
- Give each pupil some A4 lined paper which has a margin.
- Put a dot at the margin on alternate lines to remind them to double space their work. This makes it easier to read and mark.

- Tell the pupils the chosen topic and ask them to put the title at the top of the page.
- Give them five minutes to plan the essay.
- Then tell the pupils they have twenty minutes to write.
- Using a stopwatch, tell them to stop writing after twenty minutes.

Suggestions for calculating words written per minute

- Count the total number of words.
- Include words that have been crossed out.
- Count groups of initials such as GCSE as whole words. If a full stop has been used between initials count each initial as an individual word.
- Count numbers written without punctuation, such as 2004, as one word.
- A hyphenated word such as 'word-processor' counts as a single word.
- Two or more crossed out letters count as one word.
- An ampersand counts as one word.
- If two words such as 'a lot' are written as 'alot' they count as one word.

7–13-year-olds

- Choose a suitable sentence that includes all the letters of the alphabet such as 'The quick brown fox jumps over the lazy dog', 'The five boxing wizards jumped quickly' or 'Pack my box with five dozen liquor jugs'.
- Before setting the task establish that each child can say and spell the words to write the sentence.
- Ask the candidates to write the chosen sentence continuously for five minutes.
- Use a stopwatch.
- Count the total number of letters written.
- Calculate the number of letters written per minute.

Table 1 Norms for handwriting letter speeds

Year 3	Year 4	Year 5	Year 6	Year 7	Year 8
7–8 years	8–9 years	9–10 years	10–11 years	11–12 years	12–13 years
28 letters per minute	36 letters per minute	45 letters per minute	52 letters per minute	60 letters per minute	67 letters per minute

Source: Jones (2003).

The issues and implications of writing speed for individuals

Individual children with specific learning difficulties usually develop writing skills more slowly and often incompletely. They frequently do not progress through the normal stages of development in skills although their trajectory depends on the severity of their difficulties as well as the support and sensitivity with which these are treated. Someone who has been encouraged to 'have a go' and whose bad spelling has not been regarded as due to carelessness will often have the confidence to persist even if he can only spell phonetically. The widespread use of word processors and increasing availability of laptops has had a significant impact on the lives, employment and career prospects of many dyslexic individuals. The new generation of affordable portable word processors such as the AlphaSmart DANA which has a full-size keyboard has had a life-enhancing impact on many users with dyslexia and dyspraxia. There are still many unresolved issues surrounding the use of laptops including:

- At what age should a child be given a personal laptop?
- Who should be given a personal laptop at primary school?
- Should he be allowed to use it in all lessons?
- What criteria should be used when deciding who should use a laptop?
- Should all dyspraxic writers who have illegible handwriting be given one as a right?
- Who should diagnose and prescribe the use of ICT?
- Who should be responsible for providing laptops?
- Who should pay for the laptop of a child who does not have a statement?
- Should it be used in tests and examinations?
- Should schools have banks of machines to loan to pupils?
- What guidelines are there about the use of a spellchecker and grammar checker?
- How significant is writing speed when requesting the use of laptops for dyslexic children?
- Does writing speed apply to copying and writing to dictation as well as 'free writing'?
- What constitutes slow handwriting?

Many of these issues are addressed for children who have statements of SEN. The equipment they are recommended is usually specified in the statement. Pupils at senior schools who have used a computer 'as their normal means of communication' are normally allowed to use one in examinations if application for access arrangements is made to the JCQ or to the NAA for 'access arrangements'. A major issue is deciding who is entitled to additional time because of slow writing speeds. Other factors including the following also need to be considered:

- a free writing speed of ten words or less per minute
- whether poor handwriting is mainly due to fine motor and co-ordination difficulties, as in the case of a dyspraxic child who may write so slowly that he does not convey his knowledge or understanding
- whether the writing is so illegible that the examiner cannot decipher the words
- whether very poor spelling makes it impossible to decipher what the writer wants to say, as in the case of some dyslexic candidates
- whether the candidate has difficulties with organising information due to sequencing and working memory difficulties as well as with the writing processes including the secretarial aspects?

Bishop (2001) studied the effects of additional time for candidates with SpLD and obtained the following results from a group of 113 boys and 106 girls: 'An average of 11% extra words were written in extra time.' The 'marks increased as well', particularly for the slower writing pupils. The effects tend to be more noticeable at the slower, lower end of the spectrum and 'giving extra time will help those who need it most but will not significantly benefit a student who is already writing a high number of words'.

Assessment by specialist teachers who hold a qualification approved by the Joint Council for Qualifications (JCQ, 2004) will be accepted as supporting evidence on behalf of examination candidates with learning difficulties. This list is revised annually in the QCA Regulation and Guidance Relating to Candidates who are Eligible for Adjustments in Examinations and is posted on its website (www.info@jcq.org.uk). Evidence is usually provided by assessments and reports carried out by educational psychologists, particularly for pupils in independent schools. The report of the assessment must be completed and signed within 'two years of the date of the start of the examination series'.

Backhouse, G. and Morris, K. (eds) (2005) *Dyslexia? Assessing and Reporting: The Patoss Guide* (Hodder Murray, www.hoddereducation.co.uk) is a useful publication.

Key findings from a DfES-funded project which established pupils' responses and needs in 'dyslexia-friendly' schools

The Department for Education and Skills funded a project carried out by Manchester Metropolitan University and the BDA to develop a course for newly qualified teachers to teach in 'dyslexia-friendly' schools (DfES, 2003). This involved sending a questionnaire to pupils with dyslexia who were helped to complete it by their parents. A total of 138 were completed by 52 pupils aged up to 10 years and 66 by pupils aged 11 years and upwards. The key findings indicated that good teachers:

- 'don't just tell', they 'give us time to listen' and 'tell us exactly what to do'
- allowed pupils to ask questions if they had not fully understood
- gave help when pupils 'got stuck' and reassured them they were doing the right thing
- were enthusiastic and supportive and were ready to give further explanations
- were patient and understanding when mistakes were made
- spoke clearly and concisely and were prepared to repeat, preview and review lessons
- gave handouts in preference to notes
- encouraged homework to be written in homework diaries, dictated on to a tape recorder or PDA
- gave enough time to finish written work and copy from the board or OHP
- interacted with pupils, smiled and encouraged them to put their hands up to ask questions when necessary.

Pupils dislike being shouted at, singled out as being different or being made to feel stupid in public (Johnson, 2004). This feedback from pupils reinforces the argument that good practice is part of a whole school ethos which includes knowledge and understanding of the special needs of dyslexic/dyspraxic pupils as well as willingness and flexibility to 'make reasonable adjustments' by 'adapting the curriculum' to provide equitable provision for those with disabilities as imposed by the DDA 1995 and SENDA 2001.

Evidence and examples

- Try not to keep a dyslexic pupil in at break or lunchtime to finish off work. He does get very tired because he has to make an inordinate effort with all he does. He has to make three times the effort that the majority of his peers make because he does not write, read or spell automatically like the rest of the class. Constantly struggling to keep up is stressful. Rest and recuperation are essential for mental, emotional and physical wellbeing. Childhood depression and stress are sometimes a secondary difficulty associated with SpLD. Awareness of this is important.

- Note taking may be very difficult for some because of their short-term memory and working memory difficulties. Listening skills may be poor because processing information is challenging. Some have difficulties because of word retrieval and some have difficulties because of their poor secretarial skills arising from their dyspraxia. Give them copies of notes from which they can learn and which they can annotate during lessons. Some remember little of what has been said if they are simultaneously taking notes. Multi-tasking is often very challenging for them. Note taking from an oral presentation can be introduced by videoing a news programme such as the BBC six o'clock news. Replay it and teach the pupil to listen to the headings which are given at the start of news bulletins. Practice with a mini disk or digital recorder with speech recognition which can be downloaded on a computer and transcribed into notes helps. Later the pupil can use an AlphaSmart or a laptop to make notes.

- The dyslexic pupil may often arrive late for lessons because he has little sense of time as well as poor time management skills. He may be slow at changing before and after games because he has poor co-ordination skills. Try not to punish him for this. Help him to establish routines and give him support and rewards when he remembers to use them.

- The dyslexic pupil's problems do not just apply to literacy; numeracy may also be affected. Up to 50 per cent have some mathematical difficulties. According to Miles and Miles (1992), 'no dyslexic man or boy can remember his times tables'. He will need to use a table square and number lines. Older pupils need to be taught how to use a calculator. Use one with a bold display and as large keys as possible. Remember that 9 per cent of these children are outstanding mathematicians. However, many of these potentially good mathematicians can remain poor arithmeticians because of their problems with short-term memory, sequencing, orientation and the language of mathematics. For some, the language part of a word sum may interfere with their ability to calculate the answer.

- Dyslexia-friendly schools provide training for all staff. The ideal is to have at least one member of staff who has had specialist dyslexia training. Staff need regular INSET training on the use of, for example, technology in classrooms such as interactive whiteboards and laptops. The BDA (2001) carried out a survey of provision in 473 schools and it showed that 67 per cent of schools had never had an INSET day on dyslexia.

There would appear to be a wide gap between knowledge and understanding of many pupils' special needs both in theory, policy and practice in many schools throughout the UK despite the many government initiatives including legislation. There is a gap between need and provision. SENDA 2001 makes it unlawful to treat a pupil 'less favourably because of a disability'. The dilemma is how schools fulfil these requirements if many staff are unable to identify or understand the needs of vulnerable or SEN pupils. Many initiatives in SEN provision have been established as a result of the voluntary sector working in collaboration with the educational sector and with government officials. The changes in disability and discrimination legislation mean that co-operation and collaboration are no longer optional. *Removing Barriers to Achievement* (DfES, 2004) has now become a statutory requirement in schools and educational establishments.

The BDA set up an initiative with LEAs and its Local Dyslexia Associations (LDAs) to devise standards for a Dyslexia-Friendly Schools Scheme (Tresman, 2005). A Dyslexia-Friendly Schools Information Pack including details of the BDA standards was devised and funded by the DfES. The standards apply to (1) Leadership and Management, including Policy and Practice; (2) Teaching and Learning Resources; (3) Staff Awareness and Training; (4) Partnership. The rationale for the initiative was, according to O'Brien (2006), that 'a dyslexia-friendly school is a better school for all children. It is an effective school, which develops the potential and ability of all.'

Summary and conclusions

- Gross and fine motor skills can be developed and enhanced with appropriate intervention. However, the impact of underlying weaknesses may be alleviated but are not often cured for those with severe dyspraxia or dyslexia who may continue to be awkward and clumsy despite the anecdotal claims made by some purveyors of expensive magic bullets. Adams (1990) argues: 'despite the fact that many of the activities may be good for children in any number of ways, they seem not to produce any measurable payoffs in terms of learning to read.'
- Some children have persisting difficulties with handwriting often because of poor fine motor skills associated with cerebellar deficits and dyspraxia. Diagnostic assessments provide evidence of the pattern of difficulties that individual children have. They also show that symptoms vary and that there are discrepancies in individual levels of strengths and weaknesses. They do not write with automaticity. They need to make an additional effort to write neatly and often fail to use cursive writing consistently.
- Some children have difficulties with PE, games, craft and word-processing. Allowance needs to be made for individual differences in the classroom. The DDA 1995 requires schools 'not to treat disabled pupils less favourably' if they have 'a physical or mental impairment which has an effect on his or her ability to carry out normal day-to-day activities'.
- Handwriting skills have an impact on performance in examinations and may affect the outcome of those with slow writing speeds. Bishop (2001) reported that 'cursive handwriting resulted in a significantly greater amount of words written down than printed handwriting style'. According to a study conducted by Barnett *et al.* (1999), 'for boys failure to join up correctly is associated with an average drop of half a grade in GCSE English. For girls it is associated with an average drop of a whole grade'. Bishop (2001) conducted a study among pupils of average age 13 years 9 months doing a forty-minute essay in as close to examination conditions as possible, and found that 11 per cent of 'extra words were written in extra time'.
- 'Access arrangements' which include special arrangements when taking tests and examinations may be warranted and are now a statutory right for those with special educational needs. The Education Act 1996 states that 'A child has special edu-

cational needs if he or she has a learning difficulty that calls for special educational provision.'

- The JCQ and the NAA continue to update and amend access arrangements for candidates taking tests and examinations in secondary and primary level. The trend is for provision that mirrors normal classroom practice and a documented 'history of need'.
- Modifications should be made to the curriculum to accommodate the needs of those with specific learning difficulties. Support needs to be practical and immediate and targeted at the specific difficulties of individuals. A teaching assistant's help with note taking, for example, when brainstorming for an essay can make a big difference on the final outcome for someone with poor organisational skills.
- Access arrangements including the additional time allowance of up to 25 per cent have a major impact on the examination results of SEN pupils and can in some circumstances make a difference between failure and pass. For older pupils there can be a significant difference in the grades obtained when additional time is given to those who are slow readers and poor comprehenders as well as to those who write slowly and do not complete the question paper. The additional time allowance is one of the most significant factors in the increased access to higher education for dyslexic and dyspraxic candidates. Sawyer (1993) interviewed 124 sixth formers and found that 42 per cent did not have enough time to finish at least one paper.
- Tests need to be chosen carefully to ensure that they provide the evidence that the QCA and JCQ require when requesting specific access arrangements. It is important that the new literature they provide is reviewed annually.
- 'Dyslexia-friendly' schools' staff have had training in the recognition of specific learning difficulties and in the needs and rights of all their pupils. SEN is a whole-school issue and is incorporated in planning and management. The BDA's Quality Mark Initiative involving LEAs in promoting dyslexia-friendly schools is among the most exciting initiatives for decades.

Chapter 4

Why does learning to read require explicit teaching?

Outline

- Why do many individuals fail to learn to read?
- Evidence of low literacy from international studies
- Issues raised by the debate about reading standards
- Government policy for teaching literacy in the UK
- Transatlantic evidence that the UK 'reading crisis' is not unique
- What are the implications of low literacy?
- Why do we still lack universal literacy despite compulsory education?
- What is reading and why do some individuals fail to crack the code?
- Practical suggestions for developing alphabetic awareness using multi-sensory strategies
- Research and theories about underlying causes of reading difficulties
- Evidence of the importance of phonemic skills, and what practitioners can learn from research studies with suggestions for teaching phonics
- Evidence of the importance of phonological awareness, and what practitioners can learn from research studies with suggestions for teaching
- Word recognition tests
- Reading accuracy tests/reading comprehension tests
- Diagnostic reading tests
- Suggestions for doing a miscue analysis of reading errors and when doing assessments
- Hallmark features of dyslexia in reading
- Background to the debate about IQ and its significance for diagnosis and provision for children with SEN
- Tests of cognitive ability used by specialist teachers for assessment
- Tests of cognitive ability used by psychologists for assessment
- The discrepancy factor
- What is the significance of IQ scores for individuals and what are the implications for their teachers?
- Theory of multiple intelligences: its implications in the roll of honour of successful and talented dyslexic people.
- Summary and conclusions

Why do many individuals fail to learn to read?

Man is programmed biologically to speak, with parts of the brain pre-wired for speech and language. This is why children learn to speak when in an environment where they can listen and speak and are spoken to. Speech evolved over 200,000 years but writing was invented about 4,000 years ago. Writing and reading are not innate skills which is why they have to be explicitly taught. Throughout history only a minority of individuals were literate. During the twentieth century universal education became the norm and com-pulsory in most industrialised and developed countries. Basic literacy is now considered a birthright for the majority of humanity. However, various international studies show that a quarter of the population of some of the world's richest countries still have low literacy levels.

Evidence of low literacy from international studies

The International Adult Literacy Survey (IALS) (OECD, 2000) assessed literacy by using a questionnaire with a sample of 38,358, peopled aged 16–25 in twenty-one countries. It included questions about background, prose literacy, document literacy and quantitative literacy (numeracy skills) and examined functional literacy which was defined as 'using printed and written information to function in society, to achieve one's goals, and to develop one's knowledge and potential'. It tested reading comprehension including the ability to extract information from text. It showed the percentage of the population at the lowest literacy level (IALS Study, 1997) in a number of countries such as the United States (20.7); Ireland (21.8); United Kingdom (22.6). The Progress in International Reading Literacy Study (PIRLS) provided evidence that 10-year-old English school children were rated third out of thirty-five countries for reading ability but, when linked to national test results, about 20 per cent of children do not achieve the level of reading expected of them at 11 years old.

Issues raised by the debate about reading standards

For more than half a century there have been on-going concerns about reading standards, questions continuing to be raised in the public domain. A number of government inquiries were set up resulting in publications such as the Tizard Report (DES, 1972) Bullock Report (DES, 1975) and Kingman Report (DES 1988). An article in the *Times Educational Supplement* (*TES*, 1990) about claims by Turner (1990) and nine fellow educational psy-chologists' data for eight LEAs showed that there had been a decline in scores on a range of reading tests, indicating a fall in reading standards in schools. They blamed this 'downward trend' on the teaching methods used in schools. This ignited public interest in how children were being taught to read. According to Turner (1995) 'a progressive' move-ment had attempted to influence teacher behaviour away from phonic instruction and towards learning through 'real books' as advocated by supporters of 'whole language'. His booklet *Sponsored Reading Failure: An Object Lesson* (Turner 1990) fanned the flames and sparked a media frenzy with headlines such as 'Scandal of our young illiterates' (*Daily Mail*, 1990). It instigated a national debate about reading standards which turned it into a polit-ical issue. The educational establishment was divided in its response. Opinions varied from accusations that Turner was spearheading 'a well-orchestrated media campaign, carefully timed and planned' (Stierer, 2002). Wray (1995) accused him of 'sparking off a wave of teacher bashing' and used evidence from Her Majesty's Inspectorate's (HMI, 1990) report to refute Turner's claims that 'reading in 20 per cent of schools was in need of attention'. The House of Commons Select Committee (1991) set up to consider reading standards concluded that if there had been a decline in reading standards the 'real books' method was unlikely to be the cause. Wray (1995) argued that 'there is no support here for the idea, advanced by phonics theorists, that beginning with direct teaching about phoneme–grapheme relationships will thus accelerate reading progress'.

Subsequently Turner resigned as senior psychologist for the London Borough of Croydon. In 1991 he became principal psychologist of the Dyslexia Institute's Psychological Service. His responsibilities included teacher training in the use of multi-sensory methods in literacy including a preponderance of systematic phonics. His whistleblowing on the shortcomings of 'progressive' reading methodology (whole language) has been shown by research evidence and with the benefit of experience and hindsight to have been timely and correct.

The House of Commons Select Committee on Education and Skills (2005) concluded that 'in accordance with the available evidence, the DfES now seems to have accepted that phonics is an essential methodology in teaching children to read.'

Government policy for teaching literacy in the UK

In 1997 the newly elected Prime Minister Tony Blair proclaimed 'education, education, education' as a key policy for the government, resulting in a number of political initiatives including the implementation of the recommendations of the Literacy Taskforce established by the previous governments. The Secretary of State for Education and Employment David Blunkett nailed his colours to the mast by drawing attention to an Ofsted (1996) report on the teaching of reading in forty-five inner London primary schools which showed that 40 per cent of 11-year-old pupils in Year 6, their final year of primary education, had reading ages of two years or more below their chronological age. *The Times Educational Supplement* (TES, 1996) reported that he pledged during the election campaign 'that every child leaving primary school does so with a reading age of 11 by the end of the second term of office [of the Labour Government]'. He later offered to resign if this target was not met.

The National Literary Strategy (NLS, 1998)

As a result of the recommendations of the English Literacy Taskforce Report the National Literacy Strategy was launched in 1997. The *NLS Framework for Teaching* (DfEE, 1998) gave non-statutory guidance, including the teaching objectives from Reception to Year 6 to enable pupils to become fully literate with a target of 80 per cent of 11-year-olds achieving the standards of literacy expected for their age by 2002. It proposed that 'pupils become successful readers by learning to use a range of strategies to get at the meaning of the text'. John Stannard, the main author, described the range of strategies readers should use as 'a series of searchlights, each of which sheds light on the text'. This implied simultaneous use of, for example, sounding out, contextual cues and recognising shapes from previous experience. It also gave details about what should be taught during a 'Literacy Hour', an idea developed from Australian theory. It recommended that English should be taught five days a week for sixty minutes, with the main focus on literacy instruction including a mixture of the synthetic and the analytic phonics approaches. Fifteen minutes were to be spent on shared reading or shared writing of a text by the whole class. Fifteen minutes should be spent on 'word' work which should include whole-class teaching of phonics, phonological awareness and spelling at Key Stage 1 (5–7-year-olds) and of grammar, spelling and punctuation at Key Stage 2 (8–11-year-olds). Twenty minutes should be spent on independent reading or writing. Meanwhile the teacher was to do guided reading with a group of four to six children. Each child should have a copy of the text which they read mostly silently. Reading was to be taught by a 'mixed method' approach, including word recognition of the 150 high frequency words at Key Stage 1 and the 100 high frequency words at Key Stage 2, as well as phonics, grammatical knowledge and the use of contextual cues in running text. Guided writing could be an extension of the class-shared writing activity and could involve planning, drafting, editing, comprehension, handwriting practice or proofreading an essay. Ten minutes were to be spent with the whole class; known as the plenary session, this allowed the teacher to review and revise new skills and enabled pupils to clarify and practise what they had been taught. In 2003 the National Literacy Strategy and the National Numeracy Strategy were combined as the Primary National Strategy.

Secretary of State Estelle Morris resigned in 2002 because NLS targets had not been met. The Chief Inspector of Schools David Bell ordered a review of the way literacy was taught in schools because of a fall in reading standards for two successive years and because one in four children was leaving school with poor literacy. Later when responding to an Ofsted report he argued that too many teachers do not know how to teach reading properly and a 'third of pupils are unable to read and write well enough by the age of 11 in 2,235 primary schools – around one in eight schools' (Harris, 2004). 'Heads of secondary schools reckon that a third of their pupil intake cannot understand their school textbooks' (Clare, 2005). The House of Commons Select Committee on Education and Skills (2005) report, *Teaching Children to Read*, made ten recommendations based on the evidence it received, including a review of the National Literacy Strategy. The Rose Review was set up in 2005 to review the best way to help children learn to read and support those with reading difficulties.

Transatlantic evidence that the UK 'reading crisis' is not unique

Concerns about reading standards and how reading was taught had been an on-going issue in educational circles in the USA since Rudolph Flesch's (1955) *Why Johnny Can't Read* brought the issues surrounding reading into the public spotlight and in doing so polarised opinions and inflamed passionate debate about how children should learn to read. Fashions and theories resulting in different methods were tried, tested and set aside. Nevertheless, 'for the last three decades, a significant number of children in America's public schools have not learned to read' (Lyon *et al.*, 2004).

The 'reading crisis' once again became a political issue in 1996 in the USA when President Bill Clinton revealed that 40 per cent of fourth grade students (9-year-olds) could not read at grade level. Various initiatives including legislation were introduced to help tackle the issues. The report *Preventing Reading Difficulties in Young Children* (PRD) (Snow *et al.*, 1998) concluded that:

all members agreed that reading should be defined as a process of getting meaning from print, using knowledge about the written alphabet and about the sound structure of oral language for the purpose of achieving understanding. They also agreed that early reading instructions should include direct teaching information about sound symbol relationships to children who do not know about them and that it must also maintain a focus on the communicative purposes and personal value of reading.

The US Congress asked the National Institute of Child Health and Human Development to set up the National Reading Panel (NRP) to 'assess the status of research-based knowledge, including the effectiveness of various approaches to teaching children to read'. The findings of the *PRD* and NRP reports were incorporated in the No Child Left Behind Act 2001. It included a Reading First programme which provided federal funds to states and local school districts of $1 billion a year for six years provided that they could show that their teaching of reading is 'based on the scientific evidence, the essential components of any reading programme must include *systematic* and *direct* instruction in phonemic awareness, phonics, reading fluency, vocabulary development, and comprehension strategies' (Reid Lyon *et al.*, 2004). The US National Assessment of Educational Progress (NAEP) (NCES, 2003) showed that 37 per cent of pupils in the fourth grade had reading ages below their chronological age, making them functionally illiterate.

What are the implications of low literacy?

They include the following:

- Reasonable reading skills are required for 60 per cent of all jobs and ICT literacy is also essential for many jobs.
- Of unemployed people, 75 per cent are illiterate (Orton Dyslexia Society, 1986).
- Many secondary pupils truant or leave school with few qualifications. Young and Browning (2004) drew attention to the 'drop out of high school of a rate twice to three times compared to the general population' and stated that 'fewer students enroll in college and post secondary education'.
- Many of the 42,000 students in the UK who 'drop out' of education do so because they are unable to read the course content. 'This costs the tax payer more than £300 million in tuition fees and subsidised student loans' (*Daily Mail*, 2004). According to the Higher Education Statistics Agency 37 per cent of students do not complete their course at Napier University, Edinburgh, and at eleven other institutions more than a quarter fail to finish their courses. The Royal Literary Fund (2006) described as a 'public catastrophe' its findings that many university students do not know 'how to write grammatically correct prose, how to use punctuation, how to define what they think and say it, how to structure an essay'.
- Many offenders have poor literacy. In the UK a report showed that 75 per cent of the prison population have a reading age under 8 years (Blunkett, 2000). A Swedish study by Samuelsson *et al.* (2000) found that 10 per cent of the prison population had dyslexic symptoms.
- The Leitch review of skills (TES, 2005b) found that 'four million adults would still not have the expected literacy skills in 15 years' time'.

Many teachers will be dealing with pupils whose parents cannot read. In the UK 7 million adults cannot read a daily newspaper or what appears on a computer screen. The challenge is to prevent history repeating itself so that their children learn to crack the code.

Why do we still lack universal literacy despite compulsory education?

1 Social factors

Poverty and low income often mean that there will be few books, if any in the home. Parents may not have the time or inclination to read to their children at the end of a day's work. Poverty may mean that they cannot afford transport to borrow books from the library or to buy newspapers. The parent or carer may not be able to read herself.

Lyon *et al.* (2004) pointed out that:

> in New York City alone, over 70 per cent of minority students cannot read at a basic level. To be clear, it is not race or ethnicity that portends this significant under-achievement in reading – it is poverty – and minority students happen to be over-represented among disadvantaged pupils.

A study carried out in Belgium by Morais (1991) showed that children from low-income families made virtually no progress in reading when the look-and-say or whole-word method was used to start their learning because they had little experience of words, print, vocabulary or sounds.

Children who come from families who move home or school frequently, such as travellers' children, often have poor language skills and reading difficulties. Some immigrant children also have problems with literacy, particularly when English is not spoken at home. Contrast these children's language skills with those who have been read to every day by parents or carers. These fortunate children have the essential foundations of language on which to build further skills.

2 Emotional factors

- Bereavement
- trauma, such as terminal illness
- siblings with serious conditions such as autism
- divorce or separation
- immigration or migration.

3 Cognitive factors – the intelligence quotient (IQ)

Common sense tells us there is a wide distribution of abilities among the population and that some individuals are 'brighter' than others. At the ends of the ability spectrum there are very 'bright' and very 'dull' individuals. The differences are attributed to variations in intelligence.

There are many definitions of intelligence but no definitive one. Chambers defines it as 'an ability to use memory, knowledge, experience, understanding, reasoning, imagination and judgement in order to solve problems and adapt to new situations'. Wechsler (1944), who devised the universally popular and most widely used set of intelligence tests, described it as 'the aggregate of the global capacity to act purposefully, think rationally, to deal effectively with the environment'.

The other important factor to be considered is the discrepancy between ability and performance. The teacher is often puzzled by the child who does not perform well when doing written tasks but is verbally bright or the child with excellent spatial skills which may include mathematical ability who struggles with literacy. The challenge is to find the underlying causes. The buzzword in educational circles for this is the 'discrepancy factor' which is the difference between ability and performance on IQ and achievement tests, such as standardised reading and spelling tests. Critics such as Siegel (1989, 1992) argue that the content of IQ tests can be discriminatory for some individuals. The concept of discrepancy is contentious among educationalists and legislators and has significant political implications for society and individuals. In reality it has resulted in a 'waiting for failure culture' often because children will not be formally assessed until they are 2–3 years below their chronological age in attainment tests. This can result in a child falling further and further behind his peers.

4 Behavioural factors

This will include, for example, pupils with ADHD or Asperger's Syndrome. Often emotional and behavioural problems ensue because of a primary learning difficulty.

5 Physical factors

These need to be considered and should be eliminated as underlying causes of reading difficulties. They include the following:

- deafness or hearing impairment such as otitis media (glue ear) which may cause significant and/or intermittent hearing loss. It normally responds to treatment by antibiotics or by the insertion of grommets. Literacy, language and learning may each or all be affected during the period of hearing loss, just as a right-hander with a broken wrist has an 'intermittent loss' of fine motor skills which may affect his handwriting, but when he recovers the symptoms are resolved
- visual problems, whether long-sightedness, short-sightedness, squints, Meares-Irlen Syndrome, lack of acuity, visual processing difficulties when the two eyes do not work in tandem, or visual stress. All should be investigated and dealt with by an optician
- reports of specific language impairment including receptive or expressive oral language difficulties (Scarborough, 1990). The late onset of speech is highly significant for a diagnosis or prognosis of reading difficulties (Snowling, 2001).
- Some children have dyspraxia – DCD – others ADHD or Asperger's Syndrome which sometimes co-occurs with dyslexia. A third of children with attention disorders have co-existing problems often in mathematics and sometimes in reading (Shaywitz and Shaywitz, 1991). Portwood (1999) found a co-occurrence of dyspraxia with dyslexia in 50 per cent of 600 pupils in her study. Estimates of the co-occurrence of dyslexia and ADHD vary from 20 to 50 per cent (Deponio, 2004).

6 Constitutional factors

Family history may show that a sibling had similar reading difficulties. Hallgren (1950) found that 88 per cent of 112 families with dyslexia had one or more relatives who were affected. Parents may have had difficulty learning to read and some may still have unresolved reading difficulties. The Colorado Family Reading Study begun in 1973 (De Fries, 1991) studied 250 families and 1,044 relatives. They found 96 boys and 29 girls with reading problems, a gender ratio of 3.3:1. Family histories were examined to find children 'at risk' of inheriting dyslexia.

A hereditary risk factor of dyslexia has been established as follows (Vogler et al., 1985):

Dyslexic father	40 per cent son	20 per cent daughter
Non-dyslexic father	6 per cent son	2 per cent daughter
Dyslexic mother	35 per cent son	15 per cent daughter
Non-dyslexic mother	7 per cent son	2 per cent daughter

Smith et al. (1983) found a gene on chromosome 15 in a study of families where three generations had reading and spelling disabilities. Studies show that a number of genes are involved. Evidence has been found on chromosomes 15 and 6 by DeFries (1991) and DeFries et al. (1997) and replicated by Grigorenko et al. (1997).

Researchers seeking explanations for underlying causes of dyslexia have continued in the footsteps of the pioneers in the field but with the aid of technology it is now possible to study the brain structure and brain mechanisms in detail. These studies have shown that the brain contains many different specialised organs that carry out different functions but need to be co-ordinated. This has resulted in scientists exploring the following theories and hypotheses to explain possible underlying areas of dysfunction associated with dyslexia.

- Asymmetrical brain structure was described by Galaburda (1989) when he found evidence of brain abnormalities which he identified as a cause of specific language difficulties. This was confirmed by a study by Larsen et al. (1990) which showed on MRI scans that dyslexics with severe phonological deficits had symmetrical planum temporale regions.
- The Magnocellular Deficit Theory was described by Livingstone et al. (1991b) who found evidence that if the large neurons called magnocells are impaired and cause visual problems this can contribute to reading errors (Stein, 2001).
- The Cerebellar Deficit Theory was described by Fawcett and Nicolson (2001), who found evidence that dyslexics have a 'cerebellar abnormality' which results in poor motor skills including balance, posture and co-ordination particularly of rapid, skilled movement, as well as poor automatisation of skills (Nicolson and Fawcett, 1990) whether cognitive or motor.
- MRI scans show that there are seventeen different regions of the brain involved in the reading process (Shaywitz et al., 1998). Some dyslexic readers have been shown to have over-activated frontal areas of the anterior region of the brain and under-active posterior regions in the left hemisphere of the brain. All the regions of the brain need to be integrated and functioning accurately and with automaticity for fluent, accurate reading to take place.

What is reading and why do some individuals fail to crack the code?

A glimpse at the history of how written language developed helps to shed light on some of the difficulties readers face.

There are twenty-six letters in the English alphabet to represent the forty-four speech sounds we hear. There are about 140 different possible letter combinations for spelling. Words are made up of sounds called phonemes. Phonemes are the smallest units of sound that change the meaning of spoken words. Some of the letters have to be blended to represent the sounds, and letters can also be affected by their position in a word. For example, the /k/ sound at the end of a word which can be spelt in five different ways; the /sh/ sound can be spelt in ten ways, as in: *ship, sugar, social, nation, suspicion, mansion, ocean, conscious, chef, fuchsia*. This overload of sounds and shortage of letters is a core problem for those who fail to decode and encode English when reading and writing.

Reading is a complex process depending on a number of sub-skills such as an ability to recognise letters as well as comprehend the content. Children have to be taught how to read. It is not an evolutionary process. Reading is not a natural, innate or a 'spontaneous' skill (Beech, 1987); it requires direct and explicit teaching. Adams (1990) proclaimed that 'in summary, deep and thorough knowledge of letters, spelling patterns and words, and of the phonological translations of all three are of inescapable importance to both skillful reading and its acquisition'.

Others such as Goodman (1967) and Smith (1973, 1977) claimed that just as speech evolves naturally from exposure to language, reading evolves 'spontaneously and effort-lessly' from exposure to print in the environment. They declared that all that is needed is for children to learn a few sight words and focus on the meaning of text; the rest will take care of itself. In short, they argued that children 'learn to read by reading' which is a synopsis of the 'whole-language' theory.

The argument against this approach is that as new words are encountered it becomes increasingly difficult to keep a snapshot of them individually or find a unique cue for distinguishing them visually, such as the 'two legs' (ff) in *giraffe*. This approach to reading means that there is no strategy in place to decode new words which have not been previously encountered. Jorm and Share (1983) pointed out that 35–40 per cent of 1,500 words in beginners' reading books were used only once. Contextual cues are not always reliable because 'a cat could sit on the mat, rug, sofa or chair'. Gough's (1983) research has demonstrated that the average predictability of content words in running text is about 0.10, as compared to about 0.40 for function words (e.g. *on, the, to*) which are typically short, high frequency sight words that the child can already recognise. Children who rely on visual strategies rather than phonological strategies experience greater difficulties in reading development as they get older, according to Bruck (1992), often because they cannot recall enough of the physical details to recognise individual words or deal with new words.

How children are initially taught has a major impact on the outcome, as do the con-stitutional difficulties some children are biologically disposed to. Small wonder then that many struggle and fail to become literate. But the problems are not just confined to English-speaking peoples. It is a world-wide phenomenon, as shown in cross-linguistic comparisons (Goulandris, 2003) even in languages where there is a close match between sounds and letters to represent them such as Finnish, Spanish or Italian.

Some children fail to internalise and recognise the visual forms of letters, in some cases because they have not had the exposure to print which should begin long before they go to school. Adams (1990) argued that 'solid familiarity with the visual shapes of the individual letters is an absolute prerequisite for learning to read'.

Turner (2004) when considering baseline screening claimed that 'the simple device of counting how many letters (capital or lower case) children know by name at school entry' is a 'predictor of all later literacy-learning problems!'

The child needs to be able to say the letter names of the alphabet and he must be able to recognise the individual letters easily and quickly. Ehri and Wilce (1979) showed that children who struggle to learn the letter names have extreme difficulty with learning letter sounds and with word recognition. Aged 9, James remarked, 'I can never remember that one unless I say /w/ for Wilkins' (which was the first letter of his surname).

Some children have difficulties with sequencing and find it hard to say the alphabet because of short-term and working memory problems. Aged 12, Sholto said, 'I always get stuck when I get to "g" and I can never remember what a "g" and a "j" look like.'

Some find it difficult to remember the visual representation of a letter when they have to write it. They may ask, for example, 'How do you make a "y"?' Others confuse visually similar letters such as 'o' and 'u'. Some have persistent difficulties with directionality with letters such as b/d; p/q. Ali, observing his 8-year-old daughter confusing 'b' and 'd' when she was reading, remarked, 'I too still have to think about "b" and "d". I use my fingers to remind me. I stick up my thumb and curl my fingers to remind myself that "b" is for "bat" and the ball goes before the bat' (see Figure 4).

Tinker (1931) established that the upper-case letters are less confusable.

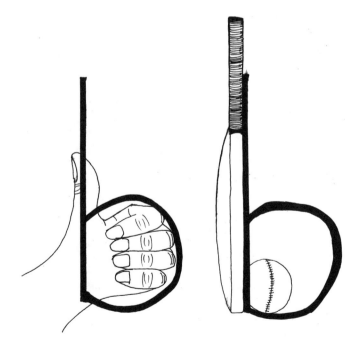

Figure 4

Practical suggestions for developing alphabetic awareness using multi-sensory strategies

- Teach the letter names first. Teach the shapes by using wooden or plastic magnetic letters which can be placed on the fridge door or on a board Adams (1990) argued that 'solid familiarity with the visual shapes of the individual letters is an absolute prerequisite for learning to read'.
- Teach tunes and jingles such as Julie Andrews's recording of 'Doe a deer – a female deer' from the soundtrack of the film Mary Poppins. BBC Educational Publishing (www.bbcschoolshop.com) produces cassettes such as Alphabet Time which teaches the letter names and sounds.
- Large wooden cut-out letters including sets of upper case and lower case can be displayed and arranged on a flat surface (wwwtaskmasteronline.co.uk).
- Sand or salt trays and carpet tiles can be used to trace over letters and make letters.
- Alphabet friezes for walls heighten visual awareness.
- Jigsaw puzzles with letter shapes such as the Alphabet Train can be used for play while developing spatial awareness (wwwlakelandeducation.co.uk).
- Games such as 'I spy something beginning with an "m"' or Simon says, 'Find me something beginning with an "f"' use language and the ears (I-Spy game www. LDAlearning.com).
- Putting individual wooden letters into bags and asking children to identify them from their shape develops kinaesthetic awareness. Lower-case and upper-case letter bags are available (www.LDAlearning.com).
- Dry-wipe whiteboards can be used to copy and trace over letters 'but independent printing holds the greatest leverage for perceptual and motor learning of letter shapes' according to Adams (1990). This can include dot-to-dot joining of individual letter shapes.
- For older dyslexic pupils a degree of sophistication can be introduced by the use of a stop watch to see how quickly the alphabet can be arranged on the table in the shape of a rainbow. Encourage the pupil to say the letter names at the same time as he is setting them out. This also helps with memorizing the sequence.
- Shaving foam can be used to make letters on the bathroom mirror.
- Sponge letters are available which are self-adhesive on the side of the bath or on wall tiles.
- Computer software programs are available to enhance alphabet skills. They include the following: Ace Monkey's Alphabet (www.r-e-m.co.uk; uses music, animation and interactive games), Alphabet Track SEMERC (www.semerc. com), teaches the names and order of the letters in the alphabet), Wordshark 3 White Space (www.wordshark.co.uk; two of the games include the alphabet and alphabet sorting), Letterland (www.letterland.com; teaches alphabet songs for letter sounds).
- Games involving 'before' and 'after' letters in the alphabet can be played. Decks of index cards can be made such as Deck 1 a–c Deck 2 ab–, Deck 3 –bc.

- Teach how to divide the dictionary into quartiles to help speed up looking up words. Use the mnemonic 'All Elephants Need Sweets' to help establish where each of the quartiles begins. Stick on protruding tabs marked A, E, N and S so that the pupil can quickly go to the required section. This can later be developed into a timed activity, seeing how quickly a word can be found.

Research and theories about underlying causes of reading difficulties

The Rapid Automatised Naming theory

RAN was developed as a result of an observation by neurologist Norman Geschwind (Geschwind and Fusillo, 1966). He studied an autopsy report by Dejerine (1892) of a patient who had suffered two strokes. The patient lost his ability to read and to name colours even though he could match colours and was not colour blind and was still able to spell and write. This led Geschwind to hypothesise that the ability to name colours must be linked to the ability to read.

Geschwind's one-time student Martha Denckla noted some of the similarities between acquired alexia and childhood dyslexia. Denckla and Rudel (1972) showed that some children though able to name colours were hesitant when doing so and had a 'lack of automaticity'. La Berge and Samuels (1974) demonstrated that accurate reading requires not only accurate but also automatic word retrieval so that attention can focus on the content and meaning.

Denckla and Rudel (1976) found that colour naming speed rather than colour naming accuracy was the main difference between normal and dyslexic readers. Colour naming ability is a cognitive, visual and linguistic process which involves retrieving a verbal label for an abstract visual symbol. They linked this to word retrieval when reading. They

Figure 5 Some children are slow at rapid naming tasks. James, when shown a picture of a red flower and asked, 'What colour is this?' replied, 'The same colour as my Dad's car!' His dad had a red Ford Sierra. This shows that he knew the colour but could not automatically retrieve the word 'red'.

devised the RAN test to test their hypothesis that rapid naming ability was predictive of later reading ability.

The double deficit theory

Wolf (1991) found that 'early naming speed at kindergarten age is the most predictive of later word recognition when reading regular, irregular and nonsense words in the fourth grade' (Year 4, 9-year-olds). Word naming speed tasks after the second grade (Year 2, 7-year-olds) predict word recognition and oral reading but do not predict reading comprehension skills. 'Dyslexic subjects appear to have depressed or faulty retrieval of known words, whereas the garden-variety poor readers have the same depressed naming performance but based on less vocabulary knowledge', according to Wolf and Obregón (1992). Some may not have word naming difficulties but they have a naming speed deficit which is often persistent and severe and in some cases lifelong.

Wolf et al. (1986) conducted a five-year longitudinal study and found that naming speed difficulties were visible from day one of the kindergarten in children who later went on to have reading difficulties: 'naming speed for basic symbols differentiated dyslexic children from average readers as well as other learning disabled children'. When these children were in the fourth grade they still had continuing difficulties with 'automatised categories, letters and words'.

Critics such as Stanovich (1986) argued that dyslexics' naming speed deficits could be explained by their lack of reading experience. He called this the 'Matthew Effect', borrowing the name from Walberg and Tsai (1983) who took it from the biblical quotation 'For unto every one that hath shall be given, and he shall have abundance; but from him that hath not shall be taken away even that which he hath' (Matthew XXV: 29). Thus good readers get better because they read more and poor readers fall further behind because of lack of exposure to print.

In response to Stanovich's (1986) remarks, Wolf (1999) conducted an experiment and analysed the data of her earlier experiment with four groups of children. She compared children two years younger but with matched reading age levels to children in the fourth grade. Her results showed that the older dyslexic children had 'significantly slower' naming speeds than the younger average readers, but not because they had less exposure to print, as Stanovich had argued. These findings were replicated in German by Wimmer (1993), in Dutch by Van den Bos (1998), in Finnish by Korhonen (1995) and in Spanish by Novoa and Wolf (1984). Wolf (1999) pointed out that in transparent languages where there is a good sound-to-symbol match, 'naming speed performance becomes an even stronger, more important diagnostic indicator and predictor of reading performance' than phonological skills. Wolf and Bowers (1999) in another study categorised their readers in four different ways:

- average group
- rate group who had a naming speed deficit and impaired comprehension but were accurate, albeit slow decoders
- phonology group who had a phonological deficit and impaired comprehension and were poor decoders
- double-deficit group who had a naming speed deficit, a phonological deficit and a severe comprehension deficit, and were slow, inaccurate readers who struggled to

remember the content of what they had read. The results showed that the double-deficit group were the most impaired readers and would be examples of classic dyslexic individuals, some of whom are known to be 'treatment resistant'.

Other researchers such as Felton *et al.* (1990) showed that naming speed deficits are persistent in adult dyslexic readers. Meyer *et al.* (1998), cited in Denckla and Cutting (1999), showed that children's performance on the RAN test in the third grade (Year 3, age 8) was 'a strong predictor of persistently poor single-word reading in the eighth grade [Year 8, age 13]'.

Evidence of the importance of phonemic skills, and what practitioners can learn from research studies with suggestions for teaching phonics

Adams (1990) concurs with Stanovich (1986) that an absence or lack of phonemic awareness appears to be a characteristic of children who are failing or have failed to learn to read.

The word 'phoneme' comes from the Greek word *phonema* meaning 'uttered sound'. A phoneme is the smallest unit of sound in a word. English is an alphabetic language, therefore the child needs to be made aware that letters are used to represent sounds in words. Phonics are used to teach reading and spelling by sounding out the individual letter sounds and blending them when reading or segmenting them when spelling. When he learns to read he must be aware that words can be segmented into the sounds represented by letters. He blends the sound when reading the word. When he learns to write he must be able to segment the individual speech sounds he hears when the word is spoken as the letters representing them at the beginning, middle and end of words; in other words, he must learn to sound out the words by using synthetic phonics. The letters of the alphabet are concrete objects whereas the sounds that represent these are numerous, confusable and can be submerged in the slip-stream of speech. Letters are visible and children are surrounded by a world of print which many discover by observation. An awareness of phonemes does not come by unaided discovery. It needs explicit teaching through a variety of strategies.

Some find phonemic skills difficult because phonemes are often co-articulated or 'merged' in standard speech (Liberman *et al.*, 1967). These are the children who say 'asposto' for 'supposed to', 'dust say' for 'just say', 'safing' for 'saving' 'hat to' for 'had to', 'wuns' for 'once'.

Snowling's (1981) research confirmed that dyslexic children have deficits in phonemic skills. An analysis of children's spelling errors can show where gaps in skills occur as well as shedding light on children's understanding of word structure. Children with poor phonemic awareness find it difficult to identify individual sound segments when blending the sounds to read and when segmenting the sounds to spell a word.

For over twenty-five years research evidence has been accumulated showing that phonemic awareness plays a crucial role when learning to read and that some individuals find acquiring phonemic skills extraordinarily difficult 'due to the elusive nature of the basic block of the alphabetic script, the phoneme' (Lundberg, 2002).

Liberman *et al.* (1974) conducted a training study to test children between 4 and 6 for their ability to tap out the phonemes in words when they were given training and feedback. None of the 4-year-olds could do the task. Of the 5-year olds 17 per cent were successful and 70 per cent of the 6-year-olds were successful. The results showed that a child's ability to segment phonemes was a good predictor of later reading achievement.

Bradley and Bryant (1983) conducted a study of sound categorisation in 4- and 5-year-olds. The children were presented with a set of three or four spoken words and they had to pick the odd one out in sounds at the beginning, middle and end of words. The children were tested three years later. The results showed a significant relationship between their scores and their later reading achievement.

Maclean et al. (1987) tested their hypothesis that a simple rhyming task such as knowledge of nursery rhymes could predict knowledge of phonemic awareness in children. Children of 3 years 3 months were asked to recite five nursery rhymes. The study showed that ability to recite nursery rhymes could predict later reading ability.

Lundberg et al. (1988) designed a study to establish whether pre-school children who were unable to read could be trained and helped to develop phonemic skills. The programme was carried out in Denmark over a full school year in a group of children who had training involving listening games, including rhymes and ditties, and playing with sentences and words, as well as identifying initial sounds and segmenting words into phonemes (Lundberg, 2002). Their results showed that pre-school children can be trained in phonemic skills without using letters or written text. These children were tested over a five-year period. The trained children outperformed a control group of children on twelve measurement tasks and there were 'rather dramatic effects on phonemic skills'.

Problems with phonemic skills are not only confined to childhood. Hoien and Lundberg (1989) studied a group of 15-year-olds with dyslexia and found that they had greater difficulties than reading age-matched controls with 'nonword reading, syllable reversal and phoneme synthesis'.

Pennington et al. (1990) showed that adult dyslexics 'have persistent problems with phoneme awareness skills'. This affects their ability to decode unfamiliar words and accounts for their slower oral reading speed.

Ball and Blachman (1991) conducted a study which taught children to analyse words into phonemes using discs to represent the sounds in words. This was adapted from Elkonin's (1973) idea of using blocks to represent each sound in sequence and putting them into squares marked on a piece of card.

Hatcher et al. (1994) designed a training study for 7-year-old poor readers which they linked with learning to read. The children were taught letter name–sound relationships, rhyming, segmentation and syllables by clapping and segmenting words. Phoneme training included sounds at the beginning, middle and end of words as well as picking the odd man out at the beginning and end of words. Each thirty-minute session began with children re-reading a book which could be read with at least 95 per cent accuracy. Later they read a book at their 'instructional level of reading' which meant they could read it with 90-94 per cent accuracy. The children also wrote a short story. There were four groups of children, each taught by a different approach. Their results showed that an adaptation of the classic Orton–Gillingham synthetic phonics approach used in specialist dyslexia programmes using 'a combined phonological literacy skills training approach is effective in boosting the reading skills of reading delayed 7 year olds'.

Nicholson (1997) conducted a study in New Zealand on children from low-income areas and showed that they benefited from training in phonemic awareness including games, posters with letters and alphabet letters.

Programmes to teach phonemic skills include the following:

Progression in Phonics (PIPs) in *Key Stage 3 National Strategy: Literacy Progress Unit Writing Organisation* (DfES, 2001).

Phonemic Awareness in Young Children (Adams et al., 1998), based on the ground-breaking research of Lundberg *et al.* (1988), teaches listening skills, rhyming, awareness of words, sentences and syllables, and phonemic skills mainly through games.

Sound Linkage: An Integrated Programme for Overcoming Reading Difficulties (Hatcher, 1994), based on the Cumbria/York research study of Hatcher *et al.* (1994), teaches syllable blending, phoneme blending, rhyme, phoneme segmentation, phoneme deletion and phoneme transposition.

Tune into Sounds and the Big ABC Book (Palmer and Morgan, 1998) is part of the Big Book Phonics series. It teaches phonics using rhymes and songs and includes activity sheets. It is linked to the NLS Key Stage 1 targets.

Fun Phonics (Sweeney and Doncaster, 2002) includes workbooks, posters, rhymes and a teacher's handbook. It is linked to the NLS Key Stage 1 targets (www.collinseducation. com).

Jolly Phonics (Lloyd, 1998) includes a video, wall frieze, workbooks and a phonics handbook for teaching 'reading, writing and spelling'. It is suitable for Key Stage 1 pupils.

Activities for Spelling Successfully (Ott, 2007b) includes multi-sensory activities and is non-age specific with differentiated activities for teaching synthetic phonics, syllables, plurals, homophones and affixes. It includes dictations, puzzles and wordsearches.

THRASS (Teaching Handwriting, Reading and Spelling Skills) is a comprehensive package of resources to teach these skills (www.thrass.co.uk).

Computer packages include WhiteShark 3 and Units of Sound.

4 Learning has some excellent videos for teaching phonics called *Rat-a-tat Phonics Special* which includes graphics, word play and rhyme. The CD-ROM Simon S.I.O. (Sounds It Out) includes voice, text and pictures (www.donjohnston.co.uk).

Evidence of the importance of phonological awareness, and what practitioners can learn from research studies with suggestions for teaching

'Children's awareness of phonics [sounds] can be hastened through appropriate training and . . . such training produces significant acceleration in the acquisition of reading and writing skills' (Adams, 1990).

Phonological awareness is the ability to distinguish the sound segments in words and includes the following.

I Syllable awareness

This is developed initially by oral activities such as:

a   clapping out syllables
b   blending syllables to make words: /De/ /cem/ /ber
c   syllable segmentation by breaking words up and denoting the number of syllables in a
    grid
d   removing a syllable and pronouncing the word remaining. What does 'caravan' say
    without 'cara'? 'Van.'

2 Rhyme awareness

This is developed by oral activities such as:

a   playing games involving movement and rhythm such as marching to 'The grand old
    Duke of York'
b   completing rhymes such as saying 'Baa, baa black sheep'
c   saying silly rhymes. Then the target is to give the correct response: 'Jack and Jill went
    up the *street*'.

3 Phoneme awareness

This can be developed by oral activities such as:

a   asking: What sound can you hear:

    - at the *beginning* of 'fog', 'fan', 'fish'?
    - at the *end* of 'dog', 'rag', 'log'?
    - in the *middle* of 'rat', 'can', 'ham'?

b   activities such as choosing the odd man out from 'log', 'cup', 'hop', 'map'.

Blachman (1987) recommended the following to teach phonological awareness:

- phonemic skills including awareness of sounds at the beginning, middle and end of
  words; blending and synthesising sounds
- reviewing regular and irregular high frequency words to develop fluency
- reading stories from phonetically controlled readers
- written dictation of regular words and sentences. A primary goal was to develop accurate and fluent recognition of the six-syllable patterns. Hatcher *et al.*'s (1994) study
  replicated this approach.

Blachman *et al.*'s (1994) study showed that children who had this training 'significantly
outperformed the control children on measures of phoneme awareness, letter-name, letter-
sound knowledge, regular word and non-word reading, a developmental spelling test and a
standardised spelling measure'.

Phonological awareness has been shown to be a sub-skill of many other linguistic tasks all of which have a role to play in the development of reading skills.

Difficulties associated with speech and language which may also affect reading acquisition include:

- word pronunciation (Catts, 1989): 'I know that word ["bibliography"], we've used it during the Literacy Hour but I can't say it', commented Jack (11 years)
- word retrieval and word naming (Wolf et al., 1986): 'I need to use those twitchy things – flying commas', said Luke (13 years) when he wanted to use quotation marks
- short-term memory for lists of words, strings of letters in spelling patterns, digit spans and the names of familiar objects seen in pictures (Brady, 1986). They also find multi-syllabic words and tongue twisters including spoonerisms very challenging to repeat: 'I had that in my spelling list for last week's test but I cannot remember whether it is "fear", "frae" or "fare"', complained Guy (10 years)
- repeating non-words (Snowling, 1981): 'I can't get my tongue round that one [Omnibombulator, a book title]', said Penny (8 years)
- reading nonsense words (Rack et al., 1992): 'These are impossible and they don't make sense', said Raj (9 years).

The identification of the role of the phonological deficit hypothesis as a core deficit in dyslexia has been hailed as one of the 'great success stories of science', according to Stanovich (1992). Lundberg and Hoien (2001) found that when they administered a battery of eleven tests, including linguistic and non-linguistic tasks, 'the most powerful predictors of later reading and writing skills in the entire battery turned out to be those requiring phonological awareness, specifically the ability to manipulate phonemes in words'.

There is a substantial body of research which shows that phonological problems can be identified in 'at-risk' children – those with at least one dyslexic parent. Scarborough (1990) studied thirty-two children of dyslexic parents from the age of 2.5 years and found that they had 'measurable linguistic disturbances' and by the age of 5 they knew fewer letters of the alphabet and 'had less phonological awareness'. Snowling and Nation (1997) found that seventy-one 'at-risk' children had 'less knowledge of letters and knew fewer rhymes and jingles than the controls'.

Gallagher et al. (1996) studied well-compensated adult dyslexic university students who had achieved almost normal ability to read and write but had residual difficulties with:

- reading and writing non-words
- dealing with spoonerisms
- reading numbers aloud
- rate of speech (it was slower).

What are the lessons to learn from the theory and research?

- Children who are taught phonological awareness using synthetic phonics become better readers. The earlier the intervention the better the final outcomes. Keeney and Keeney (1968) shows that when dyslexia was identified while a child was in the first two grades (age 6–8 years) 82 per cent caught up. When it was diagnosed in the third grade (age 8–9 years), 46 per cent caught up. When it was diagnosed in the fifth, sixth and seventh grade (age 10–13 years), only 10–15 per cent caught up.

- Teaching phonological skills simultaneously with letter names is more effective. Children require explicit teaching about letter name/sound relationships.
- Rhyming words help develop awareness.
- Saying nursery rhymes is important. The researchers found that pre-school children who could recite nursery rhymes at 3 years old had fewer problems when they learned to read.
- Children who have difficulties with phonological skills and find tapping out syllables in words difficult will often struggle when learning to read. They need explicit teaching of segmentation skills.
- Children can identify syllables orally and aurally long before they can read them in words. Oral language skills are the bedrock of literacy.

A study carried out in Scotland by Johnston *et al.* (1995) showed that children who learned about phonics made greater progress than New Zealand children who were taught by using whole words. Johnston and Watson (2005) conducted a seven-year longitudinal study of 300 children in Clackmannanshire in Scotland and compared different reading methods:

- synthetic phonics
- analytic phonics
- analytic phonics with systematic phonemic awareness.

The results showed that the children who were taught synthetic phonics were ahead of the other two groups. Later all the children were taught synthetic phonics and 'when tested were found to be achieving significantly higher levels in word reading and spelling [than] would be expected by their chronological age. Unusually boys were found to be outperforming girls' (House of Commons Education and Skills Committee, 2005). The DfES commissioned researchers at York and Sheffield universities to conduct a systematic review of the research on the use of phonics instruction (Torgerson *et al.*, 2006) in the teaching of reading and spelling. They reviewed twenty randomised controlled trials (RCT) to ensure that bias was eliminated from the experimental research. Their key finding was that 'systematic phonics instruction within a broad literacy curriculum was found to have a statistically significant positive effect on reading *accuracy*'. The effect on reading comprehension was weak but this was based on evidence from four RCT studies. These findings substantiate the US National Reading Panel sub-group (Ehri *et al.*, 2001) findings that 'phonemic awareness instruction helps children learn to read'.

A battery of standardised tests as well as diagnostic reading tests should be administered.

Turner (2004) advises teachers doing diagnostic assessments 'to give tests in pairs and hopefully the findings corroborate'. Turner (1997a) suggested that 'a diagnostic test for dyslexia is a task at which dyslexic people perform badly and non-dyslexic ones perform well'. A prime consideration is how useful the test will be for identifying current attainments as well as for diagnostic purposes. Tests should help to reveal the reading strategies the child uses to decode words which he does not instantly recognise. This information is useful when planning teaching intervention and IEPs and when applying for access arrangements for examinations. The QCA and JCQ insist on standardised scores when permission is sought for access arrangements.

An assessment of reading should include tests of:

- word recognition
- reading accuracy
- reading comprehension
- non-word reading
- diagnostic reading
- reading rate.

Word recognition is regarded as the most critical of all the reading sub-skills (LaBerge and Samuel, 1974). Reading accuracy and fluency depend on instant recognition of sight words which are stored in memory and can be read effortlessly and without hesitation. They free up mental space to concentrate on meaning and comprehension. According to Adams (1990), 'where a reader is instead wrestling with the resolution of any word, syllable, or letter of the text, comprehension is necessarily forfeited'. Lovett (1986) demonstrated that good readers can recognise sight words out of context. Sight words can be pronounced and understood rapidly, usually within a second.

Word recognition tests

Graded Word Reading Test. The Macmillan Test Unit (1985) (www.nfer-nelson.co.uk)

For the age range of 6–14 years, this is a single-word test and has two forms. It consists of a total of fifty words. It takes 5–10 minutes to administer. It includes standardised scores. The Reading Age Conversion Table for Tests 1 and 2 creates some problems of validation for practitioners. A raw score of 0–11 (which means reading the first eleven words on the test) gives a reading age of 6.0 years. At the top end of the test a raw score of forty words gives a reading age equivalent of 12 years and a raw score of forty-five words gives a reading age of 14 years. Five words represent twenty-four months of attainment. Scores at the base and ceiling are not always reliable. The manual adds a note of caution about the reliability of reading ages and points out that the 'true' score will be between plus or minus three months of the reading age. This is why standardised scores have become obligatory when reporting on attainments. They provide a means of comparison of a pupil's performance with other pupils of that age from a national average score.

Wilkinson, G.S. (1993) *Wide Range Achievement Test 3 (WRAT 3)* (www.harcourt-uk.com)

For the age range of 5–75 years, this test takes 5–10 minutes to administer. It is a letter reading and single-word recognition test of 42 words. Backhouse (2005) points out that 'the results of short tests – in terms of the number of items – should never be relied upon in a formal assessment, without a great deal of complementary supporting evidence'.

It has two forms, making it useful for example for annual reviews so that a 'teaching to the test' effect does not occur. WRAT-3 was standardised in 1993 in the USA. It has a total of forty-three words which gives a reading age from 5 to 75 years. A reading age level can be calculated. Age-equivalent scores can be misleading. A two-word difference can result in a difference of nine years in the teen years. It is an individual test. It has standardised scores, percentile ranks and grade levels.

Rust, J. Golombok, S. and Trickey, G. (1993) *Wechsler Objective Reading Dimensions (WORD)* (www.harcourt-uk.com)

For the age range of 6 years–16 years 11 months, this is used by psychologists or by teachers in conjunction with the local educational psychologist: 'The administration and interpretation of the tests must remain under the supervision of the Psychologist'.

It includes three tests including the 'Basic Reading' (word recognition) test. It is an individual test which includes standardised scores and percentile scores. It is possible when the standardised score is calculated to then calculate an 'expected standardised score' based on age and IQ scores on the WISC which is useful when establishing if there is a discrepancy between potential and attainment. This evidence can be used when requesting access arrangements such as additional time from the NAA.

Elliott, C.D., Smith, P. and McCullock, K. (1996) *The British Ability Scales II (BAS II)* (www.nfer-nelson.co.uk)

This includes a word recognition test and has an age range of 5–18 years. It is an individual test. It has UK norms which were developed in 1996. It too can be used to predict expected performance levels based on the BAS IQ scores.

Reading accuracy tests/reading comprehension tests

Reading accuracy and comprehension tests, in other words functional literacy tests, measure children's ability to deal with running text by using:

* a prose passage such as a short story
* sentences of increasing complexity
* sentence completion or passage completion tests when the appropriate missing word has to be chosen from a selection of words.

Whetton, C., Caspall, L. and McCulloch, K. (1997) *The Neale Analysis of Reading Ability*, second revised edition (NARA-2) (www.nfer-nelson.co.uk)

It has an age range of 6–12 years 11 months. It is an individually administered test and takes about twenty minutes. It provides a standardised score, percentile and a reading age. There are two parallel forms of the tests. It is part of a test battery and also includes a Test of Comprehension and Reading Rate (speed) as well as a diagnostic test (which does not include norms). There have been criticisms (Spooner *et al.*, 2004) of the Reading Comprehension Test because the manual gives the instruction to correct the child's errors while administering the test. Do these scores reflect his listening skills or his reading ability?

The individual record form has the clarity and simplicity of a Delia Smith cookery manual. Errors and miscues can be recorded and afterwards divided into categories such as mispronunciations, substitutions, refusals, additions, omissions and reversals which are useful when making a miscue analysis for diagnostic purposes and for planning later intervention. This information could also be used in an IEP.

Wiederholt, J.L. and Bryant, B.R. (2001) *Gray Oral Reading Tests (GORT-4)*, fourth edition (www.harcourt-uk.com)

It has an age range of 6–18 years 11 months. It is an individually administered test based on US norms. It has two parallel forms of fourteen developmentally sequenced prose passages, which helps to lessen the effects of over-familiarity. It includes scores for accuracy, comprehension, rate fluency and overall reading ability. It has standardised scores, percentiles, age and grade equivalents. The fluency score is derived from combining the reading 'rate' and 'accuracy' scores. The overall readability score is a combination of rate, accuracy and comprehension scores. It also provides a score for 'oral reading comprehension'. It includes a miscue worksheet to record five categories of error.

Educational Assessment Unit, University of Edinburgh (2000) *The Edinburgh Reading Tests 1–4, third edition* (www.hoddertests.co.uk)

For an age range of 7–17 years, it is a silent reading test and includes multiple choice questions. It consists of four levels for different age groups from 7–17 years. It takes 30–45 minutes (depending on the age group) to administer and is for group or individual use. It is useful for providing evidence of the need for additional time. A mark can be made on the test booklet establishing the amount completed in ten minutes. QCA (2005) states that 'pupils increase their reading comprehension age by 9 months or more when allowed 25 per cent additional time to complete a timed reading test . . .'. It has standardised scores, percentiles and reading ages.

Five sub-tests include: skimming, vocabulary, reading for facts, points of view and comprehension.

Woodcock, R.W. (1998) *Woodcock Reading Mastery Tests – Revised Normative Update* (WRMT-RNU) (www.dyslexiaaction.org.uk)

For an age range of 5–75 years, it has US norms and tests all aspects of reading including:

- letter identification
- word identification – single word recognition
- word attack (phonic/structural analysis – non-word reading)
- word comprehension including:

  - antonyms
  - synonyms
  - analogies

- Passage comprehension – including cloze procedures which involve filling in missing letters, words or parts of sentences (Ott, 1997).

It takes 10–30 minutes to administer. Turner (1997a, 1995) hailed it as 'an all-purpose reading test' and a 'landmark in the field'. Cost is the main criticism of this test, as it is of many of the tests published in the USA.

Diagnostic reading tests

Some of the aforementioned tests include a battery of sub-tests which have specific diagnostic features. New tests have been developed to help establish whether a reading problem is or is not indicative of important deficits in underlying reading skills, as well as providing significant criteria when applying for access arrangements.

Rack *et al.* (1992) established that a measure of non-word reading (an ability to read pseudo-words) has useful implications when identifying specific learning difficulties. They found that 75 per cent of poor readers have unexpected difficulties. Non-words can only be read by using phonics whereas real words can be read as sight words. This can pinpoint inaccuracies and slow reading rate as well as poor phonological decoding skills which result in difficulties learning words by sight. Turner (1995) regards it is as a 'potent diagnostic' measure.

Non-word reading tests include the following.

Fredrickson, N., Frith, U. and Reason, R. (1997) *Phonological Assessment Battery* (PhAB) (www.nfer-nelson.co.uk)

It has an age range of 6–14 years 11 months. It includes a non-word test with standardised scores. Critics question the reliability of some of the tests such as the rhyme test for older children.

Crumpler, M. and McCarty, C. (2004) *Nonword Reading Test* (www.hoddertests.co.uk)

It tests phonological decoding skills including accuracy and speed and has an age range of 6–16 years. It takes 5–10 minutes to administer. It includes two parallel forms, diagnostic error analysis and a useful guide to acceptable pronunciation of the non-words. It provides standardised scores, age-equivalent scores, percentile scores.

Torgesen, J.K., Wagner, R. and Rashotte, C. (1999) *Test of Word Reading Efficiency* (TOWRE) (www.harcourt-uk.com)

For an age range of 6–24 years 11 months, the Sight Word Efficiency tests word recognition of real words and establishes how many words can be read fluently and accurately in forty-five seconds It includes a Phonemic Decoding Test which tests how many non-words can be pronounced using phonemic decoding in forty-five seconds. It includes standardised scores, reading age equivalent scores as well as percentiles. It has two parallel forms. It takes 5–10 minutes to administer.

With older poor readers a discrepancy between scores on the two parts of the test may be used when making a diagnosis of dyslexia. The timed factor – which gives a reading rate score – is also useful because it may indicate a child who has a 'low' or 'below average' standardised score of below 90 and may need the additional time allowance in examinations.

Miller Guron, L. (1999) *Wordchains: A Word Reading Test for All Ages* (www.nfer-nelson.co.uk)

It has an age range of 7 years–adult. It can be used as an individual or a group test. The first part, Letterchains, takes ninety seconds to administer and involves dividing a string of letters into groups of three or four. It is useful for checking visual discrimination, sequencing, tracking and eye–hand co-ordination but should be used in tandem with a single word recognition test when assessing reading skills.

Wilkins, A.J., Jeanes, R.J., Pumfrey, P.D. and Laskier, M. (1996) *Wilkins Rate of Reading Test* (www.ioomarketing.co.uk)

This is a one-minute test of reading random 'very high frequency' words to test the effects of visuo-perceptual distortions such as words moving on the page, blurring of letters and 'coloured haloes' which often 'give rise to slower reading'. It can also be used to 'compare the effects on reading with and without coloured overlays'. It does not, however, provide a standardised score or a reading age, nor 'is it strongly correlated with age, or with perfor- mance on more conventional reading tests' (Wilkins *et al.*, 1996).

Suggestions for doing a miscue analysis of reading errors and when doing assessments

1   When testing reading keep a running record of each error the child makes and do a miscue analysis later. Note the pupil's response in the box underneath each word. Record the errors as the child reads the words. Later analyse the indi- vidual errors such as mispronunciations, omissions, reversals, substitutions or additions.

2   Some people may prefer to use a shorthand marking system such as: 'sp-ru' (spelling rule forgotten); 'rev' (reversal of a letter); 'ref' (refusal – no attempt to read); 'om' (omission of a letter or a word); 'sub' (substitution); 'trans' (trans- position of the order of letters in a word).

3   Other teachers may prefer to use a tape recorder to record the child reading continuous text. Later the tape can be rewound and used to transcribe and classify the errors.

Hallmark features of dyslexia in reading

- Does the pupil read in a staccato way (word for word) with little expression and with little understanding of what he is reading? (*This is sometimes an indication that the text is beyond the child's instructional level.*)
- Does he read very slowly? Check how many words a minute he can read by using a test of reading rate such as the TOWRE (Torgenson *et al.*, 1999). (*Slow reading may indicate that he has a poor sight vocabulary and/or poor word recognition skills or poor decoding skills which impact on his comprehension.*)
- Does he stumble and repeat words and phrases? (*This may indicate short-term and working memory difficulties.*)
- Does he fail to notice or use punctuation? (*This is evident in those with poor short-term and working memory.*)

- Does he lose his place when reading? Is he aware of this? (*This may indicate visuo/perceptual difficulties.*)
- Does he use self-correction strategies? (*Failure to do so to make sense of what he is reading may indicate that he is unable to remember the content of what he is reading because of the mental effort he has to make to decode the text.*)
- Does he need to use his finger to keep his place on the line? (*This may indicate poor tracking skills due to visual sequential memory deficits.*)
- Does he misread the simple, familiar high frequency words – 'a' for 'and'? (*This may indicate visuo-perceptual distortions.*)
- Does he attempt to read irregular words by using phonic skills which misfire – 'yoused' for 'used'; 'cucumber' for 'computer'? (*This may indicate phonemic and phonological difficulties.*)
- Does he sometimes omit or add parts to words – 'human' for 'hymn'; 'you was' for 'who was'? (*This indicates poor grapheme/phoneme skills and poor visual perception.*)
- Is he inclined to omit endings from words – 'play' for 'playing'? (*This is an indication of poor phonological skills.*)
- Does he sometimes confuse words of similar appearance – 'house' for 'horse'; 'of' for 'off'? (*This is an error made by someone relying on the visual features of a word but confusing the orthographic patterns perhaps because of visual distortion or underlying visual stress problems.*)
- Does he find it difficult to remember the content of what he has read correctly when asked questions about it? (*This is due to poor comprehension which may be because the text is too difficult. It could also be because of working memory difficulties or poor cognitive abilities.*)
- Does he omit syllables from words – 'rember' for 'remember'; 'begging' for 'beginning'? (*This is due to a lack of phonological awareness.*)
- Does he truncate words – 'don't' for 'downstairs'; 'active' for 'attractive'? (*This is a phonological error.*)
- Does he sometimes add letters to words – 'frog' for 'fog'; 'breast' for 'beast'; 'persuaded' for 'pursue'? (*This indicates poor phonemic skills including difficulties with consonant blending.*)
- Does he tend to look at the initial letters of the word and guess the rest – 'interrupted' for 'interceded'; 'citizen' for 'citation'? (*Children who use a mainly visual strategy to read and have poor auditory perception skills do this. They may also have expressive language difficulties including a tendency to mispronounce words.*)
- Does he make bizarre guesses at words – 'downest' for 'downstairs'? (*Poor readers do this because they are unable to match graphemes to the phonemes to pronounce words.*)
- Does he read a word correctly on one line and then misread the same word on the next line? (*These children have poor visual memory.*)
- Does he reverse whole words – 'on' for 'no'; 'was' for 'saw'? (*These children have sequencing and directionality difficulties.*)
- Does he confuse words with short vowel sounds – 'pet' for 'pit'; 'cot' for 'cut'? (*This indicates poor phonemic skills including auditory perception.*)
- Does he misread words with similar sounds – 'dim' for 'din'; 'fan' for 'van'? (*This indicates poor phoneme awareness including auditory perception.*)
- Does he invert letters – 'pig' for 'dig'? (*This indicates directionality and orientation difficulties.*)

- Does he reverse letters – 'bud' for 'dub'; 'brown' for 'down'? (*This indicates a visual sequential memory difficulty.*)
- Does he omit letters from words – 'very' for 'every'? (*This indicates phonological and phonemic difficulties.*)
- Does he transpose the order of letters in words – 'toast page' for 'postage'; 'left' for 'felt'? (*This is due to poor visual sequential memory.*)

Classifying errors when doing a miscue analysis is not an exact science. Some errors have more than one explanation and different practitioners may give different interpretations and explanations of the underlying difficulty.

Background to the debate about IQ and its significance for diagnosis and provision for children with SEN

For academic purposes intelligence can be described as abilities measurable by psychometric intelligence tests which include tests of reasoning, problem solving, spatial skills and factual knowledge. Vernon (1979) pointed out that

> genetic and environmental factors are always both involved. . . . Despite current attacks on tests in general (as well as on genetic explanations), they have much to contribute to the diagnosis of the type of education best suited to a child's needs and potentialities.

Intelligence was often considered as consisting of two factors, a general ability and a specific factor. Spearman (1904) pointed out that each test had a specific factor(s). It became evident that individuals with high ability did well on many items in a test battery but some individuals did badly on specific items, indicating an unevenness in skills and weaknesses. Child (2004) noted that many tests require verbal ability in addition to a specific ability, for example arithmetical ability. Traditionally intelligence tests included tests of verbal, non-verbal and spatial ability.

In the final decades of the twentieth century questions were increasingly raised about the reliability of IQ tests. Some critics even questioned the concept of intelligence. They argued that results were affected by an inherent cultural bias as well as by racial differences. This resulted in arguments about nature versus nurture affecting the outcomes of the test measures. A further issue was raised by Siegel (1989) which concerned the impact of learning difficulties on the measured outcomes. Stanovich (1991) suggested that 'at their best, IQ test scores are gross measures of current cognitive functioning'. According to Siegel and Smythe (2004), 'IQ tests require expressive language, understanding of vocabulary, culture-specific knowledge, and verbal memory. . . . Therefore they are intrinsically biased against the dyslexic multi-lingual individual.'

Tests of cognitive ability used by specialist teachers for assessment

Dunn, L. and Dunn, L. (1997) *British Picture Vocabulary Scale* (NFER-Nelson, www.nfer-nelson.co.uk). This is a test of receptive vocabulary for ages 3–15 years 8 months.

Raven, J.C., Court, J.H. and Raven, J. (1988) *Raven's Standard Progressive Matrices* (Oxford Psychologists Press, www.oxford.opp.co.uk). This is a test of visuo-spatial reasoning for ages 6 years–adult.

Glutting, J., Adams, W. and Sheslow D. (2000) *Wide Range Intelligence Test (WRIT)* (www. dyslexiaaction.org.uk) (4–84 years).

Tests of cognitive ability used by psychologists for assessment

Wechsler, D. (1992) *Wechsler Intelligence Scale for Children*, third edition UK (WISC-III UK) (www.harcourt-uk.com).

Elliott, C.D., Smith, P. and McCullock, K. (1996) *British Ability Scales*, second edition (BAS II) (NFER-Nelson) (www.nfer-nelson.co.uk).

Verbal sub-tests

WISC-III UK (1992) includes the following sub-tests which are presented orally. They test information and general knowledge and ask questions using long-term memory.

Information

This is a test of general knowledge and ability to recall information.

Similarities

This is a test of verbal reasoning and measures the understanding of analogies. It tests the ability to generalise one piece of information from another and gives an indication of aptitude for abstract thinking.

Arithmetic

This test of mental arithmetic requires a knowledge of multiplication tables and the use of short-term auditory memory to solve word sums.

Vocabulary

This is a test of the ability to give meanings/definitions of words and of the ability to articulate these.

Comprehension

This tests understanding of social conventions and explanations for everyday situations/ events.

Digit span

This tests auditory short-term memory when repeating a series of digits in a forward order. It also tests working memory when repeating numbers in a backwards order.

Performance non-verbal sub-tests

These are presented visually.

Picture completion

This tests visual perception when missing parts of a picture have to be identified.

Coding

This tests visual short-term memory and eye–hand co-ordination when digits have to be copied to match symbols from a given key.

Picture arrangement

This tests the ability to re-arrange pictures which illustrate simple stories so that the sequence of events makes sense.

Block design

This tests the ability to break down a geometric pattern into its component parts and re-arrange blocks to match a given design. It tests manual dexterity and visuo-motor co-ordination as well as spatial abilities.

Object assembly

This tests visual memory and manual dexterity, requiring pieces to be put together as in a jigsaw puzzle.

Symbol search

This tests visual perception, scanning and speed when shapes in a series of rows of symbols have to be matched.

WISC-III includes four individual index scores: verbal comprehension; perceptual organisation; freedom from distractibility (working memory); processing speed. They play an increasingly significant role in the diagnosis of dyslexia and dyspraxia when they indicate a discrepancy in scores.

- The verbal comprehension index includes scores from tests of information, similarities, vocabulary and comprehension.
- The perceptual organisation index includes scores from tests of picture completion, picture arrangement, block design and object assembly.

- The Freedom from distractibility index includes tests of arithmetic and digit span.
- The processing speed index includes scores from tests of coding and symbol search.

Dyspraxic children often do badly on the perceptual organisation index because of their lack of speed in manipulating pieces of puzzle or blocks. Some dyslexic children do badly on the freedom from distractibility index often because of short-term memory difficulties.

Critics such as Stanovich (1991) argue that IQ test scores do not 'measure potential in any valid sense' but are 'gross measures of current cognitive functioning', and that 'verbally loaded measures are allegedly unfair to dyslexic children'. The two main issues are:

1   the impact of dyslexia on performance in individual sub-scores
2   whether IQ tests are useful/reliable when making a diagnosis of dyslexia.

Newton *et al.* (1979) reviewed the literature on the data from eleven studies about performance on WISC sub-tests and carried out a study showing 'the dyslexic group scored significantly lower than the control group on Information, Arithmetic, Digit Span and Coding (ACID)' scores. Thomson (1990, 2001) reiterated that many dyslexic children's performance is poor on the ACID profile of tests on the basis of the scores of 300 pupils at a specialist dyslexia school.

Explanations and hypotheses for poor performance in the following sub-tests

Information

Performance is dependent on general knowledge, most of which is gleaned from reading. Many dyslexic children are poor readers, so read less than their peers. Anecdotally the discrepancy on this score is not as widespread as it was twenty years ago perhaps due to the influence of television. Denckla and Rudel's (1976) theory indicated that word retrieval and word naming difficulties may account for an inability to recall vocabulary for the oral responses in timed conditions.

Arithmetic

Short-term memory and working memory are required to recall the content of the question before providing the answer. Multiplication tables require sequencing skills and automaticity to provide a timed response.

Digit span

Some cope with the forward presentation of numbers but find saying digits in reverse order very difficult because of having to attend to the individual digits, then manipulate them using working memory.

Coding

The sub-skills involved are visual memory and eye–hand co-ordination as well as the ability to remember symbolic information.

The role of the individual sub-tests took centre stage in diagnosis with the use of WISC-III UK which included more sophisticated diagnostic measures and use of the Wechsler Objective Reading Dimensions (WORD) (Wechsler, 1993) which tested basic reading, spelling and reading comprehension and provided a predicted standardised score based on IQ.

The discrepancy between attainment scores and predicted scores is 'a critical first stage in the identification of specific learning difficulties because it points to a specific under-achievement' in Thomson's (2001) view. Thomson (2003) takes issue with the British Psychological Society (BPS) Working Party who argue that the ACID profile is 'clinically meaningless'. He disagrees with the BPS findings and refutes its claims by providing evidence from a sample of 250 dyslexic children which showed that 40 per cent had a complete ACID profile. 50 per cent had a SCAD profile with lower scores in symbol search, coding, arithmetic and digit span. He makes a strong case for the significance of IQ scores in the diagnosis of dyslexia and he demonstrates how scores help to predict attainment scores on tests. The reality of this is that at SEN tribunals parents have lost their action to have their child statemented because the criteria used, matching attainment scores with chronological age rather than IQ scores, resulted in the discrepancy not being 'severe enough' to warrant intervention.

Turner (1997a) is critical of the 'ACID profile of folklore' particularly of the 'Information component' which, he argues, 'is the most loosely implicated in specific learning difficulties'. He points out the usefulness of the digit span and arithmetic scores.

British Ability Scales BAS ll (1996) includes the following sub-tests:

Word definitions

This tests vocabulary and word knowledge including giving explanations and meanings of words.

Verbal similarities

Three items are given and the objective is to explain how they are similar. It tests verbal reasoning and knowledge.

Matrices

The objective is to point out the design that completes a pattern of shapes. It tests an ability to work out a sequence of steps by reasoning, naming and verbalising the shapes. This involves working memory and an ability to use language appropriate for the task.

Quantitative reasoning

The objective is to perceive sequential patterns and the relationship between pairs of numbers. It tests non-verbal reasoning.

Recall of designs

The objective is to reproduce simple abstract designs from cards which are then removed. It tests visual memory.

Pattern construction

The objective is to construct a pattern using four or nine blocks to match a given pattern. It tests visuo-spatial ability.

Recall of objects – immediate verbal

This is a test of visual short-term memory and spoken language.

Recall of objects – immediate spatial

This is a test of visual short-term memory and spatial ability.

Recall of objects – delayed verbal

This is a test of long-term visual memory using spoken language.

Recall of objects – delayed spatial

This is a test of long-term visual memory using spatial ability.

Speed of information processing

This is a test in which the highest number in a row of numbers has to be marked repeatedly in timed conditions.

Recall of digits forward

This is a test in which digits presented have to be repeated. It tests short-term memory.

Recall of digits backwards

This is a test of recall of digits presented in reverse order. It tests working memory.

There are three further ability scores called clusters:

Verbal ability cluster measures verbal and auditory ability, from the scores of the word definitions and verbal similarities tests.

Spatial ability cluster measures visuo-spatial ability from the scores of the recall of designs and pattern construction tests.

Non-verbal ability cluster measures how well verbal and spatial abilities are integrated from the scores of the matrices and quantitative reasoning tests and includes the BAS spelling; and BAS word Reading Attainment Test.

Scores are combined to provide a general conceptual ability score (GCA), in other words the full-scale IQ score. Thomson *et al.* (1981) found that dyslexics scored significantly less well on speed of information processing, immediate and delayed visual recall, recall of digits, basic arithmetic and word reading across all age ranges, when compared to other abilities on the BAS.

The cluster scores provide a measure of strengths and weaknesses in verbal, non-verbal and spatial skills with percentiles for abilities and attainments. Higher verbal ability and spatial ability scores and lower non-verbal ability scores are often due to working memory difficulties, indicating a discrepancy in attainments and, often, a specific learning difficulty such as dyslexia.

The discrepancy factor

The discrepancy factor refers to a gap between cognitive ability and performance in attainment tests of reading, spelling and numeracy. In practice it is often applied to the discrepancy between chronological age and reading age. It lies at the heart of the debate about diagnosis and provision and is a key factor in the implementation of special educational needs legislation and in the allocation of resources including the policy documents produced by LEAs in response to the Education Act 1993 and the Code of Practice. The major issue is what is stated in the policy document in regard to the criteria for carrying out a statutory assessment of children with special educational needs. One of the legacies of the Education Act 1981 was that parents became increasingly aware that they often needed the protection of a statement to ensure that their child with a 'significant level of learning difficulty' received 'special educational provision which cannot reasonably be provided within the resources normally available to mainstream schools in the area'.

This resulted in a major increase in appeals to the SEN Appeals Tribunal for provision for dyslexic pupils and accounted for over 40 per cent of appeal cases. It is reported for example that Buckinghamshire County Council spent over £1 million a year on the costs involved in tribunal work. Professionals had different objectives when considering whether a child should be put forward for a multi-professional formal, statutory assessment with a statement as the expected outcome.

According to the Education Act 1993 which incorporated earlier legislation the LEA must identify and make an assessment for a child who has special educational needs because his difficulties:

- 'are significant/and or complex
- have not responded to intervention
- may call for special educational provision beyond normal mainstream resources'.

When considering the needs of children who 'may have significant learning difficulties in reading, writing, spelling or manipulating numbers, which are not typical of their general level of performance', the results of standardised tests of cognitive ability and standardised tests of reading, spelling or mathematics must be taken into account. A child of 7–8 years in Year 3 would have to have a reading age of 5 years 8 months or less and a child of 10–11 years in Year 6 a reading age of 6 years 2 months to be considered for a request for a statutory assessment and a statement of SEN.

According to the legislation, 'Access to the curriculum is taken to be a central issue'. Sawyer et al. (1994) gave guidelines about the reading age necessary to access reading materials in classrooms to read to learn when following the National Curriculum which they based on the Neale Analysis of Reading (NARA) test results. They stated that a child of 7–8 years in Year 3 needs a reading age of 7 years 6 months and a child of 10–11 years in Year 6 a reading age of 9 years 7 months to access classroom reading resources.

> Normally however attainments by pupils of high ability at or above the [Reading] Age 9½ level would not be considered for special support by the authority. . . . Mathematics and spelling are not regarded as access skills in the same way as reading. Consideration will not be given for specific difficulties in these areas for pupils within or above the normal cognitive ability range, the responsibility for which will be expected to remain with the school.
>
> (Royal Borough of Berkshire, undated)

It was not surprising that LEAs had to set aside substantial sums from their budgets to cover the costs of litigation generated by parents who sought help for their child with SEN, including dyslexia and dyspraxia. The London Borough of Richmond had the highest number of appeals for SEN in 2004–5, Warrington and Coventry councils having the lowest (TES, 2006.)

LEAs claim that only 1 per cent of children need to be statemented. The BDA claims that 4 per cent of the population are severely dyslexic; their needs often cannot be met in classrooms. Many need additional support from specialist teachers often on a one-to-one basis to close the gaps between their attainments in basic skills and, at least, their chronological age but ideally their mental age.

Is a discrepancy between reading age and IQ all that is needed to make a diagnosis of dyslexia? Miles et al. (2003) argued that many dyslexic children overcome earlier reading difficulties and that the 'needs of dyslexics with only mild literacy problems should not be overlooked'. They point out that dyslexia is a syndrome and 'the important thing is the overall pattern rather than any one particular symptom'. Miles (2004), reviewing fifty years of dyslexia research including his personal experience, asserted that

> if I had to summarise in a single sentence what I thought was the main characteristic of dyslexia as I have described it I would be tempted to say that it involves a mismatch of skills. Phonological skills (that is, the ability to organise and recall speech sounds) are relatively weak and do not match up to the person's reasoning power (or the ability to 'process for meaning') which in some cases may be strong.

To establish what the 'mismatch' is, it is necessary to have a measure of 'reasoning power'.

Others such as Siegel (1989) argue that we should 'abandon the IQ test in the analysis of the child with learning difficulties' because the tests are measures of achievement rather than intelligence. They are discriminatory often because of cultural bias and sometimes because some of the sub-tests are more challenging for children from ethnic minority, immigrant or socially deprived backgrounds. Some do badly because of their short-term memory or phonological difficulties. She claimed that poor readers known as the 'garden variety' (Gough and Tunmer, 1986) of readers with low ability have the same difficulties as dyslexic children, so the use of IQ tests and the discrepancy criteria is not justified. Stanovich (1991) concurs with this view.

The British Psychological Society (1999) DECP defined dyslexia as 'evident when accurate and fluent word reading/and or spelling develops very incompletely or with great difficulty'. They dismissed 'the relationship between intelligence and attainments'. This was a retrograde step.

The Wechsler and British Ability Scales IQ tests include tables to establish a discrepancy between IQ scores and predicted scores of attainment. These are particularly useful for pupils whose reading and spelling skills are on a par with their chronological age but who have persisting difficulties with writing, speed of processing and memory. The QCA has added its support to the discrepancy debate, highlighting scores which show a significant gap between performance and verbal scores. It describes a 'significant discrepancy between cognitive ability and performance, shown by:

- a difference of 20 points or more between verbal and performance IQ or
- at least average verbal reasoning, non-verbal reasoning or quantitative scores alongside below average literacy scores'.

The formal scores apply to WISC verbal and performance scores. The latter scores apply to NFER-Nelson Verbal Reasoning and NFER-Nelson Non-Verbal Reasoning tests and Cognitive Abilities Tests (CATs).

There is much evidence that dyslexia is a 'continuum' of skills and strengths (Miles *et al.*, 2003). There are varying degrees of the condition ranging from severe, moderate and mild cases to 'atypical or incomplete' examples, described Critchley and Critchley (1978) as 'formes frustes'.

Degrees of dyslexia

Severe	The child has a high IQ and excellent verbal skills but cannot communicate because he has difficulty reading. His spelling is appalling and his handwriting is illegible. He forgets personal details such as his date of birth or e-mail address.
Moderate	He has been assessed and given specialist individual help. Nonetheless he struggles with reading text because he is a poor decoder. He struggles to write all he knows and wants to say within the time allowance.
Mild	This includes the child who may have had difficulties when learning to read. Now he can read on a par with his chronological age but is a slow, inaccurate decoder. His spelling is on a par with his chronological skills but when he writes fiction and non-fiction he has a high error rate, notably with homophones, irregular spellings and punctuation.
Borderline (*formes frustes*)	This includes those who have residual difficulties including dyslexia tendencies with short-term memory, who may find taking notes from

a lecture challenging because of poor processing skills, and he sometimes has difficulty finding the word he wants to use and finds essay writing challenging because of difficulties with organisation and sequencing.

Turner (2004) produced a 'Dyslexia Index' which describes degrees of severity based on the Dyslexia Institute's assessments data. He gives six categories based on performance on standardised tests:

1   no dyslexia signs
2   few dyslexia signs
3   mild dyslexia
4   moderate dyslexia
5   severe dyslexia
6   very severe dyslexia.

What is the significance of IQ scores for individuals and what are the implications for their teachers?

- IQ scores can differentiate between pupils who have global learning difficulties, including those who have been called the 'garden variety' of poor readers, and those who have a specific learning difficulty such as dyslexia or dyspraxia.
- They can give some indication of skills, weaknesses and strengths. Knowing this helps with timely intervention including appropriate learning support which will affect current and future academic progress.
- They can provide evidence of a bright child with a high IQ who has average or below average scores on individual tests such as the NFER verbal reasoning (VR) tests. His scores on the SATs reading test indicate that he is 'just average' or, even worse, 'slow' and 'stupid'.
- They influence parents' and teachers' perceptions which change when, for example, they are told that Jayme has a full scale IQ of 140. Knowing that one sibling has an IQ of 105 and another has an IQ of 135 helps teachers and parents have more realistic expectations for individual children.
- The relief for the pupil when he is told that he has a high IQ is immeasurable – 'knowing that I am not stupid or thick changed my life', said 14-year-old Martin. However, it is important to be mindful that not all children fulfil their potential or live up to the expectations of parents or teachers despite scores obtained on measures of ability. Some individuals outperform clever siblings in later life often because of personal characteristics or skills in non-academic areas such as the multiple intelligences described by Gardner (1983).
- The results of IQ tests are not infallible and educational testing is not an exact science and should not be promoted as such. They provide a snapshot of individual development as well as pinpointing strengths and weaknesses which can be used to predict educational outcomes as well as indicating what learning support or teaching may be required.

The use and interpretation of IQ scores as the sole criterion when assessing the educational potential of children needs careful consideration. Jackson (2005) cautions that 'all assessment results must be interpreted with caution, recognising that they represent a sample of performance in a specific assessment situation, and that, in reality, many factors interplay to affect educational achievement and performance'. Ability may be masked by under-achievement, under-achievement may be masked by lack of confidence, and lack of confidence may be masked by a specific learning difficulty such as dyslexia/dyspraxia.

Theory of multiple intelligences: its implications in the roll of honour of successful and talented dyslexic people

Howard Gardner (1983) while professor of graduate education at Harvard University was given funding to establish the nature of intelligence 'with no prior assumption of what intelligence might be'. This research was named Project Zero and is cited in Jensen (1995). Gardner's (1983) findings included a new way of defining intelligence – 'An intelligence is an ability to solve a problem or to fashion a product which is valued in one or more cultural settings' – and his ground-breaking theory of seven 'multiple intelligences'. He devised the following categorisations for these:

1   *logical-mathematical* skills which include an ability to solve mathematical or scientific problems, work through puzzles and make sense of the physical world including mending and fixing objects
2   visual-spatial skills which include an ability to design, draw and navigate as well as to visualise patterns, shapes and colour
3   intrapersonal skills which include an ability to reflect, plan, analyse and self-motivate
4   interpersonal skills which include an ability to communicate effectively with others, persuade and motivate others as well as inspire co-operation
5   *musical-rhythmic* skills which include an ability to create, play and perform music and rhythm
6   *bodily-kinaesthetic* skills which include an ability to manipulate and control bodily movements and objects
7   *verbal-linguistic* skills which include an ability to speak coherently, argue, conduct public debate.

Gardner (1999) added:

8   *naturalistic* skills which include an ability to recognise plants, animals, rocks and other natural phenomena.

Roll of Honour of successful talented dyslexic people with evidence of multiple intelligences

I Visual/spatial intelligence

David Bailey (photographer); Leonardo da Vinci (artist and sculptor); Lord Richard Rodgers (architect); Auguste Rodin (sculptor).

2 Musical/rhythmic intelligence

Harry Belafonte (singer); Sarah Brightman (singer and actress); Cher (singer/actress); Noel Gallagher (Oasis rock band member, song writer).

3 Interpersonal intelligence

Sir Richard Branson (entrepreneur and businessman); Sir Winston Churchill (statesman); Michael Heseltine (politician); Nelson Rockefeller (Vice-President of the USA).

4 Intrapersonal intelligence

Hans Christian Andersen (author of children's fairy tales); Walt Disney (cartoonist); Jerry Hall (model and actress); Eddie Izzard (comedian); Jamie Oliver (chef); Zoe Wanamaker (actress).

5 Logical/mathematical intelligence

Charles Dodgson (Lewis Carroll) (mathematician, author of *Alice in Wonderland*); Thomas Edison (inventor of the light bulb); Albert Einstein (scientist and mathematician); Bill Gates (computing); Nicholas Negroponte (founder of media lab, Massachusetts Institute of Technology); Henri Poincaré (mathematician); Charles Schwab (investment banker and financier).

6 Bodily/kinaesthetic intelligence

Magic Johnson (basketball champion); Greg Louganis (two Olympic gold medals for swimming); Sir Steve Redgrave (five times rowing Olympic gold medallist); Sir Jackie Stewart (motor racing, Formula I world champion).

7 Verbal/linguistic intelligence

Tom Cruise (actor); Sir Anthony Hopkins (Oscar-winning actor); William Butler Yeats (poet, Nobel laureate); Benjamin Zephaniah (poet).

8 Naturalistic intelligence

Charles Darwin (explorer and author); Dame Anita Roddick (Body Shop founder and conservationist); Tim Smit (gardener/designer of the Eden project); Rick Stein (chef and author).

This theory of talents and skills has been warmly welcomed by the dyslexia community because it makes sense of anomalies in test results and the anecdotal evidence of gifts and talents in individuals who struggle with literacy (West, 1991). Child (2004) pointed out that giftedness included:

- high measures of human abilities such as linguistic or mathematical abilities
- high creativity such as musical or scientific ability

- high talent such as technological or athletic ability
- high information processing such as knowledge and memory abilities.

No standardised measures have been developed to define and test specific talents but checklists such as Montgomery's (1998) include a list of the main characteristics of gifted children. This may explain why Gardner's multiple intelligence theory is controversial.

Summary and conclusions

- Reading is an unnatural act. For most individuals learning to read requires explicit teaching as well as time and experience including exposure to print. The reader needs to be given tools to 'unravel' the printed code.
- Low literacy is a global issue affecting developed as well as Third World countries.
- The 'reading wars' have become a political issue in the USA and the UK not least because of their economic and social consequences for individuals and society.
- There are many underlying causes of reading difficulties which must be considered and eliminated when seeking an explanation for why a particular child finds it more difficult to learn to read than the majority of his peers. Reid Lyon (1998) argued that for 90–95 per cent of poor readers, prevention and early intervention programmes that combine instruction in phonemic awareness, phonics, fluency development and reading comprehension strategies, provided by well-trained teachers, can increase reading skills to average levels.
- Social, emotional, cognitive, behavioural, physical and constitutional aspects need to be factored in when considering the reasons why some individuals struggle to decipher and make sense of the printed word. Frith (1997) pointed out that 'there is a general consensus that dyslexia is a lifelong development disorder with a biological origin'.
- There is scientific evidence of a hereditary factor in reading difficulties. There are three times as many boys as girls with specific reading difficulties. The gender ratio is surely a significant factor in why boys always do less well in national tests. This is frequently overlooked by commentators. Explanations such as lack of motivation and lack of parental role models, few trips to the library and watching television are often given as prime causes of the imbalance in scores between boys and girls.
- International studies and research programmes from many countries highlight the importance of first teaching systematic phonics to beginner readers including phonemic and phonological skills, rather than teaching whole words through an analytic phonics approach and memorising the NLS high frequency word lists.
- The way forward is first teaching and learning synthetic phonics to give readers the key that unlocks the door to the treasure house of literature that awaits those who can decode accurately and fluently. Readers will then need to learn to use contextual cues, sight vocabulary and grammatical clues to read for meaning, pleasure and understanding, as well as using books that are appropriate for their age and ability.
- A battery of reading tests needs to be used when identifying dyslexia because fluent, accurate reading depends on a number of sub-skills. Some children may have a word recognition age on a par with their chronological age. Others may score two/three years above their chronological age and on a par with their IQ level and yet have reading difficulties on a reading comprehension test with standardised scores below what would be expected for their age and ability. Others score well on group multiple

choice tests of silent reading comprehension but remain slow and inaccurate readers. These test results should not be used as the sole criteria of reading ability when assessing a child who may have a specific learning difficulty. Frith (1997) argued that 'test scores are only the starting points for the scientific study of dyslexia'. It is advisable also to use individual tests of word recognition, non-word reading and reading rate when making an assessment. Other poor readers have low reading rates.

- The scores on the individual tests are important but close observation needs to be made of the strategies the reader uses to deal with words that are not instantly recognisable as 'sight words'.
- The vogue is for shorter tests because of time constraints for busy professionals. A one-minute reading test does not provide enough information (as some claim) to identify dyslexia in a reader. When carrying out an assessment it is important to use test instruments that provide enough information for a diagnosis.
- A miscue analysis of reading errors may be time consuming but the information it provides about reading strengths and weaknesses pays handsome dividends for the diagnostician and the teacher. It is important to remember that many children will make some errors from time to time when reading. The dyslexic reader makes more errors and does so more frequently than the 'garden variety' of poor readers (Gough and Tunmer, 1986). Teachers, teaching assistants and parents are well placed to note the pattern of errors that dyslexic children make over weeks and months despite regular intervention and support.
- A discrepancy between 'observed' standardised scores and 'expected' standardised scores which are linked to age and IQ is very important, particularly for children who are very bright and for older children who may have compensated for some of their earlier reading difficulties. Some compensated dyslexic pupils no longer have difficulties with reading but retain many of the associated characteristics of the condition.

Chapter 5

The theory and processes involved in teaching reading: suggestions for closing the gaps in reading attainments

Outline

- Timeline of significant events, influential publications and reading resources
- How do good readers read and what lessons can be learned from their experience?
- A review of Chall's 'essential principles' for successful teaching of reading using the 'code emphasis' (phonics) method
- A review of Goodman's principles for teaching reading using the 'meaning emphasis' ('whole language') method
- A review of Adams's findings about reading processes and instructions for teaching reading
- Orton–Gillingham principles: multi-sensory teaching methods
- What do teachers need to know and do to deliver a well-balanced reading diet?
- The significance of the different developmental stages when learning reading
- Look-and-say: the 'whole word' recognition reading method
- Hints and suggestions for learning sight words, including the high frequency words
- The 'code emphasis' phonics method: suggestions for resources to develop phonic skills, including reading books
- The 'whole language' or 'meaning emphasis' method
- Hints for developing and enhancing reading comprehension skills
- The rough guide to helping reluctant readers become accurate, fluent and confident
- Suggestions for calculating the readability of a text
- Suggestions for selecting fiction and non-fiction titles
- Summary and conclusions

During the second half of the nineteenth century and for most of the twentieth century battles were fought by educationists and interested professionals about how to teach reading and how children learn to read. Major warfare erupted with important and influential 'education generals' winning the hearts and minds of their foot followers and troops on the ground. Many casualties occurred when new methods were introduced. The heaviest casualties can be found among those with SpLD including the dyslexic population. An overview of popular reading methodologies provides information and insights for current users, including teachers and learners.

Timeline of significant events, influential publications and reading resources (adapted from Morris, 1984)

1857   L.F. Bevan's *Reading Without Tears* was the first phonic reading primer published in the UK.

1899   Nellie Dale's *On the Teaching of English Reading* was published.

1900–2 This was followed by *The Dale Readers* which used synthetic phonics, colour and multi-sensory methods.

1914   Ballard's Standardised Reading Scale was the first reading assessment tool.

1922   As Morris (1984) pointed out, 'the year 1922 was important in the history of British reading instruction' because American reading schemes – 'basal readers' – were first introduced to the UK. An example is *The Beacon Readers* (Fassett, 1922). They included initial phonic instruction and tables of phonics but crucially introduced look-and-say methods. Phonics teaching went into decline.

1925   Winch (1925) conducted an experiment and found the phonic method was more successful than 'look-and-say'.

1929   Jagger's *The Sentence Method of Teaching Reading* was published and had many followers. It advocated a 'meaning emphasis' approach and denounced the phonic approach.

1939   Schonell's *Happy Venture Readers* used the look-and-say method with controlled vocabulary 'so that maximum use can be made by learning through discrimination of visual patterns of words'.

1947   *The Duncan Readers* were published. The author, J. Duncan, launched a seven-prong attack on phonic teaching in a Ministry of Education publication.

1949   O'Donnell and Munro's *Janet and John Books* were published and included a 'mixed approach' of look-and-say and phonics. In reality the teaching of phonics went out of fashion. 'Progressive' education methods were in the ascendancy. Concerns were raised about declining reading standards, particularly the high levels of illiteracy in the Armed Forces.

1954   Daniels and Diack's *Royal Road Readers* were published. They led the 'Phonic Revolt' and attacked the 'Chinese' approach of teaching reading through the whole word approach which they compared to learning Chinese logograms.

1964   Murray's *Ladybird Key Words Reading Scheme* became a bestselling look-and-say reading scheme based on McNally and Murray's (1962) *100 Key Words to Literacy*. It included some phonics from Book 4 onwards.

1969   Cox and Dyson (1969), in *Fight for Education* (the so-called 'Black Papers') launched an attack on 'progressive' teaching methods, arguing that they were responsible for the prevailing low reading standards.

1970   A House of Commons Select Committee listened to submissions from various workers in the field. There was a major emphasis on training standards in initial teaching institutions and recommendations were made for improvement in the teaching of reading.

1970s   Phonic readers went out of print as did the Initial Teaching Alphabet (ITA) resources of Pitman and St John (1969).

1970–90 The 'whole language' or 'real books' movement influenced by Goodman (1967) and Smith (1973) was widely adopted in schools until the publication of the National Literacy Strategy (NLS).

1998   The NLS *Framework for Teaching* brought the wheel full circle and put phonics back in the teaching of literacy. Its 'searchlight' model for teaching encouraged the child to draw on a range of strategies simultaneously to 'work out' the word by using context or syntax, sounding out the letters or recognising the shape from previous exposure including the high frequency lists. 'Searchlight' was a metaphor for the use of different strategies to decode words. The more cues that were used, the better the chance of reading the word.

2000   Arguments raged and commentators disagreed about whether children should be taught synthetic phonics – /c/ /a/ /t/ – or analytic phonics – /c/ /at/ – first or whether to use the 'mixed' methods including memorising the 'high frequency' lists recommended by the NLS.

2003   The Fullan Report, *Watching and Learning*, an external evaluation of the NLS, concluded that 'there is considerable disparity across teachers in subject knowledge, pedagogical skill . . .', including how to teach phonics.

2005   The House of Commons Education and Skills Committee examined evidence and published its report *Teaching Children to Read*. It accepted that 'phonics is an essential methodology'.

        The Rose Reading Review was established to examine examples of good practice in the use of phonics in the teaching of early reading.

2006   The DfES commissioned the universities of York and Sheffield to conduct a systematic review of experimental research on the use of phonics in the teaching of reading and spelling (Torgerson *et al.*, 2006).

        The Rose Report, Independent Review of the Teaching of Early Reading concluded that 'synthetic phonics offers the vast majority of young children the best and most direct route to becoming skilled readers and writers' (Rose, 2006).

How do good readers read and what lessons can be learned from their experience?

Doctors can learn how to treat their patients by studying disease. The converse is true for teachers. They can learn to teach their poor readers by studying what skilled readers do.

Ehri (1997a) showed that if a word is not instantly recognisable and is not in the reader's sight vocabulary, the good reader will use a variety of strategies including:

1   phonemic decoding of the word when trained to use synthetic phonics to sound out the letters – /m/ /a/ /n/ – and then blending and reading the word. The more experienced reader may use analytic phonics to break it down into chunks – /sh/ /ip/, /d/ /ash/ – and blend these or divide the word into syllables such as /rab/bit/

2 recognising common spelling patterns – 'ight', 'ough' in words like 'night', 'bought' – as well as roots – *form* – prefixes – *re*form – suffixes – former – or both – *performing*
3 reading words from memory by recognising visual similarities from previous reading experience
4 contextual cues to make sense of what they are reading, which is why IQ plays an important role in reading attainment levels, particularly in comprehension.
5 analogy: if readers know the word 'might', for example, they can often read 'sight', 'night'.

Awareness of these strategies is useful when assessing attainment and when identifying where a breakdown or gap in poor readers' skills occurs. Good readers recognise sight words instantly and read them effortlessly, rapidly and smoothly without pausing (Meyer and Felton 1999). This enhances comprehension and the meaning of the text. But what of those who just cannot crack the code?

The spark that ignited the reading time bomb in the USA was Rudolph Flesch's (1955) book *Why Johnny Can't Read*. He argued that the fault lay in the teaching methods used in most classrooms including look-and-say and basal readers, that children should be taught to identify the letters and sounds and that they should learn to write these. The book caused a national debate and was on the US bestseller list for thirty weeks. The outcome was that educators became more polarised in their opinions. The 'code emphasis' versus 'meaning emphasis' battle which began in the 1920s and rumbled on until the 1960s finally exploded with major upheavals in the 1970s and 1980s.

A review of Chall's 'essential principles' for successful teaching of reading using the 'code emphasis' (phonics) method

Chall studied and reviewed the literature on the scientific research on reading from the 1900s to the 1960s. Her recommendations were published in *Learning to Read: The Great Debate* (1967). They include:

- Instruction in phonics should be given.
- Phonics should be integrated into meaningful texts (rather than learning lists by rote fashion).
- Word recognition should be encouraged for reading and understanding words.
- Meaningful reading material should be given, including stories.
- A sight vocabulary of whole words should be built up.
- Words in reading books should be controlled to match reading ability. Books should match reading age levels.
- Reading readiness should be considered, for example underlying skills such as alphabet knowledge.
- Pupils should be grouped and taught according to reading ability.

This seminal text explained why the explicit teaching of phonics is fundamental and why it should be embedded in meaningful text. She identified the research evidence which showed that teaching phonics using the 'code emphasis' method was the most effective method of teaching literacy for all children and particularly for slow learners. Her message fell on barren ground and was largely ignored at the time.

A review of Goodman's principles for teaching reading using the 'meaning emphasis' ('whole language') method

Kenneth Goodman, Frank Smith and Carol Chomsky were the principal advocates of the 'whole language' ('meaning emphasis') methods which were popularised and widely adopted between 1975 and 1995 in the USA and also in the UK. They were influenced by Noam Chomsky's work on linguistics which asserted that language skills are innate in humans. They claimed that children could acquire reading skills by exposure to print. Their principles included:

- A hypothesis based on the assumption that 'children learn to read like they learn spoken language' was central. They pointed out that language skills, both oral and written, develop naturally so that some children begin to write before they can read.
- The goal was to develop a love of reading. They argued that the ability to read would then follow on naturally from this.
- Children should be given interesting and exciting books which could be read by 'whole word' and 'meaning emphasis' methods. This was described as a 'psycho-linguistic guessing game' by Goodman (1976) who claimed that children could guess at meanings, using contextual cues, pictures and their general knowledge to make sense of what they were reading.
- They recommended that sentences should not be taken apart or divided 'into words, syllables and isolated sounds' on the grounds that children would be able to deduce sound–symbol relationships for themselves when reading meaningful stories. In other words, children could teach themselves to read when exposed to interesting texts. Phonics and spelling should only be taught on a 'need to know' basis after the child makes an error. Their position was in stark contrast to the scientific findings which Adams (1990) reported which showed that 'skilled readers tend to look at each individual word and to process its component letters quite thoroughly'). Their theory was based on ideology rather than rigorous scientific research on how children learn to read. Liberman and Liberman (1990), when considering 'what's right with whole language?', commented ironically that 'Some of what it espouses is undeniably right and inherently appealing which may account for the wide currency it now enjoys.' But, 'only to the extent that it offers suggestions about instruction that sensible people like your grandmothers and ours would regard as truisms. . . . Other, more funda-mental aspects of the Whole Language position are demonstrably false'.
- Goodman (1967) and Smith (1973, 1978) reasoned that learning phonics would result in 'word callers' and would slow children down and interfere with comprehension.

This method of teaching reading was introduced into many schools by law throughout the USA. British schools soon followed the trend. 'Reading schemes' in the UK, known as 'basal' readers in the USA, were gradually abandoned by many schools. Children were encouraged to go to the 'reading corner' and choose and read a library book. This approach worked well for many of the population who learn to read whatever method is used. Liberman and Liberman (1990) confirmed that '75 per cent [of children] will discover the alphabetic principles, which is what they must understand if they are to read, no matter how unhelpful the instruction'. However, thousands of individuals did not crack the reading code because they simply did not have the knowhow. They were unable to 'discover' how to read without direct intervention and without the appropriate teaching of skills.

A review of Adams's findings about reading processes and instructions for teaching reading

The catalyst for change in teaching reading came as a result of the publication of data from the US National Assessment of Educational Progress. It showed that in the state of California 60 per cent of 9-year-olds could not read at their grade level (9 years reading age (RA)). The federal government set up a Commission on Reading and its results were published in *Becoming a Nation of Readers* (Commission on Reading, National Academy of Education, 1985). It advocated 'phonics first and fast'. It later appointed Marilyn Jager Adams to review best practice and to examine the international scientific research findings. Her report constitutes what is considered the 'most complete view' and the most important book of the twentieth century on the teaching of reading: *Beginning to Read: Thinking and Learning About Print* (1990). She concluded that a 'deep and thorough knowledge of letters, spelling patterns and words, and of the phonological translation of all three, are of inescapable importance to skillful reading and its acquisition' and are not forthcoming without special instruction. She added that 'by extension, instruction [should be] designed to develop children's sensitivity to spellings and their paramount importance in the development of reading skills'. She endorsed the 'place of elementary phonics' but pointed out: 'to be most productive, it may best be conceived as a support activity carefully covered but largely subordinated to the reading and writing of connected text'. In other words, phonics skills should not be taught as isolated drills and in lists but should be used in running texts and in reading books.

President Bill Clinton in his State of the Union address in 1996 caused shock-waves throughout the United States when he announced that 40 per cent of the fourth grade children (Year 4, 9-year-olds) could not read at grade level (9 years RA), showing that the USA had a 'reading crisis'. In response, the Reading Excellence Act (REA) 1998 was passed. Its main goals were:

- to provide children with reading readiness skills
- to teach every child to read by the end of the third grade (age 8 years)
- to improve the instructional practices for teachers and staff by using 'scientific based reading research'.

It defined reading as 'including the understanding of how speech sounds (phonemes) are connected to print, the ability to decode unfamiliar words, the ability to read fluently, and the development of sufficient background information and vocabulary to foster reading comprehension'.

Orton–Gillingham principles: multi-sensory teaching methods

The National Institute of Child Health and Human Development (2000) *Report of the National Reading Panel Teaching Children to Read: An Evidence-Based Assessment of the Scientific Research Literature on Reading and its Implications for Reading Instruction* concluded that from 'the scientific evidence, the essential systematic and direct instruction in phonemic awareness, phonics, reading fluency, vocabulary development and comprehension strategies' are 'the essential components of any reading programme'. It argued that 'reading must be taught – directly and systematically – and that the children most at risk require the most systematic instruction with the best prepared teachers' (Lyon et al., 2004). This encapsulates much of what Samuel Orton, 'the founding father' of the dyslexia movement, and his associate Anna Gillingham had advocated and taught the teachers they trained to work with their dyslexic pupils. They had begun to do this in the 1940s. The Orton–Gillingham methods which used synthetic phonics were shown to be the most effective method of teaching literacy. It has now been proved in a review of the international scientific research by Snow et al. (1998) that what is essential for dyslexic pupils is also crucial for all readers. Many workers in the dyslexia field in the USA and UK have long waited for universal recognition and acceptance of their methods. Teaching phonics was reintroduced and became an integral part of the National Literacy Strategy (NLS, 1998). There have been on-going criticisms of weaknesses in the teaching of phonics by Ofsted and by the Ontario Institute for Studies in Education (Fullan Report, 2003). This resulted in the convening of a Phonics Summit chaired by Greg Brooks (2003). He recommended that it was 'clear that within the 100 most frequent words, only those that are irregular should be taught as sight words' (by look-and-say methods).

Orton–Gillingham multi-sensory methods teach the pupil that letters have four properties: (1) names; (2) sounds; (3) shapes A a a; (4) feel. These four properties are taught simultaneously using a multi-sensory approach which involves using the lips to say the letter, the ears to listen to the sound, the eyes to look at the letter and the hand to write and touch plastic or wooden letter shapes. Alphabetic skills are taught, followed by individual letter/sound association, which are taught systematically and in a structured manner. Then the child learns to look at a word. If he does not recognise it, he sounds out the letters, then blends them and reads the word. When he wants to spell a word, he segments the sounds and spells it orally. The skills are systematically taught and are reinforced by reading and writing from dictation (Ott 2007a).

According to the connectionist theory (Adams, 1990), fluent, accurate reading depends on teaching the following four key processes: (1) orthography; (2) phonology; (3) meaning; (4) context. Readers must be taught to recognise letter shapes, relate the letter symbol to the individual sounds, recognise common letter patterns such as prefixes or suffixes, understand meaning and use context to extract meaning from text. Critically they must apply, practise and reinforce these skills by reading books. According to research by Vellutino et al. (1996), direct, intensive phoneme and phonics instruction improves word recognition and decoding skills in poor readers but their fluency remains poor. This is why an assessment of pupils with SEN requires the use of a battery of reading tests to identify weaknesses in each of these component sub-skills.

It is now established that there is no one best method of teaching reading. Research has confirmed what successful practitioners know: all readers need a balanced diet including a variety of strategies which they learn and use at different stages of development, such as beginning to learn to read by using synthetic phonics.

All pupils benefit from being taught phonics but for dyslexic readers phonic skills are a lifeline to literacy. They initially need explicit instruction in synthetic phonics and later in analytic phonics. Pupils with SpLD will often require longer and more intense, discrete instruction than their peers.

What do teachers need to know and do to deliver a well-balanced reading diet?

They need to:

- teach in a structured, sequential, cumulative and thorough manner and know what strategies and skills to teach and when to teach them. Skills need to be taught in a hierarchical order including alphabetic skills, grapheme/phoneme knowledge including synthetic phonics, sight vocabulary, phonological awareness, spelling patterns and analytic phonics such as affixes. Semantic and syntactic skills need to be learned as well as awareness and use of pictorial cues
- know and understand the processes or stages children go through as part of normal reading development including the pre-alphabetic stage, partial alphabetic stage, full alphabetic stage and consolidated alphabetic stage (Ehri, 1997a)
- encourage children to read a variety of texts such as stories, poems and information books matching their 'instructional' level; that is, texts they can read with 95 per cent accuracy
- emphasise and teach fluent, accurate and critical reading using a range of strategies such as shared reading (when the teacher reads the text and models the use of cues and strategies), guided reading (when the teacher works with a group of children on a text at an appropriate level for their skills; the pupil reads independently but with support and guidance) and independent reading (when the pupil reads silently and unaided). This approach was recommended by the NLS (1988) which pointed out that the teacher needs to model and support children to use the 'critical understanding and informed reflection' necessary for comprehension. Without understanding, reading is 'barking at print'
- Paired reading, devised by Morgan (1976), is useful because it includes encouragement and support from a parent or a teaching assistant, lessening the effort for those who find reading a daunting task. The adult and child read aloud together. The child is given prompts when needed and praised frequently. Topping and Wolfendale (1985) recommend it as 'particularly valuable for less able readers who gain access to texts of greater richness or complexity' when supported by an adult. The NLS (1998) calls it 'shared reading'. The class have a common textbook or an extract from a text. The teacher may use a 'Big Book' for shared reading which all the children can see. Alternatively an interactive whiteboard can be used
- know about the different reading methods and when and how to use these
- understand and use different assessment tools to evaluate progress and to identify those who have reading difficulties
- respond to the needs of individual children with appropriate resources including books which can be read fluently with pleasure, interest and understanding by all pupils including those with dyslexia
- evaluate reading resources to ensure that a particular text is appropriate for a particular child's current reading attainment level. Meyer and Felton (1999) argue that 'using materials that can be read accurately is the basis for fluency training in poor readers'

Because of innate difficulties some children fail to become fluent, accurate readers which is the ultimate objective of reading instruction. Some dyslexic readers have to laboriously decode many words in running text (depending on the degree of their dyslexia and on the level of difficulty of the text) rather than having instant recognition of the word.

The significance of the different developmental stages when learning reading

Learning to read is a developmental process. Most normal children pass through the different reading phases, some moving quickly, some more slowly. They usually move in a sequential manner depending on experience, the strategies they use, the practice they have, and the interest they develop in reading. However, some readers' skills develop unevenly and overlap occurs. For example, a child may struggle to sound out a word but use contextual cues effectively. Dyslexic children often reach a bottleneck in their reading development. They may therefore require more time and more practice to develop the characteristics usually associated with each stage when learning phonemic and phonological skills.

Furthermore, there is little consensus as to how many stages/phases readers go through when they begin to learn to read. Frith (1985) describes three, Chall (1983, 1987) describes six and Ehri (1995) four. Chall (1983) draws attention to the progression of skills in children's reading. Chall (1987) describes the stages of literacy development in adults which is particularly illuminating for teachers of older beginner readers including adult learners. Frequently specialist teachers deal with older dyslexic children rather than 6–7-year-old beginner readers, but the similarities and differences between a child and adult beginner are striking. According to Chall (1987), 'the major task to be learned by both the 6 year-old beginner and the 40 year-old beginner is to recognise in print the words they already know when heard or spoken'.

Their problem is often that they struggle to build a sight vocabulary and are what is called 'word-blind' (Kussmaul, 1877) in the literature, unable to remember familiar words or recognise the same word on the next line. The use of the term 'word-blind' (though vivid and succinct) is now part of folklore but is an inaccurate and inappropriate explanation of reading difficulties and should be confined to history textbooks.

Compared with the progression of skills given in Table 2, Frith (1985) simplified and rephrased the hierarchy of reading developmental skills as:

1   the logographic phase when the child recognises words from features such as colour, shape, pattern as in 'Beanz Meanz Heinz' or the golden arches in 'McDonald's'. It is involved in:

- recognition of whole words
- building a sight vocabulary
- look-and-say strategies

2   the alphabetic phase when the child begins to realise that words can be represented by sounds. He begins to learn phonics and to decode words by sounding them out. It is involved in:

- recognition of sight and sound correspondence
- phonic skills for decoding

Table 2 Characteristics of the six stages in reading development

Stage	Reading level	Key characteristics
Stage 1: Pre-reading	Below first grade level (6 years) (Year 2)	Develops awareness of print. Can read labels, signs. Learns letter names, knows some letter sounds. Can write own name
Stage 2: Decoding	First–second grade levels (6–7 years) (Years 2–3)	Can read over 1,000 common high frequency words. Understands grapheme/phoneme correspondences
Stage 3: Fluency	Second–third grade levels (7–8 years) (Years 3–4)	Uses context and meaning as well as phonic skills to decode new words. Can recognise familiar words
Stage 4: Reads to learn	Fourth–eighth grade levels (Years 5–8)	Can use reading as a tool for new information, vocabulary and to gather background information and knowledge
Stage 5: Reads a variety of texts of varying genres and for different purposes	High school, ninth–twelfth grades (14–17 years) (Years 10–13)	Can read a broad range of complex materials including narrative and expository texts with varying levels of comprehension including finding 'answers' for literal, inferential and evaluative questions
Stage 6: Reads for personal and professional purposes	College and beyond	Can read for personal and professional purposes to integrate personal knowledge with that of others

Source: Adapted from Chall (1983).

3   the orthographic phase when whole words including the spelling pattern or chunks of letters such as onset (initial consonant(s)) and rime (vowel and final consonant(s)), syllables and affixes including prefixes and suffixes are recognised. The use of context helps develop the ultimate objective – comprehension, the *raison d'être* of reading. It is involved in:

- automatic recognition of words
- using contextual cues to make sense of what is read.

Look-and-say: the 'whole word' recognition reading method

Look-and-say methods began to be used in the 1920s in the UK and gradually became increasingly popular, aided and abetted by the use of reading schemes with graded vocabulary. Keywords were taught as sight words and were often reinforced by the use of flashcards. The popularity of this method reached its zenith with the publication of the *Ladybird Key Reading Scheme* (Murray, 1964).

Many pre-school children can read words like 'television' or 'Teletubbies' just as they recognise a photograph. They remember the visual features of their own names; for example, 3-year-old Freddie knows /F/ because he can visualise 'Fireman Fred' in the *Letterland ABC* (Carlisle and Wendon, 1985). Observation of this ability resulted in children being taught initially to recognise whole words. In consequence, reading schemes were developed and used extensively to teach reading. They comprised graded reading books with progressive levels of difficulty and controlled vocabularies. They were the daily bread of readers in most classrooms in the UK for over sixty years.

This meant that the poor readers had to grapple with high frequency words many of which are irregular such as 'go', 'to', 'come', 'book' where the /o/ sound is spelt in four different ways. This proved difficult for those with poor visual memory. 'Basal readers continue to be the major tool for reading instruction in elementary classrooms throughout the country' (USA) according to Lerner (2000).

This method works for 80 per cent of the population but for those who have poor visual perceptual skills or poor visual memory it is frustrating and futile. Ehri and Wilce (1983) found that poor readers take longer and require more exposures to recognise individual words. Adams (1990) observed that 'what really matters is not the frequency with which a word occurs in print but the frequency with which it has been encountered by the reader in question'.

For some readers including those with dyslexia the look-and-say logographic 'Chinese' method of learning whole words can be a slow, frustrating and negative experience. The more complex the word the longer it takes to learn, according to the evidence of Manis *et al.* (1993). Perfetti's theory (Perfetti, 1985) showed that those who have slow word recognition and lack automaticity with sight vocabulary are poor comprehenders because so much mental energy is used to decode the letters used to pronounce words. Rack *et al.* (1992) confirmed that dyslexics find learning sight words very difficult. This is why look-and-say methods including using flashcards was often an unmitigated disaster. Critics described it variously as the 'look and guess' method or the 'look and forget' method.

Adams (1990) reported that 'word counts of school children's books reveal fifty per cent of the print . . . is accounted for by only 109 different words. 90 per cent by only 5,000 different words'. In adult books high frequency words account for only 5 per cent of words. Yet in the UK many teachers put great emphasis on teaching and learning the 'high frequency' lists in the NLS for reading and spelling. Reading schemes are being produced to incorporate these including the many irregular 'odd-bod' words which have to be guessed and recognised by their visual conformation.

Hints and suggestions for learning sight words, including the high frequency words

Being able to recognise a word instantly by sight is the most efficient way to read. Building a sight vocabulary is essential for achieving reading fluency and accuracy (Ehri, 1997a).

- Choose books with vocabularies at the child's instructional level. A rule of thumb for establishing readability is to ask the child to read a page from the text. If he makes more than five errors on the page it is too difficult. However, this generalisation may not be applicable or reliable for some dyslexic readers, including those with poor visual memory, poor processing skills and working memory difficulties, because they often misread the word they read correctly on the line above because of their underlying difficulties whereas normal readers misread because of an absence of a sight vocabulary.
- Play games and use sound and music to develop and learn rhyme and rhythm. This can be reinforced by using books of poetry, riddles and jokes.
- Use plastic or wooden letters, games available from www.LDAlearning.com. Oxford Spelling Kit Games includes Silent Bingo for High Frequency Words (www.oxfordprimary.com).
- Children need first to be made aware that many high frequency words are regular and are spelt as they are sounded, like 'up' and 'he'. (They can read many words when they know open and short vowel sounds.) Teach the irregular 'odd-bod' spelling such as 'said' using the letter names. Use multi-sensory strategies, mnemonics, tracing and colour to reinforce these, depending on the individual child's preferred learning style.
- Reinforce these sight words by getting children to use them in their personal writing including stories.
- The NLS (1998) includes forty-five high frequency words to be taught as 'sight words' in Reception and 150 'sight recognition words' to be taught by the end of Year 2. However, it should be remembered that the irregular words may be a significant obstacle for dyslexic pupils. Initially they should only be asked to read and spell phonetically regular words.
- There are many ways of practising these, including playing some commercial games available from: LDA (www.ldalearning.com), Smart Kids (www.smartkids.co.uk), Taskmaster (www.taskmasteronline.co.uk), Winslow (www.winslow-cat.com). Success will often depend on the learning style of the individual pupil. Strong visualisers will find them easier. The High Frequency Word Wall (www.nesarnold.co.uk) can be used in the classroom. Some dyslexic pupils with poor visual memory may find the task futile and frustrating. Other dyslexic pupils may require 'significantly more trials' than normal readers (Ehri, 1997a). She concluded that there is a 'deficit rather than a delay in sight word learning ability among disabled readers'.
- In the initial stages it is important to use words with regular spellings, in other words a sound/symbol match, to help develop phonic skills and confidence. The

irregular 'odd-bod' spellings and homophones usually prove the most difficult to remember for readers: for example, 'wear'/'where'. Those with poor phonological skills may not be able to distinguish the sound differences. They are doubly handicapped when words are visually similar and only differ by the orientation or sequence of the letters: 'left'/'felt', 'diary'/'dairy'.

- Re-reading texts helps children to learn and remember sight words as well as developing confidence. Georgina, 2½ years old, listened to *The Tiger Who Came to Tea* four times in one day. Part of the fun was being able to supply some of the words as the pages were turned. Clay (1985) used the strategy as part of the Reading Recovery programme. The child re-reads two or more familiar books and re-reads the new book introduced the previous day to help develop sight vocabulary. The difficulty of text affects the fluency level (Young and Bowers, 1995), which is why it is crucial to use books at the reader's appropriate level.

The 'code emphasis' phonics method: suggestions for resources to develop phonic skills, including reading books

The systematic teaching of phonics gradually went out of fashion in the twentieth century. The wheel has now turned full circle. The NLS puts a major emphasis on teaching phonics 'first and fast' in schools. The government's position can be summed up by the statement of Her Majesty's Inspectorate (Ofsted, 2001): 'the debate is no longer about whether phonic knowledge and skills should be taught but how best to teach them.' Synthetic phonics should be taught 'first and fast' for effective reading according to Johnston and Watson's (2005) research findings.

In the USA, at the instigation of the government, Snow *et al.* (1998) summed up the findings of the report *Preventing Reading Difficulties in Young Children*, and stated that:

> all members agreed that reading should be defined as a process of getting meaning from print, using knowledge about the written alphabet and about the sound structures of oral language for the purpose of achieving understanding. All thus also agree that early reading instruction should include direct teaching of information and sound–symbol relationships to children who do not know about them.

The crux of teaching reading to beginner readers is to help them to link the sounds in speech to the letters which make the words. In other words, they need to tune in their ears. Phonics should be integrated into meaningful texts and should be reinforced by reading practice. This is why phonic readers are essential for all beginner readers irrespective of age or ability.

Synthetic phonics should be taught first. The child learns to identify the individual letters and to match these to the sounds that represent them: /a/ in apple, /b/ in bus. First he learns initial sounds, then medial sounds and then the final sounds in words. He learns using words with regular spellings. He decodes words, sounding out /p/ /i/ /g/ and then he blends the sounds and reads the word 'pig'. He segments the letters to make consonant-vowel-consonant (c–v–c) words and uses these to write simple sentences using multi-sensory strategies.

Resources for teaching phonics

Activities for Successful Spelling (Ott, 2007b) includes multi-sensory activities to teach phonemic and phonological skills.

Jolly Phonics Cards can be used for practice (www.jollylearning.co.uk).

THRASS (The Teaching of Handwriting, Reading and Spelling Skills) includes games and activities (www.thrass.com).

Toe-by-Toe is a structured programme for individual use (www.toe-by-toe.co.uk).

ICT support includes the following:

Phoneme Track can be used to teach identification, blending and segmentation skills for the age range 5–13 years (www.dyslexic.com).

WordShark3 includes games and activities (www.wordshark.co.uk).

Phonomena can be used to teach phonological awareness including auditory perception and discrimination for the age range 6–14 years (www.dyslexic.com).

Suggestions for choosing phonic reading books

Bloomfield and Barnhart's *Let's Read* series (www.betterbook.com; www.dyslexiabooks.com) uses a carefully graded vocabulary and only words that consistently match sounds to their symbols. These books have no pictures and the running text is sometimes incongruous. Critics dismiss them as boring, repetitive tongue twisters, lacking in entertainment. Supporters treat them as an additional tool – a means to an end – to be used sparingly but frequently. Cox (1982) recommended that the pupil should read 1–2 pages each day to reinforce phonological and decoding skills in text.

Supersonics Fun Readers are twenty-four books published by Ginn (www.myprimary.co.uk). There are four levels with little text and many illustrations which are suitable for Key Stage 1 children. They have a very juvenile feel and could not be used with older poor readers.

Superphonics Storybooks, published by Hodder Children's Books (www.hoddereducation.co.uk), contain four levels which are colour coded to denote difficulty. Each level has five titles. They include a riot of colourful illustrations clearly aimed at Key Stage 1 readers. Some of the vocabulary, such as 'darning' and 'asteroids', is challenging for novice readers who may be frustrated when trying to use phonic skills to decode these.

Multi-sensory Learning Structured Story Books (www.msl-online.net) have three levels, each with five books which are linked to individual spelling patterns such as the vowel digraphs 'ai', 'ay', and are suitable for older beginning readers. The stories are suitable for use with Key Stage 3 pupils. There are approximately 5–13 pages of text, the remaining 4–5 pages giving various activities. Some of the spelling patterns are quite advanced at the higher levels, with vocabulary such as 'picturesque', 'delusion'.

Sound Out Chapter Books (www.annarbor.co.uk) consist of five sets, each of six books. They have attractive covers and the stories have the appeal of 'real books' and are popular with Key Stage 1, 2 and 3 pupils. They use 22-point type. They have a reading age of 6–7 years and an interest age of 7–11 years. Each book includes different skills such as consonant blends as well as a useful list on the inside of the back cover of the high frequency words used in it which are introduced gradually.

The *'Sounds Easy' series* by R. Burkett (www.egon.co.uk) includes pre-reading books (five titles), introductory level (eight titles), Level 1 reading books (four titles), 'Reading Made Easy' (seven titles). These are suitable for children aged 4–6 years. These are well illustrated and graded to teach specific sounds included in the basic stories.

Phonics – Read with Ladybird (www.ladybird.co.uk) comprises twenty stories with controlled vocabulary which 'are designed to help beginner readers grasp the important link between sounds and letters that represent them' such as the long /ē/ sound. The spelling pattern is highlighted in red, as in: 'Peter Cheetah pushes Neil Seal in his green wheelbarrow'. The stories are humorous and lively and include a CD-ROM.

Bangers and Mash, published by the Longman Group (www.longman.co.uk), comprises eighteen phonic readers with supplementary readers and games.

Fuzzbuzz, published by Oxford University Press (www.oxfordprimary.com), includes a set of phonic readers.

Stages 1–9 Story Books, published by Oxford University Press (www.oxfordprimary.com), has nine levels which 'combine high frequency vocabulary with phonetically decoded words'.

Care needs to be exercised in the choice of these resources. Some cover 'difficult' sounds and have challenging vocabulary despite attempts to control it.

The 'whole language' or 'meaning emphasis' method

This approach uses 'real books' rather than reading schemes to teach reading. The pupil uses pictures, text, syntax and grammar to help him make sense of what he reads. He is given stimulating books which should develop a love of reading and enable readers to teach themselves to read. The 'real book' approach works for some readers but for many it is a recipe for disaster. Time and experience have shown that many of Goodman and Smith's hypotheses and much of their ideology was fundamentally flawed. Adams (1991) maintained that it was a philosophy rather than a method for teaching reading. Nonetheless, according to Pressley and Rankin (1994) most teachers and 80 per cent of special education teachers in the USA used whole language as their main reading approach. How can that level of support be accounted for? What is there to commend it and what should practitioners retain when they throw out the 'bath water' when teaching beginner readers? The positive factors include:

- the choice of attractive titles to appeal to the individual child's interests
- a system that encourages the use of contextual cues including guessing strategies to make sense of the text through a meaning emphasis approach and illustrations to help with understanding
- the development of comprehension skills.

Hints for developing and enhancing reading comprehension skills

The adult and child should consider the following.

- Look at the cover of the book. Is the author's name familiar? Has your child read another book by the same author and if so did he enjoy it?
- Is the book part of a series already familiar to you, such as Francesca Simon's *Horrid Henry* titles?
- Look at the illustrations for their relevance to the story and characters, for example Quentin Blake's in *The Twits*. Discuss the timelines that Terry Deary gives in *The Horrible History* series to familiarise your child with the characters' names.
- Read the blurb at the back of the book and explain the setting more fully if necessary.
- Offer the reluctant reader such as someone who tends to reject all books as 'boring' a choice of three alternative titles appropriate for their age, interest and instructional level. One of them must be read within a week.
- The adult should preview the plot and explain the setting, for example the wartime background of *Good Night Mr Tom*. When reading myths or fables, talk about the moral of the story, in for example Aesop's 'The hare and the tortoise', so that the child understands it.
- Discuss the names and summarise the roles of the main characters so they are easily identified when, for example, *Romeo and Juliet* is being read.
- It helps older poor readers if they read an abridged version before studying the full version of the prescribed text for a literature course. Watching the video of *Lord of the Rings* or the Longman School Shakespeare CD-ROMs (www. longman.co.uk) helps those who are strong visualisers.
- Before allowing the child to read a book check the readability of the text. Use the Five Finger Readability test by asking the child to read one page. If he makes more than five errors this usually indicates that the text is beyond his current decoding skills. Lundberg (2002) pointed out that 'if more than 20 per cent of the words in a text are unknown, the resulting comprehension will probably be very modest'. Hatcher (1994) recommended that children should be asked to read 100–200 words of the running text. If this is read with 90–94

per cent of accuracy it is suitable and is at what is 'commonly called the instructional level of reading'. However, some severely dyslexic readers may make more than five errors on a page and still be able to read and enjoy the text. This is because they mispronounce names or reverse words and not because they find the vocabulary challenging. Often it means that the choice of book has to be made on an ad hoc basis.

- Low scores on reading rate tests can often be used to predict comprehension difficulties. Those who read very slowly often have difficulty comprehending text because of poor sight vocabulary or working memory difficulties. Word recognition must be rapid, automatic and accurate to 'free up' mental space for processing meaning and for understanding. This is particularly important for older pupils who are studying for examinations. ICT software such as www.texthelp.com which reads the text may be the way forward for them.
- When he has finished reading ask him, for example, to say what he thinks of Harry Potter's cousin Dudley the Dursley's son.
- The two major types of texts, including fiction (usually narrative) and factual (usually expository), have to be considered when doing comprehension activities. Each has important individual features.

The reader of fictional material may need help to consider:

- title
- setting – including time and place
- characters, including names, feelings and emotions
- the main events in the plot
- the resolution and conclusion.

The reader of factual material may need help to consider:

- the title, overview, summary and conclusion
- multi-sensory methods such as pictures and diagrams
- background knowledge; for example, when reading about the 'greenhouse effect' in geography, including the effect of climate change, destruction of the rainforests, the emission of gases from fossil fuels or CFC gases
- terminology, for example the 'dissolution of the monasteries' in history; this avoids errors, such as those of the pupil who thought Henry VIII was responsible for putting 'the monks in a solution of salt to clean them up'.

The rough guide to helping reluctant readers become accurate, fluent and confident

- Use a pencil to point to the words on the line. It works better if the adult places the pencil above the word. Children who tend to lose their place should use a bookmark or ruler two lines below the text so that meaning is not degraded by having to pause at the end of a line. Encourage the child to move the ruler himself using both hands to develop independent use. Touch him on the shoulder to remind him if he forgets to move it to the next line. Using a finger to point to individual words is not advisable because some children develop a staccato style of 'barking at print' and their comprehension of text is affected. Crossbow Eye Level Reading Rulers (www.crossbow education.com) include a tracking line and plastic overlays which come in a variety of colours. They reduce glare for those sensitive to white paper. Teacher and child can experiment to find the optimum colour. Some children find these very helpful, others find them unnecessary. The ruler can be used to 'reveal' one/two lines of text or alternatively a short passage. Choice will depend on individual need and the nature of the visual difficulty.

- Preview the text. Give explanations of technical terms before the child reads it. It may be necessary to list these for reference.
- Explain difficult vocabulary as the words arise.
- Ask him questions from time to time to ensure that he has followed and understood the story. This also helps to develop expressive language skills.
- Interaction with the text is important. Choose a text that appeals to the individual's tastes and interests. Research evidence shows that many boys prefer reading non-fiction. Interest levels are even more important for older readers.
- Daily reading is the ideal, including oral and silent reading. A little and often is best, with an adult's time and support, including the busy parent's. Children need role models to provide evidence of the importance of reading.
- Use the 'pause, prompt and praise' method devised by Glynn and McNaughton (1985) to allow the child time to attempt a word. Pause for five seconds before giving the child the word if he hesitates or makes a mistake. This allows him to make a self-correction which is considered an important sub-skill and gives the slow processor extra time to 'retrieve' a word. Prompt the child after the pause by giving the word or meaning. Praise the child's efforts, particularly attempts at sounding out words and correcting errors. However, it is important to pre-empt and tell him unfamiliar words such as names and irregular words that cannot be 'sounded out' phonetically. This avoids frustration and helps with understanding.
- The dyslexic pupil will continue to need support with reading throughout his primary school years. This should include practice in reading aloud long after the majority of the class have ceased to read to the teacher. Parents and teaching assistants play a crucial role in listening to children read.
- Home/school reading diaries are useful for recording and monitoring progress. It is important that messages are regarded as a two-way process and that comments and suggestions are acted on. The teacher needs to be told if the reading book sent home is too difficult. It is important that texts promote fluency and accuracy. This depends on resources which are appropriate for the child's reading age and interest age levels.
- 'The Matthew Effect', so called by Keith Stanovich (1986), says that good readers get better by reading, but poor readers don't get better because they don't read. This is an important truism which should frequently be considered. Daily reading to a parent or an adult is the ideal.
- Vocabulary needs to be graded. Complex, multisyllabic words can cause problems. On the other hand, some dyslexic readers struggle more with function words including the high frequency words. The vocabulary should be appropriate, including the num-

ber of syllables. Familiarity and frequency need to be considered. Those with poor phonological skills often struggle to pronounce long words like Dick King-Smith's title *Omnibombulator*. The sentence length and structure need to be uncomplicated. Those with poor working memory lose the meaning if sentences are too long. The choice of words need to be graded at the appropriate readability level. The active voice is easier to understand than the passive voice. The publisher Barrington Stoke has carved out a niche market by producing books specially written for reluctant readers by well-known authors such as Malory Blackman and Michael Murpurgo. They 'test drive' the manuscripts by asking up to thirty reluctant readers for comments and suggestions about the readability of the text, thus ensuring readability. In recent years most of the major publishing houses have responded to the need for resources for readers who have low reading ages and high interest levels. Unfortunately some titles do not succeed in their objectives, some of the material being too difficult for their intended audience. Having fewer words on the page or a large font does not in itself make the text easier to read if the vocabulary is too challenging.

- Re-reading a favourite text helps develop accuracy, confidence and fluency and enhances sight vocabulary, comprehension and understanding.
- Brooks *et al.* (1998) evaluated twenty studies of early intervention schemes 'in an attempt to boost the reading attainment of lower-achieving but non-dyslexic pupils in at least one of Years 1–4'. The aim was to describe the schemes and their effectiveness for the 20 per cent of children who 'do not get it right the first time' (from Key Stage 1 National Curriculum test, 1994–7). The authors, eminent academics, make the refreshing and revealing statement at the outset that 'reading research is a jungle, and quantitative evaluations of early interventions are among its very densest thickets'. Their review is very useful for all involved in teaching reading to beginner readers including dyslexic readers. The conclusions have important pedagogic implications. Brooks *et al.* (1998) provided evidence which showed that:

  - Normal schooling [such as following a reading scheme] ('no treatment') does not enable slow readers to catch up.
  - Work on phonological skills should be embedded within a broad approach [meaningful texts – real books – and personal writing].
  - Children's comprehension skills can be improved if directly targeted [for example, by questioning and by written activities].
  - Working on children's self-esteem and reading in parallel has definite potential.
  - IT [information technology] approaches only work if they are precisely targeted [as by learning a specific sub-skill such as phonological skills].
  - Large-scale schemes like the BSA [Basic Skills Agency] Family Literacy and Reading Recovery, though expensive, can give good value for money.
  - Where reading partners are available and can be given appropriate training, partnership approaches can be very effective [as in paired reading].
  - Most of the schemes which incorporate follow-up studies continued to show gains.

Many individuals are put off reading for life by being asked to read books that are too difficult. Try to help children to resist peer pressure to read books that are too difficult for their current literacy levels, for example the Harry Potter titles. To enjoy these a child needs to have a reading age of 11 years or above. Read them to him or alternatively he can listen to them on tape. Listening to a book on tape means that if all his friends have read it he can share the contents. Audio books are widely available and many lending libraries have collections and are a constant delight to many, including reluctant readers. For optimum benefit and to improve decoding skills, from time to time try to encourage the reader to follow the text line by line at the same time as listening to the tape. Many publishers' lists include audio books such as www.booksondemandonline.co.uk. They also include a useful top ten bestselling titles list for each section.

- Grade books on the spine by colour coding them. Then the reader can choose a book at the appropriate reading level. Some teachers dislike grading books, arguing that it is discriminatory and that children who are on the 'yellow' label know they are in the bottom set. On the other hand in busy classrooms with teaching assistants and parent helpers it saves time and embarrassment for the child if a suitable book is readily and easily available. According to various reports boys still lag behind in the literacy stakes. One of the great challenges has been finding suitable resources. Many boys have a preference for non-fiction titles rather than fiction. Interest levels are a paramount consideration. Prior knowledge or specialist interest helps pupils read more challenging text; for example, 10-year-old Rowan who was passionately interested in dinosaurs could easily roll off the multisyllabic names such as 'tyrannosaurus rex' even though he often stumbled over high frequency irregular words such as 'are'/'our'.
- Avoid sending poor readers to the book shelf or library to choose a book to read. Reading resources should be carefully monitored to ensure that they are at the child's readability level.
- Some readers report that they can 'read in their heads' (read silently) more easily. This may be because they do not have to worry about listening to what they are saying, nor do they need to think about pronunciation. Thus few sub-skills are being used, creating more mental space for meaning and understanding. Beginner readers, however, need an audience to monitor their accuracy and progress, to help them use decoding strategies and to praise them and prompt them with difficult words.

Suggestions for calculating the readability of a text

The readability factor is arguably the most important consideration when choosing books for timid, reluctant and poor readers.

It is important to remember that the following suggestion is contrived and is not based on an exact scientific formula. Neither does it allow for prior knowledge or the interests of individual readers.

The SMOG readability formula – simplified (from BSA, undated)

1 Select a title
2 Count 10 sentences
3 Count [the] number of words which have three or more syllables ☐
4 Multiply this by 3 ☐
5 Circle the number closest to your answer [in the following row]

    1   4   9   16   25   36   49   64   81   100   121   144   169

6   Find the square root of the number you circled [look at the following table]

Number of words	1	4	9	16	25	36	49	64	81	100	121	144	169
Square root	1	2	3	4	5	6	7	8	9	10	11	12	13

Add 8   ☐ ————————► ☐   Readability Level

The Text Checker to establish readability

Owen (2004) devised the Text Checker based on the Fry Graph (Fry, 1977) (www.tic1.co.uk) which can be used to check the reading age level of any text or document. This ensures that texts and curricular resources are accessible and matched to the individual's current reading attainment level. The Text Checker also includes a laminated set of cards with examples of text for reading ages from 6 to 12 years inclusive. At the back of each card tips are given on how to 'have the best chance' of making sure that texts in a worksheet, for example, can be read and understood by someone of a given reading age. For example, for age 6, it recommends using Comic Sans font and 'at least a point size 14 font'. It recommends that instructional worksheets should have a reading age level two years below the reader's current reading age level.

Using the Text Checker and the Fry Graph seems to be the easiest and most accessible method of matching reading age and text.

Physical factors for consideration

- The size of font and typeface are very important. Many poor and reluctant readers across the age spectrum are instantly switched off by small dense print. Good line spacing is vital. The length of the sentences is also relevant: 50 per cent of readers get lost if a sentence exceeds fourteen words, 80 per cent get lost if a sentence exceeds twenty words (Peer, 1996). They lose the sense of what they are reading because of working memory difficulties. Proper names can be difficult for some readers, particularly those with phonological difficulties. When reading the classics such as Greek myths they continually stumble over names. Providing a key to pronunciation is helpful, such as /ee/sop/ for 'Aesop' or /you/lis/sees/ for 'Ulysses'.
- The number of pages is also a major factor. Many poor and reluctant readers automatically turn to the last page before choosing a book to see how many pages they are being asked to read. Paragraphs should not be too long. Chapter headings rather than just numbers are helpful for meaning and understanding.
- Illustrations help by providing contextual cues, particularly for those pupils who have good visual skills. This is probably why *Where's Wally: The Wonder Book* (Handford, 1997) is a popular choice for many young readers of non-fiction. Comic-style books such as the *Jet* and *Colour* series are enticing for those timid readers who lack reading stamina. Older newly independent readers enjoy the *Graffix* series (www.acblack.com) which uses integrated devices such as speech bubbles to cut down on the reading content.

- Cost is important. Some of the specialist publishers' materials are not good value for money, page for page. It is difficult to justify paying the same amount for a book of 200 plus pages as for one of 60 pages.
- The binding is important. Children's books need to be durable. A useful resource is adjustable plastic covers – 'Adjustable Lifejackets' Book Protectors (www.book protectors.com.uk).
- The type of paper and the colour are important. According to anecdotal evidence from the BDA and the Adult Dyslexia Association, many dyslexic readers find reading from cream paper easier. Smythe (2005) reported on a poll carried out at www. dyslexia.com/qaweb.htm on 6,500 voters about background preferences for computer screens: '28 per cent preferred white, 22 per cent blue and 19 per cent cream'.

Barrington Stoke has established an unrivalled reputation for producing short novels by leading award-winning children's authors for interest ages from 8 to 16 years and reading ages below and above 8 years. They are very useful for building reading skills and stamina and for use as stepping stones to later reading of the authors' full-length titles (www. barringtonstoke.co.uk).

Children should aim to read a book in a week, otherwise they lose interest and forget the story line. Many like to read 'proper' stories rather than contrived abridged versions or the dire reading schemes that were once standard fare in most schools. Some dyslexic pupils dislike books with a selection of short stories. Some like the 'choose your own adventure' format, others hate it probably because it imposes too much effort on their working memory skills which distracts them from the plot.

Suggestions for selecting fiction and non-fiction titles

A variety of texts including fiction and non-fiction and ranging from novels, poetry, myths, legends and plays to different genres including science fiction, humour, fantasy, biography, historical novels – a rich diet – is encouraged to whet the appetites of all readers including reluctant readers. It is important that the books children are asked to read have a readability age level on a par with their current reading skills.

Encourage readers to try various authors ranging from the perennially popular Roald Dahl, J.R.R. Tolkien and Enid Blyton to current favourites including Jeremy Strong, Dick King-Smith, Jacqueline Wilson, Philip Pullman, J.K. Rowling, Anthony Horowitz and Michael Morpurgo. We ignore the importance of suitable reading material at our peril and its importance is still underestimated.

The following are examples of titles which have proved popular with beginner readers.

- The *Happy Families* series by Allan Ahlberg is enthralling (bookson demandonline.co.uk). Many children find the illustrations very stimulating. The text is cleverly presented to help develop a sight vocabulary but without sounding contrived. The Oxford English Picture Readers are well illustrated.

These abridged versions of the classics such as *Hercules* often open the door to a rich classical resource, especially for those who have seen the Hollywood film of *Hercules*. The *Hairy Maclary* series by Lynley Dodd includes lively pictures and verse and has catchy onomatopoeic titles to 'grab' the interest of reluctant readers (www.booksondemandonline.co.uk). The Irish publisher O'Brien's Panda books are well illustrated, funny and models of clarity (www.obrien.ie). Rose Impey's books are hugely popular, including the *Titch-Witch* series (www.wattspublish.co.uk).

- *Coloured Crackers* has amusing illustrations and a joke section at the back and is always awarded ten out of ten by dyslexic beginner readers (www.watts publishing.co.uk). The *Horrid Henry* series are great favourites and children always ask for further titles (Orion Publishing Group).
- *Historical Tales* by bestselling author Terry Deary are dark and exciting stories based on the lives of real people and real events (www.acblack.com).
- *Graffix* comprises over thirty titles by award-winning authors and the integrated text and illustrations are instantly appealing to reluctant readers. The *Jet* series is also very popular because of the way the text and illustration work often with the use of bubbles and cartoons. Readers quickly realise that there is less to read. When they get to this level most pupils are then ready to progress to the myriad of paperbacks available.
- For older readers the *Goosebump* series (www.acblack.com) has been extremely popular. Another current favourite is the *Horrible Histories* series by Terry Deary. According to the Public Lending Right Register (www.plr.uk.com/trends/most borrowedtitles/top20/2002–2003), sixteen of the twenty most borrowed children's non-fiction titles were by Terry Deary. Jacqueline Wilson was the most borrowed fiction author with sixteen out of the top twenty titles. Anthony Horowitz's *Horror Stories* are scary and exciting (www.wattspublishing.co.uk). There is anecdotal evidence of a gender difference, many boys preferring to read non-fiction. *Sparks Historical Adventures* series is linked to history in the National Curriculum Key Stage 2. The books have arresting titles and many eye-catching illustrations, and are easy reads. The *Animal Ark* series by Lucy Daniels also has a strong following (www.madaboutbooks.com). To get the all-important 'feel good factor' and 'street cred' poor readers must keep abreast with what their friends are reading.
- Nothing switches pupils like these off reading more than giving them books that are too difficult and that they have to read word for word, which is sometimes described as 'barking at the print'. If they don't follow the content, they won't enjoy reading and will often remain or become reluctant readers. On the other hand, it is humiliating for a teenager to be given a book which was obviously written and illustrated for an 8-year-old.
- Abridged classics are useful, such as those produced for English as an additional language (EAL) students. Longman Classics is a useful series which is graded at four levels and written in short sentences, with a glossary and useful questions about the contents (www.longman.co.uk).
- Oxford University Press's Oxford Bookworms Library, also available on cassette, is a rich source of suitable reading books for older unenthusiastic readers. The

vocabulary in these is carefully controlled, as is the length of the sentences and chapters. They have an adult appeal and include useful modern classics ranging from biographies of sporting heroes to pop stars, fantasy and horror titles.

- Penguin Readers are available in simplified text and have seven levels from Easystarts (200 words) to Advanced (3,000 words). They include contemporary authors as well as bestselling media titles. The font is small but the line spacing is adequate.
- Hodder and Stoughton's Livewire series includes *Livewire Chillers*, *Livewire Real Lives*, *Livewire Myths and Legends* and *Livewire Youth Fiction*. They are beautifully illustrated and are aimed at those Key Stage 3 and young adults with reading ages of 7+ (www. hoddereducation.co.uk).
- Ginn Impact series are written for a similar audience. They are full of comic-type illustrations and the minimum of text yet retain their appeal for older readers (www. myprimary.co.uk).

ICT resources include Start-to-Finish Reading Scheme. It is available in cassette, CD-ROM and book format. It includes text-to-speech. Gold Library has an interest age of 7–16 years and a reading age of 7–9 years with over forty titles. Blue Library has an interest age of 7–16 years and a reading age of 9–11 years (www.dyslexic. com).

A number of useful guides for busy teachers and parents are available. They include the following:

- *The Rough Guide to Children's Books for 0–5 years* (Tucker, 2002a) (www. roughguides.com).
- *The Rough Guide to Children's Books for 5–11 years* (Tucker, 2002b). It includes reviews of over 100 individual titles and series. It divides the selections into Small Readers 5–7, Bigger Readers 7–9 and Pre-teens 9–11, and includes sections on 'Myths and legends', 'Classics', 'Animals', 'Fantasy', 'Adventure', 'Historical and funny stories' as well as 'Poetry'.

    It includes a selection of old favourites as well as new authors. Reviews are restricted to one book per author but usefully other titles by the same author are listed. The guide is written primarily to help choose titles for young readers to enjoy. The reviews lend themselves to being read as a 'taster' of the pleasure to come and to whet the appetite of even unenthusiastic or timid readers. However, the age guidelines are not reliable or realistic especially for reluctant readers. For instance Roald Dahl's *The BFG* is included in the 5–7 years section. *The Hobbit* is recommended for 7–9-year-olds.
- *The Rough Guide to Books for Teenagers* (Tucker and Eccleshare, 2002). (See www.roughguides.com.) It includes reviews of over 200 titles, fiction and non-fiction, including many of the classics. There are eleven categories. Outlines of plots are given.
- The National Literacy Association produces an annual guide to literary resources including the reading resources of all the main publishers with their websites. It also lists ICT resources for literacy (www.nla.org.uk; www.literacy guide.org.uk).

- Waterstone's (2004) *Guide to Books for Young Dyslexic Readers* gives the interest age and reading age for each selection and was produced in association with the Dyslexia Institute (www.waterstones.co.uk).
- *The Ultimate Book Guide* (Hahn *et al.*, 2003) includes recommendations by popular children's authors, the editors and children for over 600 books. It is an award-winning source for books for 8–12-year-olds. It includes short, snappy reviews and reproduces some of the covers. A clever feature is a box entitled 'Next?' This makes suggestions for other titles with similar content for those who want to read 'more of the same'. Another attractive feature is that contributing authors write about different types of stories, each choosing their ten favourite books in a particular genre. It also includes readers' top ten 'sad', 'exciting' and 'funny' books. This is an indispensable reference for anyone who wants to find books that children will enjoy.
- Badger Primary Reading Boxes, Badger Publishing Ltd (www.badger-publishing. co.uk) include an eclectic mixture of over thirty books from a variety of authors and publishers which are appropriate for the language and interest age given. There are boxes of fiction, non-fiction and poetry – books for the least interested readers from infant to junior school (4–11 years). They helpfully give the interest ages and reading ages for each category.

Summary and conclusions

- A study of the history of reading instruction helps to explain why fierce divisions still exist among educational professionals about how children should begin to learn to read and how they should be taught.
- The fallout from the polarisation of views between followers of the 'whole language' 'meaning emphasis' method and the 'code emphasis' phonics method in the USA and of the synthetic versus analytic phonics first method and the NLS's 'searchlight' model in the UK, has resulted in many individuals leaving full-time education still unable to read well enough to cope with daily living.
- Low literacy has lifelong implications for individuals and society, socially, emotionally, psychologically and financially. Sixty per cent of all jobs require reasonable reading skills and according to a report by Ernst and Young (1993) 'poor literacy, in terms of lost business, remedial action, crime and benefit payments are estimated to cost £10 billion a year' in the UK.
- Reviews of international studies by Chall (1967), Adams (1990), Ehri *et al.* (2001) and Torgerson *et al.* (2006) of scientific research such as Johnston and Watson (2005) show that pre-school children should learn about the sounds in language by speaking and listening in games and oral activities. Beginner readers initially need direct systematic instruction in synthetic phonics 'fast, first and only' (House of Commons Education and Skills Committee, 2005). Later, accurate, fluent readers need to be taught through a variety of strategies and different methods inculcating grapheme–phoneme skills, word recognition skills, contextual knowledge and semantic skills. Adams (1990) pointed out that 'laboratory research indicates that the most

critical factor beneath fluent word reading is the ability to recognise letters, spelling patterns and whole words effortlessly, automatically and visually. The central goal of all reading instruction – comprehension – depends critically on this ability.' Reading is an acquired skill which does not develop naturally or spontaneously in humans, unlike language.

- In the third millennium reading has been accepted as a birthright for each and everyone in societies with universal education. Reading is not caught by individuals, it has to be taught. How it is taught does matter. There is a body of knowledge based on research and evidence based on practice which points to the best methods and principles to teach reading to all children. There is a large amount of literature about how to close the gaps in reading attainments for those with special education needs, including those with specific learning difficulties including dyslexia.

- Learning to read is a developmental process with variations between individuals who 'hardly remember how they learned to read' and those who 'struggle, no matter how many times they see the same word on the page' because they have very poor visual memory which is why they have to be taught to decode letter by letter.

- A distillation of evidence of what works best when teaching reading to all readers shows that different methods need to be used at various stages of development because skills develop in a hierarchical way. The cornerstone of literacy is teaching alphabetic knowledge which is then linked to teaching and learning synthetic phonics for the 85 per cent of regular words. Then the reader learns to use contextual cues and guessing strategies to make sense of text. A sight vocabulary can gradually be developed from 'looking and saying', especially for the irregular words. It behoves us to learn from the lessons of history and not to repeat the mistakes that have left too many individuals struggling because they cannot read.

- Children's reading improves with practice and experience, which is why choosing reading books which are at the individual's current reading age level and interest level is absolutely critical. Without practice and experience of seeing and using words in print, a reader cannot internalise them for automatic recognition, which is what makes fluent and accurate readers. Comprehension is affected without a sight vocabulary adequate for reading with pace and fluency. Phonic activities, games and computer programs which teach these skills in isolation will have little long-term impact unless the words are seen and used frequently in running text. Children learn, improve and develop as readers by being active, engaged and enthused by reading interesting and entertaining books.

- Reading aloud with an adult either during shared reading or in the Pause, Prompt and Praise method is the cohesive link needed to support, monitor and encourage newly emergent readers. Schools are making increasing use of teaching assistants and parent volunteers to carry out this vital function, allowing individual children to practise their reading in the classroom as well as at home each evening with parents or carers. Those readers with SpLD need to continue to read aloud long after their peers read silently, often until they leave primary school.

- The 2001 Progress in International Reading Literacy Study (PIRLS), 2001 found that 13 per cent of children in England disliked reading, compared to an international average of 6 per cent (www.literacytrust.org.uk/research). English children spent more time watching television or playing computer games than those in other countries.

- Research carried out for the Literacy and Social Inclusion project conducted by the

Organisation for Economic Co-operation and Development (OECD) (*Daily Mail*, 2002) showed that in a study involving thirty-one countries

> encouraging children to read for pleasure could compensate for social problems that would usually affect their academic performance . . . students who have access to a larger number of books have a tendency to be more interested in reading a broader range of materials.

- Children need to be provided with a balanced and broad selection of fiction and non-fiction and poetry to read. They need guidance and support to help them match personal preferences to appropriate titles.
- Publishers such as Barrington Stoke have responded to the particular needs of readers across the age range. More resources are being produced to meet those with special educational needs, including books with beautiful illustrations and high-quality writing and content to engage and entertain even the most timid and reluctant readers.
- Audio books have levelled the playing field and given poor readers access to titles such as *Harry Potter* or *Lord of the Rings*. Technology, including voice recognition programs, helps to enhance reading skills as well as being useful for reinforcing basic skills. For students and adult learners packages such as TextHelp (Texthelp.com) read text from the screen and give access to materials and resources that in the past were as inaccessible to them as if they had been written in Old Irish Ogham script. Electronic tools such as the Wiz Com Reading Pens (www.wiz.com) which is a handheld device can scan and read a word or a line of text aloud. This also includes a dictionary.
- In the words of Irish-born man of letters Richard Steele, 'reading is to the mind what food is to the body'. We now know what can and should be done to close the gaps in reading attainment from the cradle to the grave, especially when dyslexia is successfully managed, and when we learn from the lessons of history.

Chapter 6

Why spelling is often a major stumbling block for dyslexic children and what to do about it

Outline

- How do we account for the way we spell in English?
- Attempts to reform and simplify spelling
- Will electronic spelling forms ever become the norm in formal writing?
- The implications of poor spelling from historical and current perspectives
- Are there differences in individual spelling abilities?
- Stages in the development of spelling skills
- Using spelling errors as a 'magnifying glass' to help understanding of dyslexia
- Guidelines when choosing spelling tests
- Different categories of tests
- Spelling Test to Evaluate Phonic Skills (STEPS)
- Evaluating spelling used in spontaneous writing
- Spelling error analysis and its significance for diagnosis and assessment
- Scientific research evidence of specific spelling difficulties
- Do dyslexic children's spellings differ from those of normal spellers?
- Can spelling errors be classified? What are the practical implications of this information when teaching?
- Checklist for a miscue analysis of spelling errors
- What skills and strategies do good spellers use and what do all spellers need to know?
- Checklist and keywords of the bare essential phonics spellers need to know and learn
- Does it matter what methods are used to teach spelling to dyslexic pupils?
- An overview and rationale for the most frequently used spelling methods
- The rough guide to teaching and learning spelling rules and conventions
- Why syllables and syllable division strategies are great allies for spellers
- Suggestions for the organisation and use of a personal 'spellofax'
- Guidelines and recommendations for a 'whole-school' spelling policy document
- Summary and conclusions

How do we account for the way we spell in English?

English spelling remained non-standardised for hundreds of years. Books were handwritten by monks who wrote in Latin about ecclesiastical matters. This influenced their spelling, as did the use of French in court and government documents from the time of the Norman Conquest. Spelling was often determined by regional pronunciation and reflected local accents. Caxton's printing press established at Westminster in 1476 resulted in about 100 books being published, some of which were in English. From 1550 to 1650 a stable spelling system developed among printing houses but there was a lack of consistency in spelling in personal writing.

Mulcaster was the first headmaster of Merchant Taylors' School and later High Master of St Paul's School in London. In his book *The Elementarie* (1592) his prime objective was to ensure that words were always spelt in the same way. He set out rules which did not just depend on the pronunciation of words but included 'reason and custom' and he included an alphabetic list of recommended spellings. 'The first step had been taken towards the provision of an authoritative work of reference for spelling' and for the standardisation of English orthography (Scragg, 1974).

Robert Cawdrey's *A Table Alphabeticall* (1603) or dictionary of 'hard wordes to spell' was published to help users understand meanings and pronounce words such as those borrowed from other languages. 'There were no norms of spelling or punctuation' (Crystal, 2002) and people generally spelt words as they pronounced them. Errors crept in, such as extra letters in words derived from Latin forms. An example is the 'c' in 'scissors' which it was claimed was derived from the Latin word *scissor* meaning 'tailor' whereas in fact it came from the Old French word *cisoires* meaning 'cutting tool'.

Nathaniel Bailey's *Dictionarium Britannicum* was published in 1730 and was universally popular in the eighteenth century. It was used by Samuel Johnson as a source for his *Dictionary of the English Language* (1755). From then on dictionaries became the arbiters of spelling usage for printers and private individuals in England and America.

Attempts to reform and simplify spelling

In the late eighteenth century Noah Webster became aware that the newly independent American states wanted political and linguistic independence. He saw this as a golden opportunity to tidy up the language and rid it of what he considered superfluous, unnecessary or troublesome letters. This was the rationale for *A Grammatical Institute of the English Language* (1783), *The American Spelling Book* and *An American Dictionary of the English Language* (1828) (the American counterpart to Johnson's dictionary). Webster's spelling reforms have stood the test of time and still differentiate American from British English. Rumblings continued about perceived difficulties in spelling, however, and many, including members of the American Spelling Reform Association founded in 1876, advocated simplification.

Isaac Pitman was the driving-force of the reform movement in England. In 1837 he invented phonotype, a shorthand based on phonetics, and promoted phonetic spelling through a phonotype alphabet. The British Philological Society was founded to promote spelling reform and attracted support from Victorian figures such as Charles Darwin and Alfred, Lord Tennyson. The teaching profession's support was shown by a motion passed by the National Union of Elementary Teachers in 1876 calling on the government to set up a Royal Commission to examine spelling.

The American Spelling Reform Association was founded in 1906 and had influential supporters including Andrew Carnegie. President Theodore Roosevelt was an enthusiast. He gave a directive to White House staff advocating the use of 300 simplified spellings (which resulted in ridicule in the national press).

The Simplified Spelling Society founded in 1908 was still active after the Second World War. Mont Follick, MP, proposed a Private Member's Bill in Parliament in 1949 and again in 1953 seeking funding for research on spelling reform. The persistence of the reformers was ultimately defeated by public reaction. George Bernard Shaw donated some of his royalties to establish a new British alphabet because the English 'spell it so abominably'. In 1959 Sir James Pitman continued his grandfather's mission and developed the Initial Teaching Alphabet (ITA) and Nue Spelling, with forty-four lower-case letters to match the forty-four sounds in English to help children learn to read. ITA resources were used in many schools throughout the UK from 1961, and later abroad. Spelling was phonetic and based on received pronunciation. This resulted in misspelling by some with regional accents. The Bullock Report (1975) stated that 'the best way to learn to read in traditional orthography is to learn to read in the initial teaching alphabet'. Like other attempts at spelling reform, it fell out of favour and was ultimately rejected by the teaching profession.

There is, however, still some support for the reform and simplification of English spelling. When the Department for Education and Skills (DfES) indicated that American English spellings of scientific terms such as 'fetus' for 'foetus' should be used by British school children there was a public outcry. The then Minister for Education Estelle Morris had to withdraw the directive. Official attempts at direct or indirect simplification of English spelling had again bitten the dust despite the efforts of reform groups.

Will electronic spelling forms ever become the norm in formal writing?

The proliferation of mobile phones and their short messaging service (SMS) facility, known as texting, as well as the popularity of e-mail have resulted in new forms of communication. An argument can be made that a chink in the armour of the upholders of standard spelling has appeared. The restricted size of the keypad necessitates the use of abbreviations and acronyms. Electronic communication has rejected traditional punctuation. Lower-case font is the norm largely due to the necessity of brevity when e-mailing. Upper-case letters are often used exclusively in texting. The Internet has also spawned innovations including:

- new terminology such as 'crash'
- adding prefixes and suffixes to coin new words: 'hypertext'
- the preposition 'at' written @
- upper-case letters are sometimes used in the middle of a word: AskJeeves
- use of the letter 'e': 'e-bay'.

That 'Netspeak' (Crystal, 2002) has simplified and 'reformed' how we communicate is an irrefutable fact but can its use be considered legitimate in the English language? It is accepted as an informal means of communication but its use is frowned upon and banned by custodians of English such as the examination boards. Conventional spelling is still the gold standard by which writers are judged. The public still has 'zero tolerance' of errors in punctuation as was shown by the publishing phenomenon *Eats, Shoots and Leaves* (Truss, 2003) which was in the bestseller lists for weeks. The author argues that punctuation and standard spelling should not be interfered with and pleads for correct usage in English.

The implications of poor spelling from historical and current perspectives

One of the most frequently quoted examples of censure of poor spelling is Lord Chesterfield's letter written in 1750 to his son Philip Stanhope.

> I come now to another part of your letter, which is the orthography, if I may call bad spelling *orthography* . . . orthography is so absolutely necessary for a man of letters or a gentleman, that one false spelling may fix a ridicule upon him for the rest of his life.

Anecdotal evidence from individuals about the importance of spelling includes job applications being rejected or promotion being denied because of 'atrocious' spelling. Public figures' spelling errors are recycled to taunt them, long after the event that elicited the error has been forgotten, for example US Vice-President Dan Quayle's misspelling of 'potato'. School Standards Minister Stephen Byers when addressing an international congress for school effectiveness was castigated after being photographed in front of a blackboard on which he had written a list of points including 'underachevement' for 'underachievement' (*The Times*, 1998). Many adults still shudder when they recall their public humiliation in the classroom as their spelling test results were called out (Ott, 2007a).

Are there differences in individual spelling abilities?

Frith (1980) pointed out that spelling ability occurs in the following variations among school populations:

- good readers who are good spellers
- good readers who are 'atrocious' spellers
- above-average readers who are average spellers but have unexpected spelling problems.

> What is unexpected in unexpected spelling problems is that on the one hand the person can recognise and read a word very well, but on the other hand cannot recall the correct sequence of letters when trying to write the same word.
>
> (Frith, 1980)

Added to this list should be average readers who read very slowly, are poor comprehenders and have poor spelling. In each of these categories (except the good readers/spellers) will be some individuals who struggle because of dyslexic difficulties. 'Poor spelling is an inevitable concomitant of dyslexia' (Critchley, 1975). Another category comprises chronically poor spellers. It is important to differentiate the chronically poor from the dyslexic spellers. The underlying causes of their difficulties are usually different. Dyslexic spellers will also usually manifest concurrent dyslexic difficulties including problems with sequencing, short-term memory, phonological difficulties, word retrieval or word naming difficulties and slow processing. Chronically poor spellers and dyslexic poor spellers can be differentiated by diagnostic assessment which includes standardised tests of cognitive ability although they may often present with the same symptoms. The treatment and prognosis are different. Before attempting to find evidence of this it is necessary to consider normal development of spelling in children.

Stages in the development of spelling skills

Evidence based on analysis of children's errors shows that they go through different stages when learning to spell. Ellis (1994) reviewed the literature and summarised the stages in development. The consensus is that skills develop in the following sequence:

1. The pre-communicative stage occurs usually before formal education. Random letters are used (Read, 1975): 'k' for 'cat'.
2. In the semi-phonetic stage there is an attempt to match letter sounds to the letters at the beginning or end of words: 'u' for 'you' (Bissex, 1980). Vowels in the middle of words and final consonants are omitted: 'hd' for 'holiday'.
3. In the phonetic stage the sounds match the letters that represent them in regular spellings. Children may omit or confuse certain sounds such as schwa vowels (the unstressed vowels: sofa; terrace). They know the letter/sound correspondences but are unsure of what spellings are permissible: 'boks' for 'box'.
4. The transitional stage occurs when vowels are used in every syllable but there may be errors in spelling vowel digraphs or diphthongs: 'trian' for 'train'; 'tri' for 'try'. Visual strategies such as letter patterns are used often incorrectly: 'fite' for 'fight'.
5. At the correct spelling stage prefixes, suffixes and plurals are used. Some errors may occur: 'all together' for 'altogether'.

Using spelling errors as a 'magnifying glass' to help understanding of dyslexia

Frith (1994) pointed out that 'we learn from abnormal developments, facts that are vital to our understanding of normal development and vice versa'. She furthered her argument, saying: 'spelling has always afforded a privileged window into the mind, and spelling errors are a magnifying glass in that window'. To find this evidence and to understand how errors have been generated requires understanding as well as an analysis of individual spelling errors. This can be done by using spelling tests and free writing and then by analysing the individual errors generated.

Figure 6

Guidelines when choosing spelling tests

When deciding on tests consider the following:

- What is the purpose of this test and what skill does it measure?
- Is the manual user friendly and clearly set out?
- What type of information will it provide?
- Will it help to indicate where a breakdown of skills occurs?
- Will it provide enough examples for a miscue analysis?
- Can it be used when planning teaching intervention and when choosing appropriate teaching strategies?
- Does the test use regular spellings?
- Are irregular 'odd-bod' spellings included?
- Is it helpful when pinpointing the pupil's stage of spelling development?
- Can the results be used to target specific spelling difficulties and be included in IEPs?
- Can it be used across the age range?
- Does it have standardised and age-equivalent scores and percentiles?
- Does it have reliable parallel forms for review purposes?
- Is it acceptable by the examination boards such as the NAA and JCQ when submitting evidence for access arrangements?
- Is it an up-to-date test with reliable norms?

Different categories of tests

Informal spelling tests

These are derived from a variety of sources including:

- a compilation of words learned for school spelling tests
- words linked to spellings or on a basis of need across the curriculum
- published lists such as the NLS (1998) medium frequency words
- spelling lists from the NLS (2001) *Year 7 Spelling Bank*
- subject spelling lists NLS (2001) *Year 7 Spelling Bank*.

Standardised spelling tests

The following can be used for screening, assessment, planning intervention and monitoring progress. They include the following categories.

Category 1

The following are single word standardised dictated tests.
Vernon, P.E. (1998) *Graded Word Spelling Test* 2nd edition (www.hoddertests.co.uk)

For age range 6–16 years, it consists of eighty words. There are on average six words for each twelve months of spelling age. It provides a range of words for a miscue analysis of errors. The wide age range is very useful when assessing dyslexic children who often have wide discrepancies in their attainment levels. It includes regular and irregular spellings as well as words with silent letters. It gives standardised scores, percentiles and spelling ages. It is accepted by the NAA and JCQ as evidence in support of access arrangements in examinations.

Sacre, L. and Masterson, J. (2000) *Single Word Spelling Test (SWST)* (www.nfer-nelson.co.uk)

For age range 6–14 years, the target words include NLS high frequency list words and NLS spelling bank words. There are nine individual tests for each year group. There are thirty target words for 6-year-olds, increasing to fifty words for 14-year-olds. It gives standardised scores, percentiles and spelling ages. It includes a 'Pupil Check Sheet' with a list of the spelling patterns used for seven of the nine test levels. This can be ticked after marking the test. Gaps in individual pupils' knowledge can then be identified and included in IEPs.

The manual recommends that a pupil with SEN aged 10 years who is suspected to be performing eighteen months below his chronological age should be given Test C for 8-year-olds. The raw score in the manual does not provide a standardised score above a chronological age of 9 years 2 months for this 10-year-old pupil.

Wechsler, D. (1993) *Wechsler Objective Reading Dimensions (WORD) Spelling* (www.tpc-international.com)

For age range 6–16 years 11 months, it consists of fifty target words which include six single-letter items, regular and irregular spellings and homophones. The range is wide, so there are enough words at the lower and upper ends of the test. It gives standardised scores, percentiles and spelling ages. It can be used to compare cognitive ability and spelling attainment, which is useful when seeking evidence of a discrepancy between attainment and potential. This test and the following test are normally restricted to use by educational or clinical psychologists. Teachers may be allowed to use it under the supervision of an educational psychologist.

Elliott, C.D. (1995) *British Ability Scales (BAS II) Spelling Scale*

For age range 5–18 years, it is part of the BAS test battery. It is a 'closed' test restricted to use by psychologists. It consists of seventy-five items. It provides a standardised score, percentiles and spelling age score. The test booklet provides space to categorise the different types of spelling errors. It can be used to compare scores of cognitive ability and spelling attainment. All but two of the first forty target words are of one syllable. There is only one irregular spelling in the test.

There are a number of popular US tests which are becoming more widely used and are now generally available in the UK, including the following three.

Wilkinson, G.S. (1993) *Wide Range Achievement Test 3 (WRAT-3)* (www.tpc-international. com)

It has forty target words. It also includes a test of writing fifteen letters from dictation. It includes two parallel forms, the blue and the tan. There are no irregular spellings or words with suffixes in either of these tests.

Although it is an American test there is only one American English spelling, 'ize' rather than 'ise'. Either form can be accepted. The test gives standardised scores, percentiles and grade equivalent scores which can be compared with British National Curriculum years. The manual does not provide spelling age equivalent norms but these can be calculated according to Turner (2000).

The JCQ and NAA accept its results as evidence in support of an application for access arrangements in examinations. It is useful for providing a quick snapshot of attainment but because of its brevity fails to provide sufficient information for an analysis of underlying skills, an important factor when identifying specific learning difficulties.

Category 2

The following are part of a battery of tests and have specific diagnostic features. They can be used for screening, assessment, planning intervention and monitoring progress.

Woodcock, R.W. and Johnson, M.B. (1989) *Woodcock–Johnson Psychoeducational Battery (Revised)*

For age range 6–17 years, it includes word spelling and proofreading. Moats (1995) says that 'it does yield enough information to support qualitative analysis of error types'.

Kaufman, A.S. and Kaufman, N.L. (1985) *Kaufman Test of Educational Achievement (K-TEA)*

For age range 6–17 years, it includes a spelling test and a format for error analysis of prefixes and suffixes, syllable patterns and vowel spellings. 'There are not enough items to measure lower level (first-grade) spelling skills reliably', according to Moats (1995).

Category 3

These comprehensive spelling tests provide information about a range of spelling sub-skills. One example is:

Vincent, D. and Crumpler, N. *British Spelling Test Series (BSTS)* (www.nfer-nelson.co.uk)

For age range 5–24 years, it has five levels with gaps sufficiently wide to make it usable for high-achieving spellers as well as poor spellers. It includes parallel forms, standardised scores, spelling ages and percentile ranks. It comprises:

- single word dictated spelling
- cloze questions
- dictated passages
- proofreading including the correction of spelling errors.

It is useful for testing spelling sub-skills which are important when carrying out diagnostic assessment. It is a long test and takes about 20–30 minutes to administer.

Category 4

These multiple choice tests are sometimes found in test batteries. An example is:

Hieronymous, A.N., Linquist E.F. and France, N. (1988) *Richmond Tests of Basic Skills* (second edition)

For age range 8–14 years, it is a multiple choice test which requires the correct word to be chosen from a list of four options. This is primarily a test of visual skills rather than a test of ability to generate spellings used in writing. Production of spelling is necessary for writing and is harder than reception of spelling.

Spelling Test to Evaluate Phonic Skills (STEPS)

Pupil's test form

Instructions for use

The teacher:

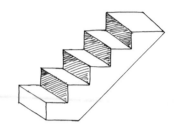

- dictates the target word
- says the sentence
- repeats the target word.

The pupil writes the word.

	Initial consonants	Target words	Sentences	Response
1	s	sat	I sat in the sun.	
2	m	mug	This is a big mug.	
3	r	rat	The rat is fat.	
4	t	tap	Turn the tap off.	
5	b	bun	I had a big bun.	
6	f	fan	Turn on the fan.	
7	n	net	Ben has a fishing net.	
8	p	pig	The pig is in the pen.	
9	d	dog	Pam has a little dog.	
10	h	ham	We had ham and eggs today.	
11	c /k/	cup	Do not drop the cup.	
12	g /g/	gun	The policeman had a gun.	
13	j	jug	That is a jug of milk.	
14	l	lap	Ann sat on Mum's lap.	
15	k	kid	A kid is a young goat.	
16	v	vet	Ben took his dog to the vet.	
17	w	wig	Sue has a red wig.	
18	z	zip	Jack broke the zip.	
19	c /s/	cent	This is a one cent coin.	
20	g /j/	gin	Gran had a glass of gin and tonic.	
21	qu	quiz	Dad likes to do the pub quiz.	
22	y	yap	My dog likes to yap.	

	Final consonants	Target words	Sentences	Response
23	s	bus	We went on a bus.	
24	m	gum	He likes bubble gum.	
25	r	car	Ben has a new car.	
26	t	cot	The baby is in the cot.	
27	b	nib	Jim broke the nib of the pen.	
28	f	of	The box is made of wood.	
29	n	pin	Pin this up on the wall.	
30	p	pup	The pup likes to play.	
31	d	mud	Pat had mud on his shoes.	
32	h	ash	That is an ash tree.	
33	c /k/	public	That is a public footpath.	
34	g /g/	bag	He had a bag of crisps.	
35	l	pal	He is my best pal.	
36	k	milk	I like to drink milk.	
37	w	cow	The cow is in the field.	
38	c /s/	mice	The cat chased the mice.	
39	g /j/	page	He read a page of the book.	
40	y	cry	His friend began to cry.	
41	ck	duck	The duck is on the pond.	
42	x	fox	The fox stole the chicken.	
43	ss	boss	The boss is in the office.	
44	ll	bell	Mel rang the door bell.	
45	ff	cliff	We went for a walk along the cliff.	
46	zz	jazz	Dad likes jazz music.	

	Short vowels at the beginning of words	Target word	Sentence	Response
47	a	ant	The ant bit my leg.	
48	e	egg	Jack put the egg in a pan.	
49	i	ink	He had an ink pen.	
50	o	odd	He had an odd sock.	
51	u	upon	Once upon a time he lived here.	

	Short vowels in the middle of words	Target words	Sentences	Response
52	a	hat	He had a hat on his head.	
53	e	hen	The hen laid an egg.	
54	i	tin	He hid the tin of biscuits.	
55	o	pot	That is a pot of jam.	
56	u	rug	The rug is on the floor.	

	Initial blends (consonant clusters)	Target words	Sentences	Response
57	bl	blot	That is an ink blot.	
58	cl	clap	He can clap his hands.	
59	fl	flat	They live in a flat.	
60	gl	glad	Dan was glad to go home.	
61	pl	plan	The plan is to go home.	
62	sl	slip	Do not slip on the ice.	
63	br	bran	Mum has branflakes for breakfast.	
64	cr	crab	He caught a crab in his net.	
65	dr	drum	Alex will bang the drum.	
66	fr	frog	The frog is in the pond.	
67	gr	grab	Grab hold of the rope.	
68	pr	pram	Roddy is sleeping in his pram.	
69	tr	trot	The pony will trot along the path.	
70	sc	scab	The scab fell off his hand.	
71	sk	skin	Her skin is clean.	
72	sm	smog	Smog is a kind of fog.	
73	sn	snap	I can snap my fingers.	
74	sp	spit	It is rude to spit.	
75	st	stop	We waited at the bus stop.	
76	dw	dwell	Do not dwell on the accident.	
77	sw	swim	Ali can swim in the pool.	
78	tw	twin	My dad has a twin brother.	
79	scr	scrub	Jill had to scrub the floor.	
80	spl	splash	I will splash my face with water.	

continued

	Initial blends (consonant clusters)	Target words	Sentences	Response
81	spr	spring	Last spring we went on holiday.	
82	str	strap	He bought a strap for his watch.	
83	squ	squad	He is in the football squad.	
84	shr	shrub	He planted a shrub in the garden.	
85	thr	throb	I can feel my heart throb.	

	Final consonant blends	Target words	Sentences	Response
86	ft	lift	We went up in the lift.	
87	lt	belt	I lost my belt.	
88	mp	jump	I like to skip and jump.	
89	nd	sand	We like to play with sand.	
90	ng	ring	He had a ring on his finger.	
91	nk	ink	I write in black ink.	
92	nt	tent	We slept in a tent.	
93	pt	adapt	We had to adapt to the food.	
94	sk	disk	We have a parking disk.	
95	sp	wisp	He only has a wisp of hair on his head.	
96	st	frost	There was a frost last night.	
97	ct	fact	It is a fact of life.	
98	ld	gold	He has a gold watch.	
99	lf	shelf	The box is on the shelf.	
100	lk	silk	That is a silk shirt.	
101	xt	text	He sent me a text message.	
102	nch	bench	He sat on the bench.	

	Initial consonant digraphs	Target words	Sentences	Response
103	ch	chum	Max met his chum at the pub.	
104	sh	ship	The ship went to sea.	
105	ph	phone	I have a mobile phone.	
106	th	thrush	The thrush is in the garden.	
107	wh	whip	The rider lost her whip.	

	Final Consonant digraphs	Target words	Sentences	Response
108	ch	rich	Sam is a rich man.	
109	sh	bush	The bird is on the bush.	
110	th	length	I swam a length.	

	Long vowels at the beginning of words	Target words	Sentences	Response
111	a	acorn	An acorn is a nut.	
112	e	emu	An emu has a long neck.	
113	i	iron	Iron this for me.	
114	o	open	Open the lid of the box.	
115	u	uniform	He has a smart uniform.	

	'y' as a vowel says /e/	Target words	Sentences	Response
116	e	baby	The baby sat in his cot.	
117	i	fry	I can fry an egg.	

	Vowel consonant -r	Target words	Sentences	Response
118	ar	star	There is a star in the sky.	
119	er	term	This term I did well.	
120	ir	bird	The bird is in the bush.	
121	or	corn	We had corn on the cob.	
122	ur	fur	My gran has a fur hat.	

	Silent letters	Target words	Sentences	Response
123	kn	knit	I can knit a sock.	
124	wr	wrist	He broke his wrist.	
125	gh	ghost	Have you seen a ghost?	
126	sc	scent	I can smell the scent.	
127	gn	gnaw	The dog will gnaw the bone.	
128	tch	match	He was playing in a match.	
129	dge	judge	The judge sent him to prison.	
130	gh	cough	He has a bad cough.	
131	lk	talk	I will talk to you.	

	Vowel digraphs	Target words	Sentences	Response
132	ai	paid	I paid for my ticket.	
133	ay	day	It is a fine day.	
134	oa	boat	The boat is sailing.	
135	ee	tree	The bird is in the tree.	
136	oe	toe	He cut his toe.	
137	oi	join	Can you join the queue?	
138	oy	toy	He will buy a new toy.	
139	ew	chew	He likes to chew bubble gum.	
140	ou	soup	I like tomato soup.	
141	au	haul	Can you haul yourself up the cliff?	
142	aw	saw	He cut the logs with a saw.	
143	ea	preach	The vicar will preach at us.	

	Vowel digraphs	Target words	Sentences	Response
144	ea	deaf	The deaf man did not hear.	
145	ow	crow	The crow is in the nest.	
146	oo	boot	He lost the left boot.	
147	oo	hook	Hang the coat on a hook.	
148	ie	pie	I like apple pie.	
149	ie	thief	The thief stole the cash.	
151	ey	they	They went shopping today.	
152	ey	donkey	The donkey is in the field	
153	ei	ceiling	He painted the ceiling.	
154	ui	fruit	We eat lots of fruit.	
155	ou	cloud	That is a very blue cloud.	

	Prefixes	Target Words	Sentences	Response
156	dis	distrust	I distrust him.	
157	mis	misspell	I must not misspell his name.	
158	im	imperfect	The diamond was imperfect.	
159	in	insane	The patient is insane.	
160	pre	preheat	We must preheat the oven.	
161	re	retake	I had to retake the test.	
162	un	untie	He had to untie the rope.	

	Suffixes	Target Words	Sentences	Response
163	able	lovable	The puppy was very lovable.	
164	en	quicken	You need to quicken your speed.	
165	er	teacher	The teacher works in a school.	
166	ful	helpful	She is a helpful person.	
167	ible	edible	The meat is edible.	
168	ion	situation	It is a dangerous situation.	
169	less	harmless	That dog is harmless.	
170	ly	slowly	He walked very slowly.	
171	ness	kindness	She has great kindness.	
172	ment	punishment	He was given a severe punishment.	

continued

	Suffixes	Target Words	Sentences	Response
173	or	actor	He is a very good actor.	
174	ing	running	The horse is running in a race.	
175	ed	hoped	I hoped to win a prize.	

The test can be administered for diagnostic purposes, in sections, at different times, depending on the stage of development of spelling skills. Results can be used to target appropriate intervention and included in IEPs.

Spelling Test to Evaluate Phonic Skills (STEPS)

Pupil's response form

Name:

Date of birth:

Date tested:

Age:

Year:

CONSONANTS

	Initial		Final
1		24	
2		25	
3		26	
4		27	
5		28	
6		29	
7		30	
8		31	
9		32	
10		33	
11		34	
12		35	
13		36	
14		37	
15		38	
16		39	
17		40	
18		41	
19		42	
20		43	
21		44	
22		45	
23		46	

SHORT VOWELS (C-V-C WORDS)

	Initial		Middle
47		52	
48		53	
49		54	
50		55	
51		56	

INITIAL BLENDS (CONSONANT CLUSTERS)

FINAL BLENDS (CONSONANT CLUSTERS)

	Initial
57	
58	
59	
60	
61	
62	
63	
64	
65	
66	
67	
69	
70	
71	
72	
73	
74	
75	
76	
77	
78	
79	
80	
81	
82	
83	
84	
85	

86	
87	
88	
89	
90	
91	
92	
93	
94	
95	
96	
97	
98	
99	
100	
101	
102	

INITIAL CONSONANT DIGRAPHS

103	
104	
105	
106	
107	

FINAL CONSONANT DIGRAPHS

108	
109	
110	

LONG VOWELS AT THE BEGINNING OF
WORDS (C-V-C WORDS)

111	
112	
113	
114	
115	

Y AS A VOWEL

116	
117	

VOWEL CONSONANT -R

118	
119	
120	
121	
122	

SILENT LETTERS

123		128	
124		129	
125		130	
126		131	
127			

VOWEL DIGRAPHS

132	
133	
134	
135	
136	
137	
138	
139	
140	
141	
142	
143	
144	
145	
146	
147	
148	
149	
150	
151	
152	
153	
154	
155	

PREFIXES

156	
157	
158	
159	
160	
161	
162	

SUFFIXES

163	
164	
165	
166	
167	
168	
169	
170	
171	
172	
173	

Evaluating spelling used in spontaneous writing

The child can be given a title such as 'If I had three wishes' or 'My favourite television programme' and asked to write for ten minutes. The spellings generated are the child's own. They reflect what he can spell in his own writing rather than in a spelling test. Before he begins ask him to write on every second line as this makes for easier marking. For younger pupils a dot can be inserted in the margin before the paper is distributed to remind them to leave a free line. Count the total number of words written. Count the number of errors and work out the percentage of errors. An analysis of the individual spelling errors can be made which may provide evidence of a pattern of difficulties associated with the dyslexia syndrome (Ott, 1997, 2007a). Moats (1993) justifies this approach as follows: 'spontaneous writing samples were analyzed because they are a natural expression of students' linguistic processing and linguistic knowledge and are less contrived than dictated spelling tests which may include words not in students' writing vocabularies'.

An analysis of the errors in a child's school English exercise book can be made. This is time consuming but very worthwhile for the busy class teacher or SENCO. An analysis of spelling errors produced over a period of months may highlight a recurrent error pattern. These errors may give a better overview of the spelling skills and strategies than results on certain standardised tests give. Moseley (1997) pointed out that 'standardised spelling tests, however reliable and valid, do have their limitations'.

Spelling tests are invaluable measures in the hands of the experienced practitioner. They are not, however, infallible despite being carefully developed to provide standardised scores. It is important to be aware of the inherent flaws in individual tests such as the following.

- Different tests which appear to measure the same skills can produce different scores, contrary to the claims of Turner (1997b) who stated when considering discrepant scores that all spelling tests correlate extremely highly – typically 0.9 or above. Chew and Turner (2003) compared performance on the WRAT (1993), Vernon (1977) and Schonell (1932) spelling tests and found that 'Schonell tends to produce a consistently lower "spelling age" especially with older pupils'. There is still a myriad copies of the Schonell Graded Spelling Tests in circulation in schools throughout the country even though they do not have standardised scores. When used year on year as an informal measure of progress they still have their uses and this accounts for their popularity and longevity. However, the NAA and JCQ do not accept the results obtained as evidence for special examination arrangements. Standardised scores are obligatory when application is made for access arrangements. Turner (1997a) advises teachers 'to communicate only in percentiles and stoop only reluctantly to age equivalents' (spelling age). But the reality is that most parents and many teachers are intimidated and confused by technical jargon.
- The choice of vocabulary and particularly word length are significant factors, notably for the dyslexic child. 'Two-syllable words pose greater memory demands in working memory than one-syllable words because, when producing them, one syllable must be held in working memory while the other is pronounced' (Snowling, 1994).
- Some test word lists provide more examples for misspelling analysis than others. Better tests include homophones, irregular spellings and multisyllabic words.
- Some test manuals recommend that testing should stop after six consecutive errors. When doing an assessment it is useful to continue for longer for diagnostic purposes

(unless the child shows signs of stress) because 'misspellings are regarded as a better source of information than correctly spelling words'.

- Some tests use a multiple-choice format. They do not provide evidence of how the speller generates words although this is important when identifying where the breakdown of skills occurs. Moats (1995) argues that 'It is also useless to give a test of proofreading ability or one that has multiple choice' when doing a diagnostic assessment. Generating spelling patterns requires different underlying skills from recognising spelling patterns.

- Ultimately, carrying out an assessment and making a diagnosis of spelling difficulties associated with dyslexia involves sifting through the evidence from a number of sources including standardised test results, classroom observation and evidence gathered over time about spelling including examples of errors in exercise books with writing activities, as well as a family history including details of literacy difficulties in other family members. These help to provide corroboration of unexpected strengths and weaknesses. Standardised tests are the handmaidens of the experienced practitioner and an adjunct to the observations of the skilful practitioner's judgement.

Spelling error analysis and its significance for diagnosis and assessment

Should this be considered an art or a science? Spelling errors have traditionally been considered as a failure to remember the word pattern and the letters required for this. Treiman (1993) confirmed that 'traditionally, learning to spell was thought to be a purely visual process'.

In the 1970s a young doctoral student at Harvard University, Charles Read (1975) identified young bright 2–3-year-olds who began to write (without formal teaching). He hypothesised that these children must be using strategies other than visual memory, relying on the sounds of words rather than visual representations when they wanted to spell. It became evident that 'misspelling analysis is a potentially fruitful assessment device for exploring what knowledge and strategies children bring to the spelling task' (Cook, 1981).

Researchers began to study children's spelling errors as 'an appreciation of the knowledge that lies behind children's errors can help teachers respond to the errors appropriately' (Treiman, 1993). The quest for the answers to why, how and what spelling errors children make is the rocket fuel that drives research projects about spelling skills. Miscue analysis of spellings helps practitioners establish when skills fail to develop and where children have stalled, and may help to identify the causes of underlying difficulties.

Treiman's (1993) study of the spelling errors of first grade pupils (6–7 years) was influential. She studied children's spelling errors and linked these to the stages in the development of spelling skills. Lennox and Siegel (1994) argued that 'the use of error analysis is based on the assumption that the analysis of errors provides clues as to the strategy used in spelling.'

The hunt began to identify individual errors and to explain their significance. Moats (1995) categorised spelling errors as:

- phonological errors linked to how a word is spoken and how this matches the letters that represent the sounds, resulting in poor segmentation of individual phonemes and consequently omissions or substitution of similar-sounding phonemes

- morphological errors made when adding suffixes, as when root words are changed when adding a suffix, resulting in difficulties with verb endings, plurals or adjectival or adverbial forms.
- orthographic errors involving the addition or deletion of letters because of a failure to remember spelling patterns, resulting in difficulties remembering common spelling patterns, irregular spelling of high frequency words and words derived from Latin and Greek.

Scientific research evidence of specific spelling difficulties

- Vowels are more difficult to spell than consonants (Schlagal, 1992): 'bote' or 'bot' for 'boat'.
- Short vowels are challenging for beginner spellers and 'special care needs to be taken with short vowel spellings' (Schlagal, 2001).
- It is difficult to discriminate between auditorily similar words: 'fin', 'thin'.
- Long vowel spellings are hard to remember: 'nite' for 'night'; 'rrwen' for 'ruin' (Schlagal, 1992).
- It is difficult to discriminate between some consonants such as 'l' and 'r', 'm' and 'n', 't' and 'd': 'junp' for 'jump'; 'pad' for 'pat'.
- Consonant blends are more difficult to spell than single consonants: 'crips' for 'crisps'; 'bush' for 'brush' (Treiman, 1993).
- Vowel consonant 'r' syllables are difficult to spell for some: 'sistr' for 'sister'; 'gril' for 'girl'.
- Doubling the correct consonants is a challenge: 'eeg' for 'egg'; 'teniss' for 'tennis' (Moats, 1995).
- The schwa – the unsounded murmur vowel – causes many difficulties: 'libry' for 'library' (Kreiner and Gough, 1990).
- Fry *et al.* (1984) dubbed certain words 'spelling demons'. They included: *accommodate; aisle; conscientious; lieutenant; muscle; noticeable; pneumonia; receipt; sergeant; unnecessary; vacuum; yacht.*
- A significant number of errors occur when the past tense of verbs is used (Moats, 1995): 'walkt' for 'walked'; 'mendid' for 'mended'; 'wishd' for 'wished'.
- When children reach sixth grade (11 years) many common errors occur when suffixes are added: 'likeing' for 'liking'; 'swimer' for 'swimmer' (Schlagal, 1996).
- Long words with difficult spelling patterns, especially those derived from Latin or Greek, cause problems for many spellers: 'senteenry' for 'centenary'; 'cignachur' for 'signature'.

The bottom line is that many normal spellers have difficulties at some stages during development of their spelling skills with some of the aforementioned words. Dyslexic children make more errors and do so more frequently and continue to do so even in words with regular spelling patterns long after their peers have learned to spell.

Do dyslexic children's spellings differ from those of normal spellers?

Researchers such as Boder (1973) and Snowling (1981) identified meaningful differences in the spellings of dyslexic individuals. Moats (1995) conducted an important study of nineteen boys aged 14–17 years old who had spent two or more years at a specialist boarding school for dyslexic pupils. She examined the errors in 'remediated adolescent' boys with dyslexia by analysing their spelling in their spontaneous writing in beginning, middle and end of year essays as well as in four recent essays available for each subject (not specified).

The following 'spelling demons' were the most commonly misspelt words (the frequency is given in brackets): *from, do, of, other, my, some, something, than/then, through, what, which, would, until* (3); *when, because, every, knows, really, were, where* (6); *buy, friend, have to* (7); *want* (9); *your/you're, to/too* (10) *their/there* (16).

Her key findings can be summarised as follows:

- There was no relationship between verbal IQ, severity of spelling disorder, and rate of growth in spelling achievement in this group of subjects: the implications are that some pupils are 'treatment resisters' because of the severity of their difficulties.
- There were two groups, with clearly distinguishable features. The poorer spellers never progressed beyond sixth grade level (11-year-old spelling age) and made 'many more errors', suggesting phonological and morphological processing difficulties were highest for the poorer spellers. The implications are that severely dyslexic pupils reach a ceiling in their spelling attainments and make spelling errors comparable to children at the beginner's stage of spelling.
- The poorer spellers made 'specific phonological error types that differentiated the poorer from the better spellers [which] included a much higher rate of omissions, insertions and substitutions'. They made more morphological errors including omissions of plurals and when adding endings such as 'ed'. The implication is that dyslexic poor spellers have persisting and often intractable difficulties with spelling which they do not grow out of over time. These errors cannot be accounted for as due to carelessness or laziness. They are distinguishable features of the condition.
- 'Individuals with intractable spelling disabilities do produce specific errors of a phonological nature in their spontaneous writing'. The implication is that the persistence of phonological spelling in children of 11 plus years should set alarm bells ringing and should be the trigger for a diagnostic assessment.
- Despite 'intensive instruction' specifically designed to overcome spelling problems, 'the most prevalent error types were evidently resistant to remediation over several years of instruction. For many subjects their learning curve for spelling had flattened by the end of High School'. The implication is that poor spelling is sometimes resistant to the best efforts and best training methods deployed by learners and teachers.
- Orthographical difficulties persisted particularly in the high frequency Anglo-Saxon function words such as 'their'/'there'; 'were'/'where'. The implication is that 'small' words (many of which occur on the NLS high frequency lists) that most normal spellers remember and use automatically are constantly spelled incorrectly.

According to Moats (1995) of the 100 most frequently used words, most of which are Anglo-Saxon, up to a quarter are spelled irregularly including the following:

are, as, been, come, could, do, from, have, many, of, one, other, people, said, some, their, there, they, to, was, water, were, what, word, would, you, your.

Thomson's (1991) training study showed that 'dyslexics learn less efficiently than normal spellers' and are 'an atypical group and do not lie on a continuum from bad spellers to very good spellers'. 'Good spellers use their good phonological processing skills in spelling while poor spellers show a different pattern, primarily using visual memory strategies in spelling difficult words' (Lennox and Siegel, 1994).

Figure 8

The conclusion must be that it borders on misanthropy to castigate or ridicule these children for their spelling errors. Their work has to be marked and evaluated on the contents rather than on the secretarial aspects. Chronically poor spelling is a lifelong characteristic of dyslexia, as many adults with dyslexia are willing to testify. Bruck (1987) reviewed the adult education and employment status of four groups who had had intensive help as children. She found that the learning-disabled adults' 'major deficits were most apparent for single word decoding and spelling skills'.

Can spelling errors be classified? What are the practical implications of this information when teaching?

Spelling errors have traditionally been classified by reference to the correct spelling of the letters in a word (Spache, 1940). This purely visual approach was linked to the customary method of learning spelling by rote memorisation. Treiman (1993) in her seminal study of children's spelling errors pointed out that 'orthographic classification schemes are based on the idea that children spell by recalling the letters in printed words that they have seen and memorised'. She concedes that this does not 'fully capture the intricacies of children's spellings'. The pronunciation of the word and the letters used to represent the phonemes also need to be considered. Frith (1979) established that 'unexpectedly poor readers read "by eye" while the spelling results have suggested that they write by ear'. Beginner spellers initially use phonological strategies to spell and usually learn and adapt other spelling strategies. Dyslexic spellers often continue to use phonetic spelling, in some cases as their sole spelling strategy. This tendency is identifiable when the diagnostician classifies spelling errors and may pinpoint underlying weaknesses in the speller's knowledge of phonological and/or orthographical skills.

Miles (1993) issued a note of caution when classifying his lifetime collection of examples of dyslexics' spelling. He pointed out that 'one of my difficulties was that when a word is misspelled there may be several different things wrong with it'. This observation should be considered when doing an assessment, just as different doctors make different diagnoses when examining the same symptoms in a patient. His classification of errors (see '13 milestones' (Ott, 1997)) provides a useful rule of thumb list.

Checklist for a miscue analysis of spelling errors

Pupil's name:

Date of birth:

Age:

Year:

Instructions for use

Find examples similar to those given below in the pupil's spelling tests and free writing.

- Put the correct spelling in the 'Target word' box.

- Put the example nearest to the error in the 'Example of error' box.

- Put a comment and teaching suggestion, to include in IEPs, in the 'Explanation of error' box

Phonemic and phonological errors

Example of target word	Example of error	Explanation of error and teaching suggestions for IEP
1 cot	cod	Confusion of final consonant due to poor phonemic skill
2 van	fan	Confusion of initial consonant due to poor phonemic skill

continued

Example of target word	Example of error	Explanation of error and teaching suggestions for IEP
3 bit	bet	Confusion of short vowel in medial position due to poor phonemic skill
4 submarine	sunbarine	Substitution of nasal sounds due to poor auditory perception and phonological awareness difficulties
5 house	houes	Sequencing error, could also be due to poor visual memory
6 anxiously	ankshusly	Phonetic spelling with a mismatch between the correct letter and sound due to poor phonological awareness
7 nephew	new	Syllable omitted due to poor phonological awareness and working memory difficulties

Example of target word	Example of error	Explanation of error and teaching suggestions for IEP
8 parsnips	parcenips	Syllables added due to poor phonological awareness
9 policeman	plissman	Vowel omitted from a syllable due to poor phonological awareness
10 shark	shrk	Vowel omitted due to poor phonological awareness
11 asylum seekers	seekers salem	Incorrect sequence and poor working memory
12 helicopter	hely copter	Incorrect boundary and word division due to poor phonological awareness

continued

Example of target word	Example of error	Explanation of error and teaching suggestions for IEP
13 supposed to	asposto	Incorrect boundary, words joined due to poor phonological awareness
14 egg	eeg	Incorrect double letter partly phonological, partly visual error
15 client	silent	Confusion of initial consonant blends due to poor phonemic skills
16 favourite	favret	The schwa vowel is omitted due to poor phonological awareness
17 rash	rach	Confusion of the consonant digraphs in the final position due to poor phonemic skills

Example of target word	Example of error	Explanation of error and teaching suggestions for IEP
18 slide	slied	Magic 'e' spelling confusion indicated by a phonetic attempt misfired

Morphological and grammatical errors

Example of target word	Example of error	Explanation of error and teaching suggestions for IEP
1 played	plad	Spells the past tense phonetically using /d/ sound: phonological/morphological error
2 mixed	mixst	Spells the past tense phonetically using /t/ sound: phonological/morphological error
3 wanted	wontid	Spells the past tense phonetically using /id/ sound: phonological/morphological error

continued

Example of target word	Example of error	Explanation of error and teaching suggestions for IEP
4 coaches	coachis	Unsure of the spelling convention for plurals ending in 's', 'x', 'sh', 'ch': morphological error
5 dogs' tails	dogs tails'	Unsure of the spelling convention for apostrophe's denoting ownership: morphological error
6 I'll	ile	Unsure of the spelling convention for contractions: morphological error

Orthographic errors including spelling conventions

Example of target word	Example of error	Explanation of error and teaching suggestions for IEP
1 tomatoes	toormartoss tmarto tortos tomrtos	The same word spelt in different ways on the page

Example of target word	Example of error	Explanation of error and teaching suggestions for IEP
2 suitable	sotabell	Reliance on the sound rather than the spelling pattern
3 chemistry	kemistrey	Inability to remember spelling conventions
4 they	thay	Struggle with high frequency Anglo-Saxon 'odd-bod' spellings
5 loving	loveing	Unsure of suffixing rules for words ending in 'e'
6 thinner	finer	Unsure of the doubling rule when adding a suffix to a word with a short vowel and with one consonant; confusion of initial phonemes

continued

Example of target word	Example of error	Explanation of error and teaching suggestions for IEP
7 queen	cween	Failed attempt to apply a spelling rule: 'q' and 'u' always stay together and say /kw/

Making an analysis of misspellings is not an exact science. Nevertheless it is a valuable tool when identifying and assessing children with abnormal spelling. Spelling error categories are not discrete and there is often an overlap in the features as well as the underlying causes of an individual's spelling errors. Errors can arise from weaknesses in visual or auditory channels. The dyslexic child makes more errors, often continues to spell phonetically, struggles with high frequency 'odd-bod' spellings long after his peers have learned the regularly spelt and high frequency words. He is often totally perplexed by words derived from other languages such as 'dachshund'. His spelling remains erratic but not irrational. It has a pattern of errors that can be recognised and when analysed can offer explanations for on-going unexpected difficulties. Misspelling analysis offers a key to those seeking to help unlock the causes and consequences of poor spelling as well as indicating what needs to be done to compensate and overcome problems. Dyslexics' spelling errors may have many similar features to poor spellers' errors but the underlying causes of the difficulties are more complex and different. Knowing and understanding helps the planning of effective intervention.

What skills and strategies do good spellers use and what do all spellers need to know?

These depend on:

- stage of spelling development.
- preferred learning style.
- cognitive skill and individual differences.

Phonological skills

Matching the sounds of speech to the letters that represent them is the starting point for most spellers. Bryant and Bradley (1980) said that 'we are suggesting that initially their reading depends very heavily on visual chunks but that they spell primarily by using phonological segments'. Bradley and Bryant (1983) showed in their training experiments that children who can segment phonemes find spelling an easier task. Read (1971) showed how precocious 2- and 3-year-olds used invented spellings and worked out that words are represented in print according to their sounds. 'Phonological skills are vital when learning to spell because they enable children to understand the alphabetic link between the sounds heard in spoken words and the letters used to represent them in written language' according to Goulandris (1994). Children need to understand and use alphabetic principles including letter names, sounds and shapes and they need to be able to segment the sounds in words to encode them when spelling and blend the sounds to decode them when reading. To do so requires phonemic and phonological skills breaking words down by sounding them out – /f/ /a/ /t/; in other words, using synthetic phonics. Then they must be able to quickly synthesise the individual sounds to make and pronounce the whole word.

Visual skills

Visual memory has long been considered a crucial factor in spelling. Children used to be given lists of spellings and told to memorise them. Those who made spelling errors were often told to write out each correction five times. Those who have strong visual memories can recall a visual image of a word or letter pattern in their mind's eye just like a photograph. They can remember salient visual features such as the 'ff' in 'giraffe' corresponding to the giraffe's two long front legs. Those who have good visual memory learn by frequent exposure to print and learn to recognise further examples when reading. These are the individuals who learn new spellings when they use word-processing. Instant feedback from the spellchecker helps them to memorise the spelling or spelling pattern they are learning.

Analogy

Children can learn by using analytic phonics – the word family approach which looks at the whole word and breaks it into chunks: /if/ /at/ /ch/ /at/. Knowing the spelling pattern 'ight' can generate ninety words (Goswami, 1994), including multisyllabic words such as 'frighten', 'frightening', 'frightened'. This is described as the onset and rime approach. The child learns the initial consonant (onset) and then learns to add on the rime which is the vowel and remaining consonants: bl-ack, cr-ack, tr-ack. However, it is essential that synthetic phonic skills are well established first.

According to Marsh et al. (1980), children do not make spontaneous use of analogical spelling strategies before the age of 10 in their free writing. However, Treiman (1993) showed that children of 7–8 years can be trained to use this skill and can use analogy as part of a spelling exercise activity. Goswami (1994) showed that using onset and rime was effective when children were trained to use analogy when learning to read. She pointed out, however, that those with poor phonological skills will need extra work on rhyme and alliteration to use analogies. She concluded that according to the research of Bruck and Treiman (1992) it 'is not a panacea' but 'can provide a useful means of learning how spelling patterns and sound correspond'.

Applying spelling rules

Individual spellers can learn and use rules depending on their learning styles. Adams (1990) pointed out that 'for neither the expert nor the novice can rote knowledge of an abstract rule, in and of itself, make any difference'. Spellers can be trained and learn to use rules, such as that 'q' and 'u' always go together.

Spellings can also be meaning based: for example, words related to fear which are derived from the Greek *phobia* such as 'claustrophobia' or 'xenophobia'.

Mnemonic devices

These are memory devices improvised to help recall how a word is spelt. They can be visual, auditory or kinaesthetic memory aides. They are often used for 'odd-bod' spellings of high frequency words and homophones. They should be used consistently and learned in a multi-sensory manner if possible: looked at in a classroom display; said for personal spelling; and written in a personal 'spellofax'.

- To remember confusable words by auditory memory, put the initial letters in a phrase or sentence: *are/our*: *are rats evil? old unicorns roar.*

Figure 9 Mnemonics for 'are'/'our': 'are rats evil?' 'old unicorns roar'.

- To remember homophones by visual memory, link a word to an illustration: *piece/peace*: Eat a piece of pie. World peace is ace.

Figure 10 Mnemonics for 'piece'/'peace': 'Eat a piece of pie', 'World peace is ace'.

- To remember difficult words by using kinaesthetic memory, write the word 'necessary', and underneath write the sentence: 'To be a successful businessman it is necessary to have a shirt and tie'. Then ask the child to touch his collar and two socks. He then copies out the writing, which adds a tactile dimension, and helps to remind him that the word has one 'c' (collar) and two 'ss' (socks).

Rhyme and rhythm

The often quoted example for learning the word 'difficulty' is to say the rhyme: Mrs 'd', Mrs 'i', Mrs 'ffi' Mrs 'c', Mrs 'u', Mrs 'lty'.

The *Primary Rhyming Dictionary* (Chambers, 2004) includes sixty verses by dyslexic poet Benjamin Zephaniah. Words are organised in word families – rimes which are helpful for spelling and rhyming sounds for personal writing including poetry. An example for the 'tion' spelling is:

Dear teacher.
Did I mention
That I don't like detention?

This approach would be even more effective (especially for good visualisers) with the use of colour to denote the phonemes.

Spelling rules and spelling conventions

Goulandris (1994) argued that 'learning [spelling] is a protracted process and it consequently takes many years for a speller to master our written language system'. Like explorers, spellers need signposts and map references as they journey through the spelling jungle. Spelling rules should be taught to match the speller's current stage of development Ott (2007a, 2007b). These could for example include teaching a child how to spell the /i/ or /e/ sound at the end of a word: words ending in the /ī/ sound often end in 'y' because no English word ends in 'i': 'cry', 'spy'. The rule-breakers are foreign words – 'ski', 'spaghetti' – and abbreviations – 'taxi', 'mini'.

Words ending in the /ē/ sound take 'y', like 'baby' or 'sunny'. When these two generalisations have been established, on another occasion teach the words ending in 'ey': 'donkey', 'money'. The regular form of the rule should be taught separately. Later teach the rule-breakers. When deciding on what rules to teach it is important to teach those that cover a wide selection of words.

Skinner's (1968) advice for all teaching is very relevant to spelling:

- Present information in small measurable steps. Teach the rule that in the plural nouns ending in 'f' or 'fe' add 'es'. Next lesson, teach the rule-breakers which just add 's'.
- Give rapid feedback about accuracy. Mark spellings as soon as it is possible to correct them. Write the correct spelling clearly on the page above or beside the word if possible. Do not just add 'sp'. Do not obliterate errors, leave for diagnostic purposes.
- Learners make better progress when they learn at a pace appropriate for their strengths and weaknesses as well as for their developmental stage. There have been criticisms of the NLS because children are taught what alliteration and onomatopoeia are while some of them are still unable to identify a sentence or know when to use a capital letter.

Adams (1990) provided another argument: rules should be part of a 'backup system' when the recognition system fails and 'the articulation of a rule is a reasonable means of pointing a reader's attention to an aspect of a spelling under study'. Some dyslexic children have difficulty in verbalising rules and definitions because of their underlying expressive language because of poor word retrieval and poor rapid automatised naming skills. These children can be helped if the rule is written on an index card, poster or personal 'spellofax' (using an alphabetical notebook). Then looking at the example will associate the rule with the words it applies to. They should be encouraged to read and rehearse the rule orally rather than trying to remember it by rote memory. Rules should be used in conjunction with running meaningful text.

Syllables

Knowing how to segment words empowers all spellers but particularly poor spellers. Being able to break words into manageable-sized pieces takes away the fear of long words and helps with pronunciation and reading. The speller needs to learn about the six major syllable patterns. He needs to learn the technical vocabulary so as to be able to use and understand the principles. He will need preliminary oral activities on rhyme and alliteration to 'tune in' his ears. He needs first to practise orally, clapping out syllables with his hands or beating out the syllables on his leg: rab/bit, ten/nis, pup/pet. This is a multi-sensory activity. Start with children's name, days of the week, months of the year. Games such as Sound and Syllables (taskmasteronline.co.uk) can be used. Later, dividing words into syllables can be a written activity. Begin with two closed syllable words and increase the number as skills and understanding develop: /in/ter/est/ing; su/per/mar/ket.

Semantic skills

Knowing the origins of words and their derivations from for example Latin and Greek roots, including prefixes and suffixes, is useful. Most of these are spelled regularly. Root words are the building blocks of language. According to Cox and Hutchinson (1988), Latin roots can be identified in 50–60 per cent of the words in any English dictionary'. Knowing that the Greek root *arch* means power and this helps with spelling 'monarch', 'oligarchy', 'archbishop'.

Knowing that the Latin root *terra* means 'land'/'earth' helps with spelling 'territory', 'terrestrial', 'terrain'.

High frequency list of word roots

form	port	rupt	sign	struct

Knowing that the Greek prefix 'anti' means 'against' helps with spelling: '*anti*clockwise', '*anti*biotic', '*anti*septic'.

Knowing the Latin prefix *circa* means 'around' helps with spelling: '*cir*culation', '*circum*-ference', '*circum*locution'.

High frequency list of prefixes (Becker et al., 1980):

com	con	de	dis	ex	im
in	or	pre	re	un	

Knowing the Greek suffix 'logy' means 'knowledge'/'science' helps with spelling over sixty words: 'bio*logy*', 'eco*logy*', 'psycho*logy*'.

Knowing the Latin suffix 'ism' means ideas/principles helps with spelling over 100 words in Chambers (1999) *21st Century Dictionary*: 'alcohol*ism*', 'commun*ism*', 'social*ism*'.

High frequency list of suffixes:

al	able	ant	ate	ed	en	ent
er	ful	ie	ing	ise [ize]	ist	ition
ive	less	ly	ment	ness	ous	[y]

'Knowledge of morphemes including affixes makes it possible to spell thousands of words', according to Hanna *et al.* (1971).

Checklist and keywords of the bare essential phonics spellers need to know and learn

Consonant	Initial	Middle	Final	
b	bag	cabin	bib	☐
c	cat	picnic	music	☐
d	dog	ladder	lad	☐
f	fan	coffee	elf	☐
g	gun	figure	pig	☐
h	hat	behind		☐
j	jug	project		☐
k	kid	blanket	ink	☐
l	leg	pillow	goal	☐
m	mug	common	gum	☐
n	net	dinner	pin	☐
p	pen	puppet	cup	☐
qu	queen	enquiry		☐
r	rug	carrot	car	☐
s	sad	missile	bus	☐
t	tap	button	bat	☐
v	vet	vivid		☐
w	wig	shower	cow	☐
y	yoga	yoyo	try	☐
z	zip	razor	quiz	☐

Final consonants

bb	ebb	☐
dd	add	☐
ff	cliff	☐
ll	bell	☐
ss	dress	☐
tt	mitt	☐
zz	jazz	☐

Consonant digraphs

		Initial	Final	
ch		chum	bench	☐
sh		ship	dish	☐
th	(voiced)	three	path	☐
	(unvoiced)	that		☐
wh		whip		☐
ph		phone	graph	☐
gh			cough	☐

Consonant blends (clusters)

	Initial	Final	
bl	blink		☐
br	brush		☐
cl	club		☐
cr	crab		☐
dr	drum		☐
fl	flag		☐
ft	gift		☐
fr	frog		☐
gl	glum		☐
gr	grip		☐
id	gold		☐
lt		belt	☐
mp		camp	☐
nd		band	☐
ng		ring	☐
nk		ink	☐
nt		tent	☐
pl	plan		☐
pr	pram		☐
qu	quiz		☐
sc	scan		☐
scr	scrap		☐
shr	shrub		☐
sk	skin	mask	☐
sl	slot		☐

sm	smog	spasm	☐
sn	snap		☐
sp	spot	crisp	☐
spl	split		☐
spr	spring		☐
squ	squash		☐
st	stop	crust	☐
str	string		☐
sw	swim		☐
thr	throb		☐
tr	trap		☐
tw	twin		☐

Short vowels

	Initial	Middle	
a	apple	hat	☐
e	egg	peg	☐
i	igloo	lip	☐
o	orange	cot	☐
u	umbrella	pup	☐

Long vowels

	Initial	Middle	
a	acorn	baby	☐
e	emu	legal	☐
i	ivy	tiger	☐
o	open	polo	☐
u	uniform	pupil	☐

Vowel consonant digraphs

	Initial	Final	
ar	arm	car	☐
er	error	sister	☐
ir	irk	tire	☐
or	order	doctor	☐
ur	urn	murmur	☐

Long vowels and magic 'e'

Final

a – e	cake	☐
e – e	athlete	☐
i – e	wine	☐
o – e	note	☐
u – e	tube	☐

Vowel digraphs

Middle

ai	train	☐
au	haul	☐
ay	play	☐
aw	straw	☐
ea	peach	☐
ee	weed	☐

Final

ew	grew	☐
ei	receive	☐
ie	die	☐
ow	show	☐
oo	boot	☐
oo	cook	☐
ui	fruit	☐

Vowel diphthongs

	Initial	Middle	Final	
ou	our	house		☐
ow	owl		cow	☐
oy	oyster		enjoy	☐
oi	oil	voice		☐

Does it matter what methods are used to teach spelling to dyslexic pupils?

Towards the close of the twentieth century there was an increasing awareness of individual differences in learning and of the need for teaching methods to take account of them. The driving force for this understanding often came as a result of a master teacher's clinical experience of teaching those with 'inexplicable spelling difficulties'. Aylett Cox (1978) pointed out that dyslexic children learn differently and that 'the educational system must begin to meet the individual child's learning needs rather than continue to require the child to meet the system's needs'. Chasty (1990) paraphrased this as: 'If the child does not learn the way we teach him, we must teach him the way he learns'. Understanding of individual differences has come mainly from neuropsychologists' and medical professionals' study of brain function using brain imaging techniques. This has given new insights about brain architecture and differences. In a post-mortem examination of the brains of dyslexic adults Galaburda and Kempner (1979) found that they had symmetrical brains. These findings may account for their weakness in, for example, spelling and strengths in spatial skills. The results of PET and MRI scans such as those used by Posner *et al.* (1988) showed that visible words and audible words activate different parts of the brain. Post-mortem examinations showed differences between dyslexics' and controls' brains. Differences were found in blood flow in various regions of the brain (Corina *et al.*, 2001). Eckert *et al.* (2003) were able to identify dyslexic adults from matched controls by the differences in the frontal area of the brain (Broca's area) and the right cerebellum. This evidence is a scientific breakthrough and has resulted in a growing understanding of individual children's special educational needs.

An overview and rationale for the most frequently used spelling methods

I Visual inspection methods

Figure 11

- Lists from spelling books such as Schonell's (1932) 3,200 words.
- Lists from personal spelling or from classroom-based vocabulary, graded according to spelling difficulty.
- Random list of words copied from the board into a spelling notebook with the number of spellings to be learned averaging from 10 to 20, depending on age and ability.
- The NLS lists including the High Frequency Lists I and II and the Spelling Banks (DfEE, 1999 for Key Stage 2 and DfEE, 2001 for Year 7).

Often the instruction on Monday was to learn 'twenty words' for a test on Friday. Child and parent would look at the spellings and the child usually learned them by spelling the words letter by letter orally. Other children may have learned them by visualising the words and then practising writing them to dictation. This method is satisfactory for children with good visual memory, for others it often results in a very poor score on the test.

Hildreth (1955) was highly critical, proclaiming that:

> the conventional list methods of teaching spelling leave much to be desired for at least three reasons: first, the standardised nature of the word lists and the rigid way in which the lists tend to be used; second, the disparity between practising the spelling of words in isolated lists and the way in which words are used in writing; third, the assumptions that *every* word to be spelled needs separate memory drill and precisely the same amount of drill or type of practice as every other word, that all the pupils require practice on identical word lists, and that a week's drill on twenty words will ensure permanent learning. Although pupils may be letter perfect in 'list' spelling immediately after a period of intensive study, they may not be able to spell the same words correctly when they write, and may not recognise the correct spelling of these words in print or writing because there has been little carry-over from rote drill to purposeful use.

This description, written over fifty years ago, could have been written yesterday to describe a methodology that is still used in many classrooms. Many children are still wasting time on spelling activities that teach them little except frustration and pain.

Brand (1984), influenced by her experience of working with dyslexic children and adults, asserted that 'too much emphasis has been placed on learning to spell through visual methods. The ears and the mouth have been forgotten and the power of the hand ignored'.

2 Horn's look-say-cover-write-check method

This was devised in the USA by Ernest Horn (1919). Peters (1985) adapted it in the UK, omitting the 'say' element. The NLS (1998) recommended its use and has helped to make this approach more widely known. It involves the following processes:

- Look at the word (note its visual features in the mind's eye).
- Pronounce it while at the same time looking at the letters.
- Say the letter names aloud while looking at them.
- Cover the word.
- Write the word in cursive writing.
- Check by looking at the original version.

This is a multi-sensory approach to spelling when the 'say' element is included and is useful for those with good auditory skills. Cursive writing is also important for those with good kinaesthetic skills. It is effective

Figure 12 Look-say-cover-write-check.

for different kinds of spellers because of the use of the eyes, ears, hands and lips simultaneously and is appropriate for different learning styles.

3 Fernald's method

Figure 13 Fernald's method.

This is based on the work of Grace Fernald (1943) who said that children learn best by practising spellings they need/want to know for use in their own writing. It involves the following (adapted from Cotterell, 1970):

1   The word is written by the teacher in cursive writing on a piece of A4 paper.
2   The teacher pronounces the word slowly and clearly. Then the pupil repeats it.
3   The pupil looks at the word carefully and notes any particular tricky letters, prefixes or suffixes (which can be highlighted).
4   He then traces over the letters using the index finger of the hand he writes with, while simultaneously saying the letter names aloud as he traces over them.
5   Then he folds over the paper.
6   He writes the word from memory, using cursive writing.
7   He then turns the paper back and checks his spelling with the target word on the page. He repeats the process if necessary until he is able to write the word correctly from memory.
8   Then he uses the word in a meaningful context either in a sentence or in a piece of his own writing.

This method matches the learning style of those with good visual memory. They use their eyes to look at the letters and could use colour to highlight morphemes including plurals, affixes and silent letters. Kinaesthetic learners benefit from using their tactile sense when they trace over the letters as well as their motor memory when they write the letters in a cursive script to enhance motor memory skills. It works well for spellers who have reached the conventional spelling stage when they know and use word patterns and derivations. It emphasises whole words rather than focusing on individual sounds. This approach is recommended for the irregular 'odd-bod' words but is not necessary for regularly spelt words.

4 Simultaneous oral spelling (S-O-S) method

- It uses the following mnemonic

S   Say the word aloud
O   Spell it Orally
S   Look at the word and Say the word you have written.

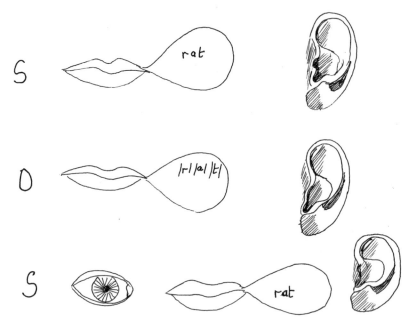

Figure 14 S-O-S.

This was devised by Gillingham and Stillman (1956) in conjunction with Samuel Orton and is the method used by most specialist teachers of dyslexic children. It is a straightforward multi-sensory approach. It is used as follows:

- The teacher says the word while the child looks at her lips (using his ears to listen and his eyes to look).

- The child repeats the word orally (using his lips to say and his ears to listen).
- The child spells the word aloud using the letter sounds (later he will use the letter names when spelling irregular words) (using his lips to say and his ears to listen).
- Then he writes the word, while saying the letter sounds (using his hands to write and his ears to listen).
- Then he reads what he has written (using his eyes and ears).

In Bradley's (1981) training study comparing different spelling methods she found that the dyslexic children 'gained significantly from this [S-O-S] multi-sensory approach'.

Thomson (1991) carried out a study on the effectiveness of different spelling methods for dyslexic pupils. He used controls with the same spelling age as the dyslexic pupils. He compared the visual inspection method with the S-O-S method. He used regular and irregular words such as biscuit, enough, special, beauty, yachtsman in the experiment. He found that the S-O-S method was effective for regular spellings but did not bolster relevant skills for irregular words. He concluded that 'the visual inspection condition gives very poor results in the dyslexics'.

Topping (1995) adapted the S-O-S method as a paired spelling method.

Figure 15 Paired spelling method.

5 Neuro-linguistic programming (NLP) method

O'Connor and Seymour (1990) developed a method of identifying individuals' learning styles by observing eye movements. They hypothesised that visual learners when asked to spell a word will turn their eyes upwards as they try to visualise a picture of the letters. The auditory learner turns his eyes aside as he tries to remember the sounds. The kinaesthetic learner may trace out the letters with his finger or he may tap out the syllables.

Brooks and Weeks (1998) carried out an experiment using ten different spelling methods 'to assess whether giving a child an insight into how to learn best' could increase spelling ability in comparison with using normal classroom methods. They found that 'after 5 months, the rate of increase in spelling age of the group using the individual methods [to match preferred learning styles] doubled, while the others increased at the usual "chronological rate".'

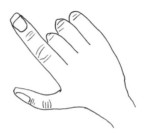

Figure 16 NLP method.

The rough guide to teaching and learning spelling rules and conventions

'In order to understand the spelling system of English, children need to be given reasons for why the spellings are as they are, and told about how these spellings relate to the way they pronounce the words': this is Crystal's (2002) cogent argument for teaching spelling. English spelling has the reputation of being complex and feckless. Some commentators say that the teaching of rules in English is unproductive, because the child cannot verbalise the rule, because of word retrieval difficulties or working memory difficulties, as well as because of not being able to know when a rule can or should be applied. Boder (1973) showed that learning rules paid dividends for dyslexic pupils because they then made fewer errors. These errors were better phonetic approximations which resulted in making their spelling more comprehensible. Rules should not be taught in a rote way. They need to be explained and how they work should be shown to pupils, with examples of good reasons for their use, such as for using 'ed' for the past tense of a verb rather than the /t/ /d/ /id/ sound.

The best news any poor speller can be given is to be told that over 84 per cent of words are regular and follow grapheme/phoneme rules (Hanna *et al.*, 1971). Crystal (2002) pointed out that 'there are only about 400 everyday words in English whose spelling is wholly irregular'. Hanna *et al.*'s (1971) study identified only 3 per cent of words in English as wholly unpredictable 'odd-bods'.

Law and order can be brought to English spelling with the use of rules and regulations including the following:

- The most commonly used letter in English is 'e', followed by 't' and 'a'.
- The most common way to spell a vowel sound is with one letter.

- Magic Mrs 'e' makes the vowel say its name but she keeps quiet: *măt – māte*; *pĕt – Pēte*; *pĭp – pīpe*; *nŏt – nōte*; *tŭb – tūbe*.
- Most words belong to word families and rhyme with other words. The exceptions with no rhymes are: *angel, burger, circle, friendly, good-natured, month, orange, pint, purple, temple*.
- Every word must have a vowel sound.
- Every syllable must have a vowel.
- Proper nouns including the names of people and place names do not follow spelling rules or conventions and should be treated on an individual basis. This explains why Mr Wilde is not 'wild'. This also applies to their pronunciation which is why Lord Hârewood lives at Hârewood.
- Hard 'c' says /k/: *cat, cot, cup*.
- Soft 'c' says /s/ when the next letter is 'e', 'i' or 'y': *cent, city, cycle*.
- Hard 'g' says /g/: *gap, gun*.
- Soft 'g' says /j/ when the next letter is 'e', 'i' or 'y': *gem, gin, gym*.
- The 'j' sound has six different spellings:

  'j' at the beginning and middle of words: *jam, job, major*
  'g' at the beginning of words when the next letter is 'e', 'i' or 'y': *germ, giro, gypsy*
  'ge' at the end of words when there is a long vowel and magic 'e': *page, rage, stage*
  'ge' if it is before a vowel digraph: *courage, gouge, stooge*
  'ge' if there is a consonant before the /j/ sound: *hinge, large, lounge*
  'dge' if it is at the end of a word after a short vowel: *badge, fridge, judge*.

- The /k/ sound is spelt 'k' at the beginning of a word: *kennel, king, kiss*; or 'c' at the beginning, middle or end of a word: *camp, broccoli, heretic*; or 'ch' at the beginning, middle or end of a word: *chemist, school, stomach*.
- The /k/ sound at the end of word is spelt 'ck': *back, chick, duck*; or 'k' at the end if there is a consonant before the /k/ sound: *pink, thank, trunk*; or 'ke' if there is a long vowel and magic 'e': *bike, coke, duke*; or 'que': *antique, boutique, mosque*.
- 'q' and 'u' are like Siamese twins and always stay together in a word: *quad, queen, quick*.
- The /s/ sound at the beginning, middle and end of a word is spelt 's': *sand, basin, minus*; or 'se' at the end of a word: *base, horse, mouse*; or 'ss' at the middle and end of a word: *classic, gossip*; *pessimist, fuss, glass, moss*; or sc: *muscle, scene, science*; or sometimes 'st': *castle, listen, whistle*. And remember soft 'c' (above).
- 'v' says /v/ at the beginning, middle and end of words. There is always an 'e' after 'v' at the end of words: *five, love, van*.
- 'w' says /w/: *wag, wig, wolf*
  'wa' says /wo/: *swan, wasp, water*
  'war' says /wor/: *swarm, ward, warm*
  'wor' says /wer/: *word, work, world*.
- 'y' when it is a consonant says /y/: *yap, yell, yolk*. When it is a vowel it can say /ī/: *cry, sty, type*. It can also say /ē/: *body, funny, happy*.
- The 'double trouble' rule:

  – In one-syllable words with one short vowel which end in 'f', 'l', 's' or 'z', the final consonant doubles: *staff, bell, miss, jazz*.

Rule-breakers are: *pal, gas, bus, his, has, pus, plus.*

- – The 'double or drop dead' rule:
- – When a word has two syllables, if the first syllable has a short vowel and ends in one consonant, double that consonant if you can hear it at the beginning of the second syllable: *button, gallon, tennis.*
- – When a word has two syllables, if the first syllable has a short vowel and ends in one consonant, double that consonant when adding 'le': *apple, middle, paddle.*
- – When a word has two syllables, if the first syllable has a long vowel and ends in one consonant, do not double the consonant when adding 'le': *bible, fable, table.*

- The 'i' before 'e' rule is best remembered by saying the following rhyme:

  'I' before 'e'
  Except after 'c';
  Or when sounded as 'a'
  As in neighbour and weigh.
  Either, neither, leisure, and seize
  Are four exceptions
  If you please.

  (Adams, 1990)

- The prefix 'all' drops 'l' when it is added to a root word: *albeit, almighty, almost, already, also, although, altogether, always.*
- There are ten different ways to spell /shun/: cean (*ocean*); cheon (*luncheon*); cian (*musician*); cion (*suspicion*); shion (*fashion*); sion (*version*); ssion (*passion*); tian (*Alsatian*); tion (*definition*); xion (*crucifixion*). However, 'tion' is the most commonly used spelling and can be used to generate over 500 words: *creation, nation, station.*
- Words ending in the /l/ sound usually end 'le': *apple, table.* Some high frequency words ending in 'el' have to be memorised: *angel, barrel, channel, funnel, kennel, label, mussel, parcel.*
- Words ending in the /er/ sound relating to a person or a job can be spelt 'ar', 'er' or 'or': *burglar, teacher, doctor.* Words derived from Latin or French use 'or': *professor, orator.* Words derived from Greek use 'er': *astronomer, photographer.*
- The past tense of the verb adding 'ed' is notoriously difficult as a spelling concept for dyslexics as it can say /t/ /d/ or /id/ (which is how phonetic spellers spell it): *walked, looked, rented.* This needs specific attention and overlearning.
- Adding 'ing' to a verb is a concept that spellers need to know and understand before they learn the more advanced rules for adding suffixes. The rules are as follows:

  - – Words ending in 'e' drop 'e' before adding 'ing': *write – writing.*
  - – If there is a vowel digraph keep 'e': *see – seeing.*
  - – If there is a vowel digraph or consonant blend add 'ing': *rush – rushing; jump – jumping.*

- If there is a short vowel and it ends in one consonant – double the con: adding 'ing': *shop – shopping; swim – swimming.*

The seven seriously super suffixing rules (Ott, 1997, 2007a, 2007

1 The one-one-one rule

Words of *one* syllable, containing *one* short vowel and ending in *one* consonant double that consonant before adding a suffix beginning with a vowel: *fun, funny, funnier, funniest; top, topper, topped, topping.*

   Verbs ending in double consonants keep them before adding a suffix: *err, erred, error, erring; purr, purred, purring.*

2 The lazy 'e' rule I

Drop 'e' before adding a suffix beginning with a vowel: *happy, happier, happiest; love, lover, loving, loved.*

3 The lazy 'e' rule II

Keep 'e' before adding a suffix beginning with a consonant: *like, likely, likeness; care, careful, careless.*

4 The lazy 'e' rule III

Keep 'e' in words ending 'ce' or 'ge' when adding the suffixes 'ade', 'able', 'ous': *courageous, orangeade, pronounceable.*

5 The 'y' rule I

Change 'y' to 'i' when adding a suffix unless it begins with 'i': *rely – relies, relied, reliant, reliable; try – tries, tried.*

6 The 'y' rule II

Keep 'y' when adding the suffixes 'ing', 'ish', 'ist' (because 'ii' is not an English spelling pattern): *study, studying; baby, babyish; copy, copyist.*

7 The 'y' rule III

Keep 'y' if there is a vowel before the 'y' when adding a suffix: *obey, obeys, obeying; pray, prays, prayed, praying.*

The rules for making nouns plural need special attention. They should be introduced to match the different stages of development of individual spellers and learned one at a time. The following is a summary of the ten rules (Ott, 1997, 2006a, 2006b).

1   The most common way to make a noun plural is to add 's': *hat – hats*; *rug – rugs*.
2   Nouns ending in 's', 'x', 'z', 'ch', 'sh' add 'es' in the plural: *glass – glasses*; *box – boxes*; *buzz – buzzes*; *coach – coaches*; *dish – dishes*.
3   Nouns ending in 'f' or 'fe' change 'f' to 'v' and add 'es': *shelf – shelves*; *wife – wives*.
    The rule-breakers just add 's', such as; *cliff – cliffs*; *chief – chiefs*.
4   Nouns ending in 'y' change 'y' to 'i' and add 'es'. If there is a vowel before the 'y' just add 's': *baby – babies*; *donkey – donkeys*.
5   Nouns ending in 'o' add 's' or 'es' (most words add 's'): *piano – pianos*; *potato – potatoes*. (Words related to music add 's'.)
6   Foreign words mostly follow the rules of their own language: *criterion – criteria* (Greek); *gateau – gateaux* (French); *radius – radii* (Latin).
7   Some words are always plural: *scissors, tights*.
8   Some words are the same in the singular and the plural: *people, sheep, trout*.
9   Some compound nouns add 's' to the first part, others add 's' to the second part: *mother-in-law – mothers-in-law*; *lay-by – lay-bys*.
10 Old English words from Anglo-Saxon times follow their own rules: *child – children*; *tooth – teeth*.

The horrible homophones (Ott, 1997, 2007b)

They cause many spellers difficulty, particularly those who spell phonetically and those who find visualising words difficult. Strategies have to be devised to help with memorisation such as the use of mnemonics and illustrations. The high frequency homophones should be tackled first such as:

are	our	
by	buy	bye
hear	here	
new	knew	
peace	piece	
some	sum	
their	there	they're
to	two	too
which	witch	

Why syllables and syllable division strategies are great allies for spellers

Long words are frequently perceived as difficult to pronounce and spell. For those who have the knowhow and can divide words into syllables, breaking them into parts makes reading and writing easier.

Syllables need to be taught and learned as an oral activity. Awareness of rhyme, rhythm and sound develops from an early age in normal children with the help of games and word play. Those who have difficulties with phonological awareness will require explicit teaching about the sound structure of the language and will require longer to learn.

Key terminology

The language associated with syllables is sometimes challenging, particularly for pupils with SpLD. They need to know and understand the following: vowels, short/long vowels, consonants, digraphs, blends, breves, macrons, syllable division lines.

The six main types of syllables can be learned by using the mnemonic C-L-O-V-E-R (Schneider 1999; Rome *et al.*, 1993).

C   Closed syllables end in a consonant and have a short vowel: *cŭp, răb/bĭt.*

L   'le' syllables end in: ble, cle, fle, gle, kle, ple, tle, zle, but the final vowel 'e' does not say a thing: *ăn/kle, tā/ble, kĕt/tle.*

O   Open syllables end in a vowel and have a long vowel: *ū/nĭt, pō/lō, bĭn/gō.*

V   Vowel digraphs/diphthongs stay together as one sound or as a diphthong: *trāin/ĕr, drāw/ĭng, slēep/ȳ.*

E   e: magic 'e' makes the vowel say its name but it is silent: *hōme, ĭg/nōre, prō/mōte.*

R   r-controlled vowels are made by adding 'r' to the vowels: ar, er, ir, or, ur. The vowels can be short or long: *ăr/row, sĭs/tĕr, ĭr/rĕl/ē/vănt, ăc/tŏr. ŭr/gĕnt*

Suggestions for the organisation and use of a personal 'spellofax'

- Use an A3 or A4 ring-back personal organiser.
- Choose one with a strong durable cover.
- Include alphabet dividers.
- Put tabs on the side of the dividers for speedy access to various categories.
- List basic terminology such as the diacritical marks.
- Include the following:

    - the phonics checklist (this can be reduced in size if necessary on a photo-copier)
    - photocopy of NLS target spelling list for each term
    - class spelling tests
    - personalised list of 'odd-bod' spellings which should be constantly updated
    - list of spelling rules and conventions in the order they have been taught
    - list of personal 'spelling demons'
    - syllable division strategies including the seven suffixing rules
    - horrible homophones
    - silent letters
    - marvellous mnemonics for 'odd-bod' spellings
    - high frequency word lists including those from NLS (1998)
    - checklist for the ten commandments for plurals of nouns
    - checklists of common roots, prefixes and suffixes
    - list of common word families
    - list of hard-to-spell words

- test results indicating preferred learning style
- test results indicating favourite spelling strategy
- computer packages and games used for learning and reinforcement
- list of essential subject vocabulary.

Each of these categories should include examples from the child's own work. It could also include worksheets from *Activities for Spelling Successfully* (Ott, 2007b) linked to the target activity.

Guidelines and recommendations for a 'whole-school' spelling policy document

- This document should be drawn up by the school SENCO in consultation with the English specialist in primary schools and by the head of the English department in secondary schools.
- There should be a list of the names of children who are on the SEN register including those assessed as dyslexic and those with statements. Children who have been assessed by external agencies should also be included.
- Those found to be 'at risk' by the Dyslexia Screening Test or the Cognitive Profiling System (COPSI) should be listed.
- A list of the names of siblings of dyslexic children should be included and their literacy progress should be kept under review and carefully monitored.
- Children who are regarded as chronically poor spellers, especially those who tend to spell phonetically, should be listed and monitored. The performance of children who show evidence of a 'surprising' discrepancy between good oral language skills and poor written work on standardised spelling tests should be scrutinised for evidence of a pattern of errors and kept under review.
- Tutors/heads of year should review and update lists annually on the basis of test results and/or comments from staff.
- Annual reviews of children with IEPs should be used to raise awareness among colleagues about children who struggle in different areas of the curriculum with written work often because of their poor spelling.
- Standardised spelling tests should be administered annually. Records should be kept and logged throughout the child's school years. Tests with parallel forms are preferable. Standardised scores overcome the difficulties associated with spelling ages. The NAA and the JCQ insist that 'results must be given as Standardised Scores' when applications are made for access arrangements in examinations. However, when communicating with parents spelling ages are often more enlightening.
- Lists of subject vocabulary should be agreed on, such as the top twenty most frequently used spellings. The NLS (2001) *Year 7 Spelling Bank* provides such

lists. They could be photocopied and enlarged, and pupils should be asked to stick them in the front of individual subject files for reference.

- The *Framework for Teaching* (NLS, 1998) medium frequency words checklist is recommended for Years 4 and 5. It gives a phonics list summary for Reception and Years 1 and 2 in the Appendix. It is important to be aware that the 'odd-bod' irregular spellings on the lists may be too challenging for some dyslexic children.

- DfES (1999) Spelling Bank for Key Stage 2 contains lists of words and objectives. These can be used during word and sentence work in the Literacy Hour. It is essential to be aware, however, that a number of the targets, for example learning the various ways to spell the long /i/ sound, may be too complex for a child with dyslexia who is still confusing the short vowel sounds.

- A useful strategy is to photocopy and enlarge Lists I and II of the NLS 'high frequency'. Colour code the initial letter in green to help those with poor alphabet skills and highlight the 'tricky' letters in red such as the 'i' in friend. Then laminate this and stick it on the desk for instant reference. For the very poor speller, put an asterisk by the 'odd-bod' spellings on the list and encourage him to check these when he proofreads. Put a tick by the regular spelling which hopefully he will remember with time and practice.

- Differentiation is important for all spellers. Give the poor speller ten words to learn rather than twenty. The stage of spelling can be established by using, for example, the STEPS Informal Phonics Test. Children can then work in groups of similar skills. A spelling rule or convention which is appropriate for the current stage of development can be taught and spelling lists including word families can be generated and given to be learned. Lists can be downloaded from the computer package.

- Some SpLD children because of the severity of their difficulties will be unable to cope with the average weekly class spelling test. These pupils should be exempt from the public humiliation and frustration it causes.

- These children could work on a computer package such as White Space Word Shark 3S 2.2 (www.wordshark.co.uk) or StarSpell (www.dyslexic.com) while the other children do the test.

- Individual learning styles should be established. Pupils should then be encouraged to use this method to memorise spelling as part of their homework. The preferred style can be matched to the most effective spelling method. Parents and teaching assistants need to be made aware of individual children's needs.

- It is important to be aware that some children have very poor visual memory. The universal habit of asking children to copy out their spelling corrections three or four times is a complete and utter waste of time in some cases. Some of these children even misspell the corrections while 'correcting' them.

- Results of spelling tests should not be read out in public as far as possible in the light of legal responsibilities set out in the Human Rights Act 1998 and the Disability Discrimination Act 1995.

- Spelling corrections should be 'given' to poor spellers. Writing 'sp' in the margin does not usually teach the child the spelling nor does it help him to remember the letters, particularly if it involves adding an ending to a root word for example. Encourage him to add spellings to his personal 'spellofax' and to use it.

- Lists of spellings for homework should be computer print-outs if possible. They can be generated easily using a whiteboard. Use a bold font of at least 14 point size and double space the lists to make them easier to read. Encourage the child to put the list in his personal 'spellofax'.
- Word patterns can be highlighted and a different colour can be used for silent letters. Try not to ask dyslexic or dyspraxic children to copy lists of spellings for the test from the board if they misspell words because of their poor eye–hand co-ordination. In some circumstances parents are themselves unaware of the error because they may be dyslexic or they may not spell English well if it is their second language. If there is a teaching assistant she may be able to copy the spellings or check what a child has written before he takes it home for homework.
- A copy of the spelling policy document needs to be circulated to all members of staff. It should be kept for reference alongside the marking scheme or mark record file.
- QCA (2003a) gives guidance on science spelling and states that 'it is not essential that children use completely correct spelling to gain marking credit for these words [of scientific processes and equipment]. Provided the terms are recognisable, e.g. major phonemes present and in the correct order, children will gain credit from marks.' This is a very positive approach and gives encouragement, particularly to those children who are poor spellers but good scientists.
- The spelling policy document needs to be discussed and reviewed annually so that changes can be made and to ensure that all new members of staff know of its existence.
- A spelling policy is important when marking, for example, an essay.

  (a) It is sometimes more effective initially to target just 4–5 errors (depending on age and spelling ability) such as high frequency words with regular spellings for correction.
  (b) Mark errors with a pencil if the child is working with a pen and vice versa. Try not to use a red pen. It can be embarrassing for a child for his exercise book to be covered in red marks. There is anecdotal evidence of a dyslexic pupil comparing these marks to drops of his own blood on the page.
  (c) Sensitivity and differentiation have to be used when marking dyslexic pupils' spelling errors. Mark only the errors in spellings that they have been specifically taught. Comment on what is 'good' about the work before targeting the error. Essays may have to be marked for content and ideas. Spelling errors may have to be ignored to help develop confidence and to encourage the child to use his vocabulary. Some children become inhibited writers if all their spelling errors are marked as incorrect.
  (d) A spelling rule can be given and reinforced at the bottom of the page and the child may be asked to learn and work on similar words, for instance in the same spelling family. This could be included in the IEP.

(e) Marks should not be deducted for poor spellings in subjects other than English (and not in English if possible), particularly for dyslexic pupils.

- Staff training and whole staff awareness are important. The DDA 2002 has implications for schools, governors and individual staff. The BDA (2001) reported an audit of 4,732 schools in 84 parliamentary constituencies about in-service training on the subject of dyslexia in schools. Sixty per cent of schools had never had an INSET day on dyslexia. Staff need awareness training about the key characteristics of the condition as well as advice on how best to help those children in the classrooms of dyslexia-friendly schools. There are 'about 375,000 schoolchildren affected in Britain – 40 per cent are classified as severely dyslexic, the rest as mild' (Gold, 2004). Almost all these children will have persistent difficulties with spelling.
- There needs to be awareness as well as agreement on the use of different spelling strategies such as the simultaneous oral spelling (S-O-S) method or Horn's look-say-cover-write-check method for regular spellings and the Fernald method for irregular 'odd-bod' spellings. Using multi-sensory learning methods has been shown to be the most effective way of learning and remembering spelling for dyslexic pupils.
- Children should be encouraged to use the same dictionary consistently so that they become familiar with its layout. Some of the newer school dictionaries are more child friendly. Some use colour for the headword and the entry word. Others have the alphabet printed down the side of the page which is a great help to those with sequencing difficulties. The inclusion of full forms of plurals and tenses of verbs is liberating for poor spellers. The *Oxford Young Reader's Dictionary* (Dignen, 2005) has large print, as recommended by the RNIB. The definitions are given as full sentences and the inflected forms are given in full. It is a model of clarity. *Chambers Primary Dictionary* (2002) deals with homophones by putting them in a box. The entry word for each includes a sentence to clarify meaning. However, being told 'to look the word up in the dictionary' is futile and frustrating for some very dyslexic children who struggle to say the alphabet. A handheld spellchecker such as Franklin Literacy Word Bank Children's Dictionary and Thesaurus (www.franklin.com/uk) which is linked to the NLS word lists may be the answer. The *Dictionary of Perfect Spelling* (Maxwell, 2005) is the solution to the problems of those who spell phonetically. If the speller wants to spell 'knowledge' and looks under 'nowledge', he will find 'nowledge' in red print, indicating that it is wrong. In the right-hand column opposite it he will find 'knowledge' in black print.
- Children need to be taught how to use handheld spellcheckers effectively. Spellcheckers have had a life-enhancing impact on many users' daily lives but they are not a panacea for all poor spellers who are often unable to read and pronounce a word to check the correct option.
- There should be agreement and guidelines on the use of spellcheckers taking the disability discrimination legislation into account. They may, for example, be used when word-processing homework and when doing coursework. The

spellchecker may or may not be allowed in internal tests or examinations depending on need. The NAA and QCA (2005) issued new guidelines for assessment and reporting arrangements and stated that:

> Spellcheckers are allowed in English (except the spelling test), mathematics and science for pupils:
>
> – learning English as an additional language
> – with special educational needs
> – who use them as part of normal classroom practice.

- Resources should ideally include an agreed structured progressive spelling programme as well as ICT packages which can be used throughout the school for individual and group work. The Rose Review (Rose, 2006) recommended that when a phonics programme was chosen schools should use it consistently and not 'pick-and-mix' from other programmes.

Summary and conclusions

- English spelling has evolved over the centuries, reflecting many influences from other languages and cultures.
- Many attempts have been made to simplify spelling but the British public has stoutly defended the status quo. Five hundred years after the first High Master of St Paul's School, London, Richard Mulcaster, championed good spelling, the present High Master, Dr Martin Stephen, continues to insist that spelling is 'absolutely crucial. It is the initial testing point for anyone filling in a job application form or wanting to go to university. It is a crucial skill a young person needs to make a favourable impact.' (*Sunday Times*, 2004)
- Many commentators forecast the demise of conventional spelling as a result of the impact of ICT technology such as SMS and e-mail. On the other hand upholders of spelling standards as well as new champions of good spelling have emerged in the media and in government agencies. The QCA has announced that they are to impose tougher penalties on examinees whose work is 'littered with errors'.
- The BBC is reported to have been influenced by the popularity of the American film *Spellbound*, which was based on The National Spelling Bee (knockout spelling competition), when it decided to make a programme about spelling. It launched a competition to find the nation's best 11–14-year-old speller. *Hard Spell* was shown on prime-time television and attracted millions of viewers as well as raising the profile of spelling. Over 1,000 schools used the 1,000 practice words supplied by the BBC to prepare pupils for the preliminary heats of the competition held in schools throughout the UK. The spelling prowess of many of the finalists was impressive as was their use of different strategies such as closing their eyes to visualise or tracing out the words with their fingers. It was also a poignant reminder of the difficulties poor spellers have.

- At the other end of the spelling continuum are the persistently poor spellers who are frequently castigated for laziness and carelessness. Miles (2004), reflecting on fifty years of research, assessment and teaching, recalls encountering his very first case of dyslexia: 'her entire inability to spell is her great weakness'. Fifty years later, this comment is as true as ever for children with dyslexia.
- The classic dyslexic spelling symptoms include poor phonemic skills, poor phonological awareness, visual errors, sequencing difficulties and poor recall of spelling patterns. Miscue analysis of spelling errors can be used as a magnifying glass to identify where the breakdown of skills occurs. Moats (1993) pointed out that

  > if spelling is analysed for this purpose, words of high and low frequency, real and nonsense words, words of one to four syllables, words with inflected endings, and words generated to dictation and in spontaneous writing would provide the comprehensive sample needed for making a valid inference [of dyslexia].

  Accurate diagnostic information is essential if teaching is to be successfully targeted to meet individuals' special educational needs.
- Testing spelling involves the use of standardised dictated tests as well as an extended sample of free writing to provide examples of spelling errors for a miscue analysis.
- Teaching and learning spelling rules is a worthwhile investment for all. The English language has a structure, including spelling patterns and conventions; 84 per cent of words are regular and follow these rules.
- There is a variety of spelling methods to use, depending on individual strengths and weaknesses and on whether words are regular or irregular as well as on individual learning styles.
- Children learn best when they are motivated, stimulated and taught with sensitivity and understanding of their strengths and weaknesses and when their preferred learning style for spelling is taken into account.
- Spelling rules can be broken down into essential elements, such as the rules for pluralisation, syllabification and suffixing. Indian-born Gayathri Panikker (*Daily Telegraph*, 2004), who became the *Hard Spell* national spelling champion at 13, when interviewed said, 'The Latin I do at school definitely helps me with my spelling because it teaches me where words come from'. This example of an Indian-born girl who did not speak English until she came to live here when she was five years old shows that good spelling is an acquired skill which can be taught and learned.
- Individual spellers can build on skills over time with practice and experience, including seeing and using spellings in running texts. How successful poor spellers are depends on intrinsic factors including the degree of their dyslexia and extrinsic factors including appropriate intervention.
- A 'whole-school' spelling policy helps when establishing dyslexia-friendly schools and classrooms and raises the profile of spelling across the whole of the curriculum.

  > The aim should be that by the end of compulsory schooling pupils should be able to spell confidently most of the words that they are likely to need to use frequently in their writing; to recognise those aspects of English spelling that are systematic; to make a sensible attempt to spell words that they have not seen before; to check their work for misspellings and to use a dictionary appropriately.

The aim cannot be the correct unaided spelling of any English word – there are too many words in English that can catch out even the best speller.

(Cox, 1991)

Technology such as the spellchecker including the use of the speech option has moved the goal posts for all spellers. Accurate spelling is no longer beyond the reach of many poor spellers. There is now a way to spell consistently well for those with SpLD who are allowed to use a spellchecker as 'part of normal practice'.

Chapter 7

Strategies for success for writers: tricks of the trade and hints galore to lighten the load for dyslexic and dyspraxic writers

Outline

- Teaching writing skills
- Timeline of influential international developments for teaching writing, with a synopsis of best practice for learners
- Practical suggestions for teaching children writing skills
- The role and contribution of word-processing to literacy
- Stepping stones to make a framework of underlying skills
- What stumbling blocks obstruct poor writers and cause specific challenges?
- Code of practice for good essay planners
- The major approaches to planning
- Checklist for effective writers when planning, drafting, editing and revising
- Practical suggestions for proofreading with the C-O-P-S strategy
- How do teachers assess writing skills and mark writing assignments?
- Checklist of questions for a good writing detective
- Guidelines for helping apprentice writers
- Top twenty tips for successful writers
- Genre theory for non-fiction writing
- Factsheets with guidelines for teaching the main non-fiction genres to pupils with SpLD
- Suggestions for using writing frames as scaffolds
- Ways and means of awakening and fostering children's interest in poetry
- Toolbox of nuts and bolts for apprentice poets
- An A–Z of poetry forms
- Handy hints for budding poets
- Key points for consideration when drafting, editing and revising poetry
- Guidelines for writing a personal response to a poem
- A spectrum of underlying causes of writing difficulties
- Summary and conclusions

Teaching writing skills

In 1711 Alexander Pope in his *Essay on Criticism* gave sound advice to apprentice writers when declaring that 'True ease in writing comes from art, not chance, / As those move easiest who have learned to dance'. If reading is to the mind what food is to the body, then writing is the lifeblood that sustains and nourishes it, helping to develop thinking skills and improving reasoning powers.

Written language requires five times more effort than oral language because many sub-skills need orchestration. Speech occurs naturally, written language is an acquired skill requiring explicit training.

> Writing is an amazingly complex activity. The writer is simultaneously involved with thinking of what to write, coherence and comprehension of the text formation and legibility of individual letters, spelling, grammar, including punctuation, layout, tone and register, organisation and selection of appropriate content for an intended audience.
>
> (*First Steps*, 1997)

Written records are necessary to remember or recall information over a period of time. The examiner assesses the pupil's knowledge and understanding and judges him on the quality of his written responses, recall of facts, information and interpretation of questions.

Teaching writing has been a significant part of schools' English curricula since pupils were given quill pens and ink. Performance in almost every subject in the curriculum has been evaluated and largely dependent on what is written. The objectives varied as did the time spent on writing practice. Time was spent transcribing texts such as the Scriptures. Younger children would rewrite Aesop's *Fables*. Older children wrote out Shakespearean soliloquies or extracts from essayists such as Bacon. Great emphasis was placed on correct spelling and neat legible handwriting (often in a copperplate style). Many innovations took place in schools in the nineteenth and twentieth centuries, including the teaching of writing skills.

Timeline of influential international developments for teaching writing, with a synopsis of best practice for learners

1887   Alexander Bain of Aberdeen University published *English Composition and Rhetoric* which described and classified narrative, descriptive, expository (factual) and argumentative essay writing.

1931   The Hadow Report reflected the continuing influence of Bain's formal approach and recommended that children should learn a range of writing forms.

1954   The Ministry of Education's publication *Language: Some Suggestions for Teachers of English and Others* recommended that children be taught the purpose of writing.

1960s The 'Creative Writing Movement' developed under the influence of Marjorie Hourd's (1949) *The Education of the Poetic Spirit*. It emphasised imagination, spontaneity and creativity in children's writing, suggesting that they could be stimulated by using their senses and feelings to write about 'a stormy sea', for example. Alec Clegg (1964) and Barry Maybury (1967) were two of its best-known exponents.

1967   The Plowden Report (DES, 1967) expressed concern about writing standards, particularly story writing, and made recommendations for improvement.

1970 James Britton's *Language and Learning* drew attention to writing for different purposes including oneself, one's teacher or a wider or unknown audience.

1971 In the USA James Kinneavy's *A Theory of Discourse* described the aims and main purpose of writing: 'to share news, to inform, to persuade, to entertain'. These should be based on the writer's personal experiences.

1975 The Bullock Report (DES, 1975) *A Language for Life*, was influenced by Britton and was critical of the teaching context and some of the features of 'creative writing'. It recommended the inclusion of expressive, transactional and poetic writing.

1980s 'Genre theory' was developed in Australia and was based on the work of Michael Halliday (1975). It described and distinguished between different kinds of writing used by individuals in their day-to-day lives in various situations and for a variety of events. Jim Martin *et al.* (1987) and Beverly Derewianka (1990) identified the most commonly used genres and described their language features and the structure used to organise the text.

1983 Donald Graves's *Writing: Teachers and Children at Work* described the process approach in a study in New Hampshire in the USA. It advocated 'modelling' (demonstration) by the teacher, generation of comments from the pupils, brainstorming, drafting and editing processes. Children were taught to write for a specific audience and purpose, and to review and revise their work before publication.

1985 The Schools Curriculum Development body instigated the National Writing Project (1990) to establish how writing was taught. It raised the status of teaching writing and helped teachers to evaluate writing and to use models of good practice. It included a marking policy emphasising positive feedback about the contents, not just comments about the secretarial functions such as spelling, punctuation and handwriting.

1986 George Hillocks reviewed the research on different writing approaches and identified three main methods in current use in schools. The 'presentational' approach was used when the teacher set a title and the child then wrote about it. The teacher marked it and told the child what was wrong with his work. The 'process' approach taught general procedures and encouraged drafting and revision. The 'environmental' writing approach involved guided writing and drew attention to models and the specific features of texts. This was found to be the most effective method.

1987 Canadian researchers Carl Bereiter and Marlene Scardamalia established that certain procedures helped when composing written work, including making an initial list of useful vocabulary, planning the main points, and deciding on a concluding sentence. They noted that pupils needed support with each of these tasks.

1989 The National Curriculum was imposed in 1988 and implemented the following year. In English it included Statements of Attainment and attainment targets for eight levels which were to be assessed by statutory tests at the end of each key stage.

1991 Statutory Standard Assessment Tasks (SATs) including a statutory writing task were introduced for 7-year-olds.

1992 SATs were introduced for 11-year-olds. Ofsted, a schools inspectorate, was established. Ofsted reports (1993, 1997) highlighted pupils' difficulties with attaining target levels. 'Standards of writing . . . were weaker in Key Stage II than Key Stage I. . . . Much remains to be done to improve competence of pupils of all ages. [In the 11–14 age range] the weakest aspect of English . . . is writing.'

1995 The Revised National Curriculum (DfEE, 1995) was introduced and it included recommendations for teaching:

- composition
- planning and drafting
- writing for a range of purposes
- writing for remembering and developing ideas
- a range of forms.

1998 The National Literacy Strategy *Framework for Teaching* was published. It 'targeted how teachers teach [and] when to teach' (Beard, 2000) fiction, non-fiction and poetry. It recommended a 'focus on specific aspects of the writing process, rather than on a completion of a single piece of work'. The emphasis was on building skill by learning a sequence of strategies, including the explicit teaching of genres.

2000 The *Second Revision of the National Curriculum* was introduced.

Practical suggestions for teaching children writing skills

Ask the pupils to look at examples of 'good' writers' work, give them some tricks of the trade and show how these can be used in their own writing. Tell them that good writers put on their thinking C-A-P-S (Figure 17) when they write. Encourage them to use the acronym as a mnemonic to remind them what to think about:

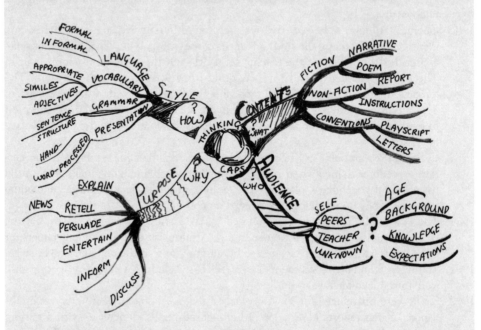

Figure 17 Thinking C-A-P-S, Content, Audience, Purpose, Style

Content

What are they writing about? Is it:

- fiction: a made-up story with imaginary characters – 'A ghost in the attic'?
- non-fiction: based on facts and real events such as instructions for 'How to wire a plug' or a newspaper report about the 'Flash floods in Boscastle'?
- poetry: using rhythm and rhyme to convey feelings and emotions and following a specific structure like William Wordsworth's 'Daffodils'?

What writing form or conventions should be used? Will it be set out as a play script or as a letter or in some other form?

Audience

Who are they writing this for? Is it for:

- themselves?
- teacher/parent/examiner?
- peers/friends?
- unknown readership – general public?

They need to think about their audience because it influences the tone, style and language. They should consider their readers' age, background, experience, knowledge and expectations.

Purpose

Why are they writing this? Is it:

- to give instructions or to describe procedures?
- to persuade someone to do/use something?
- to report facts/events?
- to entertain with a short story?
- to discuss issues?
- to give an explanation?
- to re-tell a story?

Style

How are they going to word their writing? They need to think about:

- language: should it be formal or informal?
- vocabulary: what is appropriate for the task?
- grammar: sentence structure and division into paragraphs
- whether it will be handwritten or word-processed.

The role and contribution of word-processing to literacy

The computer is as significant for literacy in the twenty-first century as Gutenberg's printing press was in the fifteenth century and likewise should be seen as a vehicle and means to an end. ICT is established as part and parcel of everyday life and is a statutory entitlement in the National Curriculum. The computer can provide a lifeline to a lifetime of success for all writers but especially for those with SEN including dyslexia and dyspraxia. A word-processing package can improve, enhance and develop the quality and quantity of writing and is often an answer to the prayers of poor writers.

However, just as the popular television programme *Ready, Steady, Cook* has shown that good ingredients in themselves do not always result in good dishes, and preparing and cooking a good meal requires understanding of the basic principles. Writing is a skill and for some a talent but it is also a craft that can be taught. It can be nurtured and improved with practice as well as being polished with experience.

A number of studies have shown that the computer improves motivation. There is much anecdotal and clinical evidence from dyslexic people of how the spellchecker and grammar checker empower and enhance their writing and solve their secretarial difficulties, including speeding up the whole process. Some wax lyrical about how they help to reduce 'pain and frustration' and prevent embarrassment. With each new technological marvel come predictions of the demise of pen and paper. Whatever the medium used to write, the writer still needs skills and knowhow because the contents, choice of language, knowledge, understanding and the emotions expressed reflect the individual's personal response.

Writing involves two main skills, composition and transcription, as well as a number of sub-skills. Composition involves generating ideas, describing responses and an ability to write in different forms for different audiences. Barrs (1987) pointed out that 'composition is what powers the writing. It is vital that the focus, in relation to children's writing, is first and foremost on composition'. Transcription involves the secretarial skills including spelling, punctuation and grammar. Word-processing helps with most aspects of the sub-skills.

Bangert-Drowns (1993) analysed the results of thirty-two 'before and after' studies on the effects of word-processing on primary school pupils and failed to demonstrate that it improves the quality of their writing. Van Haalen (1990) showed that children revised their compositions better and wrote to a better standard when they used pencil and paper. However, many older pupils and most adults would disagree with and question these findings.

Speech recognition software such as Dragon Naturally Speaking 8 Preferred and Professional IBM ViaVoice (www.dyslexic.com) can be used to dictate thoughts and ideas and it will transcribe these into text. It will also read back, edit and correct by voice. It has given a 'voice' to those who could not otherwise communicate in writing. Human intelligence is still mightier than cyber intelligence. Children can be taught how to use ICT to enhance performance and empower their creativity while exploring and exploiting sources of information and performance such as the Internet.

Stepping stones to make a framework of underlying skills

Many of the following activities involve a multi-sensory approach.

The Rose Review (2006) pointed out the importance of teaching speaking and listening skills. Expressive Language Activity Cards help to develop vocabulary to describe sequences of events, thoughts and feelings to use in narrative and descriptive writing. Children need to develop receptive and expressive oral language skills. Social Sequences (www.LDAlearning.com) encourage predictive skills and discussion about 'what might happen next'. Establish these concepts before asking the pupil to write simple sentences. *Target Listening and Understanding in Primary Schools* (Reilly and Murray, 2004) includes practical activities and suggestions to help identify and develop many aspects of language essential for spoken and written skills. Multimedia resources including CD-ROMs and videos which exploit sound and vivid colours as well as humour are fun to use. An example is Jumpstart Kindergarten (www.dorlingkindersley.co.uk).

Initially the teacher or teaching assistant may need to act as scribe for the pupil who is unable to write. Start by making labels and lists, such as what presents he would like for his birthday. A computer package such as Clicker 5 (www.clickersoft.com) can be used to write whole words and phrases and to build sentences with the help of pictures. The child can hear the word before he writes it and listen to what he has written. It includes over 1,000 pictures and can be used for subjects across the curriculum. It is suitable for 5–11 years.

Words and phrases that have been written and then cut up into laminated strips of cards can help to teach syntax – correct word order. These can then be copied into exercise books in long hand. Computer packages such as Easy Book Sunburst (TAG) (www.taglearning.com) have pages with graphics at the top and space to include text below. Use at least a 16 point font, or 20 is even easier to read. It is important not to underestimate the effectiveness of larger fonts.

Children can write by making labels and captions for objects and for their work. Pictures can be used to generate a series of actions. Using a sequence of pictures helps to develop sequential skills and sentence-building skills. The card game Sightword Spellings (www.crossboweducation.com) is helpful for this. Cut out captions and headings in different typefaces and fonts to help show how they can convey different messages and can be used to meet a variety of objectives. Advertisements are a useful resource. Logos can be used when writing about, for example, food and later when learning about persuasive writing.

Cuttings and photographs from magazines, OHPs and videos are also useful to help generate descriptive vocabulary orally in the class and to help name the objects shown. They are particularly useful for those with word naming difficulties. Raiding the toy-box is another useful resource to generate vocabulary. Chatter Boxes help to develop these skills (www.LDAlearning.com).

When brainstorming for vocabulary the words can be written by the teacher on the blackboard or interactive whiteboard. Pupils can be given a print-out and use these spellings later when writing has been discussed. Objects such as an orange, a comb, a pair of scissors, a clock and a bag of rice can be handed out to the class. A pupil is chosen to say five things about the object he has been given. Then all the pupils write five sentences about that object, without naming it. Gather up the objects and put them on the teacher's desk. Then the teacher reads aloud a description written by a child. She then asks an individual pupil to identify the specific object from the description. This activity helps to develop listening skills as well as spoken language skills. LDA Sound Stories use cards and cassettes to develop auditory sequencing memory skills.

To teach writing instructions and procedures, use a multi-sensory activity involving role-play to model and mime a series of steps, for example writing a letter. Write a brief letter, fold it, then put it in an envelope. Stick down the flap, put the address on the envelope. Stick on a postage stamp. Then ask the pupil to say six words about what he watched. The teacher puts the spellings on the board. The pupil then writes six sentences using the imperative form of the verb, such as 'Take a sheet of paper', and continues to describe the actions he watched. This helps to develop sequential thinking skills as well as visual awareness, especially if a video clip is used.

Glove puppets are another useful resource. Children can re-enact a well-known fairy tale such as 'Cinderella'. Then they can be asked to retell the story using their own words. Those with good visual skills respond to seeing objects associated with the story – white mice, a pumpkin, a coach. These can be miniature cutouts from a computer graphics package (www.microsoftoffice.com).

To develop narrative skills ask a pupil to describe last night's episode of a favourite television programme such as *Pop Idol*. Then ask another pupil to paraphrase what the first pupil said. This also helps to develop short-term memory skills as well as expressive language skills. It also helps to develop listening skills. A video clip could be shown first.

Many dyslexic pupils have inordinate difficulty with using even basic punctuation. It is not unusual for them to write a page of A4 without one full stop. To help overcome this tendency work on the three main types of sentences, simple, compound and complex, using 'meaningful contexts' such as their own writing. Give them a piece of writing which has used 'and' instead of full stops. Read the passage aloud without punctuation. Then ask the pupil to highlight the 'ands'. Then re-read the passage aloud with the punctuation. Ask them to divide the passage into sentences. This is also a multi-sensory approach to teaching punctuation. The Punctuation Show is a CD-ROM which has multi-sensory applications (www.sherston.com).

Aesop's fable 'The hare and the tortoise' can be read during shared reading. TAG Living Books (www.taglearning.com) has a CD-ROM suitable for this. The children make up their own fable after brainstorming and revision of their factsheet for recounts. This can then be illustrated with computerised graphics.

A traditional fairy tale such as 'Little Red Riding Hood' can be read to the class. Pupils can then be asked to rewrite it from, for example, the wolf's point of view.

Nursery rhymes are accessible and ideal for developing language, including an awareness of rhyme and rhythm. They can be used to model a narrative.

> Jack and Jill went up the hill
> To fetch a pail of water.
> Jack fell down and broke his crown
> And Jill came tumbling after.

Jack and Jill are the characters, the hill is the setting. The plot is about a pail of water and the events are what happens when Jack fell down and the resolution is what happened to Jill.

Using a 'powerful' verb (a verb that goes further than the basic concept) is important for style. Teachers might use the word 'said' and then give a list of about fifteen different alternative verbs. This idea can be demonstrated in a multi-sensory way by asking a pupil to mime a scene such as a classroom row. A cross-curricular link could be made as part of a drama lesson. Someone could 'bang' the door, 'burst' into the room, 'stomp' up to the teacher's desk and 'scrape' his chair as he sits down with a 'thump'. The oral response develops skills. The synonyms can be put on a poster and displayed prominently on the classroom wall for easy reference. A computer print-out can be added to the personal 'writeofax'. Cloze procedures can be used to help develop the use of verbs and adjectives. The pupil could be asked to insert the right verb from a list of ten in the spaces in a passage; likewise with adjectives. This is the modern way of teaching grammar rather than asking children to underline the verbs and adjectives in random sentences. An ICT resource is Sherston's Grammar Show (www.sherston.com).

Cutting out and studying advertisements and slogans develops an awareness and understanding of persuasive writing (as does watching television advertisements). They can be stored as models under different categories. Later pupils can design and make an advertisement for the sixth-form disco or for their favourite trainers. They can make a poster for a campaign to prevent battery hens being kept in small cages.

The computer art package Kid Pix Studio (www/taglearning.com) is useful for producing advertisements, brochures and flow charts which are motivational and give a very professional impression, creating confidence and a sense of achievement. They can be used effectively in classroom displays.

The concepts of fact and opinion can be introduced at an early age. Work on this by discussing the jingles children hear on the radio and television. Generate further examples from class members.

Exercises on 'incomplete sentences' which the pupil has to finish off, such as 'The firemen wears (?) [a helmet] and he uses (?) [a hose] to put out (?) [fires]', improve word naming and vocabulary skills. StoryBoards (www.LDAlearning.com) help children visualise and sequence ideas and develop the essential elements of stories.

Build up a portfolio of coloured pictures from magazines and brochures. Laminate them and keep them in files in categories such as footballers, pop stars, soap characters and media personalities. They can be distributed and children can choose to tell the class about David Beckham or the Simpsons. This often helps even the most tongue-tied pupil to talk about his idol. Microsoft's Creative Writer 2 has a number of useful resources such as Getting Ideas (www.microsoft.com). This has pictures classified into themes such as adventure, mystery and sport which can be used to write a story.

Descriptive writing skills can be developed by showing pictures on numbered cards of well-known landmarks such as Edinburgh Castle or the Eiffel Tower. Then shuffle them. The pupils each choose a numbered card. Using an interactive whiteboard to show these landmarks provides a strong visual stimulus. Then pupils are asked to write six sentences about the picture on their card without naming the landmark. The sentences are then read aloud, which also helps to develop listening skills. The pupil whose description is recognised by the most pupils is the winner. A prize adds spice and interest to the activity. Children enjoy these activities hugely and the multi-sensory teaching approach appeals to individuals' different learning styles.

Another useful multimedia resource is a video. Turn it on without the sound and play a sequence of events. Then switch it off and ask the pupils to guess what the characters might have been talking about. This could be a popular film such as Disney's *101 Dalmatians* or an extract from a television series such as *Dad's Army*. The British Film

Institute's Education resources pack Story Shorts Teachers' Guide shows teachers how to tie in film clips and television programmes when teaching literacy.

Ask the pupils what they would ask Jamie Oliver or J.K. Rowling if they walked in through the classroom door. They could write about this for homework or older pupils could do it as an interview.

Teach the pupil with good spoken skills and poor written skills to use a cassette recorder. It needs practice, just as dictating a letter does for an adult or even, for some individuals, leaving a message on the answering machine. Digital recorders such as an Olympus (www.dyslexic.com) can transfer dictated text to the computer.

Encourage use of the five senses in descriptive writing, for example about climbing Ben Nevis or visiting the Tower of London.

To teach adjectives and to heighten awareness of similes and metaphors help to compose a comparative poem as suggested in the NLS resource materials such as:

> He is funnier than Lee Evans on a banana skin.
> He is slimmer than a stick insect on a diet.

This helps to create an awareness of and develop descriptive writing.

Descriptive writing can be modelled, for example, by reading an extract from Clive King's perennial favourite Stig of the Dump, which gives a vivid account of when 'the ground gave away' as Barney stands by the edge of the pit.

A useful and amusing idea is to go through the letters of the alphabet from A to Z to generate descriptive language. For example, writing a story about 'My granny's dog' could produce 'he is awful and angry', 'he is weird and woolly'.

Computer graphics make composition more vivid and help generate enthusiasm and fun, making the experience more memorable, especially for good visualisers.

Pupils can also be introduced to writing about personal feelings and opinions and to recording events. The teacher or teaching assistant helps with brainstorming, providing prompts and background information and writing the children's one-word responses and short phrases randomly on the board, interactive whiteboard or paper. Older children can brainstorm in pairs. It is useful to match a good writer with a child who has good oral skills. Teaching assistants can play a major role in implementing many of the processes. Then the various contributions can be drawn together and divided into paragraphs. These can be numbered and the vocabulary can be matched to the paragraphs.

What stumbling blocks obstruct poor writers and cause specific challenges?

- Misreading titles and not following instructions accurately
- difficulties in processing information, including storing and organisation
- failure to identify the correct form and layout required
- lack of planning
- fear of the blank page and a tendency to panic sometimes because of word retrieval difficulties
- finding it hard to get started
- poor drafting and revision of contents

- the use of restricted vocabulary by writers who think they cannot spell, often due to previous experience of overemphasis on secretarial aspects
- inappropriate use of paragraphs
- failure to invent characters who are plausible and who express feelings
- inappropriate use of language, vocabulary, grammar, figures of speech
- poor proofreading because of a tendency to 'read' what was meant rather than what is on the page
- slow writing speed, making it difficult to complete assignments within the time allowed.

Children need a selection of strategies including models of writing forms to write successfully. It is important to be mindful of the different learning styles, visual, auditory or kinaesthetic, of individual pupils. These often ultimately influence the type of plan they find most useful. How children use plans varies with age and experience as well as cognitive ability. Talk ideas through with him before he attempts to write an essay plan. This can take away his fear of the blank page. Oral rehearsal is important because if you can't say it you won't be able to write it (Ott, 2001a). Essay planning is now taught as part of guided writing in the NLS. The SATs booklet for the writing test has a separate planning page endorsing the importance of making a written plan and submitting it to the examiner. In the past candidates were often not required to hand in their plan even if they had been provided with a piece of rough paper for it in the examination room, for example in the Common Entrance examination set by public schools. In reality this meant that many children omitted this vital stage underpinning the construction of their composition.

Encourage children to write their plan at the top of the page for easy reference. Some children find it helpful if the plan is written on the left-hand page of an A4 school exercise book. They then write on the opposite right-hand page. Alternatively they can use file paper. Those with sequencing difficulties need to constantly keep an eye on the plan when doing an essay, test or examination. Numbered paragraphs help them keep their place and remind them to use paragraphs. Plans are props and a simple but powerful means of helping the nervous writer put his foot on the essay-writing ladder and move up one step at a time. Learning to plan and to use planning strategies when writing is an important skill for all pupils but is crucial for those with SpLD.

'The gruesome twosome' (Figure 18) are a reminder to 'think before you ink or they'll kick up a stink'. These two characters constantly wave their banner to impress on writers the importance of always making a plan before they write. This is important for all writers and is a life-support line for delicate writers and for those with underdeveloped or fragile writing skills as well as those prone to writing phobia. Pupils need to learn and use different types of plans for different types of writing and to match planning strategies to their individual learning styles.

Figure 18 'The gruesome twosome'.

Code of practice for good essay planners

Display the following prominently on the classroom wall or put it on a pin-board at home. Discuss its significance:

'Time spent in planning is never wasted'

'A good plan makes a good essay'

- Writers need to consider which of the main types of essay is indicated by the title. Will it be a narrative, telling a real or imaginary story, for example 'The lost cat'? A title such as 'Humphrey, the Prime Minister's cat' requires a descriptive essay calling on the five senses to paint a picture in words. 'Cats' suggests a factual essay, requiring all the main facts about cats. 'Should cats be used in laboratories for scientific research?' indicates that an argumentative essay is required in which both points of view should be discussed.
- Who is telling the story and who is the audience?
- Who are the main characters? The following checklist is helpful for beginner writers:

  - What is his name?
  - How old is he?
  - What is his appearance like?
  - Where does he live?
  - How does he like to dress?
  - What is his job?
  - What sort of personality does he have?
  - Does he have any particular mannerisms?
  - How does he behave?
  - What do other people think of him?
  - What typical things would he say?

  Ideas can be generated and modelled from examples in texts such as Terence Blacker's description of MS Wiz, Millionaire or Jacqueline Wilson's Ruby and Garnet in Double Act.
- What is the setting? This should include a description and details about the name, place, time (a short time scale – a week or month – works better). Use the senses of seeing, hearing and smell to describe the scene. Extracts from J.K. Rowling's descriptions of the start of term banquet in Harry Potter and the Philosopher's Stone can be read. A film clip of Roald Dahl's Charlie and the Chocolate Factory could be used.
- What is the story about? A good plot has a trigger to get the action moving and it develops. Four events are sufficient. It works well to think in terms of scenes as in a film.
- How is the story going to begin and how is it going to end? It could begin with a quotation or dialogue. 'Where's Papa going with that axe?', the opening line of E.B. White's Charlotte's Web, arouses the reader and helps to create atmosphere. Roald Dahl gets straight to the point in Matilda: 'It is a funny thing about mothers and fathers. Even when their own child is the most disgusting little blister you could ever imagine they think that he or she is wonderful'. Examples of authors' opening lines can be collected and recorded as models for later use.
- What is the critical event?
- How is the atmosphere built up?
- What happens as a result?
- How is the situation resolved?
- What will the ending be? This could refer back to the title. There could be a moral or there could be lessons to be learned.

The major approaches to planning

I Written plans which are traditionally written down in note form

The simplest plan is Sid's Super Spidergram (Figure 19) which can be drawn by hand or by using a software package. The title is written in the spider's body. This works well when the vocabulary and ideas generated by the class during oral discussion are jotted down on the spider's legs, initially by the teacher using an interactive whiteboard or by the teaching assistant and eventually by the pupil himself. Later paragraph headings will be numbered.

Figure 19 Super Sid's Spidergram Plan.

Another version of this plan which is more sophisticated because of its emphasis on paragraphs, is shown in Figure 20.

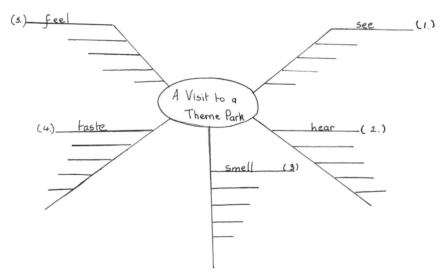

Figure 20

The plan for the story about the millennium celebrations can be generated on the computer. It has a multi-sensory dimension, drawing on the five senses as a result of modelling by an adult (Figure 21).

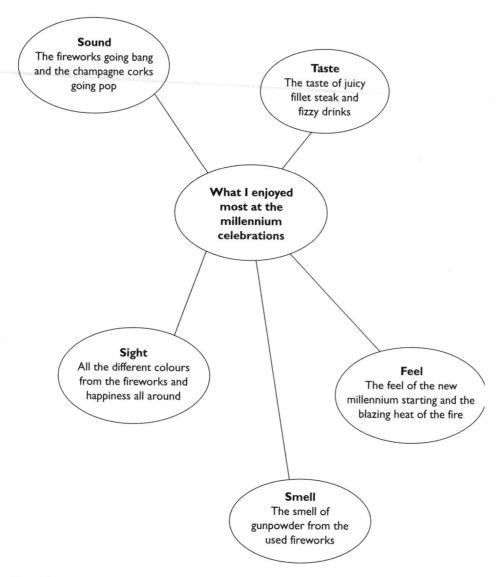

Figure 21

Pupils can follow the sequence of ideas as well as having the keywords and the spellings. Young children may need reminding that they can make up their story. It does not have to be true. They may find it difficult to embellish, borrow ideas or 'add on' to personal experiences. Alternatively they may prefer to make their narratives purely autobiographical. This tendency can be overcome by reading examples of good stories and attending to their features. A demonstration of how the teacher and writers gather ideas from a variety of external sources also helps. Narrative writing is the backbone of much of the early writing of children in many subject areas in school including English, history and Religious Studies (RS).

Doctor Do-Little's skeleton essay plan uses the format that says a story has a beginning, a middle and an ending. Some dyslexic pupils take this concept literally.

1. Orientation
2. Complication

3. Series of events
4. Resolution
5. Conclusion

Figure 22 Doctor Do-Lots' prescription plan.

It is much better to use his big brother *Doctor Do-Lots' Prescription Plan*. This acts as a trigger to set the scene, including the time and place. It is a reminder to decide who the characters are and to describe their appearance, feelings and behaviour. The plan also includes a conflict, climax and a resolution to the story. These five points can be numbered and used as paragraph headings. Many pupils find remembering to use paragraphs difficult. Numbering them on the plan acts as a reminder to use them when writing and they can be checked when proofreading. Remembering to indent for a new paragraph is difficult for some. When a word processor has been used, the appearance of a page of text without a break can sometimes be a reminder to paragraph properly during proofreading.

Writers need a lot of practice in learning what a paragraph is, where and how it begins and when it ends. Beginner writers need to learn about topic (key) sentences which define the content and are then followed by more sentences explaining and elaborating on the topic.

The 'Just So' Easy plan uses 'The six serving men's questions' taken from Rudyard Kipling's poem (Figure 23). The 'Just So' Easy plan can be used for a title such as 'The School Fire Alarm Rang':

> What happened? Who was involved? When did it happen? Where did it happen? Why was it such a disaster? How much damage did it cause?

This plan can also be used for non-fiction writing, such as a report.

Figure 23 The 'Just So' Easy plan.

2 Graphic plans

These come in many forms such as pictures, shapes, mindmaps, frames, tree diagrams, webs. They are usually known as graphic organisers and are used for different purposes such as those described by Hasenstab *et al.* (1994) who give twenty-six different examples including some of the following which can be used when writing stories.

Cause and effect

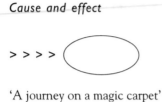

'A journey on a magic carpet'

Order of events

'Our school trip to the Science Museum'

Main points of the story

I Introduction	2 Something happens	3 Exciting part	4 Sorts itself out	5 Conclusion

'I looked at the letter again, I could not believe my eyes'

Orbit

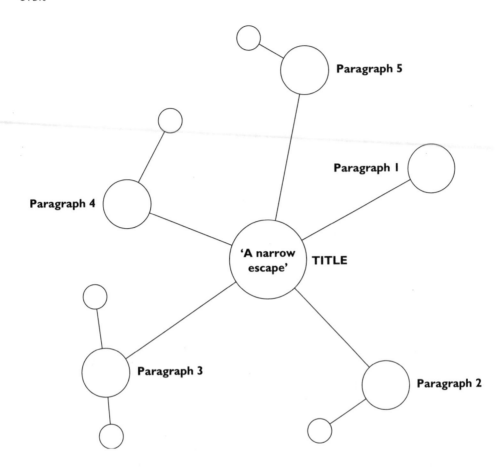

Tree diagram

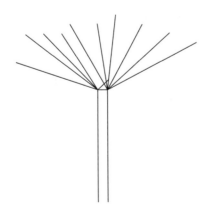

'A storm in Burnham Beeches'

Story board

Scene 1	Scene 2	Scene 3
Scene 4	Scene 5	Scene 6

'The centenary school fête'

Mindmaps

Mind maps™ were originally devised by Buzan and are now variously known as concept or ideas maps. They can be hand drawn on a sheet of unlined paper used in the landscape position, with the title in the centre (see Figure 24). Paragraph headings are used as the main lines which join to the centre. 'Twig' lines with subheadings and keywords branch off from these. Colour and symbols are used. Text, pictures and colour digital photographs can be used as well. They can also be generated on a computer packages such as Softease Ideas Map (www.softease.com).

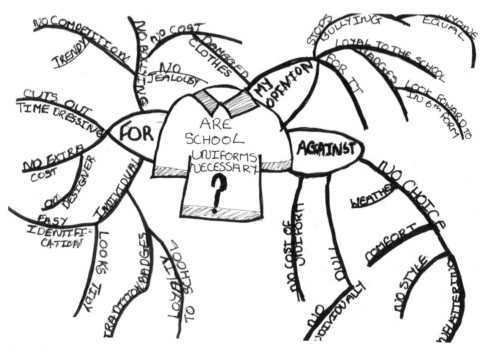

Figure 24

Hints and suggestions for using graphic organisers for genre theory (adapted from Moline, 2001)

Graphic organisers have a strong visual form and are made from hand-drawn diagrams, computer graphics or software packages for mindmapping, some of which can also be used with an interactive whiteboard (Inspiration v 7.6; Kidspiration v 2.1; www.iansyst.co.uk).

Genre	Structure	Example
1 Procedures	Storyboard	How to make spaghetti bolognese
	Flowchart	How is paper made?
2 Recounts	Timeline	The day we went to Alton Towers
	Storyboard	The Gunpowder Plot
3 Explanations	Storyboard	How does the heart work?
	Web diagram	How do governments get money to run the country?
4 Persuasion	Word wheels	Be a vegetarian
	Flow diagrams	Buy British beef
5 Non-chronological reports	Word wheels	Foot-and-mouth disease
	Tree diagrams	Tourism in the Lake District
6 Discussion	Venn diagram	Should school uniforms be compulsory?
	Web diagram	Should NHS patients pay for their food when they are in hospital?

Graphic organisers have become popular for teaching children to write in fiction and non-fiction genres in many areas of the curriculum and can also be used for note taking. They are extremely effective for strong visualisers. Norris et al. (1998) showed that some children rely on the visuals to help them think about what comes next and what to say when they write. Many dyslexic pupils are strong visualisers. Anecdotal evidence comes from the high percentage who go to art colleges. But it is misguided to assume that mind-mapping and using graphic organisers are equally effective for all dyslexic pupils. Mortimer (2004) conceded that 'there is no current empirical evidence to support these suggestions [that dyslexic learners have visuo-spatial talents, and the assumption that dyslexic learners should be taught using visuo-spatial or kinaesthetic learning methods may well disadvantage those individuals who favour a verbal style'.

Checklist for effective writers when planning, drafting, editing and revising

Planning

- Have I read the title carefully and underlined keywords or phrases? Have I been on the look-out for words such as 'compare'? Have I remembered the maxim 'Think before you ink'?

- Did I identify the most appropriate plan? Did I brainstorm for ideas? Have I written a detailed plan in note form or used a graphic organiser for this?

- Have I identified and numbered on the plan where the paragraphs are going to be, for example for each different/new idea, change of time/place or change of speaker when using a dialogue?

- Has my plan included information about the (1) characters (2) setting (3) plot (4) events (5) resolution?

- Have I used a good opening sentence? 'I opened the door and there on the doorstep . . .' or 'I never knew my father's family originally came from Alsace' are examples that create atmosphere.

- Have I used just a few main characters, three perhaps at most, and then centred the plot round them? It is worth remembering that a catchy, wacky name often helps to trigger the imagination and catch the reader's eye. Sometimes it works well if the main character is described but not named: this helps to spark the reader's curiosity.

- Does my writing use description of what the characters are thinking, saying and feeling?

- Does the dialogue sound plausible? Is it appropriate for the character? Does it add to the story line or is it just 'padding' which is punctuated too often with 'said'?

- Have I described the characters' physical appearance, clothes, accent and peculiar mannerisms? Have I established who is sad, funny, nasty or 'mysterious'? Adjectives and adverbs for description can be built up from personal and shared reading and filed in a 'writeofile' or on computer as in a rogues' gallery.

- How have I dealt with the plot? Could I have borrowed some ideas from a book, play, film or programme I have watched on television? Is it exciting, entertaining, has it plenty of action with no more than three sub-plots? The plot should be connected to a series of incidents that relate back to the title. Does the whole plot fit together and does it have a convincing ending?

- Have I used too much or too little dialogue? Have I tried to use the names of the speakers (a way of avoiding some of the problems caused by mixing first and third person pronouns)? (Dyslexic writers sometimes confuse who was saying what.)

- Have I remembered to write in the past tense? (This may sound very prescriptive but forestalls the problems some dyslexic writers have with verb tenses.) Have I used the personal pronouns consistently? Have I used 'connectives' such as 'later' or 'nevertheless' to tie my story together? Have I used descriptive words including adjectives and adverbs?

- Have I worked out a conclusion to my essay that leaves my audience satisfied, amused, entertained? This could include referring back to the title and using a moral, such as 'I will never do that again' or a thought-provoking question 'Should she ever have opened that door?'

- Have I tried to avoid the use of hackneyed endings such as 'I opened my eyes and I realised it was a dream'. Endings used by different authors can be filed in the personal writing file and used as models.

Drafting

This involves writing different versions to develop, improve and change a piece of writing.

- Keep drafts to display alongside the final copy to highlight their importance in the writing process.
- It is important that pupils are reminded to follow the plan they have written.
- They should use the words gathered during the brainstorming to help drafting.
- Children need to be encouraged to write what they know and want to say.

> The teacher who demands neat writing, correct punctuation and perfect spelling while children are learning to master new skills runs the risk of promoting the continuation of short boring texts written by children who have no interest in the message, only what the teacher demands.
>
> (First Steps, 1997)

This was also a key finding of the National Writing Project (1990).

- Novice writers and dyslexic writers need to be reassured and told not to worry about their spelling and mechanics such as punctuation when drafting. If they are unsure of how to spell a word put a question mark beside it. It should be checked later with a dictionary or a handheld spellchecker or given by an adult (depending on individual current spelling ability).
- Encourage the child to 'have a go' at the spellings and to use a phonetic approximation as this will encourage those with a good spoken vocabulary to use it in their writing. Too much emphasis on correct spelling can interfere with the creative processes, particularly for those with sequencing and working memory problems. Multi-tasking is challenging.
- Remind him to write on every second line. This makes re-reading easier and helps when inserting corrections when revising and editing.

Review and revise

- This needs to be done with the help of an adult. Text can easily be restructured and moved about using a word processor.
- Children need to be made aware that the purpose of revising a text is to improve the content. There is a difference between picking up a missed full stop or an occasional spelling error and changing sentences, adding phrases and moving them around.
- This activity needs to be done with sensitivity and an awareness of the development stage of writing skills as well as an understanding of the individual's specific learning difficulties.
- The child should ask: 'Does what I have written make sense?' He may need help to identify words omitted or incomplete sentences.
- He should then ask: 'Have I given my audience enough information to be able to follow the story?'
- Then 'Are my characters lively and interesting?' Help may be necessary to encourage the use of more and better adjectives and adverbs.
- 'Have I kept to the point and remembered the purpose of my writing and/or have I given enough detail?'

- Can the language be improved, for example by using strong verbs, similes or metaphors?

The child then incorporates the improvements and alterations discussed above.

Teach him shorthand and abbreviations for editing to save time: ∧ denotes an omission of a word; ⋏ denotes insert letter; // denotes new paragraph.

Some children may be able to pick up some of their own spelling errors with a little prompting. Some very dyslexic pupils may need help with identifying their spelling errors. A light touch when correcting spelling errors is more constructive than marking every spelling mistake. A useful strategy can be to identify personal persistent errors such as words from the high frequency list and to target a few of these for correction. Prompts like 'Can you tell me what is wrong with "thay"?' may trigger the correction that it should have an 'e'. Putting 'sp' beside a word such as 'senteeary' can be futile for the speller who does not know what letter 'centenary' begins with. The *Dictionary of Perfect Spelling* (Maxwell, 2005) lists words as they sound in red and gives the correct spelling in black in a parallel column. This is very useful for those who mostly spell phonetically. Other children can be encouraged to check spellings in their personal 'spellofax' which includes a personal list of their own spelling demons. Older children should be encouraged to use a handheld spellchecker for handwritten work and the spellchecker on the computer when they are word processing.

Practical suggestions for proofreading with the C-O-P-S strategy

- Children can be reminded to use the C-O-P-S proofreading strategy (Figure 25) to check that they have used capital letters appropriately, not omitted words or letters

C	Capital Letters
O	Omissions
P	Punctuation
S	Spellings

Figure 25

and have checked their punctuation and spelling. It heightens awareness if the child uses different colour pens for this – green for punctuation and grammar errors and red for spelling corrections. Children can be given an incentive such as the award of a star or a housepoint if they can find and correct six spelling errors in their writing.

- The spelling of the past tense of verbs ending in 'ed' is a perennial problem for many dyslexic spellers. They need to be reminded that when they hear /t/, /d/, /id/ at the end of a verb it is usually spelt by adding 'ed'.
- Apostrophes can be corrected with assistance when their attention is focused on punctuation. Contractions can be corrected with the help of an oral prompt. For example 'the dog lost it's tail' can be corrected when the child is given the prompt – 'the dog lost it is (it's) tail'.
- Speech marks can be checked and corrected by rehearsing the five features of their use. Children may be challenged to remember to use a capital letter for the first word inside the speech marks and a punctuation mark before they are closed.

Most of the foregoing comments apply to work which has been written by hand. The word processor can be used to correct many errors. The spellchecker and grammar checker are very helpful but not infallible. Some dyslexic learners find them difficult to use, for example when a list of spelling suggestions is given. James and Draffan (2004) found that 'if the correct spelling appeared first in the list 84 per cent were correctly chosen'. Problems arise because of difficulties with reading the options and with keeping the target word in working memory. Poor visual perception can result in the incorrect option being chosen. The Franklin Literacy Word Bank Children's Dictionary and Thesaurus (www.franklin.com/uk) was found to be the best handheld spellchecker option for dyslexic users.

How do teachers assess writing skills and mark writing assignments?

Children will be assessed on their ability to:

1 Write imaginative, interesting and thoughtful texts;
2 Produce texts which are appropriate to task, reader and purpose;
3 Organise and present whole texts effectively, sequencing and structuring information, ideas and events;
4 Construct paragraphs and use cohesion within and between paragraphs;
5 Vary sentences for clarity, purpose and effect;
6 Write with technical accuracy of syntax and punctuation in phrases, clauses and sentences;
7 Select appropriate and effective vocabulary;
8 Use correct spelling.

(QCA, 2003b)

Marking Key Stage 2

Long writing test

The following should be considered:

1   sentence structure and punctuation (8 marks maximum)
2   text structure and organisation (8 marks maximum)
3   composition and effect (12 marks maximum)
4   handwriting (3 marks maximum).

Short writing test

The following should be considered:

1   sentence structure, punctuation and text organisation (4 marks maximum)
2   composition and effect (8 marks maximum).

Spelling is assessed in a separate specific test at Key Stages 1 and 2. In Key Stage 3 spelling is assessed in pupils' writing of 'complex words rather than [by] counting errors'.

Marking Key Stage 3 Extended Writing

The following should be considered (Key Stage 3 National Strategy, 2001b):

1   Are paragraph breaks used?
2   Does the order makes sense?
3   Do paragraphs start where there is a shift in topic, time or perspective?
4   Are paragraphs coherent, i.e. contain information that hangs together?
5   Is there 'topping and tailing' – key sentences, a concluding paragraph?
6   Are connectives used as links between paragraphs, e.g. 'Next . . .', 'Another reason . . .', 'The next day . . .'.

The NLS uses this list diagnostically when assessing writing to establish what support pupils require. Coordination Group Publications (www.cgpbooks.co.uk) produce SATs practice papers. They include an answer book with a mark scheme and hints for users.

Guidelines for teachers when marking narrative text

- Avoid using a red pen for marking. The alternative is to use a pencil to correct a word-processed or handwritten text.
- Limit the number of corrections to match the pupil's level of skill and differentiate according to the degree of learning difficulty.
- Do not correct or draw attention to a grammatical or punctuation error if he has not yet learned the rule, for example the use of the apostrophe for possession. He will not remember the rule and will be made to feel negative about his work.
- It helps to encourage younger children when doing handwritten work if the correction is put on a post-it note. If he is working in pencil he can erase his error and make the

correction when he revises and proofreads his work. It is important not to under-estimate the effect that constant exposure to one's own mistakes (particularly when the same errors occur routinely, as they do in dyslexic pupils' writing) has on morale and self-esteem.

- Some teachers deal with corrections by writing a target at the bottom of the page such as:

'Target: to check that you have used capital letters for all names of people.' This can be included in the child's IEPs.

- Avoid writing 'sp' beside a word. Give the correction or ignore the mistake.
- Write comments about what was 'good' about the writing rather than using ticks or stars.

Checklist of questions for a good writing detective

Figure 26 The good writing detective.

- Have I read through the whole paragraph/story before I attempted editing?
- Have I read what I have written aloud/or sub-vocally to check that it makes sense and that I have not left words out?
- Have I begun sentences with a capital letter?
- Have I used a question mark when I am 'asking' something and a full stop when I am 'telling' something?
- Have I checked homophones such as 'here'/'hear' using (if necessary) a mnemonic such as 'I hear with an ear'?
- Have I checked the spellings I am unsure of by using my personal 'spellofax', dictionary, handheld spellchecker or word processor?
- Have I checked the punctuation, especially in dialogue?
- Have I used legible handwriting and differentiated for example between 'e' and 'i'?
- Have I used a 12-point font which is easier to read?
- Have I double-spaced my writing?
- Have I added graphics where appropriate?
- Have I finalised the editing?
- Have I saved a copy if I am word-processing on the computer?
- Have I made a print-out to be given to the teacher for marking?
- Have I kept a copy of the corrected version in my personal writing file for reference?

These questions can be adapted, modified and differentiated to meet the needs and skills of SEN pupils.

Guidelines for helping apprentice writers

The NLS (1998) *Framework for Teaching* puts great emphasis on the teacher modelling shared and guided writing. This has developed from Lev Vygotsky's (1978) theory that 'what a child can do with assistance today he will be able to do by himself tomorrow'. It promoted the theory that children learn like apprentices by following in the footsteps of their master.

The teacher:

- writes the keywords or phrases when brainstorming
- provides 'scaffolds' (Bruner, 1986) to support writing forms and processes which would otherwise be too difficult for the writer to implement, including pro-forma plans and/or writing frames
- models the writing process including analysing examples of good writing in texts. She helps children to find examples of synonyms of words in the thesaurus when writing descriptions
- does guided writing involving one-to-one collaboration (possibly the teaching assistant takes the teacher's place) which Graves (1983) called 'conferencing'. The adult helps with the revision and improvements that need to be made. The NLS (1998) was influenced in its recommendation of the use of guided writing by Hillocks (1986)
- needs to play a positive role in motivating the writer by always find something positive to say first. Praise should come before criticism whenever possible for all pupils but is crucial for reluctant or timid writers
- gives dyslexic and dyspraxic writers more time and realistic targets. It takes them longer to process ideas and to generate vocabulary and this may also affect the quantity and quality of their writing.

Top twenty tips for successful writers

1 Make a written plan and follow it.

2 Try not to end a sentence with a preposition ('on', 'under').

3 Verbs should always agree with their subjects: 'he and I are good friends'.

4 Avoid clichés and hackneyed expressions and never use slang.

5 Try not to start a sentence with the conjunctions 'and', 'because'.

6 Avoid contrived use of figures of speech.

7 Try not to use parentheses, however useful they (usually) are.

8 Avoid contractions ('won't', 'can't') in formal writing except in dialogue.

9 Be careful when making absolute statements or generalising: 'everyone hates bananas'.

10 Eliminate unnecessary commas such as the Oxford comma (before 'and' in a list).

11 Be careful about making too many comparisons as they can be as bad as clichés.

12 Use apostrophes correctly: 'it's', for 'it is'. Beware of using the 'greengrocer's' comma: 'cucumber's and apple's'.

13 Avoid mixed metaphors.

14 Use quotations sparingly.

15 Use plain English. Avoid complex words.

16 Remember to give sources when using them.

17 Avoid plagiarism – stealing other people's ideas – particularly from the Internet.

18 Use description and figures of speech to add colour and variation.

19 Remember to paragraph properly.

20 Proofread carefully with the C-O-P-S to check for capital letters, omissions, punctuation and spelling.

Genre theory for non-fiction writing

Joan Rothery and Fran Christie were the driving force in the creation of what is known as the 'genre theory' for non-fiction. It 'refers to different types of writing each with its own specific characteristics' (NLS, 1998).

- Its purpose is to inform, enlighten and instruct the reader.
- The contents are arranged coherently.
- There are different structures and layouts for different forms of factual writing such as letters or newspaper reports.
- It should be taught in meaningful contexts and children should be encouraged to write about their own experiences.
- Texts follow certain language conventions including grammatical structures. For example, the imperative is used when writing instructions.
- SATs examination papers at each of the Key Stages include a variety of different genres in the writing task.
- One of the most influential messages from the NLS is that children need 'explicit teaching' including learning about non-fiction genres.

Critics such as children's author Philip Pullman argue that teaching has become too prescriptive in many classrooms. Some professionals regard the emphasis on direct instruction as well as target setting as an infringement of their teaching skills and personal judgement. But although there is evidence that some great artists never had a drawing lesson or that some great chefs never use a cookery book, common sense tells us that the vast majority of individuals learn skills, including writing, by being taught by someone who knows more about the subject and has had greater experience than they have. This applies to the majority of writers but it is particularly important for poor or reluctant writers who need to be shown how to proceed and given practical examples rather than being left to flounder in a sea of ignorance.

The main non-fiction genres

There are a number of different possible sources for a list of non-fiction genres, including the National Curriculum (2000), the NLS (1998) *Framework for Teaching* and Key Stage 3 National Strategy (2001b). The lists they provide can be slimmed down to a more manageable size such as that in Derewianka (1996):

- Procedures
- Recounts
- Stories [narratives]
- Explanations
- Persuasion
- Discussion
- Information Reports.

Factsheets with guidelines for teaching the main non-fiction genres to pupils with SpLD

- Discuss and outline the objective for the particular genre.
- Explain keywords and give definitions. Put these on the board.
- Explain the language features and the processes. Write these as a factsheet for inclusion in the personal writing file for review and revision.
- Model the process orally. Support with a text which can be annotated to highlight key features and used for later reference.
- Make a plan which can be based on the outline in the factsheet.

The plan can be made using a writing frame, graphic organiser or mindmap and can be handwritten or computer generated. Many of the genres are more easily undertaken on a word processor.

It is important to point out that writing does not always fit neatly into the categories taught using National Strategy guidelines. Writing can include a mixture of features from a variety of genres.

Factsheet and hints for writing instructions or procedures

Purpose

To tell someone how to do, play or make something.

Language features

Use imperative verbs, the simple present tense and personal pronouns.

---

1   Make a list of the materials, ingredients, utensils, equipment or tools needed. Put these in a box under the heading.
2   Instructions are often written as a list and sometimes include labelled diagrams.
3   Number, bullet or use letters for each instruction.
4   Write the method as a series of steps, in the same order as you do them.
5   Begin each instruction with an imperative verb (a useful mnemonic is to call these the 'bossy' verbs).
6   Write short simple sentences.
7   Good instructions are clear and easy to follow.

Examples of possible titles

1   How to mend a bicycle puncture
2   How to make a cheese sandwich

Factsheet and hints for writing recounts

Purpose

To give a personal account of an event or something the writer witnessed or experienced.

Language features

Use the past tense, adverbs of time, the pronouns 'I' and 'we' and connectives such as 'In the beginning . . .', 'Later . . .', 'Afterwards . . .'.

1   Retell the events in chronological order.
2   Tell someone about the events as if they had been present.
3   This genre can be used for a newspaper report, magazine article, biography, obituary, autobiography, diary entry.
4   Include the 'six serving men's' questions in the plan and answer: When? Where? Why? What? Who? How did it happen? Give enough background information for the reader to understand and follow the recount.
5   Use words such as 'beginning', 'next', 'later', 'afterwards', 'meanwhile', 'finally'.

Use a 'timeline', flowchart or cards on a washing line plan.

continued

Examples of possible titles

1   The sponsored walk
2   The foot-and-mouth outbreak

Factsheet and hints for writing a newspaper report

Purpose

To inform and entertain your audience.

Language features

Use the past tense.

1   The title is called a headline and should catch the reader's eye.
2   Consider your readers (audience). Who are you writing the article for?
3   Use subheadings which are like paragraph headings. Set the report out in paragraphs.
4   Give a summary of the main points in the first paragraph.
5   Give background details including full names and ages of the people mentioned and enough facts to enable understanding of the events.
6   Include at least three eye-witness quotes, using direct speech to make the article more credible.
7   In your report answer Rudyard Kipling's questions: what? why? when? where? who? how did it happen?

Examples of possible titles

1   Lottery winner helps fund trip to Disneyland for cancer sufferer
2   Nightmare experience of girl trapped in an underground cave

---

Factsheet and hints for writing a myth, fable or legend

A myth is an ancient or traditional story about gods/goddesses or heroes and may include magic/evil. An example is the story of Icarus and Daedalus. A fable is a story about animals which usually has a moral and teaches a lesson, such as 'The hare and the tortoise'. A legend is a story which is believed to have some basis in reality, such as the stories of King Arthur and the knights of the Round Table.

Purpose

To write the events of the story in chronological order with an explanation for the outcome.

Language features

Use the past tense and adjectives to describe the characters and the setting.

1   The hero of the story is usually a god or goddess.
2   They may use magic to attain their objective.
3   Evil is done by the gods.
4   The story takes place in ancient times.
5   It explains or gives a reason for what has happened.
6   There is usually a lesson to be learned from the story.

Use a spidergram plan.

Examples of possible titles

1   The fable of the boy who cried Wolf
2   It's never too late to learn

Factsheet and hints for writing explanations

Purpose

To tell how, when and why something happens.

Language features

Explanations often use the present tense and the passive form of the verb. Connective words and phrases such as 'because', 'as a result of' and 'however' are used to say what happened and why. This is a critical feature differentiating an explanation from a description. The third person is used throughout.

1   The audience is the reader who wants to find out why or how something happens.
2   Technical vocabulary is used and defined when necessary.
3   Explanations are usually written in sequence and in paragraphs using connectives such as 'therefore', 'consequently', 'in order to', 'because', 'as a result of'.

continued

4   Use labelled diagrams and flowchart plans.
5   Explanations can be used in leaflets, reference manuals, encyclopaedia entries and reports of experiments in science.

Examples of possible titles

1   How do potatoes grow?
2   The water cycle

Persuasive writing

Establish that there are different kinds of persuasive writing including:

- *advertisements*, designed to persuade people to buy and use one product such as one brand of washing powder rather than another; they feature in magazines and newspapers or on billboards
- *brochures*, which give details including illustrations about different places or things such as holidays or schools
- *letters*, for example a formal letter to the chairman of the Highways Committee of the County Council complaining about the state of the pavements in the town which caused granny to fall and break her leg; these should go straight to the point.
- *political propaganda*, designed to persuade people to vote one way or another, in the form of posters put up in windows, on notice boards, or on large bill-boards or flyers sent to every home in the candidate's constituency describing how he would make the town a better place by improving education and school buildings, introducing better sports facilities and re-equipping old people's homes and libraries
- *charity appeals for cash or sponsorship*, for example letters to all households, known as 'mailshots', sometimes including a free pen or address labels to make giving to the charity seem more appealing; pictures of hungry children or badly treated animals are sometimes included.

Factsheet with hints for persuasive writing

Purpose

To persuade or convince someone to agree with your point of view.

Language features

The present tense is usually used but the future may also be used. Vivid language including adjectives and adverbs are used for descriptive purposes.

1   Make statements and put forward arguments that sound as if everyone agrees with you: 'You know it makes sense.'
2   Only say positive things about the product: 'An apple a day keeps the doctor away'.
3   Repetition reinforces the message.
4   Use vivid language and catchy phrases: 'Clunk! Click! Every trip!'
5   Try to appeal to the reader's emotions.
6   Give statistics to improve credibility.
7   Shock tactics are sometimes used to catch the reader's attention: 'Smoking can seriously damage your health'.

Examples of possible titles

1   Recycling waste paper and saving forests
2   Healthy food in the school canteen

Factsheet and hints for writing advertisements

Purpose

To make arguments to persuade someone to buy or use a product or object.

Language features

The language should be 'snappy' and hold the reader's attention because it is funny and lively.

1   Rhyme and assonance – 'Let the train take the strain' – or slogans or jingles – 'Go to work on an egg' – are effective.
2   Give the attractions and advantages to create a demand.
3   Use photographs, illustrations or logos to catch the reader's eye.
4   The layout is important. The headline should grab the reader's attention. The captions should keep the reader interested and help to develop brand loyalty.
5   Use the word 'you' because it makes it more personal and involves the reader.
6   There must be enough information for the reader to know the cost, where, how to buy and use the product.

Examples of possible titles

1   A poster for the school fête
2   An advertisement for jeans

Factsheet and hints for writing a travel brochure

Purpose

To make the destination sound exciting to visit because of the following:

- accommodation, cost, health factors
- travel facilities
- sports/leisure facilities
- climate
- food
- language
- customs
- scenery
- people.

Use a mindmap or spidergram plan.

Examples of possible titles

1 Come and see the charm of the Emerald Isle
2 Explore London and its unrivalled attractions

Factsheet and hints for writing discussions

Purpose

To give the arguments for and against a particular subject. The writer gives his view in the conclusion (see Figure 27)

Language features

The present tense and strong emotive language can be used.

1 Give background information.
2 Give the arguments in favour with evidence to support your opinion. (Remember one good example is worth a thousand words.)
3 Give the arguments against with evidence to support your opinions.
4 Give your personal opinion or recommendation in the conclusion.

Use 'pro' and 'con' boxes with a plus and a minus sign heading for the plan.

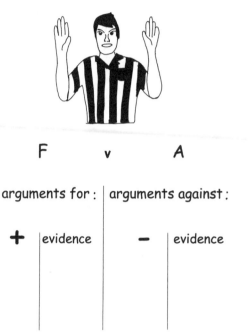

F   v   A

arguments for :   arguments against :

+ evidence   **—** evidence

Figure 27 The referee's F–A plan.

Examples of possible titles

1   Should wind farms be allowed on the Yorkshire Moors?
2   Is a ban on smoking in public places justified?

Factsheet and hints for writing information reports

Purpose

To give factual information about a subject or classification.

Derewianka (1996) recommended using 'information reports' because the term is used 'generally rather loosely to refer to many different types of texts such as school reports'.

Language Features: Use the passive voice and present tense of the verb. Order need not be chronological. The third person pronoun is used. Technical vocabulary is used and should be defined. The title is often written in the plural but deals with one subject.

continued

1   Begin with a definition.
2   Include information about when, where and why something happens. Give various characteristics of the subject.
3   Describe behaviour and functions.
4   Include examples.

Use a spidergram plan.

Examples of possible titles

1   Dinosaurs
2   The Olympic Games

Suggestions for using writing frames as scaffolds

Literacy Progress Unit: Writing Organisation (Key Stage 3 National Strategy, 2001a) includes examples and models of contextualised writing. Skeleton Poster Books for Writing Genres (Palmer, 2001) Skeleton Poster Books for Non-fiction (Palmer, 2001), Skeleton Non-fiction CD-ROM for Interactive Whiteboards (www.LDAlearning.com). The books are Big Books and include the key features of each genre including suggestions for language and form as well as graphic reminders to include when planning.

Many publishers have produced 'writing frames' which are 'templates consisting of starters, connectives and sentence modifiers which offer children a structure for communicating what they want to say' (Lewis and Wray, 1995). They are available as photocopiable resources, CD-ROMs or software packages.

Pelican Shared Writing CD-ROMs include over forty writing frames which are differentiated and are linked to the NLS writing objectives for fiction and non-fiction. There are two CDs for each year group (www.longman.co.uk).

The following are suggestions for using writing frames as scaffolds:

*   Revise the key features of the genre using the appropriate factsheet. Discuss the aim and purpose of the writing and identify the audience. Read a model text and comment on its features and form. This can also be modelled with an interactive whiteboard. *Developing Writing Skills* (Dayus and Ayres, 1999) includes models for each of the six different non-fiction genres, is photocopiable and has worksheets (Developing Writing Skills CD-ROM, www.heinemann.co.uk).
*   The teacher can then model the process on the board or interactive whiteboard while simultaneously explaining what she is writing.
*   She generates contributions from the pupils and writes them on the board.
*   The teacher distributes writing frames.
*   She guides and supports the pupils while they complete these. Some dyslexic pupils may need a teaching assistant to scribe for them.
*   Pupils should then be helped to revise and edit their work. Then they write the final copy.

- Not all children need these frames. Some children find them restrictive once they have mastered the process.
- Dyslexic writers may need to use scaffolds for longer but ultimately they should be seen as a stepping stone to independent writing.
- Scaffolds are particularly effective as a crutch for timid writers at the planning stage.
- They can be adapted and used to 'differentiate' materials and make resources more accessible to pupils with different levels of ability.
- They should be used as a prosthesis for those with a tendency to panic or develop writer's block. They work well with pupils whose exercise books have comments such as 'This is not enough' written on them.
- They help to reduce the fear of a blank page. The scaffolding they provide keeps the bricks in place and helps the pupil build his own writing skills. Like scaffolding on buildings, they should be regarded as temporary measures and should be removed when the pupil has learned the technique or process. However, some poor writers may continue to need them. They improve the quality and quantity of writing as well as developing and helping to internalise writing forms.

Ways and means of awakening and fostering children's interest in poetry

Children at an early age, when made aware, can respond to rhyme and rhythm in language. Georgina at nine months old enjoyed rhymes and action games such as:

Round and round the garden
Like a teddy bear.
One step, two steps,
Tickle me under there.

International research has shown how important rhyme is in the development of later literacy skills. Marching, clapping and playing action games such as 'London Bridge is falling down' helps children to develop an 'ear' for language.

- Read poems to children on a regular basis at home, in the classroom, and in assembly.
- Provide children with anthologies that are age and interest appropriate.
- Choose a 'poet of the week' and read different examples of the work of popular poets such as Michael Rosen and Les Magee.
- Encourage children to write their own poems. Use these for classroom displays.
- Children can be encouraged to enter poetry competitions such as: BBC Radio 4 Young Poetry Competition, BBC Broadcasting House, Bristol; Simon Elvin Young Poet of the Year Awards, The Poetry Society.
- Arrange for a poet to visit the school and to run a workshop showing how to draft, revise and edit their work.
- Arrange a poetry declamation competition in school. Children choose a favourite poem, learn it and recite it. It can be organised in year groups. The best two pupils can be chosen to go forward to a final which could be judged by an outside guest and the winners can perform in front of the whole school.
- Poetry weeks are also popular. Make these more interesting with different themes.

- Class anthologies can be compiled and published. Commercial firms arrange for schools' anthologies to be published.

Toolbox of nuts and bolts for apprentice poets

Alliteration	Use of words in which the same initial letter recurs:

She sells sea shells by the sea shore
The shells she sells are surely sea shells.

Anthology	A collection of poems by different authors, sometimes with a theme, such as war poetry.
Assonance	Verse form where the vowels but not the consonants rhyme or vice versa, sometimes called a half rhyme:

To market, to market to buy a plum cake.
Home again, home again, market is late.

Blank verse	Verse without a rhyme.
Doggerel	Poorly written poetry with little form or meaning.
Figures of speech	Language which evokes a scene or impression by making comparisons: 'All the world's a stage'.
Free verse	Verse with no regular pattern of rhyme, rhythm or line length.
Hyperbole	Words used in an exaggerated way: 'Thanks a million'.
Iambic pentameter	A form of verse in which every second beat is emphasised.
Imagery	Uses words to create a picture in the mind's eye of sounds and emotions by exploiting one or all of the five senses. Comparisons are made by using a simile or metaphor (see below).
Metaphor	A description of something as if it really were what it only resembles: 'She was a tower of strength'.
Onomatopoeia	Uses words which sound like their meaning: 'crash', 'hiss', 'slit'.
Personification	Non-human lifeless objects are treated as if they were human:

Slowly, silently now the moon
Walks the night in her silver shoon.

Poem	All poems have rhythm which can be fast, slow or smooth depending on the mood. Poets often use figures of speech such as similes and metaphors. They frequently use rhyme. Modern poetry often uses free verse which is a non-rhyming form.
Rhyme	Use of the same sounds and same stressed and unstressed syllables at the ends of lines:

> There was an old woman who lived in a shoe,
> She had so many children she did not know what to do.

Rhyming couplets	Two consecutive lines which rhyme and are the same length.

> I had a little nut tree, nothing would it bear
> But a silver nutmeg and a golden pear;
> The King of Spain's daughter came to visit me
> And all for the sake of my little nut tree.

Rhythm	A result of the use of stressed and unstressed syllables. Poems can have different rhythms. Having a regular number of syllables provides a strong rhythm.
Simile	A comparison of one thing with another, usually including 'like' or 'as': 'The old man was as blind as a bat'.
Stanza/verse	A group of lines of poetry, usually four, six or eight. The same pattern is generally used throughout the poem.
Syllable	A beat which has one vowel sound. Words can be divided into different kinds of syllables.

An A–Z of poetry forms

Acrostic	A poem in which the initial letters of each line form a word which can be read vertically. Double acrostics use the first and last letter of each line.
Alphabet poem	A poem in which the initial letters of each line are in alphabetical order. It is usually about a specific topic.
Ballad	A poem which tells a story and is often sung. The lines usually rhyme. Verses may be of varying lengths. Ballads are sometimes called narrative poems because they tell a story, for example Alfred, Lord Tennyson's 'The Charge of the Light Brigade'.
Cinquain	A type of poem, first written by Adelaide Crapsay, which has five lines of twenty-two syllables.
Clerihew	A comic poem, invented by Edward Clerihew Bentley, in which the first line is the name of the person about whom the poem is written. It consists of two rhyming couplets:

> Jeremiah Smith
> Is boring to be with.
> The company he doth keep
> Will send a person to sleep.

Elegy	A poem or song written to lament the death of someone or something, such as Thomas Gray's 'Elegy Written in a Country Churchyard'.
Epic	A very long poem often describing a heroic act or about a legendary figure, such as John Milton's *Paradise Lost*.
Haiku	First written in Japan, it has three lines of which the first and last have five syllables and the second has seven syllables:

> Loving, faithful, fun,
> Trusting and loyal and true
> Chocolate-brown suki.

Jingle	Short verse or line, often using alliteration or rhyme and designed to catch attention.
Kenning	First written in Old English or Norse, a poem which is written using metaphors and sometimes as a riddle.
Limerick	A comic poem of five lines, first written in the Irish city of Limerick. The first, second and fifth lines rhyme and so do the third and fourth.
List	A poem which uses the same word to begin each line.
Lyric	A short poem or song which is usually written in the first person and often expresses strong emotion such as John Masefield's 'Sea-Fever'.
Nonsense	A poem which is wild and wacky and plays on words such as Edward Lear's 'The Jumblies'.
Ode	A poem written for a special person or to celebrate a special event. It is written in the second person, for example Robert Herrick's 'To Daffodils'.
Rap	An oral poem with a strong rhythm first used in Afro-Caribbean countries.
Shape	A poem also known as a calligram, a poem in which lines form a shape which represents the meaning of the title. Crystal (1988) describes it as a concrete poem, for example George Herbert's 'The Altar'.
Sonnet	A poem of fourteen lines each of which has ten syllables such as William Shakespeare's 'Shall I Compare Thee?'
Tanka	First written in Japanese, a poem of five lines and thirty-one syllables. The first and third lines have five syllables and the second, fourth and fifth lines have seven syllables.

Handy hints for budding poets

1 Poetry can be written in different ways. It is always written in lines. Each line begins with a capital letter.
2 Poetry often uses rhyme but it does not have to.
3 Rhythm is part and parcel of poetry and is important when the poem is read or recited aloud.
4 The choice of language is a crucial element. Devices such as onomatopoeia – 'The snake will hiss and slither on the grass' – or alliteration – 'She sells seashells by the seashore' – are used, as are figures of speech. Such as similes – 'The old man's face was withered like a baked potato skin', metaphors – 'Georgina's toy cupboard beats Hamleys on Christmas Eve', personification – 'The stallion surveyed his harem of wives waiting for him in the field', and imagery – 'The cunning cat sprang slowly, silently and swiftly upon the unsuspecting bird'. See definitions on pp. 250–1.

5   There are many different forms, such as ballads, sonnets, etc. Each has a different structure. (See pp. 250–1.)
6   Consider the audience and decide whether you want to make them happy or sad, amused or annoyed.
7   What is the purpose of your poem? Is it an ode to lament the death of your pet?

Useful tips when writing poetry

1   Choose a title. Think about your audience. Who are you writing this for? Yourself, teacher or friend?

2   Decide what form of poem you want to write, for example an alphabet or list poem.

3   Decide whether to use rhyme. Nursery rhymes provide models for rhyme and rhythm.

4   Decide whether to use verses and whether to use four or eight line verses.

5   Each line begins with a capital letter.

6   Brainstorm and make lists of words. A useful tip is to use the alphabet to generate lists of suitable rhymes. There are some excellent rhyming dictionaries such as Black's *Rhyming and Spelling Dictionary* (www.acblack.com).

7   Think of which adjectives and adverbs you want to use. List in note form.

8   Think of figures of speech to use, such as similes and metaphors.

9   Poems are often easier to write in collaboration with another writer, so work in pairs.

10   The computer can be used and instant access to a dictionary or thesaurus is helpful.

11   Think of poems you have read on similar themes or with similar structures to those you envisage. Re-read these. Phinn (2001) concluded that children 'should be encouraged to read as much poetry as possible and take all the help they can get from what they read'.

Key points for consideration when drafting, editing and revising poetry

Structural issues

*   Is the title appropriate?
*   Have I used a form that matches the title and content?
*   Is the opening line good enough to make the audience want to read on?
*   Have I used the rhyming pattern (if using one) consistently?

- Does the rhythm sound right when the poem is said aloud?
- Have I used lively images?
- Is the language clear and interesting?
- Have I used interesting and exciting adjectives and adverbs?
- Have I used similes and metaphors effectively?
- Have I remembered to begin each line with a capital letter?
- Have I kept to the same number of lines in each stanza?

Guidelines for writing a personal response to a poem

Phinn (2001) argued that 'appreciation comes before analysis'. This underlines the importance of reading a poem silently, then saying it aloud so the language, rhythm and rhymes can be appreciated. Children can then be asked to summarise the poem. Then they can be asked to choose their favourite line or image and say why they have chosen it. This should be done as an oral activity. Later they can learn how to make a written response to a poem. The poem should be read once or twice (by a different person, maybe at a different pace). Then they can use the mnemonic A-P-R-I-L to help them analyse the poem.

Hints on writing answers to poetry questions (adapted from Evans and Lodge, 1999)

A   What is the poem *about*? Give a summary of it.

P   What is the poet's aim or *purpose*? What message is the poem giving?

R   Choose quotes and *refer* to the text to explain why they are important.

I   Then you need to say 'what *I* like about the poem'. Choose examples of your favourite parts. Give your personal opinions.

L   Comment on the *language*, for example the use of similes, rhyme, rhythm, personification, onomatopoeia, adjectives, powerful verbs, imagery, and give examples of these by referring to the text.

A spectrum of underlying causes of writing difficulties

There is a host of factors to consider when looking for the root causes of why individual pupils have difficulties with writing, just as there are when identifying special educational needs. What specific difficulties do dyslexic and SEN pupils have with writing? They include some or all of the following:

Factor 1

They have poor language skills. Some have limited vocabularies due to specific language impairment (SLI), meaning language skills significantly below what could be expected for their age and cognitive ability. There is often a considerable gap between their verbal and non-verbal skills when measured on standardised tests, which is not due to neurological impairment.

Gathercole and Alloway (2004) found that those with SLI performed badly on tests on working memory and short-term memory and that 'these deficits were 50 times more common in this group of children'.

This also often applies to EAL pupils and it can make diagnosis more complex. They do not deal with language with automaticity. Eoin was perplexed when he heard his mum saying, 'I must nail dad down and we must go and buy a new telly on Saturday. I wonder if it will fit in the boot of our new five horsepower car?'

They have difficulties with receptive and expressive language, as we have already noted. It can inhibit their writing and is an obstacle to literacy. Others may struggle to find the word they want to use according to Denckla and Rudel's (1976) RAN theory. Stirling and Miles (1988) found that adolescent dyslexic boys 'produced more examples of inappropriate usage, (saying, for example, that a 'pier "is what people walk along and fishing off"), more incomplete sentences, more repetitions, more misunderstandings of words, and more unnecessary amplifications of their original response'. Others are slow at retrieving words associated with their ideas, sometimes despite adequate vocabulary skills, according to Wolf and Bower's (2000) double deficit theory. They may also have difficulties with sequencing their ideas, facts and opinions. These are classic language features associated with the dyslexia syndrome. Oral language is the bedrock on which written language is embedded.

Geschwind (1982) reminded us that 'dyslexia appears on a foundation of delay in the development of the entire system devoted to language.'

Furthermore throughout most of the twentieth century influential psychologists such as Luria (1959) showed that 'language is central to thinking abilities'. The maxim 'If you can't say it, you won't be able to write it' is very true (Ott, 2000) and is often applicable to these pupils. Harpin (1976) showed that pupils write substantially more when given oral preparation by the teacher. This approach has been taken up by the NLS (1998) and is part of the shared and guided activities recommended during the Literacy Hour.

Factor 2

Pupils with SpLD's short-term and working memory skills are often poor so that they forget what they want to say. They find it difficult to generate ideas and the required vocabulary and to hold on to the plot while simultaneously remembering punctuation, syntax, grammar and spelling. Some lose their place, forget the plot and often omit or repeat words or phrases. These problems are compounded for children with ADD which is often co-existent with other specific learning difficulties. Ten-year-old Thomas put this very succinctly when he said, 'My brain is like a battery which only has enough energy to get the spellings right or to do good writing. It goes flat when I try to do both at the same time.' Consequently, like so many other children, he often writes in a brief truncated and mechanistic style when his writing is unsupported. In some cases children's work does not reflect what they know or can say orally. These are the pupils of whom it is often said 'If only he could do his exams orally, he would be top of his class.'

They may lose their train of thought because of sequencing difficulties. Often their ideas dry up because of the additional mental effort they need to make. Paul said to me, 'Oh, I wish I had a printer that I could plug into my head and then I could show people that I'm not stupid.'

Factor 3

Dyslexic pupils need to have explicit teaching of grammar. They struggle with syntax, particularly with the rules for sentence formation.

> Grammar is what gives sense to language. . . . Sentences actively create sense in language and the business of the study of sentences is the study of grammar intuitively from oral language, but those who have poor oral language skills do not have the tools and materials to construct a text.
>
> (Crystal, 1995)

Wilkinson (1971) was at the forefront of researchers and led a movement that proclaimed that formal grammar teaching did not improve writing. With the benefit of hindsight and at the instigation of the QCA (1998), interest has reawakened in the importance of teaching children to recognise 'parts of speech', now known as 'word classes' because they describe word function, as well as teaching rules about how sentences are constructed and linked. The arguments about whether grammar teaching should be ended or mended were raised by Noam Chomsky in the 1970s but they continue to rumble on. Some academics and practitioners have claimed that the traditional approach to teaching grammar in literacy lessons does not improve children's writing. Supporters of the NLS recommendations for grammar teaching argued that 'most children need a teacher's guidance [for writing], and guidance requires a language for talking about the items of performance, be these musical notes or words' (Hudson, 2005).

Factor 4

Pupils with specific learning difficulties often have poor gross and fine motor skills resulting in illegible or messy and untidy handwriting. This particularly affects those who have dyspraxic difficulties.

Being admonished 'to write neatly please when you do your story' may be the last straw for struggling writers who are juggling with so many other cognitive demands concurrently.

Factor 5

Poor processing and organisation skills may mean that they find it difficult to co-ordinate their ideas and gather information in a logical and sequential manner. This becomes evident, for example, when they have to write a recount or put events in chronological order for a report about yesterday's visit to the National History Museum. The reality is that extended writing can be torturous for some pupils as the following anecdote shows.

Steven's learning support teacher was dozing in front of the television one evening when she had a frantic phone call from the boy's mother. His English teacher, who was also the football coach, had called him aside after the game he had played and told him to do a report on it for homework, adding that he would read it out next day in Assembly. His mother said that when Steven came home he sat down at the kitchen table and cried hysterically, saying he would be laughed at by the other children the next day. Despite his mother's help he was overwhelmed and confused. He could not remember the names of the players or of those who had scored the goals. Neither could he remember the final score, even though he, the captain, had scored the winning goal.

The specialist teacher gave him some scaffolding and e-mailed a writing frame with questions such as the name of the opposing school's team, where the venue was and what happened in the first half and what the score was then. In the second half which side scored and what was the final score? Who were the goal scorers? Then a phone call to a fellow parent who had watched the match from the sidelines provided the missing information. Given these scaffolds, Steven was then able to complete the work (Ott, 2001a).

The lesson to learn is to give a vocabulary checklist or computer print-out including names and dates with homework. The way forward must now be for more classrooms to be equipped with interactive whiteboards which will do this at the touch of a button.

Many writers have an underlying fear of writing and tend to panic when asked to write. This is sometimes ascribed to 'writer's block'. Help is at hand in the Aladdin's cave of ICT resources, particularly with the use of speech recognition software such as Dragon Naturally Speaking Preferred 7 (www.dyslexic.com). Nonetheless, even with the best technology it is still necessary to have 'knowhow' about the different writing processes as well as knowledge of different writing forms when composing fiction, non-fiction and poetry and to be able to generate ideas and opinions.

Factor 6

The reluctant writer needs oral rehearsal and help with brainstorming for vocabulary, models for scaffolding, including frameworks, as well as help and strategies to put his ideas on paper. This may require a teaching assistant who can write down keywords and give useful spellings. A critical element in fostering confidence and skill building is initially to ignore errors and allow the pupil to guess spellings.

A study was carried out in Canada by Clarke (1989) on 100 children in four classes to investigate the effects of using conventional spelling and invented spelling. Two classes were encouraged not to worry about their spellings in their creative writing. The other two classes were encouraged to spell correctly and to use the dictionary or ask their teacher or friend to spell words they were unsure of. The classes using 'invented spellings' made 34 per cent spelling errors. The classes using conventional spellings made 6 per cent spelling errors. However, the children using 'invented spellings wrote stories of 43 words on average while the children using conventional spellings wrote 13 words on average'.

Furthermore, reluctant writers often cannot spell even the high frequency words, especially the 'odd-bods' such as 'said' or 'they', which the majority of pupils do automatically. Dyslexic pupils have to make an additional effort to remember spellings often because of poor phonological skills or weak visual memory for spelling patterns. Consequently their brain often becomes overloaded. This explains breakdowns in skills such as misspelling a word spelt correctly in this week's spelling test or even a word copied from the title written on the board. Gathercole and Alloway (2004) suggested that providing a list of keywords on the child's desk rather than on a distant board may reduce errors because of the difficulties in locating the spellings on the board. A useful suggestion is to make enlarged computer print-outs of the NLS high frequency lists and then laminate them and tape them to individual pupils' desk tops for easier access and reference. Commercial versions are available. If too much emphasis is put on correct spelling children can become very inhibited writers with impoverished vocabularies and a stilted style. Spelling should be an obedient servant, not the cruel taskmaster of the dyslexic writer. Moseley (1989) carried out research on 13–15-year-old diagnosed dyslexic pupils and found that they:

- used fewer words outside a core vocabulary of 500 words
- used more regularly spelt words
- avoided using common hard-to-spell words
- found ways of repeating words in order to 'play safe'.

His studies confirmed that 'a lack of confidence in spelling affects children's writing expression'. Therefore it is vitally important not to draw their attention to their inability to spell when writing, as far as is possible. Spelling and punctuation can be corrected when they proofread initial drafts and when they revise text. Co:Writer Smart Applet is a word prediction package that can be used to help chronically poor spellers and those with word naming and retrieval difficulties.

For the severely dyslexic pupil, phonetic spelling may in fact be the only way of communicating and may be a lifelong feature of his handwritten work. The spellchecker is now an intrinsic part of most word-processing packages and has opened up another world for many pupils and adults.

Word-processing speed

Word-processing has become universally important, particularly in schools, at home and in the workplace. ICT can have a conspicuous impact on skills, including dramatic improvements in the output of dyslexic and dyspraxic writers. To maximise the benefits, children should learn to touch-type. Response to learning touch-typing varies, depending on the individual's strengths and weaknesses.

There are a number of computer packages such as Kinlock's (1994) EasyType which teach the skill. Acquiring it is one of the best possible investments a child with SEN can make with his time. Before deciding whether a child should use a word processor in an examination it is important to know how many words per minute he can type. Typing needs to be faster than writing by hand to be worthwhile. What type of test needs to be undertaken?

1   test of free writing: ten minutes
2   test of dictation: ten minutes
3   test of copying: ten minutes.

Scores need to calculated for each of these. Many packages have in-built timed tests.

Technology is set to play an increasingly important role in the education and daily lives of all pupils. The computer ranks beside television as one of the twentieth century's greatest inventions. The message is still the same, the messenger still has to convey it. He can do this more easily and efficiently if he has learned to use some of the tricks of the trade as well as using hints and strategies for writing.

Summary and conclusions

- Teaching and learning effective writing skills has become a prime consideration in schools. The government has made the raising of writing standards a major objective of its education policy.
- The technological revolution of the new millennium has made the mechanical aspects of communication easier and faster to execute but the writer still has to have the understanding and ability to use various writing forms. They must also know why certain conventions are necessary for clarity and coherence in written communication.
- Writing skills should be contextualised for individuals and taught and practised in meaningful, realistic and relevant settings.
- All good writing involves planning, organisation and structure as well as a knowledge and understanding of the subject matter and an ability to use the sub-skills including spelling, punctuation and an appreciation of literary style.
- Checklists and guidelines help with planning, drafting, revising and editing.
- Apprentice writers need models on which to base their own writing. Master teachers can help with scaffolding and constructive criticism as well as encouragement and practical advice.
- Genre theory which was introduced as part of the National Literacy Strategy for teaching non-fiction is perhaps the most liberating and innovative feature of teaching writing to have been introduced into schools in the past century. It has applications across the whole of the curriculum. The increasing use of ICT goes hand in hand with teaching, learning and using different writing forms for different purposes and a variety of audiences.
- Desktop publishing with the use of a word-processing package is now a reality for those with access to a computer.
- Teaching and learning poetry plays an important role in developing interest, appreciation and pleasure in language.
- Those who have difficulties with expressive and receptive language may have co-existing difficulties with written language. Luria (1970) considered that 'the expression, or more precisely the formulation of thought is certainly the most important function of speech'.
- Some individuals who have specific learning difficulties have constitutional difficulties with writing which are often resistant to remediation and are pervasive and on-going. They can be compensated for, especially with the ICT support, which lightens the load of things to remember, such as spelling. However, according to Critchley (1970),

  > in the case of the 'cured' dyslexic, defective writing and spelling may continue to appear long into adult life. Where some degree of writing lies within the capacity of a dyslexic, the mistakes are of such a nature as often to make it possible to diagnose the reading defect from a mere perusal of the script.

- The computer has levelled the playing field for writers with specific learning difficulties including dyslexia, dyspraxia, specific language impairments and attention deficit disorders. When and if individual children are given the support and knowhow to use these technological marvels, the result is success. However, without the initial support of a teacher, parent or mentor these high-powered tools are often under-utilised.

- The ability to write at speed, including word-processing or using legible handwriting automatically, is still a core issue and plays a significant role for individuals in the classroom, at home and in examinations.
- Writing is an art which can be practised and a skill which can be honed and polished. Experience and using the tricks of the trade enable the writer to communicate effectively and efficiently.

Glossary

Access arrangements '[A]djustments that schools must consider in advance of [the] tests . . . should be based primarily on history of need and normal classroom practice for pupils with particular needs' (QCA, 2005).

Analytic phonics Involves looking at the whole word, then segmenting the initial consonant(s) (called the onset) and the vowel and remaining consonant(s) (called the rime) when spelling and blending them when reading. It is sometimes called the 'word family' approach. Examples: /str/ /ap/, /p/ /inch/.

Attention Deficit Disorder (ADD) Described by the American Psychiatric Association (1980) as a neurological condition characterised by difficulties in concentration, staying on task, impulsivity. It may or may not include hyperactivity.

Attention Deficit Hyperactivity Disorder (ADHD) A neurological condition characterised by difficulties focusing on important issues, getting started on a task, sustaining performance or returning to task when interrupted, poor short-term memory. Hyperactivity difficulties include fidgeting and squirming, often being constantly 'on the move' and sometimes talking excessively. Impulsivity includes interrupting others, blurting out answers, and being unable to wait for a turn to speak (American Psychiatric Association (1994).

Automaticity Applies to skills such as reading and writing and includes motor skills which become internalised and effortless when learning has become almost subconscious. Such skills can be used when required with little processing effort. Dyspraxics have problems developing automaticity with gross and fine motor skills which use the muscles in the lips, tongue, mouth, soft palate to produce speech sounds and words, and also with skills performed by the fingers, hands, toes and by the arms, legs and feet.

Blends Two or more consonants found next to each other. They sound separately but quickly and are drawn together when pronounced. They are sometimes called consonant clusters and can occur at the beginning, middle or ends of words: *stop, listing, post.*

Cerebellar deficit theory The cerebellum is the main part of the hind brain and is responsible for motor skills including precise timing and co-ordination of the muscles and postural stability including balance and muscle tone. Studies on cerebellum deficits found that some dyslexics were less well automaticised, not only for literacy but also for other tasks. They showed symptoms of cerebellar abnormality and cerebellar dysfunction including a lack of co-ordination and impaired timing of rapid pre-planned, automatic movements.

'Code emphasis' reading method This teaches the relationship between letters and sounds – the alphabetic code which teaches explicit decoding skills including phonics. The pupil decodes the letters he sees. He blends these when he sounds out a word as he reads. He segments the sounds he hears and matches these to the letters when he spells a word.

Cognitive abilities Mental skills which enable a person to know, to be aware, to think, to reason, to criticise and to be creative. Tests of cognitive ability such as the Cognitive Abilities Test (CAT) assess reasoning ability and verbal, non-verbal, numerical and spatial ability.

Co-morbidity The simultaneous existence of two or more unrelated conditions or disorders. 'Co-existence' or 'co-occurrence' is considered a more precise term in the case of dyslexia and dyspraxia.

Cursive handwriting Joined-up writing which involves a continuous flowing movement. The lower-case letters begin on the line with an entry stroke and end on the line with an exit stroke. Letters with descenders have a loop stroke to allow them to join up to the other letter.

Decoding The ability to look at the visual representation of letters and then to pronounce and read them as a word by matching the symbols to their sounds.

Differentiation A term used in the Special Educational Needs Code of Practice (2001). It may mean reducing the content of the curriculum, or giving additional time to carry out assignments such as exams, or allowing the use of ICT to access course materials.

Digraph Two letters making one sound at the beginning, middle or end of words: shop, crashed, wish. Vowel digraphs are two vowels making one sound at the beginning, middle or end of word ōāk, wēēding, sēā.

Diphthong Two vowels side by side which glide together when pronounced in rapid succession such as: bōīl, mōōn, hōūse.

Discrepancy criteria Scores indicating the difference between a pupil's current attainment scores and his potential as predicted by IQ test scores. Tests such as the Wechsler Objective Reading Dimensions (WORD), which is often used in conjunction with the Wechsler Intelligence Scale for Children 111 UK (WISC 111uk) test battery (Wechsler, 1992), have a table for such scores. The WORD test includes a test of basic reading, spelling and reading comprehension. This test also includes a predictive score which is used to ascertain how well literacy scores match ability as calculated from the overall IQ score on the test. The discrepancy between attainment, as measured by tests of reading, spelling and numeracy, and potential as measured by tests of cognitive ability such as the CATs tests is cited when requesting access arrangements in examinations.

Double deficit theory Described by Wolf (1999) as a naming speed deficit and a phonological deficit which results in slow, inaccurate reading and poor comprehension of a text.

Dyscalculia Used to describe people who have difficulties in acquiring mathematical skills. 'Dyscalculic learners may have difficulty understanding simple number concepts, lack an intuitive grasp of numbers and have problems learning number facts and procedures' (DfES, 2001b).

Dyslexia Derived from the Greek dys meaning 'difficult'/'bad' and lexis meaning language, a difficulty with receptive and expressive language in both its written and its spoken forms. It is a constitutional difficulty which is often hereditary. Individuals with dyslexia may have difficulties with reading, writing, spelling and oral language. It also involves difficulties with short-term memory, sequencing, organisational skills, motor skills and processing speeds.

Dyspraxia Derived from the Greek *dys* meaning 'difficult'/'bad' and *praxis* meaning 'practice'/'action'. It is used to describe a condition in which people have a difficulty planning and carrying out non-habitual motor skills. It involves an impairment in the ability to perform familiar or unfamiliar motor skills with automaticity and is sometimes described as Development Co-ordination Disorder (DCD).

Explicit teaching Each step in the skill being taught is taught specifically and in a structured sequence. It includes modelling by the teacher, and practice and support while the skill is being acquired.

Fernald's spelling method The target word is written by the teacher in cursive writing and pronounced slowly. The pupil repeats the word while simultaneously looking at it. Then he highlights tricky letters. He traces over the word with the index finger of his dominant hand. He folds over the paper. Then he writes the word from memory using cursive writing. Then he turns back the paper and checks what he has written.

Free writing Children's spontaneous writing about a topic. They are 'free' to write about it in any way they choose.

Genre theory Developed to describe different kinds of writing used by individuals. It includes the distinguishing features such as language and structure used to organise the text.

Grapheme A letter or a group of letters used to represent a single sound.

High frequency words Those most commonly used in writing and reading, originally derived from Dolch's sight list. The *NLS Framework for Teaching* (DfEE, 1998) produced two lists of high frequency words comprising 45 words and 150 words to be learned because 'these words usually play an important part in holding together the general coherence of texts and early familiarity with them will help pupils get pace and accuracy into their reading at an early stage'.

Horn's spelling method Usually known as the look-say-cover-write-check method. The pupil looks at the word, notes the letters and then says the word aloud. Then he writes the word and simultaneously says the letter names. Then he covers the letters and writes the word from memory. Finally he checks what he has written.

Individual educational plan (IEP) A planning, teaching and review resource. It should include short-term targets and details of teaching strategies which are '*additional to* or *different from* differentiated curriculum provision, which is in place as part of provision for all pupils' (COP, 2001)

Intelligence Quotient (IQ) Tests Psychometric tests, which measure reasoning, problem solving, spatial skills and factual knowledge and provide standardised scores and a description of ability.

Key stages A term used in the National Curriculum (QCA, 1999) to describe different age groups: Key Stage 1: Reception (R), Year 1, Year 2 (5–7 years); Key Stage 2: Year 3, Year 4, Year 5, Year 6 (8–11 years); Key Stage 3: Year 7, Year 8, Year 9 (12–14 years); Key Stage 4: Year 10, Year 11 (15–16 years).

Kinaesthetic skills These relate to physical skills involving motor memory and touch. Motor skills apply to gross motor skills involving the arms, neck, trunk and legs. Fine motor skills apply to the fingers, hands and speech muscles. Kinaesthetic learners learn by a sensation of movement either by using the muscle memory in their fingers, hands and arms when carrying out an activity such as dancing, drama; skywriting, tracing, copying or word-processing spellings or doing a project, a science experiment, making a model, writing notes or using computer packages or CD ROMs.

Learning style The way individuals process, remember and recall information and facts. There are four main pathways to learning: oral, visual, auditory and kinaesthetic.

Look-and-say A method of reading which teaches the pupil to recognise whole words. It is primarily a visual approach. It was used in reading schemes which had controlled vocabularies of 'sight words' which were to be memorised.

Magnocellular deficit theory The magnocellular pathway and parvacellular pathway relate to the two visual pathways used to see. 'Magnocellular' is derived from *magnus* meaning 'great'/'large' and *parvus* meaning 'small'/'lesser'. The magnocellular pathway is responsible for changes in the visual field and the parvacellular pathway is responsible for fine details in the visual field. Both functions work in tandem. The magnocells are large neurons and are responsible for timing sensory and motor events. Weaknesses in the visual magnocellular system may result in 'visual confusion of letter order and poor visual memory for orthography'. Evans (2001) reviewed the literature and found 'evidence for a [magnocellular] deficit' in cases of dyslexia but 'it seems that, although visual factors can contribute to some of the reading errors, they do not play the major causal role in dyslexia'. Stein *et al.* (2001) argued from the studies he has conducted that 'the visual magnocellular system is impaired' and this 'impacts on reading'. But 'it is not immediately obvious how the magnocellular system contributes to reading'.

'Matthew Effect' Term used by Stanovich (1986) to describe the fact that good readers get better by reading whereas poor readers do not get better because they do not read. The term is taken from a biblical reference.

'Meaning emphasis' Reading method used to teach beginners by focusing primarily on words which are connected to text for meaning. Children are assumed to learn about alphabetic principles by reading for meaning. The prime focus is using texts that can be read quickly and easily so that unknown words can be deciphered. Contextual cues help the reader to guess words rather than having to attempt to decode them by sounding them out letter by letter.

Meares-Irlen syndrome Also known as scotopic sensitivity syndrome, this describes visual difficulties associated with light sensitivity, sustained focus, glare and difficulties with black and white contrast.

Mind map® (Buzan and Buzan, 1993) or concept map is a pictorial representation of thoughts, words and ideas and can be used for an essay plan, notes from a textbook, lecture or revision. It can be illustrated by hand or with a computer package.

Miscue analysis This is carried out by examining errors recorded during standardised tests or when reading aloud. The errors are scrutinised, analysed and categorised. It developed from the hypothesis that readers use phonological semantic or syntactic cues when decoding text. The 'miscue' can provide evidence about underlying strengths and weaknesses. It can also be used for spelling error analysis.

Mnemonic Derived from the Greek word *mnemonikos* meaning 'memory'/'mindful', it is a memory device used to help remember facts, words, phrases or sentences. The sentence '*never eat shredded wheat*' helps the learner to recall that the points of the compass are: north, east, south and west. Acronyms can be used to remember the letters used to spell a word: the sentence '*big elephants can't always use small exits*' helps to remember how to spell 'because'. Rhymes can also be used: 'you hear with an ear'. The initial letters of the target word can be recalled by repeating the sentence.

Motor skills   These apply to muscular movements. Gross motor skills apply to the large muscles involving the arms, legs, body and neck. Fine motor skills apply to the fingers, hands and speech muscles of the tongue. Graphomotor skills apply to the hands and fingers when tracing, drawing, handwriting and keyboarding. Oromotor skills apply to musical or rhythmic memory such as remembering a tune or the words of a song.

Multi-sensory learning   This involves the eyes, ears, lips and the hands simultaneously. The eyes are used to look at words, the lips to pronounce them, the ears to listen to them and the hand to write them. All the learning pathways to the brain are activated to optimise learning.

National Literacy Strategy (NLS)   A government initiative to raise national standards in reading, writing, speaking and listening. The Department for Education and Employment (DfEE, 1998) published non-statutory guidelines to meet a national target for all pupils to become literate between Reception and Year 6. The objectives are set out in the *Framework for Teaching* which is a reference document for classroom teachers. It gives a detailed analysis as well as guidance for the implementation of the Literacy Strategy in schools and day-to-day guidance for the implementation of the Literacy Hour which should be structured to include word-level work, sentence-level work and text-level work. The objectives for each of these are sub-divided for each term of a thirty-six week school year from Reception Year to Year 6.

Non-word reading and spelling   Pseudo-words, sometimes called nonsense words, may be used to identify underlying weaknesses in phonological and phonemic skills.

'Odd-bod' spellings   A term coined by Ott (1997) to denote irregular spellings, as in words without a good sound-to-symbol match or with silent letters. They may be borrowed from other languages, and words derived from Anglo-Saxon are a prime source. They also include words which do not have that rhyming words: 'orange', 'pint'.

Onset   The initial consonant or cluster of consonants in a word: /d/ /og/, /ch/ /ap/, /str/ing.

Otitis media   An inflammation of the middle ear causing a build-up of fluid and discharge due to infection, or inflamed tonsils, It can be caused by swimming or allergies. It results in hearing loss and can interfere with language and learning, though not the primary cause. It is usually known as glue ear.

Paired reading   A beginner reader and a skilled reader read a text simultaneously. Gradually as the pupil becomes more confident he reads alone while the teacher praises his effort.

Percentiles   These show, for example, the percentage of pupils nationally of a similar age or age range who would score at the same level, or below, on the standardised scores. A percentile of 96 would show that 96 per cent of individuals would score at the same level or below while only 4 per cent would score more highly.

Pre-readers   Children who have not received any formal reading instruction.

Phoneme   Derived from the Greek word *phonema* meaning 'uttered sound', it is the smallest unit of sound that distinguishes the meaning of one spoken word from another: 'c', 'b', 'f' before 'at' make 'cat', 'bat', 'fat'. In the past there was an on-going debate about the exact number of phonemes in English. The number has varied between 33 and 44. There is now a general consensus (NLS, 1998) that there are forty-four phonemes in the English language.

Phonemic awareness Lindamood *et al.* (1997) described phonemic awareness 'as an ability to identify individual sounds and their order within words – to divide a whole word into parts'. The child must have an awareness of the individual sounds in words in oral language. This can be difficult to learn without explicit teaching, primarily because in speech many sounds are co-articulated and elide.

Phonetic errors Made when there is mismatch between the phonemes and the letters that represent them, these errors can occur at the beginning, middle or end of words: 'cet' for 'get'; 'cot' for 'cut'; 'boks' for 'box'.

Phonics This involves teaching reading and spelling by sounding out the individual letters, then blending and synthesising them to pronounce a word when reading and segmenting them when spelling (Ott, 1997). There are two methods. The analytic phonics method teaches the child to look at a whole word and break it into chunks and pronounce these when reading. The synthetic phonics method teaches the child to sound out the individual letters and then blend them when reading. According to the DfEE (2001a), 'phonics consists of the skill of segmentation and blending, knowledge of the alphabetic code and understanding of the principles which underpin how the code is used in reading and spelling'.

Phonological awareness The *National Literacy Strategy* (DfEE, 1998) defines it as 'an awareness of sounds within words – demonstrated by the ability to generate rhyme, alliteration, and in segmenting and blending component sounds'.

Phonological deficit hypothesis This shows that phonological awareness is a sub-skill of many linguistic tasks, all of which have a role to play in the development of reading skills. The identification of phonological deficit as a core deficit in dyslexia has been hailed as one of the 'great success stories of science' (Stanovich, 1992).

Processing speed deficits These indicate difficulties in interpreting language at the speed at which it is presented, and interpreting information, particularly when given in sequential form.

Psychometric tests Used for psychological measurement, these include the Wechsler Intelligence Scale for Children (WISC III) and the British Ability Scales (BAS-II).

Rapid automatised naming theory (RAN) Denckla and Rudel (1976) established that children with dyslexia had problems processing language at speed. They devised a test in which the child has to give the names of fifty stimuli, such as digits, letters, colours, objects, as quickly as possible.

Rime The vowel and final consonant(s) in a word: b(*ack*), cr(*ime*), str(*ong*). Rimes can also be single sounds fr(*ee*), sh(*e*), d(*ay*). 'Rime' is used because some multisyllabic words have more than one 'rime': 'mountain' and 'fountain' rhyme but each has two rimes 'ount' and 'ain'. 'Mountain' and 'counting' do not rhyme but they do have the same initial rime, 'ount'.

Schwa sounds Unstressed vowel sounds sometimes known as 'murmur vowels' which occur in unaccented syllables such as: /u/ in 'circus', /a/ in 'sofa', /er/ in 'discover'.

'Searchlight' Reading method recommended by the NLS (1998) which stated that 'pupils become successful readers by learning to use a range of strategies to get at the meaning of a text'. These include phonics, knowledge of context, grammatical knowledge, word recognition and graphic knowledge.

Sequencing The ability to remember a series or a succession of things in a specific order as in the alphabet, times tables, instructions, formulas, spelling patterns.

Short-term memory A temporary storage facility in the mind, used to hold a small amount of sensory information several seconds while the information is processed and interpreted. This allows the individual to carry out an intellectual task such as remembering a telephone number or recognising a picture.

Sight words Whole words which are instantly recognisable because all the letters have been memorised in long-term memory. Decoding or encoding strategies are not used because such words can be read within one second from memory effortlessly, quickly and automatically.

Simultaneous oral spelling (S-O-S) This method involves saying a word aloud, then spelling the word orally and writing the letters at the same time.

Skywriting Using an outstretched arm and the index finger of the dominant hand to trace letters in the air. It can be used to develop motor memory of letter shapes and spelling patterns. It is particularly useful for those with a kinaesthetic preferred learning style.

Special Educational Needs (SEN) According to the Education Act 1996, a child has a learning difficulty if he or she:

a) has a significantly greater difficulty in learning than the majority of children of the same age.

b) has a disability which either prevents or hinders the child from making use of educational facilities of a kind provided for children of the same age in schools within the area of the local authority.

Specific learning difficulty This is a particular learning difficulty which affects certain cognitive skills including receptive and expressive language, reading and writing, and mathematical skills. It involves developmental co-ordination difficulties and attention deficit disorders rather than a general learning difficulty which affects most aspects of learning. The term is often used in the UK interchangeably with dyslexia. The US Government's Individuals and Disabilities Education Act 1997 (IDEA) states that:

> The term 'specific learning disabilities' means those children who have a disorder in one or more of the basic psychological processes involved in understanding or in using language, spoken or written, which disorder may manifest itself in imperfect ability to listen, think, speak, read, write, spell or do mathematical calculations . . . a severe discrepancy exists between the student's apparent *potential for learning* and his or her low level of achievement.

'Spellofax' A personal workbook which enables the pupil to build a cumulative record of his learning, recording a sequence of spelling challenges. It can become a point of reference across the curriculum.

Standardised scores Calculated from the raw score test results, they compare a pupil's performance with those of other pupils of the same age group nationally. The nearer the pupil is to the mean score of 100, the nearer he is to the average for his age group.

Statement A document issued by a Local Education Authority (LEA) after a child has had a statutory assessment and is found to have special educational needs (learning difficulties). It should 'describe all the child's learning difficulties' and include details of 'appropriate facilities and equipment, staffing arrangements' as well as 'modifications to the application of the National Curriculum'. It should also 'indicate any special examination provision recommended' and 'the particular school which the LEA consider appropriate' (COP, 2001).

Statutory Standard Assessment Tasks (SATs) Imposed and implemented after the National Curriculum was introduced, they define Statements of Attainment and attainment targets for eight levels which are assessed by statutory tests at the end of each key stage.

Synthetic phonics Derived from the Greek words *synthetikos* meaning 'skilled at putting together' and *thesis* meaning 'playing', when used in linguistics and for teaching and learning phonics it means the sounding out of individual phonemes from left to right and then their being blended together to help pronounce a word, as when reading. The converse takes place when the individual phonemes are segmented to match the sounds when spelling. This method is sometimes described colloquially as the 'sounding out' or 'code emphasis' approach. The use of the term 'synthetic' can be a source of confusion because its common meaning is 'artificial' or 'insincere'.

Theory of multiple intelligences A hypothesis put forward by Howard Gardner (1983) who argued that intelligences consist of different abilities and skills and that each ability has its individual characteristics such as musical ability.

Visual discrimination An ability to detect differences in shape, size and configuration of letters and effects.

Visual memory An ability to recall or retain a mental picture of a letter, word or object including its shape, length and the order of the letters.

Whole language movement This developed from the philosophy that reading is linked to oral and written language and that reading skills develop naturally. The reader picks and chooses information just as in speech to predict and decode meaning. It is therefore not necessary to teach sound–symbol relationships formally.

'Whole word' reading method Children are given books with good illustrations and encouraged to memorise and recognise whole words rather than systematically decoding the letters.

Word recognition The ability to recognise and pronounce written words as well as understand their meaning. It results in automaticity when reading which enhances comprehension and underpins fluent and accurate reading.

Working memory Correlated to short-term memory, it involves holding a piece of information in the mind to which another piece of information can be added. Or else an element can be subtracted from the original piece of information. In other words, two things are done at once. It can include auditory memory, motor memory, visual memory and semantic memory. It is used, for example, when saying multiplication tables, keying in a pin number, remembering a car number plate or when saying a digit span in reverse order and in non-word repetition tasks. Working memory problems constitute a classic difficulty associated with dyslexia, accounting, for example, for a tendency to omit syllables or affixes when reading, writing or saying polysyllabic words and for difficulties with sequencing tasks.

Bibliography

Adams, M.J. (1990) *Beginning to Read: Thinking and Learning about Print*. MIT Press, Cambridge, MA.

Adams, M.J. (1991) 'Why not phonics and whole language?' In Ellis, W. (ed.) *All Language and the Creation of Literacy*. Orton Dyslexia Society, Baltimore, MD.

Adams, M.J., Foorman B.R., Lundberg I. and Beeler T. (1998) *Phonemic Awareness in Young Children*. Paul Brookes Publishing, Baltimore, MD.

Addy, L. (2004) 'Speed-up! Increasing the speed and fluency of handwriting using a kinaesthetic approach'. Seminar, The Education Show, Special Needs, London.

Allcock, J.A. (1972) *Sensory Integration and Learning Disorders*. Western Psychological Services, Los Angeles, CA.

Allcock, P. (1999a) 'Define "slow" – the quest for a standardised test of handwriting speed'. *Patoss Bulletin* 12 (2).

Allcock, P. (1999b) 'Directions for counting'. In Backhouse, G. (ed.) *A Practical Guide*. Professional Association of Teachers of Students with Specific Learning Difficulties, Evesham.

Allcock, P. (2000) 'An investigation on handwriting speed as a factor in learning difficulties in a secondary school'. Master's dissertation. Middlesex University.

Allcock, P. (2001) 'Update September 2001. Testing Handwriting Speed'. *Patoss Bulletin* 14 (2).

American Psychiatric Association (1980) *Diagnostic and Statistical Manual of Mental Disorders* (3rd edn). Washington, DC.

American Psychiatric Association (1994) *Diagnostic and Statistical Manual of Mental Disorders* (4th edn) (*DSMIV*). American Psychiatric Association, Washington, DC.

Andrews, R.H. (1990) 'The development of a learning style program in a low socioeconomic underachieving Carolina elementary school'. *Journal of Reading, Writing and Learning Disabilities International* 6: 307–14.

Annett, M. (1970) 'A classification of hand preference by association analysis'. *British Journal of Psychology* 61: 303–21.

Audit Commission (2002) *Special Educational Needs: A Mainstream Issue*. Audit Commission, London.

Ayres, J.A. (1972) *Sensory Integration and Learning Disorders*. Western Psychological Services, Los Angeles, CA.

Backhouse, G. (2000) *Providing for Candidates with Special Assessment Needs During GCE (A-Level), VCE, GCSE and GNVP. A Practical Guide*. Patoss, Evesham.

Backhouse, G. (2005) 'Basic concepts in psychometrics'. In Backhouse, G. and Morris, K. (eds) *Dyslexia: Assessing and Reporting. The Patoss Guide*. Hodder Murray, London.

Backhouse, G. and Morris, K. (2005) (eds) *Dyslexia? Assessing and Reporting. The Patoss Guide*. Hodder Murray, London.

Bailey, Nathaniel (1721) *Universal Etymological English Dictionary*.

Bain, A. (1887) *English Composition and Rhetoric* (enlarged edn). Longmans, Green, London.

Balcombe, K. (1998) *The Handwriting File (Photocopy Masters) A4 Information and Practice Book for Handwriting*. KBER Educational Resources, Shrewsbury.

Ball, E.W. and Blachman, B.A. (1991) 'Does phoneme awareness training in kindergarten make a difference in early word recognition and developmental spelling?' *Reading Research Quarterly* 26 (1): 49–66.

Bangert-Drowns, R.L. (1993) 'The word-processor as an instructional tool: a meta-analysis of word processing in writing instruction'. *Review of Educational Research* 63 (1): 69–93.

Barnett, A.L. and Henderson, S.E. (2004) 'Assessment of handwriting in children with development coordination disorder'. In Snyden, D.A. and Chambers, (eds) *Children with Development Coordination Disorder*. Whurr Publishing, London.

Barnett, D., Galbraith, J., Roaf, C. and Rutherford, S. (1998) *The Role of Handwriting in Raising Achievement*. Ford William's School, Thame.

Barnett, D., Galbraith, J., Roaf, C. and Rutherford, S. (1999) *The Role of Handwriting in Raising Achievement*. Teacher Training Agency, London.

Barrs, M. (1987) *Learning to Write. Language Matters (2) and (3)*. CLPE, London.

Basic Skills Agency (undated) *Making Reading Easy*. London.

BDA (2001) 'Dyslexia friendly school audit'. *Dyslexia Contact* 20 (2): 6.

BDA (2005) *Achieving Dyslexia Friendly Schools. Resource Pack*. BDA, Reading.

Beard, R. (2000) *Developing Writing 3–13*. Hodder and Stoughton, London.

Becker, W., Dixon, R. and Anderson-Inman, L. (1980) 'Morphographic and root word analysis of 26,000 high frequency words'. University of Oregon College of Education, Eugene, OR.

Becta (2005) 'Learning styles – an introduction to the research literature', http://www.becta.org.uk

Beech, J.R. (1987) 'Early reading development'. In Beech, J.R. and Colley, A.M. (eds) *Cognitive Approaches to Reading*. Wiley, Chichester.

Bereiter, C. and Scardamalia, M. (1987) *The Psychology of Written Composition*. Lawrence Erlbaum, Hillsdale, NJ.

Beringer, V.W. (2004) 'Brain-based assessment and instructional intervention'. In Reid, G. and Fawcett, A. (eds) *Dyslexia in Context: Research Policy and Practice*, 90–119. Whurr Publishers, London.

Bevan, L.F. (1857) *Reading Without Tears, or A Pleasant Mode of Learning to Read*. Hatchards, London.

Bishop, D.V.M. (1990) *Handedness and Developmental Disorder*. Mac Keith Press, The Spastics Society, London.

Bishop, E. (2001) 'Writing speed and extra time in examinations'. *Dyslexia Review* 12 (3).

Bissex, G.L. (1980) *GNYS AT WRK: A Child Learns to Write and Read*. Harvard University Press, Cambridge, MA.

Blachman, B. (1987) 'An alternative classroom reading program for learning disabled and other low-achieving children'. In Bowler, R. (ed.) *Intimacy with Language: A Forgotten Basic in Teacher Education*, 49–55. Orton Dyslexia Society.

Blachman, B., Ball, E., Black, S. and Tangel, D. (1994) 'Kindergarten teachers develop phoneme awareness in low income, inner-city classrooms: does it make a difference?' *Reading and Writing: An Interdisciplinary Journal* 6: 1–17.

Blunkett, D. (2000) News Report BBC1.

Boder, E. (1973) 'Developmental dyslexia: a diagnostic approach based on 3 atypical reading-spelling patterns'. *Developmental Medicine and Child Neurology* 15: 663–87.

Body, W. (ed.) (2000) *Pelican Guided Reading and Writing*. Pearson Education, Harlow.

Bradley, L. and Bryant, P. (1983) 'Categorising sounds and learning to read – a causal connection'. *Nature* 301: 419–21.

Bradley, L.L. (1981) 'The organisation of motor patterns for spelling: an effective remedial strategy for backward readers'. *Developmental Medicine and Child Neurology* 23: 83–91.

Brady, S. (1986) 'Short-term memory, phonological processing and reading ability'. *Annals of Dyslexia* 36: 138–53.

Bramley, W. (1984) *Units of Sound: Teacher's Notes*. Unit of Sound Productions, Corsham.

Brand, V. (1984) *Spelling Made Easy, Introductory Level Fat Sam*. Egon Publishers, Baldock.

British Ability Scales (1996) *British Ability Scales* (2nd edn) (BAS-II), ed. Elliot, C.D., Smith, P. and McCullock, K. NFER-Nelson, Windsor.

British Psychological Society (1999) *Dyslexia, Literacy and Psychology (DECP)*. British Psychological Society, Leicester.

Britton, J. (1970) *Language and Learning*. Penguin, MA.

Brooks, G. (1996) *The Knowsley Reading Project. Using Trained Reading Helpers Effectively*. NFER-Nelson, Windsor.

Brooks, G. (2003a) 'DfES Response to the March 2003 Phonics Seminar and Professor Greg Brooks' Report'. www.dfes.gov.uk.

Brooks, G. (2003b) *Sound Sense: The Phonics Element of the National Literacy Strategy. A Report to the Department for Education and Skills*. University of Sheffield, Sheffield.

Brooks, G. and Pugh, A.K. (1984) *Studies in the History of Reading*. Centre for the Teaching of Reading, University of Reading, University of Reading School of Education and the United Kingdom Reading Association.

Brooks, P. and Weeks, S. (1998) *Individual Styles in Learning to Spell: Improving Spelling in Children with Literacy Difficulties and All Children in Maintained Schools*. Research Report No. 754, Department of Education and Employment, HMSO, Norwich.

Brooks, G., Pugh, A.K. and Schagen, I. (1996) *Reading Performance at Nine*. National Foundation for Educational Research (NFER), Slough.

Brooks, G., Flanagan, N., Henkhuzens, Z. and Hutchinson, D. (1998) *What Works for Slow Readers?: The Effectiveness of Early Intervention Schemes*. National Foundation for Educational Research, Slough.

Bruck, M. (1987) 'The adult outcomes of children with learning disabilities'. *Annals of Dyslexia* 37: 252–63.

Bruck, M. (1992) 'Persistence of dyslexics' phonological awareness deficits'. *Developmental Psychology* 28: 874–86.

Bruck, M. and Treiman, R. (1992) 'Learning to pronounce words: the limitations of analogies'. *Reading Research Quarterly* 27: 374–89.

Bruner, J. (1986) *Actual Minds, Possible Worlds*. Harvard University Press, Cambridge, MA.

Bryant, P.E. and Bradley, L. (1980) 'Why children sometimes write words which they do not read'. In Frith, U. (ed.) *Cognitive Processes in Spelling*. Academic Press, London.

Bryant, P.E., Bradley, L., Maclean, M. and Crossland, J. (1989) 'Nursery rhymes, phonological skills and reading'. *Journal of Child Language* 16: 407–28.

Buckinghamshire County Council (1995) *Education Act 1993. The Code of Practice. Criteria for Statutory Assessment of Children with Special Educational Needs*, Aylesbury.

Bullock Report (1975) *A Language for Life*. Department of Education and Science, HMSO, London.

Buzan, T. (1974) *Use Your Head*. Ariel Books, British Broadcasting Corporation, London.

Buzan, T. and Buzan, B. (1993) *The Mind Map Book*. BBC Books, London.

Carlisle, R. and Wendon, L. (1985) *The Letterland ABC*. Thomas Nelson and Sons, Walton-on-Thames.

Catts, H. W. (1989) 'Defining dyslexia as a developmental language disorder'. *Annals of Dyslexia* 39: 50–64.

Cawdrey, R. (1604) *A Table Alphabeticall*.

Chall, J.S. (1967) *Learning to Read: The Great Debate*. McGraw Hill, New York.

Chall, J.S. (1983) *Stages of Reading Development*. McGraw-Hill, New York.

Chall, J.S. (1987) 'Reading development in adults'. *Annals of Dyslexia* 37: 240–63.

Chambers (2000) *21st Century Dictionary* (revised edn). Chambers Harrap Publishers, Edinburgh.

Chambers (2002) *Primary Dictionary*. Chambers Harrap Publishers, Edinburgh.

Chambers (2004) *Primary Rhyming Dictionary*. Chambers Harrap Publishers, Edinburgh.

Chasty, H. (1990) 'The challenges of specific learning difficulties'. In Hales, G. (ed.) *Meeting Points in Dyslexia*. BDA, Reading.

Chew, J. and Turner, M. (2003) 'Testing the tests: standards of ability and spelling'. *Dyslexia Review* 14 (2).

Child, D. (2004) *Psychology and the Teacher* (7th edn) Continuum, London.

Clare, J. (2005) 'Any questions'. *Daily Telegraph*, 6 April.

Clarke, L.K. (1986) 'The effects of encouraged invented spelling in first grade children's writing on learning to spell and read'. Doctoral thesis. University of Toronto, Toronto.

Clay, M. (1985) *The Early Detection of Reading Difficulties*. Heinemann, Portsmouth, NH.

Clegg, A. (1964) *The Excitement of Writing*. Chatto and Windus, London.

Close, R. (2004) 'Television and language development in the early years: a research review'. www.Literacytrust.org.uk.

Code of Practice for Providers of Post-16 Education and Related Services (2002) The Disability Rights Commission, The Stationery Office, Norwich.

Code of Practice for Schools (COPSH) (2002) *Disability Discrimination Act 1995: Part 4*. Disability Rights Commission 2002, The Stationery Office, London.

Code of Practice on Schools Admission (1999) *Circular 10/99. Social Inclusion: Pupil Support. Special Educational Needs Code of Practice*. DfES Publications.

Coffield, F. (2005) 'Kinaesthetic nonsense'. *Times Educational Supplement*, 14 January.

Coffield, F., Moseley, D., Hall, E. and Ecclestone, K. (2004) *Should We Be Using Learning Styles? What Research Has to Say to Practice*. Learning and Skills Research Centre, London.

Cogan, J. and Flecker, M. (2004) *Dyslexia in Secondary School*. Whurr Publishers, London.

Commission of Reading, National Academy of Education (1985) *Becoming a Nation of Readers*. National Institute of Education, Washington, DC.

Cook, L. (1981) 'Misspelling analysis in dyslexia: observation of development strategy shifts'. Bulletin of the Orton Society 31: 123–34.

COP (2001) *Special Educational Needs Code of Practice*. Department for Education and Skills. DfES Publications, Nottinghamshire.

COPP16 (2002) *Code of Practice for Providers of Post-16 Education and Related Services (2002)*. The Disability Rights Commission, The Stationery Office, Norwich.

Corina, D., Richards, T., Serafini, S., Richards, A., Steury, K., Abbott, R., Echelard, D., Maravilla, K. and Beringer, V. (2001) 'fMRI auditory language differences between dyslexic and able reading children'. *Neuroreport* 12: 1195–201.

Cottrell, G.C. (1970) 'The Fernald auditory-kinaesthetic technique of teaching reading and spelling'. In White Franklin, A. and Naidoo, S. (eds) *Assessment and Teaching Dyslexic Children*, 97–100. Invalid Children's Aid Association, London.

Cottrell, S. (1999) *The Study Skills Handbook*. Palgrave, Basingstoke.

Cox, A. (1978) 'The Samuel T. Orton Award for 1977 to Aylett Royall Cox. Response by Aylett Cox'. *Annals of Dyslexia* 28: 1–7.

Cox, A.R. (1980) *Structures and Techniques: Multisensory Teaching of Basic Language Skills*. Educators Publishing Service, Cambridge, MA.

Cox, A.R. (1982) Personal Communication.

Cox, A.R. (1985) 'Alphabetic phonics: an organisation and expansion of Orton–Gillingham'. *Annals of Dyslexia* 35: 187–99.

Cox, A.R. and Hutchinson, L. (1988) 'Syllable division. Pre-requisite to dyslexics' literacy'. *Annals of Dyslexia* 38: 226–42.

Cox, C.B. and Dyson, A.E. (1969) *Fight for Education*. The Critical Quarterly Society, London.

Critchley, M. (1970) *The Dyslexic Child*. Heinemann Medical Books, London.

Critchley, M. (1975) 'Specific developmental dyslexia'. In Lenneberg, E.H. and Lenneberg, E. (eds) *Foundations of Language Development: A Multidisciplinary Approach*, Vol. II, Academic Press, New York.

Critchley, M. (1981) 'Dyslexia – an overview'. In Pavlidis, G. Th. and Miles, T.R. (eds) *Dyslexia Research and its Applications to Education*. John Wiley and Sons, Chichester.

Critchley, M. and Critchley, E.A. (1978) *Dyslexia Defined*. Heinemann Medical Books, London.

Croft, C. (1983) *Teacher's Manual for Spell-Write: An Aid to Writing, Spelling and Word-Study*. New Zealand Council for Educational Research, Wellington.

Crumpler, M. and McCarty, C. (2004) *Nonword Reading Test*. Hodder Murray, London.

Crystal, D. (1988) *The Cambridge Encyclopedia of Language*. Guild Publishing, London.

Crystal, D. (1995) *The Cambridge Encyclopaedia of the English Language*. (2nd edn). Cambridge University Press, Cambridge.

Crystal, D. (2002) *The English Language: A Guided Tour of the Language* (2nd edn). Penguin Books, London.

Daily Mail (1990) 'Scandal of our young illiterates'. 30 June.

Daily Mail (2002) 'Report about OECD'.

Daily Mail (2004) 'Ex-poly universities hit by student dropout crisis', 30 September.

Daily Mail (2005) '£420 m. That's the annual cost to taxpayers from students dropping out', 18 January.

Daily Telegraph (1990) 'MacGregor to investigate reading crisis'. 30 June.

Daily Telegraph (2004) 'The young Indian who has nation under spell', 7 December.

Dale, N. (1899) *On the Teaching of English Reading*. Philip, London.

Dale, N. (1900–2) *The Dale Readers*. Philip, London.

Daniels, J.C. and Diack, H. (1956) *Progress in Reading*. University of Nottingham School of Education, Nottingham.

Davenport, M. and Hall, P. (2004) *Target Listening and Understanding in Secondary Schools*. Barrington Stoke, Edinburgh.

Dayus, J. and Ayres, T. (1999) *Developing Writing Skills*. Heinemann Education Publishers, London.

DECP (1999) *Division of Educational and Child Psychology of the British Psychological Society. Dyslexia, Literacy and Psychological Assessment. Report by a Working Party*. British Psychological Society, Leicester.

DeFries, J.C. (1991) 'Genetics and dyslexia: an overview'. In Snowling, M.J. and Thomson, M. (eds) *Dyslexia: Integrating Theory and Practice*. Whurr Publishers, London.

DeFries, J.C., Alarcon, M. and Olson, R.K. (1997) 'Genetics and dyslexia: developmental differences in the etiologies of reading and spelling deficits'. In Hulme, C. and Snowling, M. (eds) *Dyslexia: Biology Cognition and Intervention*. Whurr Publishers, London.

Dejerine, J. (1892) 'Contribution à l'étude anatomo-pathologique et clinique des différentes variétés de cécité verbale'. *Mémoires de la Société de Biologie* 4: 61–90.

Delamain, C. and Spring, J. (2003) *Speaking, Listening and Understanding: Games for Young Children*. Speechmark Publishing, Bicester.

Denckla, M.B. and Cutting, L.E. (1999) 'History and significance of rapid automaticised naming'. *Annals of Dyslexia* 49: 29–42.

Denckla, M.B. and Rudel, R.G. (1972) 'Colour-naming in dyslexic boys'. *Cortex* 8: 164–76.

Denckla, M.B. and Rudel, R.G. (1974) 'Rapid automatised naming of pictured objects, colours, letters, and numbers by normal children'. *Cortex* 10: 186–202.

Denckla, M.B. and Rudel, R.G. (1976) 'Rapid automatized naming (RAN): dyslexia differentiated from other learning disabilities'. *Neuropsychologia* 14: 471–9.

DENI (1998) *The Code of Practice for the Identification and Assessment of Special Educational Needs*. DENI, Bangor.

DENI (1998) *The Code of Practice for the Identification and Assessment of Special Educational Needs*. Department for Education, Northern Ireland, Bangor.

Deponio, P. (2004) 'The co-occurrence of specific learning difficulties: implications for identification and assessment'. In Reid, G. and Fawcett, A. (eds) *Dyslexia in Context: Research, Policy and Practice*. Whurr Publishing, London.

Derewianka, B. (1990) *Exploring How Texts Work.* Primary English Teaching Association (PETA), Rozelle, New South Wales.

Derewianka, B. (1996) *Exploring the Writing of Genres.* United Kingdom Reading Association, Royston, Hertfordshire.

DES (1967) *Children and their Primary Schools* (The Plowden Report). Department of Education and Science, London.

DES (1975) *A Language for Life* (The Bullock Report). Department of Education and Science, HMSO, London.

DES (1978) *Special Educational Needs: Report of the Committee of Inquiry into the Education of Handicapped Children and Young People* (The Warnock Report). Department of Education and Science, HMSO, London.

DfEE (1994) *Code of Practice for the Identification and Assessment of Special Educational Needs.* Department for Education and Employment, Central Office of Information, London.

DfEE (1995) *English in the National Curriculum.* Department for Education and Employment, HMSO, London.

DfEE (1998) *The National Literacy Strategy Framework for Teaching.* Department for Education and Employment, London.

DfEE (1999) *The National Literacy Strategy. Spelling Bank. Lists of Words and Activities for the KS2 Spelling Objectives.* Department for Education and Employment Publications, Nottingham.

DfEE (2001) *Key Stage 3 National Strategy. Year 7 Spelling Bank.* Department for Education and Employment Publications, Nottingham.

DfES (2001) *Key Stage 3 National Strategy: Literacy Progress Unit Writing Organisation.* Department for Education and Employment, London.

DfES (2001a) *Special Educational Needs Code of Practice.* Department of Education and Skills, London.

DfES (2001b) *SEN Toolkit.* Department for Education and Skills, DfES Publications, Nottingham.

DfES (2001c) *Special Educational Needs (SEN) Guide for Parents and Carers.* Department for Education and Skills (DfES) Publications Centre, Nottingham.

DfES (2002a) *Special Educational Needs and Disability Tribunal: Disability Discrimination in Schools. How to Make a Claim.* Department for Education and Skills Publications Centre, Nottingham.

DfES (2002b) *Special Educational Needs and Disability Tribunal: Special Educational Needs: How to Appeal.* Department for Education and Skills Publications Centre, Nottingham.

DfES (2003) *Targeting Support: Choosing and Implementing Interventions for Children with Significant Literacy Difficulties.* Department for Education and Skills, Nottingham.

DfES (2004a) *What Are the Special Needs? Percentage of Pupils by Type of Need, England 2004.* Department for Education and Skills, Nottingham.

DfES (2004b) *Removing Barriers to Achievement: the Government's SEN Strategy.* DfES Publications, Nottingham.

Dignen, S. (2005) *Oxford Young Reader's Dictionary,* 2nd edn. Oxford University Press, Oxford.

Disability Rights Commission Code of Practice for Schools (2002) Disability Rights Commission, Stratford-upon-Avon.

DoES (2002) *Report of the Task-Force on Dyslexia.* Department of Education and Science, Dublin.

Dolman, E. (2003) 'Access to assessments and qualifications: "An incredible journey"'. *Patoss Bulletin* 16 (1).

Duncan, J. (1947) *The Duncan Readers.* Harrap, London.

Dunn, L. and Dunn, L. (1997) *British Picture Vocabulary Scale.* NFER-Nelson, London.

Dutton, K.P. (1992) 'Writing under examination conditions. Establishing a baseline'. *Handwriting Review.*

Ebbinghaus, H. (1885) *On Memory.* Duncker, Leipzig.

Ebbinghaus, H. (1966) *Memory* (trans. by Ruger and Bussenius). Dover, New York.

Eckert, M., Leonard, C., Richards, T., Aylward, E., Thomson, J. and Berninger, V. (2003) 'Anatomical correlates of dyslexia: frontal and cerebellar findings'. *Brain* 126 (2): 482–94.

Educational Assessment Unit, University of Edinburgh (2000) *The Edinburgh Reading Tests* 1–14, 3rd edn. Hodder Murray, London.

Ehri, L. (1995) 'Phases of development in learning to read words by sight'. *Journal of Research in Reading* 18: 116–25.

Ehri, L.C. (1997a) 'Sight word learning in normal readers and dyslexics'. In Blachman, B. (ed.) *Foundations of Reading Acquisition and Dyslexia: Implications for Early Intervention.* Lawrence Erlbuam Associates, Mahwah, NJ.

Ehri, L.C. (1997b) 'Learning to read and learning to spell are one and the same, almost'. In Perfetti, C.A., Rieben, L. and Fayol, M. *Learning to Spell.* Lawrence Erlbaum Associates, Mahwah, NJ.

Ehri, L.C. and Wilce, L.S. (1979) 'The mnemonic value of orthography among beginning readers'. *Journal of Educational Psychology* 71: 26–40.

Ehri, L.C. and Wilce, L.S. (1983) 'Development of words, identification speed in skilled and less skilled beginning readers'. *Journal of Educational Psychology* 75: 3–18.

Ehri, L.C., Nunes, S.R., Willows, D.M., Schuster, B.V., Yaghoub-Zadeh, Z. and Shanahan, T. (2001) 'Phonemic awareness instruction helps children learn to read: evidence from the National Reading Panel's meta analysis'. *Reading Research Quarterly* 36: 250–87.

Elkin, S. (2001) 'How the exam rules are bent'. *Daily Mail*, 7 August.

Elkonin, D.B. (1973) 'U.S.S.R.' In Downing, J. (ed.) *Comparative Reading.* Macmillan, New York.

Elliott, C.D., Smith, P. and McCullock, K. (1996) *British Ability Scales*, 2nd edn (BAS II). NFER-Nelson, Windsor.

Elliot, J. (2005) 'Dyslexia myths and the feel-bad factor'. *Times Educational Supplement*, 2 September.

Ellis, N.C. (1994) 'Longitudinal studies of spelling development'. In Brown, G.D.A. and Ellis, N.C. (eds) *Handbook of Spelling: Theory, Process and Intervention.* John Wiley and Sons, Chichester.

Ernst and Young (1993) *Literacy, Education and Training: Their Impact on the UK Economy.* Ernst and Young, London.

Evans, J. (ed.) (2001) *The Writing Classroom: Aspects of Writing and the Primary Child 3–11.* David Fulton, London.

Evans, P. and Lodge, J. (1999) *Revise the National Tests. English Key Stage 3.* Letts, London.

Fassett, J.H. (1922) *The Beacon Readers.* Ginn, London.

Fawcett, A. (2002) 'Evaluating therapies excluding traditional and phonological based therapies. A review for the Department for Education and Skills, the British Dyslexia Association and the Dyslexia Institute Review'. www.dfes.gov.uk/sen/documents/ACF4312, 2 February.

Fawcett, A. (2003) 'Definitions of dyslexia'. In Johnson, M. and Peer, L. (eds) *The Dyslexia Handbook 2003.* BDA, Reading.

Fawcett, A.J. and Nicolson, R.I. (1995) 'Persistent deficits in motor skill of children with dyslexia'. *Journal of Motor Behaviour* 27 (3): 235–40.

Fawcett, A.J. and Nicolson, R.I. (2001) 'Dyslexia: the role of the cerebellum'. In Fawcett, A. (ed.) *Dyslexia: Theory and Good Practice.* Whurr Publishers, London.

Fernald, G.M. (1943) *Remedial Techniques in the Basic Subjects.* McGraw Hill, New York.

Felton, R.H., Naylor, C.E. and Wood, F.B. (1990) 'Neuropsychological profile of adult dyslexics'. *Brain and Language* 39: 485–97.

First Steps (1997) *Writing Resource Book.* Education Department of Western Australia, Rigby Heinemann, Port Melbourne, Victoria.

Fisher, A., Murray, E. and Bundy, A. (1991) *Sensory Integration: Theory and Practice.* F.A. Davis, Philadelphia, PA.

Flesch, R. (1955) *Why Johnny Can't Read.* Harper and Row, New York.

Foorman, B., Francis, D., Fletcher, J., Schat-Schneider, C. and Menta, P. (1998) 'The role of instruction in learning to read. Preventing reading failure in at-risk children'. *Journal of Educational Psychology* 90: 1–15.

Frederickson, N., Frith, U. and Reason, R. (1997) *Phonological Assessment Battery (PhAB).* NFER-Nelson, London.

Frith, U. (1979) 'Reading by eye and writing by ear'. In Kolers, P.A., Wrolstad, M. and Bouma, H. (eds) *Processing of Visible Language, 1*. Plenum Press, New York.

Frith, U. (1980) 'Unexpected spelling problems'. In Frith, U. (ed.) *Cognitive Processes in Spelling*. Academic Press, London.

Frith, U. (1985) 'Beneath the surface of developmental dyslexia'. In Patterson, K.E., Marshall, J.C. and Coltheart, M. (eds) *Surface Dyslexia*. Routledge and Kegan Paul, London.

Frith, U. (1994) Foreword. In Brown, G.D.A. and Ellis, N.C. (eds) *Handbook of Spelling: Theory, Process and Intervention*. John Wiley and Sons, Chichester.

Frith, U. (1997) 'Brain, mind and behaviour in dyslexia'. In Hulme, C. and Snowling, M. (eds) *Dyslexia: Biology, Cognition and Intervention*. Whurr Publishers, London.

Fry, E. (1977) *Elementary Reading Instruction*. McGraw Hill, New York.

Fry, E., Polk, J. and Fountoukidis, D. (1984) *The Reading Teacher's Book of Lists*. Prentice-Hall, Englewood Cliffs, NJ.

Fullan Report (2003) *Watching and Learning 3: Final Report of the External Evaluation of England's National Literacy and Numeracy Strategies*. Ontario Institute for Studies in Education, Toronto.

Galaburda, A. (1985) 'A developmental dyslexia: a review of biological interactions'. *Annals of Dyslexia* 35: 21–33.

Galaburda, A.M. (1989) 'Ordinary and extraordinary brain development: anatomical variation in developmental dyslexia'. *Annals of Dyslexia* 39: 67–79.

Galaburda, A.M. and Kempner, T.L. (1979) 'Cytoarchitectonic abnormalities in developmental dyslexia. A case study'. *Annals of Neurology* 6: 94–100.

Gallagher, A., Laxon, V., Armstrong, E. and Frith, U. (1996) 'Phonological difficulties in high functioning dyslexics'. *Reading and Writing, An Interdisciplinary Journal* 8: 499–509.

Gardner, H. (1987) 'The theory of multiple intelligences'. *Annals of Dyslexia* 37: 19–35.

Gardner, H. (1983) *Frames of Mind: The Theory of Multiple Intelligences*. Basic Books, New York.

Gardner, H. (1993) *Multiple Intelligences: Theory and Practice*. Basic Books, New York.

Gardner, H. (1999) *Intelligence Reframed. Multiple Intelligences for the 21st Century*. Basic Books, New York.

Gathercole, S.E. and Alloway, T.P. (2004) 'Working memory and classroom learning'. *Dyslexia Review* 15 (3).

Gathercole, S.E. and Baddley, A.D. (1993) *Working Memory and Language*. Erlbaum, Hove.

Geschwind, N. (1982) 'Why Orton was right'. *Annals of Dyslexia* 32: 13–30.

Geschwind, N. and Behan, P. (1982) 'Left-handedness: association with immune disease, migraine, and developmental disorder'. *Proceedings of the National Academy of Sciences* 79: 5097–100.

Geschwind, N. and Fusillo, M. (1966) 'Colour-naming defects in association with alexia'. *Archives of Neurology* 15: 137–47.

Geschwind, N. and Galaburda, A.M. (eds) (1984) *Cerebral Dominance: the Biological Foundations*. Harvard University Press, Cambridge, MA.

Gillingham, A. and Stillman, B. (1956) *Remedial Training for Children with Specific Language Disability in Reading, Spelling and Penmanship* 5th edn. Educators Publishing Service Inc., Cambridge, MA.

Given, B.K. and Reid, G. (1999) *Learning Styles: A Guide for Teachers and Parents*. Red Rose Publications, St Annes-on-Sea.

Glutting, J., Adams, W. and Sheslow, D. (2000) *Wide Range Intelligence Test Manual*. Wilmington, DE.

Glynn, T. and McNaughton, S. (1985) 'The Mangere home and school remedial reading procedures: continuing research on their effectiveness. *New Zealand Journal of Psychology* 14: 66–77.

Glynn, T., McNaughton, S., Quinn, V. and Quinn, M. (1979) *Reading at Home: Helping You to Help Your Child*. New Zealand Council for Educational Research, Wellington, New Zealand.

Gold, K. (2004) 'Struggling with words'. *TES/EXTRA for Special Needs*, October.

Goodman, K.S. (1967) 'Reading: a psycholinguistic guessing game'. In Gollasch, F.V. (ed.) *Language and Literacy: the Selected Writings of Kenneth S. Goodman*, Vol. 1. Routledge and Kegan Paul, London.

Goodman, K.S. (1976) 'Reading: a psycholinguistic guessing game'. In Singer, H. and Ruddell, R.B. (eds) *Theoretical Models and Processes of Reading*. International Reading Association, Newark, DE.

Goodman, K.S. (1986) *What's Whole in Whole Language?* Heinemann, Portsmouth, NH.

Goswami, U. (1994) 'Reading by analogy: theoretical and practical perspectives'. In Hulme, C. and Snowling, M. (eds) *Reading Development and Dyslexia*. Whurr Publishers, London.

Gough, P. (1983) 'Context, form and instruction'. In Rayner, K. (ed.) *Eye Movements in Reading: Perceptual and Language Processes*. Academic Press, San Diego, CA.

Gough, P. and Tunmer, W.E. (1986) 'Decoding, reading, and reading disability'. *Remedial and Special Education* 7: 6–10.

Goulandris, N.K. (1994) 'Teaching spelling: bridging theory and practice'. In Brown, G.D.A. and Ellis, N.C. (eds) *Handbook of Spelling: Theory, Process and Intervention*. John Wiley and Sons, Chichester.

Goulandris, N. (ed.) (2003) *Dyslexia in Different Languages: Cross-Linguistic Comparisons*. Whurr Publishers, London.

Government of Ireland (2000) *Learning-Support Guidelines*. Government Publications, Dublin.

Grant, D. (2004) 'From myths to realities: lessons to be drawn about dyslexia from over 900 student assessments'. Paper presented at the 6th BDA International Conference, Warwick.

Graves, D. (1983) *Writing: Teachers and Children at Work*. Heinemann, Exeter, NH.

Green, C. and Chee, K. (1999) *Understanding A.D.H.D.* Vermilion, London.

Griffiths, C., Norwich, B., Burden, B. and Youngs, C. (2005) 'I'm glad that I don't take no for an answer'. In Tresman, S. and Cooke, A. (eds) *The Dyslexia Handbook 2005*. BDA, Reading.

Grigorenko, E.L., Wood, F.B., Meyer, M.S., Har, L.A., Speed, W.C., Shuster, A. and Pauls, D.L. (1997) 'Susceptibility loci for distinct components of developmental dyslexia on chromosomes 6 and 15'. *American Journal of Human Genetics* 60: 27–39.

Guide for Parents and Carers (2001) *Special Educational Needs (SEN); A Guide for Parents and Carers*. Department for Education and Skills. DfES Publications, Nottingham.

Haber, R.N. (1970) 'How we remember what we see'. *Scientific American* 105, May.

Hadow Report (1931) *Report of the Consultative Committee on the Primary School*. Board of Education, London.

Hagley, F. (2002) *Suffolk Reading Scale*, 2nd edn. NFER-Nelson, London.

Hahn, D., Flynn, L. and Reubens, S. (eds) (2003) *The Ultimate Book Guide*. A. and C. Black, London.

Hallgren, B. (1950) 'Specific dyslexia ('congenital word-blindness'): a clinical and genetic study'. *Acta Psychiatrica et Neurologia Scandinavica*, Suppl. 65: 1–287.

Halliday, M.A.K. (1975) *Learning How to Mean*. Edward Arnold, London.

Handford, M. (1997) *Where's Wally?* Walker Books, London.

Hanna, P.R., Hodges, R.E. and Hanna, J.S. (1971) *Spelling: Structure and Strategies*. Houghton Mifflin, Boston, MA.

Harpin, W. (1976) *The Second 'R': Writing Development in the Junior School*. Allen and Unwin, London.

Harris, S. (2004) '1 in 3 pupils aged 11 can't read properly'. *Daily Mail*, 15 December.

Hasenstab, J.K., Flaherty, G.M. and Brown, B.E. (1994) *Teaching Through the Learning Channels Instructor Guide*. Performance Learning Systems, Nevada, CA.

Hatcher, P.J. (1994) *Sound Linkage: An Integrated Programme for Overcoming Reading Difficulties*. Whurr Publishers, London.

Hatcher, P.J., Hulme, C. and Ellis, A.W. (1994) 'Ameliorating early reading failure by integrating the teaching of reading and phonological skills: the phonological linkage hypothesis'. *Child Development* 65: 41–57.

Heaps, C. (1998) 'Assessment'. *Patoss Bulletin* 11 (2).

Hedderly, R.G. (1995) 'The assessment of SpLD pupils for examination special arrangements'. *Dyslexia Review* 7 (2).

Hedderly, R. (1996) 'Vernon–Warden Reading Test – revised'. Kirklees Version. www.dyslexia. inst.org.uk.

Hieronymous, A.N., Linquist, E.F. and France, N. (1988) *Richmond Tests of Basic Skills*. NFER-Nelson, Windsor.

Hildreth, G. (1949) 'The development and training of hand dominance. II. Developmental tendencies in handedness'. *Journal of Genetic Psychology* 75: 221–75.

Hildreth, G. (1955) *Teaching Spelling: A Guide to Basic Principles and Practice*. Henry Holt, New York.

Hillocks, G. (1986) *Research on Written Composition*. National Conference on Research on Reading and Communication Skills, Urbana, IL.

Hinson, M. and Smith, P. (1997) *Phonics and Phonic Resources*. NASEN Enterprises, Tamworth.

HMI (1990) *Aspects of Primary Education: the Teaching and Learning of Language and Literacy*. Her Majesty's Inspectorate, HMSO, London.

Hoien, T. and Lundberg, I. (1989) 'A strategy for assessing problems in word recognition among dyslexics'. *Scandinavian Journal of Educational Research* 33: 15–201.

Horn, E. (1919) 'Principles of methods in teaching as derived from scientific investigation'. In Whipple, G. (ed.) *Eighteenth Year Book*. National Society for the Study of Education, Public Schools Publishing, Bloomington, NJ.

House of Commons Select Committee (1991) *Standards of Reading in Primary Schools*. HMSO, London.

House of Commons Select Committee (1996) *Special Educational Needs: the Working of the Code of Practice and the Tribunal*. HMSO, London.

House of Commons Select Committee on Education and Skills (2005) *Teaching Children to Read*. Eighth Report of Session. House of Commons, The Stationery Office, London.

Hudson, R. (2005) Letter: 'Grammar is safe with the strategy'. *Times Educational Supplement*, 4 February.

IALS Study (1997) *Further Results from the Second International Adult Literacy Survey*. OECD, Paris.

Improving our Schools (2000) 'Special Educational Needs: the Programme for Action'. www. scotland.gov.uk/library2.

International Dyslexia Association (1998) 'What is dyslexia'. www.interdys.org.

Jackson, A. (2005) Personal communication.

Jagger, J.H. (1929) *The Sentence Method of Teaching Reading*. Grant Educational, Glasgow.

James, A. and Draffan, E.A. (2004) 'The accuracy of electronic spellcheckers for dyslexic learners'. *Patoss Bulletin* 17 (2).

JCGQ (2003) *Regulations and Guidance Relating to Candidates with Particular Requirements*. Joint Council for General Qualifications.

JCQ (2002) 'Regulations and guidance relating to candidates with particular requirements'. www.jcgq.org.uk.

JCQ (2004) 'Access arrangements and special consideration. Regulations and guidance relating to candidates who are eligible for adjustments in examinations'. www.jcq.org.uk.

Jensen, E. (1995) *Super Teaching*. The Brain Store, San Diego, CA.

Johnson, M. (2004) 'Dyslexia friendly schools – policy and practice'. In Reid, G. and Fawcett, A. (eds) *Dyslexia in Context: Research, Policy and Practice*, 237–56. Whurr Publishers, London.

Johnson, M., Peer, L. and Lee, R. (2001) 'Pre-school children and dyslexia: policy, identification and intervention'. In Fawcett A. (ed.) *Dyslexia: Theory and Good Practice*. Whurr Publishers, London.

Johnson, Samuel (1755) A *Dictionary of the English Language*. Strahan, London.

Johnston, R. and Watson, J. (1995) *The Effects of Synthetic Phonics Teaching on Reading and Spelling Attainments*. Scottish Executive Education Department, Edinburgh.

Johnston, R. and Watson, J. (2005) *The Effects of Synthetic Phonics Teaching on Reading and Spelling*

Attainment: A Seven Year Longitudinal Study. Scottish Executive Central Research Unit, Edinburgh.

Johnston, R., Connelly, V. and Watson, J. (1995) 'Some effects of phonics teaching on early reading development'. In Owen, P. and Pumfrey, P. (eds) *Emergent and Developing Reading: Messages for Teachers.* Falmer Press, London.

Jones, K. (2003) 'The Disability Discrimination Act and Special Education Needs Code – issues revolving around specific learning difficulties'. *PATOSS Bulletin* 16 (1).

Jones, N. (2003) *Dyspraxia: the School Pack.* Bridgend County Borough Council.

Jorm, A.F. and Share, D.L. (1983) 'Phonological recording and reading acquisition'. *Applied Psycholinguistics* 4: 103–47.

Kaplan, B.J., Wilson, B.N., Dewey, D. and Crawford, S.G. (1998) 'DCD may not be a discrete disorder'. *Human Movement Science* 17: 471–90.

Kaplan, B.J., Wilson, B.N., Dewey, D.M., Crawford, S.G. and Wilson, B.N. (2001) 'The term comorbidity is of questionable value in reference to developmental disorders: data and theory'. *Journal of Learning Disabilities* 34 (6).

Kaufman, A.S. and Kaufman, N.L. (1985) *Kaufman Test of Educational Achievement (K-Test).* American Guidance Services, Circle Pines, MD.

Keeney, A.H. and Keeney, V.T. (1968) *Dyslexia: Diagnosis and Treatment of Reading Disorders,* Mosby, St Louis, MO.

Kephart, N. (1963) *The Brain-Injured Child in the Classroom.* National Society for Crippled Children and Adults, Chicago, IL.

Key Stage 3 National Strategy (2001a) *Framework for Teaching English: Years 7, 8 and 9.* Department for Education and Employment, London.

Key Stage 3 National Strategy (2001b) *Literacy Progress Unit, Writing Organisation.* Department for Education and Employment, London.

Kingman Report (1988) *A Report of the Committee of Inquiry into the Teaching of English Language.* Department of Education and Science. HMSO, London.

Kinlock, R. (1994) *EasyType.* Egon, Baldock.

Kinneavy, J.L. (1971) *A Theory of Discourse.* Prentice Hall, Englewood Cliffs, NJ.

Kipling, R. (1902) *Just So Stories.* Macmillan, London.

Kirby, A. (1999) *Dyspraxia: the Hidden Handicap.* Souvenir Press, London.

Kirby, A. (2004) *The Adolescent with Developmental Co-ordination Disorder (DCD).* Jessica Kingsley Publishers, London.

Knight, M. (2004) 'A differentiated spelling scheme'. *Dyslexia Review* 15 (2).

Korhonen, T. (1995) 'The persistence of rapid naming problems in children with reading disabilities. A nine-year follow up'. *Journal of Learning Disabilities* 28: 232–9.

Kreiner, D. and Gough P. (1990) 'Two ideas about spelling: rules and word-spelling memory'. *Journal of Memory and Language* 29: 103–18.

Kussmaul, A. (1877) 'Disturbances of speech'. In Von Ziemssen, H. and McCreery, J.A. (trans.) *Cyclopedia of the Practice of Medicine,* 14. Wood Wm., New York.

LaBerge, D. and Samuels, J. (1974) 'Toward a theory of automatic information processing in reading'. *Cognitive Psychology* 6: 293–323.

Larsen, J.P., Høien, T., Lundberg, I. and Ödegaard, H. (1990) 'MRI evaluation of the size and the symmetry of planum temporale in adolescents with developmental dyslexia'. *Brain and Language* 39: 289–301.

Lazar, I. and Darlington, R. (eds) (1982) *Lasting Effects of Early Education: a Report from the Consortium of Longitudinal Studies.* Monographs of the Society for Research in Child Development, 27 (2–3, serial No 195) (Summary Report, DHEW Publications No OHDS 80 – 30/79).

Lennox, C. and Siegel, L.S. (1994) 'The role of phonological and orthographic processes in learning to spell'. In Brown, G.D.A. and Ellis, N.C. (eds) *Handbook of Spelling: Theory, Process and Intervention.* John Wiley and Sons, Chichester.

Lerner, J. (2000) *Learning Disabilities: Theories, Diagnosis and Teaching Strategies*, 8th edn. Houghton Mifflin, Boston, NJ.

Lewis, M. and Wray, D. (1995) *Developing Children's Non-fiction Writing*. Scholastic, Leamington Spa.

Lewis, M. and Wray, D. (undated) *Writing Frames: Scaffolding Children's Non-fiction. Writing in a Range of Genres*. EXEL-Exeter Extending Literacy Project, Reading and Language Information Centre, University of Reading, Reading.

Liberman, A.M., Cooper, F.S., Shankweiler, D. and Studdert-Kennedy, M. (1967) 'Perception of the speech code'. *Psychological Review* 74: 731–61.

Liberman, I.Y. and Liberman, A.M. (1990) 'Whole Language vs. Code Emphasis: underlying assumptions and their implications for reading instruction'. *Annals of Dyslexia* 40: 51–76.

Liberman, I.Y., Shankweiler, D., Fisher, F.W. and Carter, B. (1974) 'Explicit syllable and phoneme segmentation in the young child'. *Journal of Experimental Child Psychology* 18: 201–12.

Litterick, I. (2005) 'Is there a specific font that is more dyslexia friendly than others?' Personal communication.

Livingstone, M.S., Rosen, G.D., Dislane, F.W. and Galaburda, A.M. (1991) 'Physiological and anatomical evidence for a magnocellular deficit in developmental dyslexia'. *Proceedings of the National Academy of Sciences* 88: 7943–7.

Lloyd, S. (1998) *The Phonics Handbook: a Handbook for Teaching Reading, Writing and Spelling*, 3rd edn. Jolly Learning, Chigwell.

Losse, S., Henderson, S.E., Elliman, D. Hall, O., Knight, E. and Jongmans, M. (1991) 'Clumsiness in children: do they grow out of it? A 10 year follow up study'. *Developmental Medicine and Child Neurology* 33: 55–68.

Lovett, M.V. (1986) 'Sentential structure and the perceptual spans of two samples of disabled readers'. *Journal of Psycholinguistic Research* 15 (2): 153–75.

Lundberg, I. (2002) 'Twenty five years of reading research as a basis for prediction of future development'. In Hjelmquist E. and Euler C. Von (eds) *Dyslexia and Literacy*. Whurr Publishers, London.

Lundberg, I. and Hoien, T. (2001) 'Dyslexia and phonology'. In Fawcett A. (ed.) *Dyslexia: Theory and Good Practice*. Whurr Publishers, London.

Lundberg, I., Frost, J. and Petersen, O.-P. (1988) 'Effects of an extensive program of stimulating phonological awareness in preschool children'. *Reading Research Quarterly* 23: 264–84.

Lunzer, E. and Gardner, K. (1979) *The Effective Use of Reading*. Heinemann, London.

Luria, A.R. (1959) 'The directive function in speed in development and dissolution'. *Word* 15 (3): 341–52. (Reprinted in Oldfield, R.C. and Marshall, J.C. (eds) (1968) *Language*. Penguin Books, Harmondsworth.)

Luria, A.R. (1970) *Traumatic Asphasia*. Mouton, The Hague.

Lyon, G.R. (1998) *National Health Institute Report to the Committee on Labor and Human Resources*. National Institute of Child Health and Human Development, www.readby grade3.com.

Lyon, G.R., Shaywitz, S.E. and Shaywitz, B.A. (2003) 'Defining dyslexia, comorbidity, teacher's knowledge of language and reading'. *Annals of Dyslexia* 53: 1–14.

Lyon, R.G., Shaywitz, S.E., Chhabra, V. and Sweet, R. (2004) 'Evidence-based reading policy in the US'. In Reid, G. and Fawcett, A. (eds) *Dyslexia in Context: Research, Policy and Practice*. Whurr Publishers, London.

McArthur, T. (ed.) (1992) *The Oxford Companion to the English Language*. Oxford University Press, Oxford.

MacArthur, C. and Graham, S. (1987) 'Learning disabled students' composing with three methods: handwriting, dictation and word processing'. *Journal of Special Education* 21 (3): 22–42.

Maclean, M., Bryant, P. and Bradley, L. (1987) 'Rhymes, nursery rhymes, and reading in early childhood'. *Merrill-Palmer Quarterly* 33: 255–81.

McGuinness, D. (1998) *Why Children Can't Read and What We Can Do About It*. Penguin Books, London.

Macmillan Test Unit (1985) *Graded Word Reading Test*. NFER-Nelson, London.

Macmillan Test Unit with Hagues, N. and Burley, J. (1990) *Group Reading Test 6–14*. NFER-Nelson, London.

McNally, J. and Murray, W. (1962) *100 Key Words to Literacy*. Schoolmaster Publishing Co., Kettering.

Macpherson, G. (ed.) (1995) *Black's Medical Dictionary*, 38th edn. A. and C. Black, London.

Manis, F.R., Custodio, R. and Szeszulski, P.A. (1993) 'Development of phonological and orthographical skills: a 2-year longitudinal study of dyslexic children'. *Cognition* 58: 157–95.

Marsh, G., Friedman, M., Welch, V., and Desberg, P. (1980) 'The development of strategies'. In Frith, U. (ed.) *Cognitive Processes in Spelling*. Academic Press, London.

Martin, J.R., Rothery, J. and Christie, F. (1987) 'Social processes in education: a reply to Sawyer and Watson (and others)'. In Reid, I. (ed.) *The Place of Genre Learning: Current Debates*. Deakin University, Deakin, Victoria.

Maxwell, C. (2005) *Dictionary of Perfect Spelling*. Barrington Stoke, Edinburgh.

Maybury, B. (1967) *Creative Writing for Juniors*. Batsford, London.

Mercer, C. and Campbell, K. (1998) *Great-Leaps Reading Program*. Diarmuid Inc., Micanopy, FL.

Meyer, M.S. and Felton, R.H. (1999) 'Repeated reading to enhance fluency: old approaches and new directions'. *Annals of Dyslexia* 49: 283–306.

Meyer, M.S., Wood, F.B., Hart, L.A. and Felton, R.H. (1998) 'Longitudinal course of rapid naming in disabled and nondisabled readers'. *Annals of Dyslexia* 48: 91–114.

Miles, T.R. (1993) *Dyslexia: the Pattern of Difficulties*, 2nd edn. Whurr Publishers, London.

Miles, T.R. (2004) 'Fifty years of dyslexia research: a personal story'. *Dyslexia Review* 16 (1).

Miles, T.R. and Miles, E. (eds.) (1992) *Dyslexia and Mathematics*. Routledge, London.

Miles, T.R., Haslum, M.N. and Wheeler, T.J. (1996) 'Handedness in dyslexia: should this be routinely recorded?' *Dyslexia Review* 8 (2).

Miles, T.R., Wheeler, T.J. and Haslum, M.N. (2003) 'The existence of dyslexia without severe literacy problems'. *Annals of Dyslexia* 53: 340–54.

Miller, G.A. (1956) 'The magical number seven, plus or minus two: some limits in our capacity for processing information'. *Psychological Review* 63: 81–97.

Miller, Guron L. (1999) *Wordchains: A Word Reading Test for All Ages*. NFER-Nelson, London.

Ministry of Education (1954) *Language: Some Suggestions for Teachers of English and Others*, HMSO, London.

Moats, L.C. (1993) 'Spelling error interpretation: beyond the phonetic/dysphonetic dichotomy'. *Annals of Dyslexia*, 43: 174–85.

Moats, L. (1995) *Spelling Development, Disability, and Instruction*. York Press, Baltimore, MD.

Moline, S. (2001) 'Using graphic organisers to write information texts'. In Evans J. (ed.) *The Writing Classroom: Aspects of Writing and the Primary Child 3–11*. David Fulton Publishers, London.

Montgomery, D. (1998) 'Gifted education: education of the highly gifted'. In Shorrocks-Taylor, D. (ed.) *Directions in Educational Psychology*. Whurr Publishers, London.

Morais, J. (1991) 'Constraints on the development of phonemic awareness'. In Brady, S.A. and Shankweiler, D.P. (eds) *Phonological Processes in Literacy*. Lawrence Erlbaum Associates, Mahwah, NJ.

Morgan, R. (1983) *Helping Children Read. The Paired Reading Handbook*. Methuen Children's Books, London.

Morris, J. (1984) 'Phonics: from an unsophisticated past to a linguistics-informed future'. In Brooks, G. and Pugh, A.K. (eds) *Studies in the History of Reading*. Centre for the Teaching of Reading and the United Kingdom Reading Association, University of Reading School of Education, Reading.

Mortimer, T. (2004) 'Widening opportunity for dyslexic learners – is learning style theory the answer?' *Dyslexia Review* 16 (1).

Moseley, D.V. (1989) 'How a lack of confidence in spelling affects children's written expression'. *Educational Psychology in Practice* 5 (1): 42–6.

Moseley, D.V. (1997) 'Assessment of spelling and related aspects of written expression'. In Beech, J.R. and Singleton, C. (eds) *The Psychological Assessment of Reading*. Routledge, London.

MRC (Wilkins, A.J., Jeanes, R.J., Pumfrey, P.D. and Laskier, M.) (1996) *Wilkins Rate of Reading Test*. The Institute of Optometry, London.

Mulcaster, R. (1592) *The Elementarie*.

Murray, W. (1964) *The Ladybird Key Words Reading Scheme*. Wills and Hepworth, Loughborough.

NAA (2004) *Assessment and Reporting Arrangements. Key Stages 1, 2, 3*. Qualifications and Curriculum Authority, London.

National Curriculum (1989) *English in the National Curriculum*. Department of Education and Science, London.

National Curriculum (1999) *The National Curriculum Programmes of Study and Attainment Targets [English]*. Department for Education and Employment and Qualifications and Curriculum Authority, HMSO, London.

National Curriculum (2000) *The Second Revision of the National Curriculum*. Department for Education and Employment, London.

National Institute of Child Health and Human Development (2000) *Report of the National Reading Panel Teaching Children to Read: An Evidence-based Assessment of the Scientific Research Literature on Reading and its Implications for Reading Instruction*. Reports of the Subgroups (NIH Publications No 00–4754), US Government Printing Office, Washington, DC.

National Writing Project (1990) *Perceptions of Writing*. Nelson, Surrey.

NCES (2003) *National Assessment of Educational Progress: the Nation's Report Card*. US Department of Education, Washington, DC.

New Oxford Thesaurus of English (2000) Oxford University Press, Oxford.

Newton, M. and Thomson, M. (1976) 'Dyslexia: a guide to examinations'. *Dyslexia Review* 16.

Newton, M.J., Thomson, M.E. and Richards, I. (eds) (1979) *Reading in Dyslexia*. Learning Development Aids. Wisbech.

Nicholson T. (1997) 'Closing the gap on reading failure: social background, phonemic awareness, and learning to read'. In Blackman, B. (ed.) *Foundations of Reading Acquisition and Dyslexia: Implications for Early Intervention*. Lawrence Erlbaum Associates, Mahwah, NJ.

Nicolson, R.I. and Fawcett, A.J. (1990) 'Automaticity: a new framework for dyslexia research'. *Cognition* 35 (2): 159–82.

Nicolson, R.I. and Fawcett, A.J. (1994) 'Comparison of deficits in cognitive and motor skills among children with dyslexia'. *Annals of Dyslexia* 44: 147–64.

NLS (1998) *The National Literacy Strategy Framework for Teaching*. Department for Education and Employment, London.

NLS (2001) *Year 7 Spelling Bank*. Department for Education and Employment, London.

Norris, E., Kopuider, M. and Reichard, C. (1998) 'Children's use of drawing as a pre-writing strategy'. *Journal of Research in Reading* 21 (1): 69–74.

Northedge, A. (1990) *The Good Study Guide*. The Open University, Milton Keynes.

Northedge, A. (1997) *The Sciences Good Study Guide*. The Open University, Milton Keynes.

Nosek, K. (1997) *Dyslexia in Adults: Taking Charge of Your Life*. Taylor Publishing Company, Dallas, TX.

Novoa, L. and Wolf, M. (1984) 'Word-retrieval and reading in bilingual children'. Paper presented at Boston University Language Conference, Boston, MA.

O'Brien, C. (2006) *Dyslexia Friendly Schools Scheme. Dyslexia Handbook*. BDA, Reading.

O'Connor, J. and Seymour, J. (1990) *Introducing Neurolinguistic Programming*. Mandala, London.

O'Donnell, M. and Munroe, R. (1949) *The Janet and John Books*. Nisbet, London.

OECD/Statistics Canada (2000) *Literacy in the Information Age. Final Report of the International Adult Literacy Survey*. OECD, Paris.

OECD (2004) 'UK schools slip down the world's league table'. *Daily Telegraph*, 7 December.

Ofsted (1991) *English Key Stage 1: A Report by H.M. Inspectorate on the First Year 1989–1990.* HMSO, London.

Ofsted (1993) *The Implementation of the Curricular Requirements of the Education Reform Act: English Key Stages 1, 2, 3, 4. Fourth Year, 1992–3: A Report of Her Majesty's Chief Inspector of Schools.* HMSO, London.

Ofsted (1996) *The Teaching of Reading in 45 Inner London Primary Schools.* HMSO, London.

Ofsted (1997) *The Annual Report of Her Majesty's Chief Inspector of Schools: Standards and Quality in Education (1995/6).* HMSO, London.

Ofsted (1999) *Pupils with Specific Learning Difficulties in Mainstream Schools: A Survey of the Provision in Mainstream Primary and Secondary Schools for Pupils with a Statement of Special Educational Needs Related to Specific Learning Difficulties,* Ofsted Publications Centre, London.

Ofsted (2001) *Report on Phonics.* HMSO, London.

Ofsted (2004) *Reading for Purpose and Pleasure: an Evaluation of the Teaching of Reading in Primary Schools.* Ofsted Publications Centre, London.

Oldfield, R.C. (1971) 'The assessment and analysis of handedness: the Edinburgh inventory'. *Neuropsychologia* 9: 97–113.

Ornstein, R.E. (1972) *The Psychology of Consciousness.* W.H. Freeman, San Francisco, CA.

Orton Dyslexia Society (1986) 'Some facts about illiteracy in America'. *Perspectives on Dyslexia* 13 (4): 1–3.

Orton, S.T. (1937) *Reading, Writing and Speech Problems in Children.* Chapman and Hall, London.

Ott, P. (1997) *How to Detect and Manage Dyslexia: a Reference and Resource Manual.* Heinemann Educational, Oxford.

Ott, P. (1999) 'Detecting and managing dyslexia in the classroom'. Paper presented at European Council of International Schools, Nice.

Ott, P. (2000) 'Dealing with dyslexia at home'. Paper presented at European Children in Crisis Seminar. Borschette Centre, Brussels.

Ott, P. (2000) *Top Dog's Plural Enforcers.* Pictorial Charts Educational Trust (PCET), London.

Ott, P. (2001a) 'Strategies for success for reluctant writers'. Paper presented at the 5th International Conference of the British Dyslexia Association, York.

Ott, P. (2001b) 'Closing the gaps in reading attainments: when dyslexia is successfully managed'. In Sheil, G. and Ni Dhalaigh, U. (eds) *Reading Matters: A Fresh Start.* Paper delivered at the Reading Association of Ireland Conference, Educational Research Centre, Dublin.

Ott, P. (2007a) *How to Manage Spelling Successfully.* Routledge, London.

Ott, P. (2007b) *Activities for Spelling Successfully.* Routledge, London.

Owen, J. (2004) 'The Text Checker'. The Inclusion Consultancy Ltd, www.tic1.co.uk.

Palmer, S. (2001) *How to Teach Writing Across the Curriculum at Key Stage 2.* David Fulton Publishers, London.

Palmer, S. (2001) *Skeleton Books (6).* Big Books Technology Teaching Systems, Alfreton.

Palmer, S. and Morgan, M. (1998) *Tune into Sounds and The Big ABC Book, Teacher's Book.* Ginn, Oxford.

Panikker, G. (2004) 'The young Indian who has nation under her spell'. *Daily Telegraph,* 7 December.

Patoss (2002) 'Chairman's Report' (Greenwold, L.) Patoss Bulletin 15 (1).

Pauk, W. (1974) *How to Study in College,* 2nd edn. Houghton Mifflin, Boston, MA.

Paulesu, E., Frith, U., Snowling, M., Gallagher, A., Morton, J., Frackowiak, R.S.J. and Frith (1996) 'Is developmental dyslexia a disconnection syndrome? Evidence from PET scanning'. *Brain* 119: 143–57.

Peer, L. (1996) 'Reading difficulty (Fogg Index)'. *BDA Newsletter,* May.

Peer, L. (1999) 'What is dyslexia?' In Smythe I. (ed.) *The Dyslexia Handbook.* BDA, Reading.

Pennington, B., Van Orden, G., Smith, S. Green, P. and Haith, M. (1990) 'Phonological processing skills and deficits in adult dyslexics'. *Child Development* 61: 1753–78.

Pennington, B.F., Smith, S.D., Kimberling, W.J., Green, P.A. and Haith, M. (1987) 'Left-handedness and immune disorders in familial dyslexics'. *Archives of Neurology* 44: 634–9.

Perfetti, C.A. (1985) *Reading Ability*. Oxford University Press, New York.

Peters, M.L. (1985) *Spelling Caught or Taught: a New Look*. Routledge, London.

Phinn, G. (2001) 'Different ways into fiction and poetry'. In Evans, J. (ed.) *The Writing Classroom. Aspects of Writing and the Primary Child 3–11*. David Fulton Publishers, London.

Pitman, J. and St John, J. (1969) *Alphabets and Reading*. Pitman, London.

Pope, A. (1711) *Essay on Criticism*. W. Lewis, London.

Portwood, M. (1996) *Developmental Dyspraxia: A Practical Manual for Parents and Professionals*. Educational Psychology Service, Durham County Council, Durham.

Portwood, M.N. (1999) *Developmental Dyspraxia Identification and Intervention: A Manual for Parents and Professionals*. 2nd edn. David Fulton, London.

Posner, M., Petersen, S., Fox, P. and Raichle, M. (1988) 'Localisation of cognitive operations in the human brain'. *Science* 240: 1627–31.

Pressley, M. and Rankin, J. (1994) 'More about whole language methods of reading instruction for students at risk of early reading failure'. *Learning Disabilities: Research and Practice* 9 (3): 157–68.

Pumfrey, P. (2002) 'Specific developmental dyslexia (SDD). "Basics to back" in 2000 and beyond?' In Wearmouth, J., Soler, J. and Reid, G. (eds) *Addressing Difficulties in Literacy Development: Responses at Family, School, Pupil and Teacher Levels*. Routledge, London.

Pumfrey, P.D. and Reason, R. (1991) *Specific Learning Difficulties (Dyslexia): Challenges and Responses*. Routledge, London.

QCA (1998) *The Grammar Papers*. Qualifications and Curriculum Authority, London.

QCA (2002) *Guidelines for Writing Targets*. Qualifications and Curriculum Authority. www.info@ qca.org.uk.

QCA (2003a) *Assessment and Reporting Arrangements. Key Stage 1, 2, 3*. Qualifications and Curriculum Authority, London.

QCA (2003b) *The English Tests*. Qualifications and Curriculum Authority, London.

QCA (2004) *Assessment and Reporting Arrangements. Key Stage 2*. Qualifications and Curriculum Authority, London.

QCA (2005) *Key Stage 2. Assessment and Reporting Arrangements*. Qualifications and Curriculum Authority, London.

Rack, J. (2003) 'The who, what, when and how of intervention programmes: comments on the DDAT evaluation', *Dyslexia* 9 (3): 137–9.

Rack, J.P., Snowling, M.J. and Olsen, R.K. (1992) 'The nonword reading deficit in developmental dyslexia. A review'. *Reading Research Quarterly* 27 (1): 29–53.

Raven, J.C., Court, J.H. and Raven, J. (1988) *Raven's Standard Progressive Matrices*, Oxford Psychologists Press, Oxford.

Read, C. (1971) 'Preschool children's knowledge of English phonology'. *Harvard Educational Review* 41: 1–34.

Read, C. (1975) *Children's Categorisation of Speech Sounds in English*. Research Report No 17. National Council of Teachers of English. Urbana, IL.

Reid, R.G. (1998) *Dyslexia: a Practitioner's Handbook* 2nd edn. John Wiley and Sons, Chichester.

Reid, G. (2005) *Dyslexia: a Complete Guide for Parents*. John Wiley and Sons, Chichester.

Reilly, J. and Murray, S. (2004) *Target Listening and Understanding in Primary Schools*. Barrington Stoke, Edinburgh.

Riding, R. and Rayner, S. (1998) *Cognitive Styles and Learning Strategies: Understanding Style Differences in Learning and Behaviour*. David Fulton Publishers, London.

Robinson, F.P. (1970) *Effective Study*, 4th edn, Harper and Row Publishers, New York.

Rome, P. and Smith, Osman, J. (1993) *Language Tool Kit*. Educators Publishing Service, Cambridge, MA.

Rose, J. (2006) *Independent Review of the Teaching of Early Reading*. www.standards.dfes.gov.uk/rosereview.

Rose, S.P.R. (1993) *The Making of Memory*. Bantam, London.

Rosen, G.D., Sherman, G.F. and Galaburda, A.M. (1993) 'Dyslexia and brain pathology. Experimental animal models'. In Galaburda, A.M. (ed.) *Dyslexia and Development: Neurobiological Aspects of Extra-Ordinary Brains*. Harvard University Press, Cambridge, MA.

Rosner, J. (1993) *Helping Children Overcome Learning Difficulties*, 3rd edn. Walker, New York.

Royal County of Berkshire (undated) *The Education Act 1981. Criteria for Multi-Professional Assessment*, Bracknell.

Royal Literary Fund (2006) *Writing Matters: The Royal Literary Fund Report on Student Writing in Higher Education*, ed. Davies, S., Swinburne, D. and Williams, G. RLF, London.

Russell, P. (1997) 'Parents as partners: some early impressions of the impact of the code of practice'. In Wolfendale, S. (ed.) *Working with Parents After the Code of Practice*. Fulton, London.

Rust, J. Golombok, S. and Trickey, G. (1993) *Wechsler Objective Reading Dimensions* (WORD) The Psychological Corporation. Harcourt Assessment, Cambridge, MA.

Sacre, L. and Masterson, J. (2000) *Single Word Spelling Test*. NFER-Nelson, London.

Samuelsson, S., Gustavsson, A., Herkner, B. and Lundberg, I. (2000) 'Is the frequency of dyslexic problems among prison inmates higher than in a normal population?' *Reading and Writing: an Interdisciplinary Journal* 13: 297–312.

Satz, P. (1990) Foreword. In Bishop, D.V.M., *Handedness and Developmental Disorder*. Mac Keith Press, London.

Sawyer, C.E. (1993) 'Handwriting speed and special arrangements in GCSE'. *Handwriting Review* 7–9.

Sawyer, C., Potter, V. and Taylor (1994) *Reading Age Levels for Statutory Assessment*. Dorset LEA.

Scarborough, H. (1990) 'Very early language deficits in dyslexic children'. *Child Development* 61: 1728–43.

Schlagal, B. (1992) *Patterns of Orthographic Knowledge and the Foundations of Literacy. A Memorial Festschrift for Edmund H. Henderson*. Lawrence Erlbaum Associates, Hillsdale, NJ.

Schlagal, B. (1996) 'Teaching disabled spellers'. In Putham, L.R. (ed.) *How to Become a Better Reading Teacher: Strategies for Assessment and Intervention*. Merrill, Englewood Cliffs, NJ.

Schlagal, B. (2001) 'Traditional, developmental, and structured language approaches to spelling: review and recommendations'. *Annals of Dyslexia* 51: 147–76.

Schneider, E. (1999) *Multisensory Structural Metacognitive Instruction: an Approach to Teaching Foreign Language to All-Risk Students*. Peter Lang, Frankfurt am Main.

Schonell, F. (1939) *Happy Venture*. Philip and Tacey, London.

Schonell, F.J. (1932) *Essentials in Teaching and Testing Spelling* (new edition 1969). Macmillan, London.

Schonell, F.J. (1974) *Graded Word Reading Test*, 5th edn. Oliver and Boyd, London.

Scragg, D.G. (1974) *A History of English Spelling*. Manchester University Press, Manchester.

SENDIST (2003a) *Guidance for Coming to the Tribunal*. SENDIST, Darlington.

SENDIST (2003b) *Special Educational Needs and Disability Tribunal Annual Report 2002–2003*. SENDIST, Darlington.

Shaywitz, B.A. and Shaywitz, S.E. (1991) 'Comorbidity: a critical issue in attention deficit disorder'. *Journal of Child Neurology* 6: 13–20.

Shaywitz, S., Shawitz, B., Ough, K., Fulbright, R., Constable, R.T., Mencl, W.E., Shankweiler, D., Liberman, A., Skudlarski, P., Fletcher, J., Katz, L., Marchione, K., Lacadie, C., Gatenby, C. and Gore, J. (1998) 'Functional disruption in the organisation of the brain for reading in dyslexia'. *Neurobiology* 95: 2636–41.

Sheffield, B. (1996) 'Handwriting: a neglected cornerstone of literacy'. *Annals of Dyslexia* 46: 21–35.

Shorter Oxford English Dictionary: On Historical Principles (1933) ed. Onions, C.T. The Clarendon Press, Oxford.

Siegel, L.S. (1989) 'IQ is irrelevant to the definition of learning disabilities'. *Journal of Learning Disabilities* 22: (8) 469–78, 486.

Siegel, L.S. (1992) 'An evaluation of the discrepancy definition of dyslexia'. *Journal of Learning Disabilities* 25: 618–29.

Siegel, L.S. (1994) 'The modularity of reading and spelling: evidence from hyperlexia'. In Brown, G.D.A. and Ellis, N.C. (eds) *Handbook of Spelling: Theory, Process and Intervention*. John Wiley and Sons, Chichester.

Siegel, L. and Smythe, I. (2004) 'Dyslexia and English as an additional language (EAL): towards a greater understanding'. In Reid, G. and Fawcett, A. (eds) *Dyslexia in Context: Research Policy and Practice*. Whurr Publishers, London.

Simmons, K. (1997) 'Supporting parents at the special educational needs tribunal'. In Wolfendale, S. (ed.) *Working with Parents of SEN Children after the Code of Practice*. David Fulton Publishers, London.

Skinner, B.F. (1968) *The Technology of Teaching*. Appleton Century Crofts, New York.

Smith, F. (1973) *Psycholinguistics and Reading*. Holt, Rinehart and Winston, New York.

Smith, F. (1977) 'Making sense of reading and of reading instruction'. *Harvard Educational Review* 47: 386–95.

Smith, F. (1978) *Understanding Reading*. Holt, Rinehart and Winston, London.

Smith, S.D., Limberling, W.J., Pennington, B.F. and Lubs, H.A. (1983) 'Specific reading dis-ability: identification of an inherited form through linkage analysis'. *Science* 219: 1345.

Smythe, I. (2005) 'Making e-learning dyslexia friendly'. In Tresman, S. and Cooke, A. (eds) *The Dyslexia Handbook*. BDA, Reading.

Snow, C., Burns, S. and Griffith, P. (eds) (1998) *Preventing Reading Difficulties in Young Children*. National Academy Press, Washington, DC.

Snowling, M.J. (1981) 'Phonemic deficits in developmental dyslexia'. *Psychological Research* 43: 219–34.

Snowling, M.J. (1994) 'Towards a model of spelling acquisition: the development of some component skills'. In Brown, G.D.A. and Ellis, N.C. (eds) *Handbook of Spelling: Theory, Process and Intervention*. John Wiley and Sons, Chichester.

Snowling, M. (2001) 'From language to reading and dyslexia'. *Dyslexia* 7: 37–46.

Snowling, M. and Hulme, C. (2003) 'There is no evidence that DDAT is an effective treatment for dyslexia-related disorders: a critique of claims from Reynolds, Nicolson and Hamby' *Dyslexia* 9 (2): 127–33.

Snowling, M. and Nation, K. (1997) 'Language, phonology, and learning to read'. In Hulme, C. and Snowling, M. (eds) *Dyslexia: Biology, Cognition, and Intervention*. Whurr Publishers, London.

SOEID (1994) *Effective Provision for Special Educational Needs (EPSEN)*. The Scottish Office Education and Industry Department, The Stationery Office, Edinburgh.

SOEID (1996) *Children and Young Persons with Special Educational Needs: Assessment and Recording*, The Scottish Office Education and Industry Department. The Stationery Office, Edinburgh.

SOEID (1998) *A Manual of Good Practice in Special Educational Needs*. The Scottish Office of Education and Industry Department, The Stationery Office, Edinburgh.

Spache, G. (1940) 'A critical analysis of various methods of classifying spelling errors'. *Journal of Educational Psychology* 31: 111–34.

Spearman, C. (1904) 'General intelligence, objectively determined and measured'. *American Journal of Psychology*, 15: 201–93.

Special Educational Needs Code of Practice (2001) Department for Education and Skills, DfES Publications, Nottingham.

Sperry, R.W. (1968) 'Hemispheric deconnection and unity in conscious awareness'. *Scientific American* 23: 723–33.

Sperry, R.W. (1983) *Science and Moral Priority: Merging Mind, Brain and Human Values*. Columbia University, New York.

Spooner, A.L.R., Baddeley, A. and Gathercole, S.E. (2004) 'Can reading accuracy and comprehension be separated in the Neale Analysis of Reading Ability?' *British Journal of Educational Psychology* 74: 187–204.

Stanovich, K.E. (1986) '"Matthew effects" in reading: some consequences of individual differences in the acquisition of literacy'. *Reading Research Quarterly* 21: 360–407.

Stanovich, K.E. (1991) 'The theoretical and practical consequences of discrepancy definitions of dyslexia'. In Snowling, M. and Thomson, M.E. (eds) *Dyslexia: Integrating Theory and Practice*. Whurr Publishers, London.

Stanovich, K.E. (1992) 'Speculation on the causes and consequences of individual differences in early reading acquisition'. In Gough, P.B., Ehri, L.C. and Treiman, R. (eds) *Reading Acquisition*. Lawrence Erlbaum, Hillsdale, NJ.

Stein, J. (2001) 'The magnocellular theory of developmental dyslexia'. *Dyslexia* 7: 12–36.

Stein, J. (2004) 'Dyslexia genetics'. In Reid, G. and Fawcett, A. (eds) *Dyslexia in Context: Research, Policy and Practice*. Whurr Publishers, London.

Stierer, B. (2002) 'Simply doing their job? The politics of reading standards and "real books"'. In Soler, J., Wearmouth, J. and Reid, G. (eds) *Contextualising Difficulties in Literacy Development*. Routledge Falmer, London.

Stirling, E.G. and Miles, T.R. (1988) 'Naming ability and oral fluency in dyslexic adolescents'. *Annals of Dyslexia* 38: 5–72.

Sunday Times (2003) 'Doubts over £1,500 dyslexia treatment', 2 February.

Sunday Times (2004) 'Why spell it out?' 28 November.

Sweeney, J. and Doncaster, C. (2002) *Fun Phonics. Teacher's Handbook*. Collins Educational, Harper Collins Publishers, Glasgow.

Sylva, K. and Evangelou, M. (2003) *The Effects of the Peers Early Education Partnership (PEEP) on Children's Developmental Progress*. DfES/University of Oxford.

Sylva, K., Melhuish, E., Sammons, P., Siraj-Blatchford, I., Taggaet, B. and Elliott, K. (2003) *The Effective Provision of Pre-School Education (EPPE) Project: Findings from Pre-school Period*. Institute of Education, University of London, London.

Tallal, P., Miller, S., Jenkins, W. and Merzenich, M. (1997) 'The role of temporal processing in developmental language-based learning disorders'. In Blachman, B. (ed.) *Foundations of Reading Acquisition and Dyslexia*. Lawrence Erlbaum, Mahwah, NJ.

Task Force on Dyslexia (2001) Cremin, P. (Chairperson). *Report of the Task Force on Dyslexia*. Department for Education and Science, Stationery Office, Dublin.

The Teacher (1998) 'Don't ignore dyslexics', July/August.

Terman, L.M. and Merrill, M.A.(1937) *Revised Stanford–Binet Scale*. Houghton Mifflin, Champaign, IL.

TES (1990) 'A closed book'. *Times Educational Supplement*, 20 July.

TES (1996) 'Labour gets back to basics'. *Times Educational Supplement*, 31 May.

TES (2000) 'Revision guides for English'. *Times Educational Supplement*, 14 April.

TES (2004) 'Inclusion is just an illusion'. *Times Educational Supplement*, 12 November.

TES (2005a) 'Leave grammar out of English lessons'. *Times Educational Supplement*, 21 January.

TES (2005b) '12 m adults stuck at age 11. Lord Leith warns ministers that millions will still lack adequate literacy and numeracy in 2020'. *Times Educational Supplement*, 9 December.

TES (2006) 'Councils shamed over SEN'. *Times Educational Supplement*, 10 February.

Thomson, M. (1990) *Developmental Dyslexia: Studies in Disorders of Communication*, 3rd edn. Whurr Publishers, London.

Thomson, M. (1991) 'The teaching of spelling using techniques of simultaneous oral spelling and visual inspection'. In Snowling, M. and Thomson, M. (eds) *Dyslexia: Integrating Theory and Practice*. Whurr Publishers, London.

Thomson, M. (2001) *The Psychology of Dyslexia: a Handbook for Teachers*. Whurr Publishers, London.

Thomson, M. (2003) 'Monitoring dyslexics' intelligence and attainments. A follow-up study'. *Dyslexia: an International Journal of Research and Practice* 9 (1): 3–17.

Thomson, M.E. and Newton, M.J. (1979) 'A concurrent validity study of the Aston Index'. In Newton, M.J., Thomson, M.E. and Richards, I.R. (eds) *Reading in Dyslexia: a Study Text to Accompany the Aston Index*. Learning Development Aids, Wisbech.

Thomson, M. and Watkins, B. (1990) *Dyslexia: a Teaching Handbook*. Whurr Publishers, London.

Thomson, M.E., Hicks, C., Joffe, L. and Wilsher, C. (1981) 'The use of the British Ability Scales amongst children with dyslexia'. *Dyslexia Review* 4 (2): 18–22.

The Times (1998) 'Literacy skills!; underachievement by boys; qualifications', 7 January.

The Times (2001) 'Are we not such dunces after all?', 6 December.

Tinker, M.A. (1931) 'The influence of form of type on the perception of words'. *Journal of Applied Psychology* 16: 167–74.

Tizard Report (1972) *Children with Specific Learning Difficulties*. Department of Education and Science, HMSO, London.

Topping, K.J (1995) *Paired Reading, Spelling and Writing: The Handbook for Teachers and Parents*. Cassell, London.

Topping, K.J. and Wolfendale, S. (eds) (1985) *Parental Involvement in Children's Reading*. Croom Helm, Beckenham.

Torgerson, C.J., Brooks, G. and Hall, J. (2006) 'A systematic review of the research literature on the use of phonics in the teaching of reading and spelling'. University of York and University of Sheffield.

Torgensen, J.K., Wagner, K. and Rashotte, C. (1999) *Test of Word Reading Efficiency*. Psychological Corporation, Harcourt Assessment, Oxford.

Treiman, R. (1993) *Beginning to Spell: a Study of First-Grade Children*. Oxford University Press, New York.

Tresman, S. (2005) *Dyslexia-Friendly LEAs and Schools. The BDA Quality Mark Initiative*. BDA Handbook 2005. BDA, Reading.

Truss, L. (2003) *Eats, Shoots and Leaves: the Zero Tolerance Approach to Punctuation*. Profile Books, London.

Tucker, N. (2002a) *The Rough Guide to Children's Books for 0–5 Years*. Rough Guides, London.

Tucker, N. (2002b) *The Rough Guide to Children's Books for 5–11 Years*. Rough Guides, London.

Tucker, N. and Eccleshare, J. (2002) *The Rough Guide to Children's Books for Teenagers*. Rough Guides, London.

Turner, M. (1990) *Sponsored Reading Failure: an Object Lesson*. IPSET Education Unit, Warlingham, Surrey.

Turner, M. (1995a) 'Finding out'. In Gains, C. and Wray, D. (eds) *Reading: Issues and Directions. NASEN and UKRA*. NASEN Enterprises Ltd, Stafford.

Turner, M. (1995b) 'Assessing reading: layers and levels'. *Dyslexia Review* 7 (1): 15–19.

Turner, M. (1997a) *Psychological Assessment of Dyslexia*. Whurr Publishers, London.

Turner, M. (1997b) 'Assessment by educational psychologists'. In Beech, J.R. and Singleton, C. (eds) *The Psychological Assessment of Reading*. Routledge, London.

Turner, M. (2000) 'WRAT-3 supplementary information'. *Dyslexia Review* 11 (1); 20–2.

Turner, M. (2004a) 'The dyslexia screen – a resource for schools and colleges'. *Dyslexia Review* 16 (1): 12–15.

Turner, M. (2004b) 'The nonword decoding test'. *Dyslexia Review* 16 (2): 23–4.

UNESCO (1994) *Salamanca Declaration and Framework for Action*. UNESCO, Paris.

Vail, P. (1998) Paper presented at the Helen Arkell Conference, Cambridge.

Van den Bos, K. (1998) 'IQ, phonological awareness, and continuous-naming speed related to Dutch children's poor decoding performance on two word identification tests'. *Dyslexia* 4: 73–89.

Van Haalen, T.G. (1990) 'Writing and revising: bilingual students' use of word processing'. *Dissertation Abstracts International* 52 (2): 418.

Vaughn, S., Schumm, J.S. and Gordon, J. (1993) 'Which motoric condition is most effective for teaching spelling to students with learning disabilities?' *Journal of Learning Disabilities* 26: 191–8.

Vellutino, F.R., Scanlon, D.M., Sipay, E.R., Small, S.G., Pratt, A., Chen R. and Denckla, M.B. (1996) 'Cognitive profiles of difficult to remediate and readily remediated poor readers. Early intervention as a vehicle for distinguishing between cognitive and experimental deficits as basic causes of specific reading disability'. *Journal of Educational Psychology* 88 (4): 601–38.

Vernon, P.E. (1979) *Intelligence: Heredity and Environment*. W.H. Freeman, San Francisco, CA.

Vernon, P.E. (1998) *Graded Word Spelling Test*. Hodder and Stoughton, London.

Vincent, D. and Crumpler, N. (1997) *British Spelling Test Series (BSTS)*. NFER-Nelson, Windsor.

Vogel, S.A. and Reder, S. (2001) 'International perspectives on dyslexia'. In Fawcett, A. (ed.) *Dyslexia: Theory and Good Practice*. Whurr Publishers, London.

Vogler, G.P., De Fries, J.C. and Decker, S.N. (1985) 'Family history as an indicator of risk for reading disability'. *Journal of Learning Disabilities* 18: 419–21.

Vygotsky, L.S. (1978) *Mind in Society*. Harvard University Press, Cambridge, MA.

Wagner, R., Torgeson, J. and Rashotte, C. (1999) *Comprehensive Test of Phonological Processing (CtoPP)*. Pro-Ed, Austin, TX.

Walberg, H.J. and Tsai, S. (1983) 'Matthew effects in education'. *American Educational Research Journal* 20: 359–73.

Warnock, M. (1978) *Special Educational Needs Report of the Committee of Inquiry into the Education of Handicapped Children and Young People*. HMSO, London.

Waterstone's (2004) *Guide to Books for Young Dyslexic Readers*, www.waterstones.co.uk.

Webster, N. (1828) *An American Dictionary of the English Language*.

Wechsler, D. (1944) *The Measurement of Adult Intelligence*, 3rd edn. Williams and Wilkins, Baltimore, MD.

Wechsler, D. (1949) *Wechsler–Bellevue Intelligence Scale*. Harcourt Brace Jovanovitch Psychological Corporation, New York.

Wechsler, D. (1992) *Wechsler Intelligence Scale for Children – Third Edition (WISC-III)*. Psychological Corporation, London.

Wechsler, D. (1993) *Wechsler Objective Reading Dimensions (WORD)*. Psychological Corporation, London.

West, T.G. (1991) *In the Mind's Eye: Visual Thinkers, Gifted People with Learning Difficulties, Computer Images, and the Ironies of Creativity*. Prometheus Books, New York.

Westwood, P., Harris-Hughes, M., Lucas, G., Nolan, J. and Scrymgeour, K. (1974) 'One-minute addition test, one-minute subtraction test'. *Remedial Education* 9 (2).

Whetton, C., Caspall, L. and McCulloch, K. (1997) *The Neale Analysis of Reading Ability*, 2nd rev. edn (NARA-2) NFER-Nelson, London.

Wiederholt, J.L. and Bryant, B.R. (2001) *Gray Oral Reading Test – 4th Edition (GORT-4)* Pro-Ed, Austin, TX, and the Psychological Corporation, Harcourt Assessment, Oxford.

Wilkins, A. (2001) *Assessment with the Intuitive Overlays*. Institute of Optometry, London.

Wilkins, A.J., Jeanes, R.J., Pumfrey, P.D. and Laskier, M. (1996) *Wilkins Rate of Reading Test*. IOO Marketing, London.

Wilkinson, A. (1971) *The Foundations of Language*. Oxford University Press, Oxford.

Wilkinson, G.S. (1993) *Wide Range Achievement Test – 3rd Edition (WRAT-3)*. Psychological Corporation, Harcourt Assessment, Oxford.

Wimmer, H. (1993) 'Characteristics of developmental dyslexia in a regular writing system'. *Applied Psycholinguistics* 14: 1–34.

Winch, W.H. (1925) *Teaching Beginners to Read in England: Its Methods, Results and Phonological Bases*. Journal of Educational Research Monographs No 8. Public School Publishing, Bloomington, IL.

Wolf, M. (1991) 'Naming speed and reading. The contribution of the cognitive neurosciences'. *Reading Research Quarterly* 26 (2): 123–41.

Wolf, M. (1999) 'What time may tell: towards a new conceptualisation of developmental dyslexia'. *Annals of Dyslexia* 49: 3–28.

Wolf, M. and Bowers, P. (1999) 'The "double-deficit hypothesis" for the developmental dyslexias. *Journal of Educational Psychology* 91: 1–24.

Wolf, M. and Bowers, P. (2000) 'The question of naming-speed deficits in developmental reading disabilities: an introduction to the double-deficit hypothesis'. *Journal of Learning Disabilities* 33: 322–4.

Wolf, M. and Obregón, M. (1992) 'Early naming deficits, developmental dyslexia, and a specific deficit hypothesis'. *Brain and Language* 43: 219–47.

Wolf, M., Bally, H., and Morris, R. (1986) 'Automaticity, retrieval processes and reading. A longitudinal study in average and impaired readers'. *Child Development* 57: 988–1000.

Woodcock, R.W. (1998) *Woodstock Reading Mastery Test – Revised/Normative Update (WRMT-R/NU)*. American Guidance Systems Inc., Dyslexia Institute, Egham.

Woodcock, R.W. and Johnson, M.B. (1989) *Woodcock–Johnson Psychoeducational Battery (Revised)*. American Guidance Services, Circle Pines, MD.

Wray, D. (1995) In Gains C. and Wray D. (eds) *Reading: Issues and Directions*. NASEN and UKRA Enterprises Ltd, Stafford.

Young, A. and Bowers, P. (1995) 'Individual differences and text difficulty determinants of reading fluency and expressiveness'. *Journal of Experimental Child Psychology* 60: 428–54.

Young, G. and Browning, J. (2004) 'Learning disability/dyslexia and employment: a US perspective'. In Reid, G. and Fawcett, A. (eds) *Dyslexia in Context: Research, Policy and Practice*. Whurr Publishers, London.

Yuill, N. and Oakhill, J. (1988) 'Effect of inference awareness training on poor reading comprehension'. *Applied Cognitive Psychology* 2: 33–45.

Zangwill, I. (1960) *Cerebral Dominance and its Relation to Psychological Function*. Oliver and Boyd, Edinburgh.

Zaporozhets, A. and Elkon, D. (1971) *Psychology of Preschool Children*. MIT Press, Cambridge MA.

Index